**WITHDRAWN FROM
MACALESTER COLLEGE
LIBRARY**

Law and Justice in China's New Marketplace

Also by Ronald C. Keith

COMPARATIVE POLITICAL PHILOSOPHY: Studies under the Upas Tree (*co-editor*)

REGIONALISM AND MULTILATERALISM IN THE POLITICS OF GLOBAL TRADE (*co-editor*)

ENERGY, SECURITY AND ECONOMIC DEVELOPMENT IN EAST ASIA (*editor*)

THE DIPLOMACY OF ZHOU ENLAI

CHINA'S STRUGGLE FOR THE RULE OF LAW

Law and Justice in China's New Marketplace

Ronald C. Keith
Professor and Head
Department of Political Science
University of Calgary
Canada

and

Zhiqiu Lin
Associate Professor of Sociology
Department of Sociology and Anthropology
Carleton University
Ottawa
Canada

© Ronald C. Keith and Zhiqiu Lin 2001

All rights reserved. No reproduction, copy or transmission of this publication may be made without written permission.

No paragraph of this publication may be reproduced, copied or transmitted save with written permission or in accordance with the provisions of the Copyright, Designs and Patents Act 1988, or under the terms of any licence permitting limited copying issued by the Copyright Licensing Agency, 90 Tottenham Court Road, London W1P 0LP.

Any person who does any unauthorised act in relation to this publication may be liable to criminal prosecution and civil claims for damages.

The authors have asserted their rights to be identified as the authors of this work in accordance with the Copyright, Designs and Patents Act 1988.

First published 2001 by
PALGRAVE
Houndmills, Basingstoke, Hampshire RG21 6XS and
175 Fifth Avenue, New York, N.Y. 10010
Companies and representatives throughout the world

PALGRAVE is the new global academic imprint of
St. Martin's Press LLC Scholarly and Reference Division and
Palgrave Publishers Ltd (formerly Macmillan Press Ltd).

ISBN 0–333–77090–0

This book is printed on paper suitable for recycling and made from fully managed and sustained forest sources.

A catalogue record for this book is available
from the British Library.

Library of Congress Cataloging-in-Publication Data
Keith, Ronald C.
　　Law and justice in China's new marketplace / Ronald C. Keith, Zhiqiu Lin.
　　p. cm.
　　Includes bibliographical references and index.
　　ISBN 0–333–77090–0 (cloth)
　　1. Law reform—China. 2. Justice, Administration of—China. 3. Capitalism—China. I. Lin, Zhiqiu, 1959– II. Title.
KNQ470 .K45 2000
347.51—dc21
　　　　　　　　　　　　　　　　　　　　　　　　　　00–041510

10 9 8 7 6 5 4 3 2 1
10 09 08 07 06 05 04 03 02 01

Printed and bound in Great Britain by
Antony Rowe Ltd, Chippenham, Wiltshire

In recognition of China's jurists

Contents

Acknowledgements ix
List of Abbreviations xi

1 Pluralized Jurisprudence in the Socialist Market 1
   The 'value problem' problem in market jurisprudence 8
   'Running the country according to law and establishing a
      socialist rule-of-law country' 27
   Judicial justice in the new marketplace 39
   Key issues 43

**2 The 'Special Grouping' of the Human Rights of Women,
Children, Handicapped and Elderly** 49
   The new salience of 'rights and interests' 53
   Social and legal guarantees and the changing role of the state 57
   'Internationalization' and the 'special grouping' of rights 61
   The handicapped in the 'special grouping' of rights 66
   The rights and interests of women and children 68
   The law of protecting the rights and interests of the elderly 86
   Conclusion 89

3 Justice and Efficiency in Contractual Labour Relations 93
   Labour law in the 'socialist market' 102
   Assessing the shift to contract labour 109
   The trade union's role in the new era of collective
      agreement 119
   Social justice and the labour dispute settlement system 125
   Justice and equality in the scope of the 1994 Labour Law 131
   Conclusion 136

4 Sorting Out Property and Ownership Rights in Law 138
   Property versus ownership rights in the state's relation to
      state enterprise 143
   Efficiency and justice in the reform of township enterprise 159
   New perspectives on private ownership and property 169
   Conclusion 175

5 Balancing Society and the Individual in Judicial Justice 178
   The balance of interests in the revised CPL 188

    The changing substantive principles of Chinese criminal law   202
    Law and 'economic crime' in the marketplace   214
    The balance of values in the 1997 Criminal Law   222
    The redefined purposes of the 1997 Criminal Law   226
    Conclusion   228

6 The Law and the Market at the Crossroads of Justice and Efficiency   232
    The main features of 'pluralized jurisprudence'   233
    The readjustment of interests   236
    Conclusion   245

Notes and References   247

Abbreviated Listing of Prominent Jurists   287

Select Glossary of Chinese Political/Legal Terms   290

Select English and Chinese Bibliography   299

Index   308

Acknowledgements

The authors are greatly indebted to colleagues and our principal funding agency, the Social Sciences and Humanities Research Council of Canada (SSHRCC). The subject matter was very difficult to research in the absence of a relevant English-language scholarship and reference base. While, thanks to the funding assistance of the SSHRCC, the authors enjoyed significant access to Chinese journals, reference books and textbooks on law and jurisprudence, they especially appreciated the intellectual generosity of colleagues in Beijing who during interviews took the time to explain Chinese concepts of law and to walk the authors through unfamiliar and late-breaking arguments in Chinese jurisprudence. We can only hope that we have repaid our hosts with balanced, comprehensive and accurate explanation and analysis. In particular, we are indebted to the CASS Institute of Law for its academic hospitality, which was so graciously and effectively extended even in the absence of a formal scholarly exchange agreement between the Chinese Academy of Social Sciences and the Social Sciences and Humanities Research Council of Canada. The authors will look forward to the future conclusion of such an agreement as well as greater levels of international exchange in the related fields of law, political science and sociology, based upon mutual learning and reciprocity. They will also remember the energetic support of Ms Jiang Xiaohong of the Research Administration and Foreign Affairs Division of the CASS Institute of Law in helping to organize our numerous requests for interviews. Our debts to particular Chinese jurists and scholars are too wide-ranging to recount fully here, but we would like to extend a special thanks to Li Buyun, Director of the Centre for Human Rights, at the CASS Institute of Law and to the following prominent jurists and law professors: Cui Min, Fu Kuaizhi, Shi Tanjing, Zhang Guangxing, Chen Mingxia, Chen Shirong, Wu Changshen, Liu Junhai and Xia Yinlan.

Dr Ronald C. Keith is especially grateful for the long-term support of the SSHRCC. The three-year cycle of funding which resulted in the earlier Macmillan/St. Martin's publication of *China's Struggle for the Rule of Law* helped establish a continuous research base in the field of Chinese legal reform. A SSHRCC standard research grant for 1995–99 funded the present project and book. It provided critical support for travel to Beijing, the collection of Chinese materials on jurisprudence, interviews, the completion of the research and writing of the present book. Dr Keith is personally indebted to Dr Charles Morrison and the East–West Center, Honolulu. Two successive visiting fellowships at the Center, in the summers of 1998 and 1999, offered some relief from departmental administration and provided an opportunity to get a head start on the writing of this book. Dr Zhiqiu Lin would also like to thank the SSHRCC for a related Carleton University research grant which helped to fund his research and enabled him to join Dr Keith in Beijing. And last but certainly not least the authors would thank George Shouliang Dong and Dr David Ding for their research assistance as well Ms Rita Dickson for editorial assistance. It was a pleasure to work with Sally Crawford at Macmillan Press. Mr Dong prepared a preliminary draft for the book's index.

With appropriate permission, parts of recent journal articles by the authors were updated, revised and incorporated into this book. The authors would like to thank Oxford University Press and the *China Quarterly* for permission relating to Ronald C. Keith, 'Legislating Women's and Children's "Rights and Interests" in the PRC', *China Quarterly*, no. 149, March 1997, pp. 29–55; and *Problems of Post-Communism*, edited at George Washington University and published by M.E. Sharpe, for permission relating to Ronald C. Keith, 'Post-Deng Jurisprudence: Justice and Efficiency in a "Rule of Law" Economy', *Problems of Post-Communism*, vol. 45, no. 3, May–June 1998, pp. 48–57; and *China Information* and The Documentation and Research Center for Contemporary China, Leiden University, for permission relating to Zhiqiu Lin and Ronald C. Keith, 'The Changing Substantive Principles of Chinese Criminal Law', *China Information*, vol. xiii, no. 1, Summer 1998, pp. 76–105.

RONALD C. KEITH AND ZHIQIU LIN

List of Abbreviations

ACFTU	All China Federation of Trade Unions
BR	*Beijing Review*
CASS	Chinese Academy of Social Sciences
CCP	Chinese Communist Party
CCPCC	Central Committee of the Chinese Communist Party
1979 CL	1979 Criminal Law
1997 CL	1997 Criminal Law
1979 CPL	1979 Law of Criminal Procedure
1996 CPL	1996 Law of Criminal Procedure
CQ	*China Quarterly*
FBIS	Foreign Broadcast Information Service
FWCW	Fourth World Conference on Women
GPCL	General Principles of Civil Law
1994 LL	1994 Labour Law
NPC	National People's Congress
NPCSC	Standing Committee of the National People's Congress
PRC	People's Republic of China
SPC	Supreme People's Court
SPP	Supreme People's Procuratorate
WF	All China Women's Federation

1
Pluralized Jurisprudence in the Socialist Market

This book delves into the correlations and the contradictions between law and justice in China's transitional market economy. Essentially it tells the story of a newly emerging jurisprudence, *falixue*. It puts the sharp contradictions and sophisticated nuances of this jurisprudence in the immediate context of politics. Every chapter in the story begins with a deliberate explanation of the internal Chinese perspective on the controversies confronting the legal community. The many points of controversy surrounding the purposes and values of Chinese law can be plotted along a single continuum with reference to two intersecting formal concepts – 'the market economy is a rule of law economy,' *shichang jingji shi fazhi jingji*, and 'running the country according to law and establishing a socialist rule-of-law country', *yifa zhi guo, jianshe shehuizhuyi fazhi guojia*.

New Party policy regarding the market has fostered renewed interest in the essential meaning of the rule of law and the related legal adjustment and protection of 'rights and interests', *quanyi*, in society.[1] As Chinese society moved more deeply into the process of market transition, rights and interests replaced 'class' in terms of the conceptualized composition of society and the changing notion of social justice. In this fascinating and unprecedented chapter of China's social and economic change, China's jurists are struggling to consolidate a new and flexible jurisprudence, one which clearly defines the fundamental principles of social and judicial justice. However, in the contemporary context of economic reform, this justice is deliberately coordinated with policy emphasis that promotes efficiency and the rising productivity associated with marketplace competition.

As the Party has endorsed the comprehensive development of the law, there has been an extraordinary crash course of training of lawyers and jurists as professional specialists in the various departments of law. Western social scientists, and even sinologists, may view the subject of Chinese 'jurisprudence' as a politically qualified exegesis of potentially futile scholarly reasoning, or even worse as a inconsequential matter of *ex post facto* rationalization of the power of a decaying Party–State. This book takes the view that, in any national context, jurisprudence develops within the prevailing political, economic and social circumstances and that reformed Chinese jurisprudence is both vibrant and substantively critical to an informed understanding of the legal dimensions of China's fascinating transition to a 'rule of law' based market economy.

Jurisprudence is now directly addressing what is fair and just under the law in a time of uncertain property relationships and social change. Western legal and sinological study has yet to generate significant research in this area. Chinese human rights have received extraordinary international attention, but very little has been written on China's own correlation of human rights and the rule of law within a jurisprudence premised in 'the market economy is a rule of law economy'.

With so much at stake in China's rapidly changing society, the internal debates both of China's jurists and of legal scholarship have become intense and far reaching in their political implications. Not surprisingly, while these debates deliberately seek to separate out law from the raw politics of the state, these debates originate at the heart of a changing politics of reform. While the newly acclaimed 'rule of law' aspires to enhance the independent and politically objective authority of the law, it is itself the formal object of state policy. Many of China's legal reformers have advocated the law's independence from the state; and yet they are, themselves, directly involved in the fashioning of policy regarding the law and its role in facilitating the state's policies on market reform.

The role of the jurist is in question, as is the nature of jurisprudence itself. 'Jurisprudence', then, has come under review as jurists consider whether it ought to be naturally 'unified' on the basis of a single grand theory or whether 'jurisprudence' ought to reflect the pluralization of the new subjects which have emerged in response to market reform and changes in ownership and distribution.[2]

The quality and degree of development of general legal theory reflects the messy complications of unprecedented societal change and the often confused political and ideological response to the arresting development of new market relations in society. From the founding of the new People's Republic, to the inception of Deng Xiaoping's reform beginning in late 1978, the system of legal thought was well charted. There was a politically explicit notion of justice premised in class analysis and the didactic unity of state and society. Legal theory dutifully responded to the ideological articulation of the values and purposes of the law in its correlations with China's constitutionally declared stage of economic and social development.

Today's circumstances are different. There is no handy compass by which jurists can readily chart the heavenly constellations so as to confirm the direction of society and politics. 'Class' no longer serves as the pole-star of Chinese politics. There is obvious growth, but at the same time unfamiliar pluralization of subjective interests in the marketplace. The degree of development of general legal theory remains influenced by ideology. But ideology now stresses the complexity of social structure in the context of accelerated transition to the market economy. This makes for a less neat explanation of how justice in law connects with the state–society relationship.

The plain spoken Politbureau member, Li Ruihuan, in a March 1999 plea for more research on the complexities of China's contemporary transition from the planned to the socialist market economy, warned the members of the Chinese People's Political Consultative Conference of the need for greater objectivity in light of growing 'phenomena of phoniness':

> China is now in a transitional period. . . . Although we have broken the old system, its influence still exists in some areas; and the new system, which is being established, has to be improved in many respects. This has given rise to numerous complexities. Because of the *adjustment of interests between different sectors*, social contradictions have become intertwining; because of the collision between new, correct concepts and old improper concepts, people often have diverse views, or even diametrically different views, on the same issues; and because of the rapid changes of the objective realities, people's understandings are apt to become obsolete. Phenomena of phoniness are rampant in our society today.[3]

'Pluralization' may attempt to make a virtue out of sharp and unprecedented disagreement over the most appropriate contemporary values of law. The law faculties of various universities, however, are scrambling to introduce a new generation of textbooks on the subject of 'jurisprudence', *falixue*. There is a proliferation of formal thinking and writing about the purposes of law and the law's relation to the changing dimensions of distributive and procedural justice. More than ever before, the jurisprudential study of law is engaged in speculation about the changing concept of society within China's rapidly changing politics. Guo Daohui, chief editor of one of China's leading law journals, pointed out that in its response to the new demands of the socialist market jurisprudence is pushing into previously 'forbidden areas'.[4]

Guo's book, *Fade shidai jingshen* (The Contemporary Spirit of Law), precipitated discussion of a revised relation of state and society in the hope of redefining the public purposes of the state. The more optimistic jurists extolled the positive association of a 'rule of law state', *fazhi guo*, and 'rule of law society', *fazhi shehui*, and criticized the past instrumentalism in the state's co-optation of society and its use of law for the exclusive purposes of social control.[5] Some stressed the critical importance of separating law from politics, but Guo emphasized anchoring the rule of law in state activism to create a new societal attitude towards the law. In short, the state must not only be bound by law, but it must actively support the development of the 'rule of law'.

An important part of this changing reality of state and society has to do with the enhanced role of jurists, not only in the drafting of laws, but also in setting the tone and direction of legal reform in the new context of a market economy. How are jurists, given the ambiguities of the Chinese 'socialist' context of basic political cultural and institutional change, coping with their new assignment to create a more relevant and useful jurisprudence which responds to the requirements of the marketplace?

A Shandong law professor, Hao Tiechuan, in his discussion of the professional role of the jurist, pointed out that this role relates to the whole issue of 'democratization' and law-making. Perhaps forgetting that jurists may have interests too, Hao critiqued the past tendency to rely excessively on specific central ministries and government departments to draft law. Such reliance had fostered the narrow entrenchment of bureaucratic interests at the expense of focus on citizen's rights, and Hao saw an urgent need for the objective independence of jurists vis-à-vis the multiplication or 'pluralization of the subjects of interests' in the developing market economy. He hoped that objective professionalism would compensate for the messy subjective extremes of marketplace competition.[6]

As for the objective impartial dimensions of the law, there is also an unfolding controversy over the rationale for due process and judicial justice. The formal changes to procedural law over the last few years are both significant and substantive. They suggest that a paradigm shift is occurring within the domestic judicial process. How does procedural change relate to the new market economy and the related changes in the position of the state vis-à-vis society? At a more mundane and detailed level one must understand the complexity of the changes occurring across the different fields of codified law such as civil, criminal, and constitutional law, and how these departmental pieces fit together within the overall theoretical architecture of China's developing jurisprudence.

As will be detailed throughout this book, 'jurisprudence' is being tugged in two opposite directions. On the one hand, there is a strong new trend towards the separation of law and state and the related 'pluralization of jurisprudence'. This trend is comfortable with the complexity of ownership and distribution in the new market. It not only tolerates, but encourages, discussion about the coexistence of alternative basic values within jurisprudence. One might hypothesize that this trend is consistent with what is known as 'civil society' in the West. On the other hand, there is a growing political and legal concern to bring the state back into the equation. Chinese legal reformers and human rights activists often support the deployment of an activist state to reinforce a new rule of law and to secure a social and judicial justice which protects newly emerging rights and interests in society.

What are the basic connotations of 'jurisprudence', *falixue*? The general editor of the 1997 *Zhonghua faxue da cidian* (The Chinese Encyclopedia of Legal Studies), Sun Guohua, suggests that this term originated with the open door and economic reform era of Deng Xiaoping.[7] During the period 1949–78, there was a preference for alternative terms such as 'theories of state and law', *guojia yu fade lilun*. After 1978 the study of law steadily acquired a more independent basis of its own as reflected in expressions such as *faxue jichu lilun* (basic theory of law) and *fade yiban lilun* (general theories of law). The latter were conveniently boiled down into *fali*, legal theory. 'Jurisprudence', or *falixue*, explicitly addressed the origins, value, functions and development of law in its relation to other social phenomena.

While the new term, *falixue* generally prevailed as 'jurisprudence', controversy continued as to whether such jurisprudence was essentially a matter of science or of legal philosophy. Marxist preferences often equated the latter with western usage and experience and saw 'legal philosophy' as a lower form of study.[8]

In conventional ideological terms, legal theory, or jurisprudence, was part of the state 'superstructure', but it was also a constituent element of 'socialist spiritual civilization'. It assumed a meshing of the entire universe of state, social organization and action. Even in the 1997 Ministry of Justice text on jurisprudence, the law's 'internal and external correlations' are discussed in this expansive way. This text, for example, predictably cited Deng Xiaoping's famous 16 character formulation, 'there must be law, it must be relied upon; it must be enforced; and law-breakers must be dealt with'.⁹ It described all of the law's 'interior correlations' (*neixietiao*), as these cut across the various departments of law, such as constitutional, criminal, administrative, civil law, and so on, as well as the conceptual and structural dimensions of judicial process relating to the legal enhancement of human capabilities and the need for public order and social control.¹⁰

Jurisprudential study also encompassed 'external correlations' (*waixietiao*), and the Ministry's 1997 text explained these as follows:

> The law's internal correlations refer to the correlations of legal and social systems. Here the specific meaning points to the correlations of particular national circumstances and legal systems. These correlations include those relating to a country's internal environment and they include as well other methods of legal adjustment and control such as correlations of ethics, politics, customs, the charters of mass associations, village regulation, people's agreements, etc. The law's external correlations must meet all of the systemic demands of modernization reaching out to the world and at the same time these correlations must systematically agree with society's laws and regulations, the course of history and people's rights and ideals. These external correlations are built on the base of internal correlations.¹¹

This text explored a plethora of correlations while at the same time recognizing the importance of *yi fa zhi guo*, relying on law to govern the country' as a modern trend which could be discerned in a variety of comparative national circumstances. Indeed, for quite some time Chinese jurisprudence has speculated on the true meaning of the 'rule of law', *fazhi*. The first notion of the rule of law emerged in the post-Cultural Revolutionary context of Deng Xiaoping's 1978 interpretation of the need for 'legalization' and 'democratization' in light of the continuing 'feudal' tradition of 'one man rule', the brutal extremes of which, were so vividly expressed in the mid-1960s large-scale class struggle.

Western interpretation of China's 'totalitarianism' or even 'mature totalitarianism' or 'neo-authoritarianism' has often assumed that Marxism–Leninism and the rule of law are locked in resolute contradiction. The latter notion has, nonetheless, been extensively discussed in light of jurist debate over the interpretation of Deng Xiaoping's legal theory, particularly as it responded to the Cultural Revolution and the 'socialist market'. The new theory may well have served to accentuate the Party's own contradictions as it eulogized Yan'an principles of collective self-sacrifice while endorsing 'to get rich is glorious' and the Shekou slogan, 'time is money and efficiency is life'.

As a senior Marxist jurist, Sun Guohua discussed 'jurisprudence', underscoring the specifically Chinese and socialist dimensions of contemporary PRC law. Sun was at the centre of the mid-1980s politics of legal reform in the mid-1980s with this advocacy of the 'rule of law', as distinct from 'rule by law'. He has since lost influence to progressive reformers. The latter wished completely to exorcise the spirit of Soviet theory which had prevailed in what is now regarded as only the first stage of jurisprudential development. These critics now regard Sun as a latter-day Vyshinsky who has 'no market' for his ideas.[12]

The current policy correlation of the rule of law and the socialist market was directly as a result of Deng Xiaoping's early 1992 inspection tour of Southern China. His related 'Southern Tour' theory was subsequently incorporated into the Party line at the pivotal October 1992, 14th Party Congress. Deng warned against any unacceptable polarization of society; however, he also gave extraordinary precedence to market efficiency in achieving an improved material standard of living.

In the Southern Tour theory, the market become the primary mechanism for 'liberating' China's productive forces. 'Liberating' the productive forces was distinguished from 'developing' them. While the latter referred only to the scientific and technical improvement of these forces, the former sought to actually change the social structures which informed the developing productive relations in society.[13] The former in effect required a re-examination of society's 'structure of interests', *liyi jiegou*, and the legislated 'readjustment' of interests was to follow upon a new understanding of ownership and distribution. In a major ideological departure, the 14th Party Congress revised the basic principle of distribution, moving from 'each according to his/her work' to 'distribution according to work as the main body, supplemented by other economic sectors and distribution modes'.[14]

Particularly in the last several years, there has been a creative adaptation to Southern Tour theory as it relates to legal theory on the values and purposes of law. Southern Tour theory distilled Deng's essential thoughts on a further acceleration of the development of the market. This theory served as the premise for the 14 November 1993 CCP Central Committee Decision on 'socialist market structure' which endorsed the market's 'fundamental role in resource allocations'.[15]

Responding in the mid-1990s to the opportunities of this changing policy context, many legal reformers began to explore 'pluralized jurisprudence', *duoyuande falixue*. The very advocacy of pluralized jurisprudence is intrinsically interesting in that it challenges past state dictation of a 'unified' jurisprudence, based on a singular class conception of social justice. Donald Clarke and James Feinerman (Clarke and Feinerman 1995) got at the underlying issue when they explained the conventional Chinese assumption as follows: 'Chinese state ideology does not accept the legitimacy of multiple standards of morality.'[16] Now it is not uncommon to hear of 'comparative advantage' and 'survival of the fittest'. Interests are not automatically presumed to be in synthesis and the law has been featured in attempts to deal rationally with the necessary competition between the various interests in society and the economy.

As competition between the various interests is now regarded as increasingly likely, and as the law is directly related to the provision of justice and the stability of society, the greater complexity of interests and the proliferation of formally recognized 'subjects' before the law becomes increasingly inevitable. As a result of market reforms, ownership relations become more complex and there is also a pluralization of legally recognized 'subjects'.

The 'value problem' problem in market jurisprudence

The 'subjective' question of 'interest'

Whether it is 'unified' or 'pluralized', contemporary jurisprudence must now understand the developing relationships between a 'socialist market economy', the 'rule of law' and the correlation of rights and interests as law and policy deals with the formal creation and protection of human rights. In its analytical interpretation of these large concepts, jurisprudence runs the risk of unsettling incoherence. Jurisprudence has what jurists candidly refer to as a 'value problem'. Jurisprudence must sort out its own internal content relating to the ordering of values such as justice, equality, efficiency, public order and security. Of key importance is how jurisprudence will respond to the new policy, 'efficiency is primary and fairness, supplementary', *xiaoyi wei zhu, gongzheng wei fu*.

In the altered circumstances of the socialist market, conventional class-based jurisprudence has been exposed as an anachronism. In its time it had been relentlessly unified on the morally edifying basis of a single notion of justice. This jurisprudence could consider the law's social nature, but it was never allowed to stray too far from the strict assumptions of class struggle. The older theory blithely presumed an ideal synthesis of state, collective and individual interests. Such theory did not have to deal with the competition between interests in a market society.

The Maoist trinity of state, society and law has now been challenged in the multiplicity of new practical demands in the 'socialist market economy'. The hierarchical nature of state power as it was exercised in the command economy is challenged in the development of new associations and interests in society. Jurisprudence must now sort out pluralized 'subjects'. Ideally, it must expedite the impartial 'readjustment of interests' and consolidate the use of law as a buffer against corruption. All of this has reinforced the standing argument for equality before the law and the supremacy of the law.

The new precedence assigned to interests in correlation with rights signals a shift in jurisprudence. Class analysis has radically declined while subjective interest has acquired new theoretical validity. Jurists have challenged the centrality of the conventional dialectical unity of rights and obligations as a substantive 'obligational fundamentalism'. Rights had been lost in the irrational excesses of an overcentralized, planned economy. In the transition to 'commodity' and then to 'socialist market economy', there was a transparent need to move from the previous 'objective' requirements of state imposed obligation to consider the definition of 'rights' in correlation with the subjective manifestation of 'newly emerging interests' in China's transitional society. This correlation was examined within a wider national debate on the relevance of human rights and the need to support the new socialist market economy.

The focus on the subjective content and natural development of newly emerging interests in society has threatened to undermine the traditional focus on the state's 'objective' determination of interests. Sun Guohua has suggested that there are three views in Chinese jurisprudence as to the conception and affirmation of 'interests'. Some jurists treat the latter as if they are essentially subjective. Others viewed them as essentially objective, and yet another group of jurists argue for the unity of the subjective and objective in the formative development of 'interests'.[17] Sun, himself, stated flatly that interests are objective in nature. He disliked the 'subjective', considering that it precipitates the negation of state power, and he deeply distrusted the market's apparently natural predisposition towards social inequality.

Professor Xu Xianming, in his book on rights and obligations (Xu 1991), reported on the heated Shandong law society controversy over rights and obligations as they related to 'interests'. Xu detailed a new theory, which posited that rights constitute the recognition of individual and social values in socio-economic relationships. This theory had originated in the push towards commodity production and it had called for the realization of human values. Xu summed up the changing focus in theory as follows:

> One of the positive results of the years of reform has been the progressive penetration of the old model of group interest formation and the facilitation of a plural structure of social interests. The law participates in the aggregation of new and important interests by affirming or denying the demands made by various interest groups through the distribution of rights and obligations.[18]

In subsequent debate, the past assumption that the 'will of the ruling class' could be relied upon to dictate the proper distribution of rights and obligations came under increasing challenge. This attack left the door open for the alternative advocacy of the 'will of the people'. Theorists, such as Ma Changshan, went so far as to argue that the 14th Party Congress line on the socialist market allowed for the development of a 'civil society' in substitution for the 'will of the ruling class':

> In modern society, both civil society and the political state have achieved full development in their coexistence . . . Since the reform and opening [policy of Deng Xiaoping], the centralized economic system, in which group and individual interests were utterly overwhelmed by state interests, has been shattered as the criteria of rights is replacing the criteria of power.[19]

There should be no question that international human rights debate has had a far-reaching impact on the related internal debate, as well as on the development of Chinese jurisprudence. Increasing priority was assigned to 'interests' at the same time as reformers seized the opportunity to pursue new internal sanction for the development of human rights.[20]

Luo Mingda and He Hangzhou, in their correlation of 'rights and interests', questioned whether power politics had compromised China's human rights development:

> Interest is a value that is subjectively determined and pursued. It refers to the extent to which subjective needs become manifest and to the degree of this materialization. Human rights, in the broadest sense

of the term, are integral to human needs and social reality.... These needs are fundamentally and inherently human in nature; they are expressed in the subjective pursuits of man. These interests emerge within a relevant open multi-tiered interest system. If one can say that the human productive forces limit the total existing sum of interests, [then] one [can] also note the imbalance of human interests created in society. In the attainment of [these] limited rights, rights were not distributed on the basis of the [human] species, so that every member of the human species may have a share – on the contrary, distribution took place on the basis of power.[21]

The advent of 'rights and interests' raised a key cognate issue as to the appropriate power of the state in the formation of human rights. 'Human rights' were defined in the early 1990s as 'rights to which a person is entitled by virtue of his/her human nature',[22] and the national debate on human rights certainly affected formal perception as to the relative importance of the objective and subjective nature of rights and interests.

The rise and fall of rights and interests in the market economy

The reform of state enterprise generated a great deal of anxiety over who would join the ranks of the winners and losers in the inevitable societal polarization and the potential sacrifice of short-term interests for the purpose of long-term increases in productivity based upon prospective new efficiencies. No one questions that the market has helped fillip a jurisprudential focus on the conceptualization, materialization and readjustment of rights and interests, but dealing with the market is somewhat like riding the proverbial tiger and not being able to get off. The market, in other words, can create potential social injustice and inequality. Yang Haikun once pointed out: 'An urgent task of legal adjustment is to establish mechanisms to facilitate the legitimate expression of interests by social groups.'[23] And those legal reformers who extol the virtues of the market economy as a rule of law economy are vulnerable to more conservative Marxist argument which focuses on the market's negation of justice.

The question of interest formation is generally described by legal reformers as part of the overall move towards the rule of law and democratization. Also, the political highlighting of efficiency as primary has not meant that jurists are free to ignore the plight of those in society who may become more or less marginalized in the rush to seize market opportunities. The latter are not universally accessed by members of society. The consequences of contract for the rights and interests of labour, for example, is an especially pressing political and legal concern. Conventional theory provides no logical basis for understanding the contractual obligations of workers to management, and while the formal right to strike may be in the offing, workers have had to seek refuge in the ambiguities of the law in order to take an active role in respect of their jobs.

Moreover, and not unrelatedly, the potential effect of the market on specific sectors of the population and the possibility of social instability, has prompted a more enthusiastic leadership support for a special grouping, *teshu qunti*, of rights and interests for women, children, the handicapped and the elderly. This integrated approach has received almost no attention in western analysis. In fact, while one can refer to a large literature on women, only a small portion of this literature systematically deals with jurisprudence and legal issues concerning women's 'rights and interests'. There is a much smaller literature on the legal rights and interests of children under the law too, and an even more incipient literature on the lawful rights and interests of the elderly.[24]

In the early to mid-1990s in China, several important new national laws were deliberately legislated in a tight sequence. These included the PRC Law on the Protection of the Rights and Interests of Women, the PRC Law on the Protection of Minors, the Law on the Protection of the Rights and Interests of the Handicapped and the PRC Law on the Rights and Interests of the Elderly. Related jurisprudence focused generally on 'social protection law', *shehui baozhang fa*.[25] This trend partly originated in a Chinese counter to international human rights criticism. It coincided with the process of 'internationalization' involving the active comparison of domestic and foreign legal experience, but even more importantly there has been a strong domestic political focus on the implications of rights and interests for the regime in its urgent need for social stability.

While formal reference to 'rights and interests', *quanyi*, has been around since 1949, this terminology has acquired such a new pre-eminence in the contemporary context of reform that its critics have caricatured it as 'rights and interests fundamentalism', *quanyi benwei*. The criticisms largely originate with, but are not at all confined to, disaffected Marxist jurists who are concerned lest the subjective nature of interests override the state's presumably 'objective' requirement to achieve social justice through the law. While more conservative Marxist jurists are offended by such fundamentalism, they are just as concerned, if not more concerned, about the elaboration of a 'special grouping' of rights so as to protect the most vulnerable elements of society against the harsh conditions of market competition. The lines of jurist debate, in this case, are politically complex. There is widespread popular concern that China's economic growth might be compromised in wide-ranging social disturbance in the context of massive and qualitative transition to the competitive market environment. Moreover, the top Party leadership has been very concerned over the destabilizing effects of the market on the integrity of family life. The latter is seen as critically important to the stability of society as the economy undergoes more profound transition.

In fact there is a related explicit political reason for the new pre-eminent correlation of 'rights' with 'interests' in so many new basic laws. The political leadership believed that 'interests', while not strictly a formal legal concept, would nevertheless have public appeal if incorporated into popular legislation. 'Interests', in other words, offered those affected by the uncertain social consequences of economic reform a legal life preserver. The new generation of rights legislation offered moral and legally derived assurances of state remedy against the vicissitudes of the changing marketplace.

Even with a strong new emphasis on the law's comprehensiveness and the related need for clear stipulation of crime, this same systemic legislation assumed an educational function in deliberately setting out new benchmarks for behaviour appropriate to the values of society and social justice; for example, in the PRC Law on the Protection of Women's Rights and Interests, there is attempt to synthesize the social and legal protection of rights. Over the last several years the politics behind the legislative prioritization of rights and interests has become a much more interesting (and active) area of the law.

New theory has tended to liberate 'human rights', *ren quan* – as human entitlements which transcend the parameters of any particular state authority – from the past emphasis on 'citizens' rights', *gongmin quan*, as rights exclusively generated by the state. 'Rights and interests' have acquired new status within a 'special system' in reaction to past lopsided emphasis on obligations within the 'unity of rights and obligations'. While they are not totally dismissed, obligations, in this particular context, are seen as distractors, and the focus is alternatively on the more charitable correlation of rights with interests. As discussed in Chapter 3, the socio-economic utility of obligations has been alternatively stressed within advocacy of 'small government, big society'. Obligation in this context has been deployed somewhat paradoxically to emphasize individual self-determination within a multi-tiered approach to the socialized funding of benefits. Thus, support for the contemporary relevance of 'obligation' has come from opposite sides of the political spectrum. In order to protect the state's power, conservative opinion has subscribed to the relevance of obligation. Some reformers have also subscribed, but for a different reason. They are prepared to explore obligation in so far as it relates to the individual's responsibility vis-à-vis the state's responsibility for social welfare.

This overall theoretical context is analytically compelling when one considers the attack on the unified nature of 'jurisprudence' and the growing difficulties in creating a clear set of universally acceptable social criteria governing social benefits and subsidies. The critics of 'rights and interests obligationalism' have a point. Even among the scholars and jurists who are dedicated to 'pluralized jurisprudence' and the expansion of rights in correlation with interests there is some disquiet over the regime's explicit prioritization of efficiency over fairness. There is no automatic consensus on how the law should deal with its own value of social justice.

Traditional Marxist–Leninist dialectics has always required the designation of a primary element in any social contradiction. Any reform view which prefers that equal emphasis is given to fairness and efficiency is at odds with this traditional primacy of social justice. While reformers are likely to object to a state-imposed 'unified jurisiprudence', they may disagree on the degree to which an activist state is necessary to the pursuit of social justice. The current Party-endorsed emphasis on a complete legal system is a matter of the Party's own self-conscious political adjustment, and the legislation of human rights is being pursued in tandem with a familiar state-sponsored social activism which in large part represents an upgraded notion of the Party's traditional mass-line organizational strategy.

The CCP's mass-line, formally, if not always practically, required up–down, down–up communication and policy processes which constantly engaged Party leadership with the masses at all levels of political and social organization. This essential politics was to ensure a comprehensive networking between the state and society in the achievement of socialist ends. Policy relating to social justice was supposed to be defined, refined and continuously adjusted on this political basis. While the mass-line traditionally tended to emphasize the law's role within a larger process of public order which was designed to facilitate the development of 'socialist spiritual civilization' through consciousnes-raising in mass politics, the post-Cultural Revolutionary context of economic reform was more concerned about the need for social stability, and the law was newly prized for its innate predictability. In short, the law was recognized as an institutional failsafe or a hedge against the 'spirit of the leader' and the political extremes of class struggle in the modernizing era of economic reform. The law's predictability, not to mention its related dignity and authority, required a newly stated independence from the vicissitudes of mass-line politics. In light of the shift from class struggle to economic reform, what then is the role of the Chinese state in relation to law which deals explicitly with essential social values and the articulation and protection of rights and interests?

Specifically, how does law deal with the ideals and reality of China's contemporary transition to the marketplace? In a June 1998 interview with the authors, one of China's leading jurists specializing in women's law, Chen Mingxia, pointed out that, on the more abstract level, the law often contains such legislative language in the Chinese as one 'should', *yingdang*, as distinguished from the prescriptive, one 'must', *bixu*. In the former case, the law stands as moral instruction. While this instruction is in a very general sense legally binding, it need not be literally carried out until some future date when the appropriate resources are actually in place. Even in the context of greater sensitivity to rational legal culture, this is represented as progressive and as appropriate to Chinese culture. In other words, this 'special grouping' of rights and interests is being used deliberately to point self-consciously towards a future ideal society wherein rights would be comprehensively enjoyed on the basis of appropriate principles of justice.

In this respect, the more substantive articles of such law contain a specific conception of social justice which often requires the coordination of the 'responsibilities' of or the moral division of labour between the state, related 'mass,' or popular social associations, schools and public agents, families and individuals for authenticating rights in the practical transactions of society. At the same time, such legislation is said to reflect better the separation of law from politics and policy and a new jurisprudential emphasis on the importance of clearly defining crime in a changing social context.[26]

As the above discussion would suggest, justice is a critical dimension of the law's 'value'. Social justice has been correlated with the 'rule of law' in the context of the decline of 'class' concepts and the rise of 'interests', which are often packaged together with 'rights'. At the general theoretical level concerning the development of law and the related legal system, there is an abstract insistence on the separation of law from the state. In the legislated recognition of rights and interests, however, there is a qualifying focus on the state acting through law to provide remedy against the extremes of marketplace inequality. Mid-to-late 1990s jurisprudence has increasingly endorsed a number of important and familiar principles such as the protection of human rights, the supremacy of law, judicial independence, equality before the law and the rationalization of contemporary legal culture. In large part this trend constituted a response to the new market rationality of economic competition. The acceptance of the market's correlation with law, however, came with a new set of contradictions concerning the law and social justice and disagreement over the optimal formation of rights and interests under the rule of law.

'Rights and interests' have gained increasing acceptance in actual legislation and regulatory implementation; however, the Party has served notice that these cannot all be materialized at once. Apparently, the sacrifice of 'short-term' in favour of 'long-term interests' may be historically necessary. Jiang Zemin, in his 12 September 1997 speech to the Party, generally spoke of the continuing relevance of Deng Xiaoping's Thought and specifically re-affirmed 'efficiency is primary and fairness is supplementary'. Jiang performed genuflection before Deng Xiaoping and his thought but he rocked what was left of the Party's conservative establishment in his revision to the fundamental principles of ownership and distribution.

Pluralized distribution and ownership

In the first place, Jiang revised the ideologically sacrosanct Marxist formulation for distribution, which had served, since 1949, as one of two essential theoretical pillars marking the essential difference between capitalism and socialism. While Deng was still alive, Jiang, in October 1992, dropped the exclusive principle, 'each according to his [or her] work'. In September 1997, Jiang still noted the primacy of work, but he stretched the Party's conventional formula for distribution to include explicitly new and potentially heretical connotations. In 1997, Jiang subscribed to 'combining remuneration according to work and remunerating according to factors of production put in', *an lao fenpei wei zhuti, duozhong fenpei fangshi bing cun*.[27] In an unambiguous break with Mao's ideological tradition, such factors were acknowledged to include capital and knowledge.

Secondly, Jiang spoke of the 'pluralization' of the system of public ownership, providing a new interpretative gloss on 'public ownership as primary and the common development in the economy of various forms of ownership, *gongyou zhi wei zhuti, duozhong suoyouzhi jingji gongtong fazhan*.[28] While Li Peng was still the Premier, Jiang had left him out on a limb to deal with the volatile issues of ownership. Then, in 1997, Jiang, himself waded into the controversy over 'property rights' versus 'ownership rights'.

Jiang repeated his 1992 qualification about the importance of 'fairness', but he was frank about the reform of state enterprise, seeing it as an opportunity to downsize and to re-employ workers on the basis of a 'competitive mechanism selecting the superior and eliminating the inferior'.[29] Jiang aimed to ally the benefits of expediency to production. With the deepening of enterprise reform and the readjustment of economic structure, Jiang conceded that it would 'be hard to avoid the flow of personnel and layoffs'.

The Party General Secretary placed the onus for enterprise reform on the backs of the workers. Apparently the 'masters' under the people's democratic dictatorship would bear a significant part of the short-term costs of change. They were served notice to change their job concept in order to conform to a new social and economic reality. Reform might involve postponing the 'short-term' for the 'long-term' gains of the workers, who no longer enjoyed the same privileged position as proletarians. Would this entail a queue for the enjoyment of rights in society? Would the workers, for example, be exposed to a new range of inequities as they shuffled between a planned and contract economy? Would contract law and jurisprudence offer them adequate protection of their newly defined rights and interests?

Secondly, Jiang also reconsidered the second pillar of socialism mentioned above and offered qualified but new support to those jurists who were lobbying for a stronger notion of 'ownership rights' as opposed to the more conservative understanding of 'property rights'. Instead of using Li Peng's preferred term of property rights, *caichan quan*, or the more radical reform notion of 'ownership rights', *suoyou quan*, Jiang repeatedly referred to *chan quan*.[30]

Previously, the October 1992 14th Party Congress had endorsed Li Peng's notion of 'property rights of enterprise as legal person'. Reformers at the CASS Institute of Law, in particular, were frustrated by the evident influence of conservative economists who were apparently unable fully to appreciate the most fundamental aspects of jurisprudence. In 1992, the reform jurists had been politically outflanked by these same conservative economists who knew little of either 'ownership' or commercial law.

In the view of the reform jurists, the 1986 General Principles of Civil Law had not properly entrenched the subject status of private property. State property rights were still treated as 'sacred' whereas the General Principles only offered 'to protect' private property. Public and private property were not equal subjects before the law, and 'private property rights' did not have the same exalted status under law as 'private ownership rights'. Civil Law had apparently not gone far enough. It had settled for the mere existence of 'private property rights', *ziran caichan quan*, and the effect of this was to perpetuate old Soviet theory, which presumed that private property rights in law were an inconsequential exception to public ownership rights.

Some in China's legal community disliked the deliberate fuzziness of the term property rights. CASS Institute of Law advocates, for example, complained that conservative Marxist economists were clinging to the term so as to obscure the clear distinction between state enterprise ownership and operational management. Some experts responded by disingenuously reading the content of ownership rights into property rights. Still others described the term's content as 'combined rights', including rights relating to liability, intellectual property, debate, operations, trade marks and reputation. While Jiang's *chan quan* was not an immediately recognizable legal concept in the familiar continental tradition of law, it offered succour to those who claimed that clear ownership rights had to be assigned to state enterprise. On the basis of *chan quan*, progressive reformers could renew their argument that while the state may own shares in stock companies, these companies are not owned by the state and have their own ownership rights.

Even as with Mao's old pagoda of state, collective and individual interests crumbled before their very eyes, jurists scrambled to keep up with proliferating interests and the ownership implications of the socialist market. They had to consider how the law would define and readjust rights and interests in the context of a deliberate differentiation between public and private law. While market economies are thought to provide new opportunities for the legal formation of rights, Chinese politicians and jurists have had to ask themselves whether the genie of efficiency, once freed from its bottle, would threaten social stability and retard rights and interests formation in practice.

Justice and efficiency in the 'rule of law economy'

Jurists, who were seeking to disassociate the law from the state, were also faced with mounting contradictions originating in the 'socialist market economy as a rule of law economy'. The contemporary proponents of such reform are celebrating their victory in gaining ultimate political support for their notion of the rule of law. Some dared to argue that the rule of law is not the instrument of the market economy, but rather it is a self-standing rationality which accompanies the development of a modern state. Few would deny, however, that the political importance of the market served as the driver for the development of the legal system and the 'rule of law' itself.

There is perhaps a creative tension between an emphasis on the law's independence from policies concerning economic relationships and the need to incorporate social justice within the law as one of the law's own essential values or purposes. The market's existence provides the 'rule of law' with new legitimation, but at the same time policy concerning the market may threaten the independence of law from the state. Put simply, the sharp focus on adaptation to the market has intensified the 'value problem' inside Chinese jurisprudence.

In terms of an ideal reading of jurisprudence, Zhang Wenxian, in a Ministry of Justice approved text on jurisprudence, noted that, in the western context, the contradiction between 'fairness', (*pingdeng* or sometimes *zhengyi*), and 'efficiency' was accepted as an inevitable outcome of economic growth. In the socialist context of China, the two must, however, be placed within a 'balance of values'. Zhang recognized past transgressions in terms of an over-emphasis on fairness resulting in counterproductive 'egalitarianism'. Predictably, he stressed that 'efficiency' is essentially a matter of improving the productive forces. Jurisprudence was, therefore, expected to right the imbalance of the past. Without such improvement, he could not see how human rights would develop. Zhang concluded that there had to be a 'unity' of these values at the interstices of society and the economy.[31]

The issue also highlighted the correlation of social justice and the rule of law. Gong Pixiang, Vice-President of Nanjing Normal University, for example, wrote concerning the substantive nature of the rule of law: 'The modern rule of law doctrine, as distinguished from the traditional doctrine of the rule of man, must take reason and the rational value system as its starting point and its end. Without a connection with freedom, equality, justice and the rights of the subject the rule of law would be in name only.' In his view, the modernization of the legal system had to be anchored in a deep foundation of values. On this basis, Gong disagreed with Max Weber's distinction between formal and substantial rationality. In his opinion, these two rationalities had to be combined in a rule of law which balances fairness and efficiency in the scales of justice.[32]

The very difficult issues were not so easily resolved in the ebb and flow of debate. Qi Yanping, for example, objected to argument which placed efficiency and social justice in rigorous antithesis, but he also discussed the value of law in relation to principles of equality and efficiency and drew the following correlation between justice and economic relations in society:

> Social justice refers firstly to justice in distributing rights and interests and secondly, it means justice in resolving conflicts. The justice encompassed in law is neither trans-social nor trans-historical [in nature]. Justice is limited and determined by economic relations. The purpose of the market economy is to distribute the rights, interests and resources according to the rule of the market, to pluralize the subjects of rights and interests, and to lead the activities of [the legal] subject according to contract, and to legalize [related] activities.[33]

In the West, there is still vigorous criticism of Chinese human rights theory for its lack of genuine commitment, but inside China's legal circles there is a growing alarm on the part of conservative jurists who complain bitterly of an increasingly dominant 'rights orientation' and a perilous drift into pluralism. Jurists, such as Zhang Guangbo of the Jilin University law school, and Sun Guohua, at the People's University law faculty in Beijing, were deeply shocked by the rapid acceptance in legal circles of arguments concerning the emphasis on the freedom of contract, the prioritization of private, as distinct from public, law, 'internationalization' as the 'transplantation' of western law and 'rights and interests fundamentalism'.

'Socio-rights' vs 'rights and interest fundamentalism'

Zhang Guangbo has argued that there are no 'abstract interests' and '. . . to say that we need to establish a "contractual society" [*qiyue shehui*] is to go too far.' Any talk of 'pluralization' could only originate within a Marxist ideological viewpoint.[34] Zhang then distinguished the 'socialist market' from the 'great market', *da shichang*, of his reform critics. Emphasizing the continuing importance of state power, he took his cue from Deng Xiaoping on the importance of the 'liberation' and 'development of productive forces'. In his view, market efficiency had to be subordinated to the objective requirements of state power:

> Though the market economy is more efficient than the planned economy in allocating resources, it is difficult for the market in its

development to eliminate such problems as blindness, spontaneity, the destruction of balance in economic life, and polarization ... therefore, the state must of necessity exercise macro-adjustment of, and control over the economy.[35]

In a rear-guard response to the advocacy of a 'rights-oriented model' or 'rights and interests fundamentalism', these jurists rallied, somewhat unconvincingly, to support the distribution of interests on the basis of the will of the ruling class. At the same time, they attempted to bring obligations back into the theoretical fold of a reunified jurisprudence.

The key issue of 'rights and interests fundamentalism' surfaced in a Wuhan controversy over 'natural', or 'social jurisprudence' in its correlation with constitutional law. In a 1994 prize-winning essay, Professor Tong Zhiwei of the Wuhan law school offered a new grand jurisprudential theory which promoted a complete explanation of the legal complexity of the reform era.[36] Tong probed the constitutional law's response to the Leninist interpretation of a 'network of natural phenomena', *ziran xianxiangzhi wang*. Tong deployed familiar dialectics in his discussion of the transition from 'class' to 'interest'. His theory dropped 'class' and offered a new material focus on 'socio-rights', *shehui quanli*. Tong's theory defined 'socio-rights' as 'the interests of the whole of society as understood from constitutional law perspective, recognized and protected by the constitution and concretely expressed in various forms of citizen's rights and state power'.

Tong was disingenuous. He emphasized the new importance of rights, but he also noted the importance of state power. He did not explicitly negate 'the will of the ruling class'. Citing the demands of the new marketplace, he highlighted the need for clarification in law of the hitherto 'unsettled' factors of ownership. Tong not only built rights and interests into his theory, but he also reserved some room for obligations in a bid to avoid the pitfall of 'rights and interests fundamentalism'.

His ponderous theory identified two distinctive layers of 'natural phenomenon'. The first layer encompassed the abstract totality of social wealth as the sum of all the material means of society. This sum included settled and unsettled ownership rights. Within his operationally critical second layer, Tong dealt with interest relationships and the expression of wealth in socio-economic relationships. At this level, Tong expected constitutional law to respond to five identified types of interests: complete social interests, inclusive of all forms of legally and non-legally defined socio-economic wealth; overall social interests, including the previously mentioned legally defined socio-economic wealth; individual interests of both natural and legal persons; public interests, namely the interests originating with the social existence of that part of the wealth enjoyed by public institutions such as state agencies and enterprises; and the spontaneous inchoate interests of society, including interests that had yet to materialize as 'settled ownership rights'.

Tong's affirmation of 'public interests' had some resonance in the legal community. Sun Xiaoxia similarly focused his attention on the general social interests of 'public society'. He argued that the 'subject' of such interest is broader in scope than that of either the terms 'group' in sociology or 'class' in political science. Moreover, such public interest encompassed the classical differentiation of state, collective and individual interests. While stressing that the state had an obligation to protect social interests, Sun Xiaoxia preferred to balance individual efficiency with the protection of public society, but he endorsed the public interest as superior to collective and state interests.[37]

Tong Zhiwei's critics would not let the matter of 'socio-rights' rest. They detected a predisposition towards 'unified' jurisprudence and a reluctance to endorse fully the centrality of rights. The issue, in other words, was not 'rights and interests fundamentalism', but 'obligation fundamentalism'. Tong's grand theory might have been very useful in its clarification of 'settled' and 'unsettled' ownership rights, but the theory looked towards a reconstructed unity of state and society. Tong's explicit dialectical materialism effectively reduced the subjective nature of interests while elevating the importance of state power in the achievement of a unified social justice. Tong's Wuhan colleagues, Zhao Shiyi and Zou Xueping, decried his 'methods of addition and abstraction' in the generation of 'socio-rights'. Tong's theory apparently distracted attention from the primacy of rights and his methods obfuscated the distinction between citizen's rights and state power. Apparently, Tong had cleverly assigned rights and powers the same level of significance within society – both part of the same unified material structure.[38]

Tong rebutted these criticisms, claiming that he had given precedence to rights by distinguishing them from power within a revised dialectical unity of opposites. He drew his critics' attention to his own terminological focus on 'socio-rights', as distinct from 'socio-powers'. Then Tong gave his critics a lesson in elementary dialectics. He chided them for their forced opposition between citizen's rights and state power in China's context of scarce resources. Correlating the material formation of rights with particular development of society's productive forces, he argued that in the case of China's developing status, the state would have to take a positive, but aggressive role in protecting citizen's rights from within a newly forming rule of law. In light of this, Tong reaffirmed the importance of obligations. Although these were not in and of themselves 'interests', Tong believed that they were conditional to the logical development of rights and interests.

Tong has lobbied continuously to reinstate 'obligations' to its rightful place in jurisprudence. He assigned positive meaning to state power, highlighting the responsible correlation of order and justice and his own self-professedly rational clarification of categories of rights and interests:

> If the [respective] spheres of citizen's and state's rights are unclear, this would mean a lack of clarity in the categories of subject relative to rights and interests.... In light of this [we] might certainly expect a non-proceduralized conflict between the manifest subjects of public and private rights and interests; and no matter what the outcome of this, it would be detrimental to the building of the rule of law environment and the preexisting constitutional order would suffer damage.[39]

While contemporary jurisprudence has dispatched 'class', it has not been able to dispose properly of obligation. Indeed, the latter has always enjoyed a certain prestige across various legal systems. However, in a 1998 exchange with Professors Zhang Guangbo and Zhang Wenxian, Tong Zhiwei lamented that China's newly evolving jurisprudence had failed to provide adequate research and supporting theory on rights and obligations on three counts. Research had failed to determine the scope of rights and the related boundaries between rights and obligations and rights and power. Secondly, it had failed to determine accurately the relationship between rights and interests; and thirdly it had failed to explain the material essence of rights.[40] Even the most vocal Chinese supporters of rights would have theoretical difficulty in abandoning obligation altogether. 'Rights and interests' were conscripted in opposition to 'obligational fundamentalism', but not to 'obligation' *per se*.

A well known CASS champion of the rule of law, Liu Han, had already attempted to limit the retreat from obligations in his praise for Cheng Yunsheng's 1995 book on rights relativism. Liu warmed to Chen's fine dialectical balancing of rights and obligations. Like Chen, Liu rejected the 'socially harmful obligational fundamentalism of state planning' which allegedly marginalized the importance of rights within an extremist subjectivism. While some reformers stressed that obligations had undermined individual and group rights, Liu rejected the expediency of the new rights orientation, which apparently neglected group and social interests in the single-mindedly selfish pursuit of new individual rights.[41]

This debate directly invoked the relationship between state and society. Some reformers endorsed 'small government, big society' (*xiao zhengfu, da shehui*) in reaction to the gross irrationalities of past state planning and in support of the new importance of rights.[42] Even those who supported a new rights orientation were, nonetheless, divided as to the degree to which the protection of rights would necessarily require an activist state in order to combat the persisting 'feudal' dimensions of authority in contemporary society and politics.

Sun Guohua, and his People's University co-author, Huang Jinhua, challenged the apparently superficial fascination with 'rights and interests fundamentalism'.[43] As an alternatively, they championed the 'unity of rationality and power'. They contended that of course law must reflect the struggle to create interests and that this struggle is the essence of the law's 'rationality'. They also contended that, if such rationality serves as the essential content of law, the law's form must inevitably relate to state power and its ability objectively to order the relations between interests on the basis of a common set of values relating to morality and justice. They deeply regretted the extent to which jurisprudence had hyped the rationality of law at the expense of the form of law itself.

This debate also raised the issue as to what is the best legislative and law enforcement strategy for the legal and social protection of rights. Does one, in other words, accept the critical importance of the state in creating the rule of law in the first place? Subsequently, to what extent should the state actively promote the rule of law so as to insure justice, as against subjective interests which run amok in the extremes of social inequality?

Conservative jurists such as Sun Guohua, Gong Pixiang and Zhang Guangbo, consistently supported the 'rule of law' as it was distinguished from the 'rule of man', but, despite the irresistible correlation of the rule of law with the socialist market, they were not prepared willy nilly to abandon the will of the ruling class. The latter was integral to their notion of law and justice in society. Insisting that the state had its own legitimate public purpose, they hit back at their critics eschewing their morally bankrupt 'pluralized jurisprudence'.

The latter, in their view, was not so much a newly discovered moral science of justice as a depraved relativistic science of competing interests that contradicted the essential requirements of distributive justice as well as the localization of the Chinese legal system in accordance with the presumably recognizable public standards offered in contemporary Chinese culture. This is a very familiar polemic. Even the most vocal exponent of reform is seldom able to resist the temptations of 'localization' and is vulnerable to criticism of overzealous 'internationalization' at the expense of the distinctive cultural and historical interests of the Chinese people.

The strong political focus on 'efficiency as primary and fairness as supplementary' created a 'value problem'. Chinese jurisprudence has been traditionally predisposed to thinking of the value of law in terms of its rational contribution to social progress. Texts on jurisprudence often speak of the law's own efficiency or effect in providing predictable distribution of social and economic benefits. Also, these same texts will invariably place 'efficiency' as a value on the same conceptual level as freedom, equality, justice, public order and security.[44]

There has been ongoing debate as to whether efficiency, as it generates new material wealth, should supersede 'fairness' in terms of the universal enjoyment of rights and interests. Scholars and jurists divided on the issue as, for example, in the 1995 editorial review of the eminent journal, *Faxue yanjiu* (Studies in law).[45] During this debate, Zhao Zhenjiang accepted efficiency as primary and as a legitimate matter of social progress. The scarcity of resources apparently gave rise to such a principle; as he put it: 'Since rights are closely related to interests, the principle of efficiency first should also be followed in the distribution of rights.' In answer to his conservative critics, he issued a pre-emptive *caveat* that should unfair income distribution in society and unfair competition between enterprises exceed a certain limit, then this would create inefficiency. Zhao left the empirical limits of such inefficiency to others to define, but the implications for the conventional understanding of distribution were frankly explored.

The search for a better 'balance of values'

It is difficult to know whether Qiang Shigong anticipated Jiang Zemin's revision of 'to each according to his work', but in the same debate he stoutly contended that giving primacy to efficiency would require greater recognition of the importance of knowledge and capital in distribution. These features could not be adequately captured in the traditional formulation of 'each according to his work'. Moreover, past jurisprudence was incapable of understanding the importance of the individual as the primary subject of rights. The individual's rights and interests had been subordinated to the state's focus on obligations in law.[46]

Li Bing, a scholar at the Nanjing University Faculty of Law, explored the western economic preference for giving priority to 'benefit' so as to maximize social wealth in the allocation of scarce resources. Li cautioned against a unidimensional evaluation of law which focuses too exclusively on such benefit, for this, in his mind, threatened the independent character of legal science and the legal system. The value of law was not to become hostage to 'fashionable and mechanistic policy interpretation'. Law and jurisprudence, in other words, could provide only an indirect service to the policy on economic construction by helping create a just social environment and through the realization of a series of interrelated values such as freedom, equality, democracy and human rights.

Li wanted a better balance of values. He could not personally support an interpretation of 'giving due consideration to fairness' as secondary. Moreover, he contended that 'fairness' could not be simply equated with distributive justice. 'Justice' had to be more broadly conceived in terms of a more complete range of values regarding substance and procedure. To that end, Li Bing conscripted John Rawls in defence of his own viewpoint, citing the famous Harvard professor's argument: 'In fact, in justice as in fairness, the principle of justice is prior to any consideration of benefits.'[47]

Li Bing explored the appropriate correlation of market fairness to the rule of law. Underlying the importance of the independence of law and the variety of values encompassed in related jurisprudence, Li put both justice and the rule of law ahead of any particular policy regarding distribution. Li considered the differences in the Chinese and western cycles of state-building, but he concluded:

'Supremacy of benefit' as advocated by the Western school of economic analysis in legal science as the value of law for the modern market economy is based on the rule of law, which prevails in Western society.... Though the kind of market economy that contemporary China is trying to establish is the same modern market economy, we cannot ignore the fact that the building of this market economy begins in a society which is experiencing a social transition from the rule of man towards the rule of law. The contradiction between the rule of man and rule of law is the main contradiction in China's legal system construction. The basic task of contemporary Chinese legal science is to foster the rule of law spirit.[48]

The 'value problem' in Chinese jurisprudence was accentuated in the attempt to define the proper relationship between the market and the rule of law. A working definition of the 'rule of law' in jurisprudence has been urgently needed, and it is only very recently that the related contents of the rule of law have received authoritative sanction at the highest level of political power.

'Running the country according to law and establishing a socialist rule-of-law country'

The 15th National Party Congress of September 1997 endorsed the formulation and content of the 'rule of law', as it is specifically conveyed in 'running the country according to law and establishing a socialist rule-of-law country'. These connotations of the latter are distinctive, and they received ultimate constitutional sanction in the amendments of mid-March 1999.[49]

However, as was explained in *China's Struggle for the Rule of Law* (Keith 1994), the 'rule of law' had emerged as a new concept in the early to mid-1980s.[50] In fact the formal endorsement of the 'rule of law' in 1985 had been preceded by revision to the Party Constitution in September 1982 requiring that the Party conduct its activities in relation to criteria set out in state constitutional law. In addition, Article 5 of the new State Constitution of December 1982 required that all political parties, specifically including the Chinese Communist Party, would have to abide by the law and that no individual or organization would be allowed to enjoy the privilege of being above the state constitution and the law.[51]

Chinese debates during the mid to late 1980s concerning the substantive nature of the rule of law often distinguished between 'rule of law', *fazhi*, and the 'rule of man', *renzhi*. These debates were influenced by the incipient new policy on economic reform and the open door, but they were largely informed by a political reaction against the legal nihilism of the Cultural Revolution and the desire to avoid any future large-scale class struggle.

At that time, a minority of scholars attempted to disassociate the 'rule of man' from personality cult or the 'spirit of the leader' and, alternatively, to associate the 'rule of man' with the positive substance of traditional Chinese humanism that endorsed the importance of 'good men' in governance. Despite the constant search for the 'Chinese characteristics' of law and the legal system, this latter viewpoint received little support, and opinion overwhelmingly described the 'rule of man' concept in the negative terms of the utter moral supremacy of imperial rulership in China's 'feudal' past.

Commentary by Wang Liming had clarified the difference between the mere existence of law as under Chinese Legalism and the notion of an ethos in which law would enjoy supremacy over political leadership and policy change. This was perhaps best captured in the early 1989 *Renmin ribao* headline of Wang Liming, '*Yi fazhi guo bushi fazhi*' (A rule-by-law state does not equal the rule of law).[52] In fact one of the Party's most trusted jurists, Sun Guohua, informed Ronald C. Keith in a People's University interview of September 1989, that, some time after Tiananmen Square, Jiang Zemin had personally assured Sun that he appreciated the distinction between the mere existence of law in a legal system, *fazhi*, and the rule of law as a substantive ethos that placed law above the vagaries of the political leadership or the 'spirit of the leader' in Chinese politics.

Li Buyun, the current director of the Center of Human Rights, within the CASS Institute of Law, was part of the earlier mid-1980s debate. He has detailed the history of the debate, and in that light he discussed how one ought to understand Deng Xiaoping's essential strategy for ruling the country in accordance with law, *yi fa zhi guo*. Drawing on his past arguments against the rule of man as 'feudalism', Li described three theories that had circulated in the debates of the early to mid 1980s.

The first theory recommended the rule of law as distinguished from the rule of man. The former required the independence of law in order to deal with personality cult and to provide social and political stability. A second theory attempted to synthesize the rule of law and the rule of man. This synthesis was justified on the grounds that law is the tool or creation of man and man is the moral agent who puts law to work. The theory of rule of law, *fazhi lun*, and theory combining the rule of law and rule of man, *jiehe lun*, were distinguished from a third Marxist theory, *quxiao lun*, which disavowed the 'rule of law' as neither 'objective' nor 'scientific'.[53]

Li Buyun pointed out in a June 1998 interview with the authors that the mid-1980s distinction still lacked a credible political consensus. In his view, the top leadership only came to accept the 'rule of law' as a commonly held position under the leadership of Jiang Zemin in 1994–97. Li cited a series of six crucial lectures given to the Politbureau leadership in its own inner sanctum in Zhongnanhai in December 1994 to December 1997.[54]

The Party leadership's adaptation to the socialist market has had a significant impact on the debate over the content of the rule of law. Deng

Xiaoping's Southern Tour theory has been canonized since his death and it has formed a large part of the justification for a new third stage of development in Chinese jurisprudence featuring 'running the country according to law and establishing a socialist rule-of-law country'.[55]

Deng Xiaoping, himself, only rarely referred to the 'rule of law', but he explored the notion of placing the law above leadership and policy change. Deng hoped to use law to avoid the upheavals associated with large-scale class struggle and 'feudal' factionalism within the political leadership. Zhang Zhende's 1995 study of Deng's legal theory acknowledged that the politicians were not always as scrupulous as the jurists in maintaining the distinction between the 'rule of law', *fazhi*, as an ethos embracing the supremacy of law and equality before the law and 'legal system', *fazhi*, as an expedient set of legal rules and processes facilitating state policy.

Zhang, however, contended that Deng actually distinguished between these two contents. Deng's selected works often referred to entwined 'democratization' and 'legalization'. Zhang claimed that Deng envisaged a 'rule of law society', *fazhi shehui*. The latter synthesized related ideas on the objective notion of law as distinct from the subjective dimensions of politics and the synthesis of law and democracy in the transcendence of law over the 'spirit' of leaders and vicissitudes of state policy change.[56]

Such generous interpretation was sometimes challenged, as in Guo Daohui's foreword to the 1995 publication of Huang Tao's *Socialist Rule of Law*. Guo, as editor of one the country's most prestigious law journals, was not satisfied that Deng's celebrated 1978 16-character principle (*you fa keyi, you fa biyi, zhi fa biyan, wei fa bijiu*), had clearly distinguished between the rule of law and rule of man. Guo and his supporters believed that Deng should have provided an even stronger emphasis on law as superior to the will of the leader.[57] It is arguable whether Deng faithfully adhered to his own words in the later context of Tiananmen Square, but, in reaction to Mao in the Cultural Revolution, he had clearly earmarked the law as a part of a new post-Mao strategy of institutionalization to deter the extremes of leadership. Jurists and scholars have often cited the following 13 December 1978 statement in justification of legal reform:

> Democracy has to be institutionalized and written into law, so as to make sure that institutions and laws do not change whenever the leadership changes or whenever the leaders change their views....

30 Law and Justice in China's New Marketplace

The trouble now is that our legal system is incomplete.... Very often what leaders say is taken as law and anyone who disagrees is called a lawbreaker. That kind of law changes whenever a leader's views change. So we must concentrate on enacting criminal and civil codes, procedural laws and other necessary laws.... These laws should be discussed and adopted through democratic procedures.[58]

Deng may not always have acted on the basis of the 'supremacy of law', but he sponsored the creation of a comprehensive set of laws, which were intended to weather and transcend leadership and policy change. Party Congress debate on the substance of his remarks featured four related ideas encapsulated in 16 Chinese characters translated as 'to perfect the law' [i.e. to create complete codes for the different departments of law], 'to observe law and to act according to law', 'to insure equality before the law' and 'to strengthen the supreme authority of the law'. Deng's 3rd Plenary Session remarks have become the *classicus locus* in all subsequent discussion of the rule of law.

Deng's Southern Tour theory opened the door to wider discussion of the relationship between the principle of the supremacy of law as a hallmark of the rule of law in the new market context of rights and interests formation. Yang Haikun, for example, wrote in 1993 of the need for law to act as an impartial mechanism facilitating the legitimate expression of interests and to moderate the sharp competition which is contemporaneous with the increasing efficiencies of market productivity. While accepting the primacy of efficiency, Yang correlated the market, the rule of law and the supremacy of law in the following analysis:

> Chinese legal tradition reflected unitary, vertical and hierarchical interest structure and denied the interests of the individual and group in the name of *raison d'état*. There was rule by law but not rule of law: law was subordinated to power. Changes in modern society have broken down this kind of structure of interest. Various individual and group interests are recognized. Meanwhile, the complicated structure of interest groups requires an independent authority to adjust relationships among interest groups. This authority must transcend the interest of any particular group and represent the common interest of society. This supreme authority is law.[59]

In the light of Deng's death and the subsequent politics of leadership transition, what is the current understanding of the 'rule of law'?

Leading scholars at the influential CASS Institute of Law, such as Li Buyun and Chen Shirong, provided the authors with a number of important insights. They claimed the support of the top Party leadership for their views, and they argued that, since 1993–94, Chinese jurisprudence as a whole has consequently entered a new third stage of development as new thinking on the rule of law has taken hold more widely within the Party–State itself.

This historiography challenges western speculation that there was a rift within the Party leadership between Jiang Zemin's 'core faction' which exclusively stressed the critical nature of Party leadership in a time of fundamental socio-economic change and Qiao Shi's 'rule of law faction' seeking to place the law above the Party. No doubt in anxious anticipation of Deng's death, Jiang Zemin was busily establishing himself as the 'core' of Party leadership; however, it did not automatically follow that he was opposed to the growing emphasis on the 'rule of law'. One might alternatively suggest that all of the central leadership were in favour of the rule of law, but that they did not always agree on the content of the concept.[60]

In a rare interview, the then Chair of the NPC Standing Committee, Qiao Shi, did provide the following perspective which was possibly shared by many in the leadership who, like Deng Xiaoping, were 'groping for rocks on the riverbed':

> There has never been a successful transition from the central planning economy to market economy in the world, so we have to feel for way on our own, [verbatim]. The same is true of the establishment of a legal framework for market economy. Without a model to follow, we have to do it on our own too, It requires a speedy development of legislation work to accelerate the reforms and opening up and to develop the socialist market economy. . . . There must be laws to direct, regulate, guarantee and restrict the development of the socialist market economy.[61]

Qiao emphasized the unprecedented circumstances of China's transitional process. He outlined four target areas for development of a legal framework for the socialist market. He prioritized the legislative agenda in terms of the laws needed to 'standardize subjects' and their rights and obligations in the market.

Qiao contended that laws would help 'regulate the relationships among different subjects in the market' on the basis of willingness, fairness, equal price, honesty, trustfulness and legality. Qiao wanted 'macro regulation' by the state and 'harmonious economic development' and laws to create a new social security system. He concluded that the pattern of corruption could not be contained without the strict and reliable application of the law on the basis of equality before the law. Official corruption, particularly involving high officials and the leadership's offspring, was unsettling to the top Party leadership and the issue was at the forefront of unprecedented debate in the National People's Congress.

With Jiang Zemin, Li Peng, Qiao Shi, Li Ruihuan, Liu Huaqing and others in attendance, Cao Jianming, of the East China University of Law and Politics, launched the pivotal series of Zhongnanhai lectures on law with a pre-approved discussion of international trade law and agreements on 9 December 1995. This discussion put China's participation in international trade in the perspective of the November 1993 Party decision on the establishment of the socialist market and then proceeded to review the purposes of GATT and the urgency of establishing law on the protection of intellectual property rights. A second lecture, by Shen Sibao of the University of Foreign Economic Trade, focused the attention of the leadership on the legal system of international trade and Chinese involvement with foreign economic law.

The initiation of major policy change through formal leadership study, in interaction with selected concerned participants and experts, is nothing new in the united front history of Chinese Communist Party politics. The Yan'an tradition of Kangda-style public leadership study was confirmed in the headline of the *Renmin ribao* confirming a new set of lectures on law at Zhongnanhai. Under Mao's slogan of 'Study, Study and Study Some More', the *Renmin ribao* eulogized the leadership roundtable discussions on the 'legal system':

> In the self-styled university of the socialist market economy, we are all elementary school students.... In the past, in the midst of war, we studied warfare and we achieved a great victory in the revolutionary war. Today, in the midst of reform, we study reform, and in the midst of a socialist market economy we are studying socialist market economics and law, and this is so that we can well achieve reform and the great victory in establishing socialist market economic structure and the socialist legal system.[62]

Following along this well-beaten path of self-conscious study, the Party took charge of the 'rule of law' agenda. Out of a series of topics offered by the Ministry of Justice, Jiang Zemin personally selected subject matter relating to the creation of a 'socialist legal system' in the context of a socialist market economy. The resulting third lecture of the Zhongnanhai series was collectively written by a group of distinguished senior scholars at the Institute of Law, including Liu Hainian, Wang Baoshu, Xia Yong, Liang Huixing, Xiao Xianfu, Wang Jiafu and Li Buyun, and subsequently delivered by Wang Jiafu in January 1995. At the time, while Jiang was apparently himself quite receptive, there was still an important degree of Politburo opposition which interfered with the lecture's agenda and language so as to highlight the more conservative concept of 'building the socialist legal system'.

As explained, for example, in the 1997 Qiao Keyu text on jurisprudence, the formulation, 'building the socialist legal system' was the preferred one in the past Marxist–Leninist understanding of the socialist relation of law and the state. This preference was part of the reaction to the critical assumptions of capitalist regimes, which had deliberately advanced the rule of law in opposition to the integrity of China's political system. This text challenged the emphasis on 'legal system', arguing that it would be more appropriate to view the 'rule of law', *fazhi*, as it forms part of the progress from a traditional to a modern society. The rule of law then becomes a method for realizing modernization in either the modern capitalist or socialist context. Its content would include, but would not be restricted to, the modernization of the 'legal system' (*fazhi*). According to this view, the 'rule of law' had to been understood as belonging to a higher and more encompassing conceptual category than the 'legal system'.[63]

Currently, CASS Institute of Law jurists claim that jurisprudence has just entered a third stage of development just as the rule of law debate has responded to the policy emphasis on the market economy. These jurists relate this new stage to a real shift, which they believe has been unequivocally ratified by the top leadership.

After Deng's October 1992 line was set, market reform fundamentally informed the political context of theoretical debate concerning the rule of law and its particular manifestation in China's modern legal culture. On the vital issue of Party leadership vis-à-vis 'running the country according to law', the *Renmin ribao* recorded Jiang's statement at Wang Jiafu's first lecture: 'The party must, on one hand, play a leadership role in drawing up the constitution and laws and, on the other hand, consciously operate within the framework of the constitution and laws, strictly abide by laws, and running the country according to law.'[64]

The longer formulation, 'running the country according to law to create a socialist rule-of-law country' was subsequently endorsed in the March 1996 documents of the 6th Plenary Session of. the Eighth National People's Congress and the September 1997 15th Party Congress. This rather repetitive formulation was rationalized with reference to Deng Xiaoping's theory on 'socialism with Chinese characteristics'. This formulation offered a more definitive separation of the law from the state. It challenged a narrow institutional focus on building a 'legal system' as distinct from building the 'rule of law', as an ethos sustaining a political cultural notion of authority.

Professor Wang Jiafu gave a second lecture in the seminal Zhongnanhai series. He anticipated a newly emerging viewpoint in the top leadership. His previous lecture had featured Deng Xiaoping's theory to justify the 'building of a new legal system'; however, this time he made it quite clear that the creation of a legal system for a socialist market economy would constitute a profound legal reform and not merely a patching up of the extant law and legal system.

Wang's second lecture affirmed the necessity of the 'rule of law' in terms of the need for law which could assist in the creation of social stability at a time of extraordinary transition, and he reiterated a basic argument to the effect that the rule of law was part of an inevitable process of modernization in which China would finally transcend the limitations of 'feudalism'.

Wang did not hesitate to appeal to the top leaders' gut instinct for political and social stability. He connected social stability with rights protection:

> So that we can have a socialist country with a people's democratic dictatorship and so that we can have a communist party which says what it means in terms of serving the people, we must take the protection of people's rights as our essential and enduring purpose. Indeed, if the people's rights are easily violated, then in reality this is a violation of the people and this would lead to the resistance of the people. One might say then that this would rouse the people to fight among themselves, to oppose the government, and to oppose the Party.[65]

Wang linked the regime's legitimacy to the enjoyment of rights and the public perception of fairness. While noting the unity of rights and obligations, he clearly singled out rights as the more important aspect of this unity. Wang also reiterated that the best way to strengthen Party leadership was to insure that the Party act on the basis of legal methods of leadership and administration.

Wang Jiafu's first lecture had been innocuously entitled '*Shehuizhuiyi shichang jingji falu zhidu jianshe*' (Questions concerning the establishment of a socialist market economy legal system). A supplementary lecture, by Professor Shen Mingzhao of the Southwestern University of Politics and Law, as appendixed to Wang's first lecture, had made similarly cautious reference to 'legal system'. Wang's internal content referenced 'the socialist market economy is a rule of law economy', but, at the time, the sensitive politics of leadership succession precluded definitive recognition of the rule of law as distinguished from legal system.

In written remarks appendixed to Wang's published second lecture, Li Buyun highlighted the familiar distinction between legal system and rule of law. In his view, while these concepts were closely related, they conveyed qualitatively different emphases in that the first focused on the system of laws and institutions relating to legislation and judicial process while the latter connoted a broader form of governance or a method of ruling which, in Li's firmly held conviction, no longer had any relevance to class considerations.[66]

The final ascendance of the rule of law has been attributed to the personal intervention of Jiang Zemin. Liu Hainian, the current director of the CASS Institute of Law, has, for example, claimed that Jiang was the originator of two related ideas, namely, 'running the country according to law' and 'establishing a socialist rule-of-law country' since these ideas were explored in his 'Problems Concerning the Theory and Practice of Running the Country according to Law and Establishing a Socialist Legal System Country' and his 8 February 1996 remarks entitled 'Running the Country according to Law and Protecting the State's Governance and Peace for a Long Time to Come'.[67]

Indeed, the two ideas were endorsed by Jiang Zemin in his 12 September 1997 speech to the 15th National Party Congress.[68] This new formulation apparently transcended past reference to the rule of law as a subordinate constituent element of socialist 'spiritual civilization'. Referring to Jiang's 12 September 1997 speech, Li Buyun also underlined the fact that for the first time 'running the country according to law in order to create a socialist rule-of-law country' was placed on the same theoretical level as the socialist market economy. Nonetheless, many within the Party and the legal community still consider the rule of law as a dependent material and policy reflection of the socialist market economy.

In his aforementioned appendix to Wang Jiafu's second lecture, Li Buyun identified the content of 'rule of law country' under five headings relating to the creation of a complete and departmentally comprehensive legal system, the correlation of democratization and legalization, the supremacy of law vis-à-vis organizations and individuals, an improved judicial system and a modern legal culture. After the second lecture, the members of the CASS Institute of Law fanned across the country in a high-profile lecture circuit. Li Buyun, himself, subsequently committed himself to a gruelling pace, conducting 80 lectures to assembled central government ministers and their deputies, provincial governors and mayors.

In his 4 June 1998 interview with the authors, Li Buyun elaborated further on the content of the second lecture so as to provide a more comprehensive checklist of ten basic principles of legal development which, he presumed, would rest upon three related societal foundations. Li specifically enumerated ten specific principles: (1) perfecting a complete legal system; (2) sovereignty of the people; (3) protection of human rights; (4) a system of checks within a balancing of power; (5) equality before the law; (6) supremacy of law; (7) government according to law; (8) due process; (9) judicial independence; (10) the ruling Party to conduct itself according to law.

Li believed that these principles had to have their tripartite foundation in the market economy, democratic politics and a rational culture whereby both people and officials acted in accordance with a positive sense of the law. In his view, the principles and their related foundation originated in contemporary changes in Chinese society and politics. The true historical significance of the market was duly stressed in that the market, unlike the planned economy, needs a complete set of laws to deal with the international market and the developing internal aspiration to respect changes in popular perspective and social relations as well as the growing awareness of individual rights and interests.

According to Li, these changes have already encompassed a move in social relations from status to contract, and they are coincidentally reflected in support for 'small government and big society'. Contemporaneously, there is a coalescence of the sense of subject, the sense of rights, the sense of democracy and the notion of modern enterprise as rooted in a notion of democratic process. While Li noted that the Party had set a target of 2010 for the completion of the building of a comprehensive socialist market legal system, he believed that it would take 30 to 40 years for China to realize the ten principles in practice.

Li addressed a number of immediately relevant questions. As for explaining how this new qualitative stage in thinking come about, he gave due political credit to the initiative of the intellectual and scholarly community, and particularly the legal circles within this community, and he stressed the role of the 'reform faction', *gaige pai*, within the government and Party.

As for the potential contradiction between efficiency and fairness, Li Buyun acknowledged that reform could not create instant equality. Citing the disturbing rise in unemployment as an example, Li recognized that economic reform was likely to polarize things in society. Past emphasis on egalitarianism had discouraged productivity and failed to provide for the universal enjoyment of rights, and he contended that short-term sacrifice would create a longer term viability in the economy and that some short-term inequality would necessarily accompany the struggle for more freedom and liberty.

As for the relevance of western experience to the building a socialist rule-of-law country and related jurisprudential controversy over the relative importance of 'localization' vis-à-vis 'internationalization', Li returned to his ten principles to suggest an increasingly substantive congruence in the western and Chinese concepts of the 'rule of law'. Furthermore, he clarified his own usage of 'internationalization', highlighting two basic connotations, namely, the importance of the linkages with the international community and China's participation in the making of international convention and the rational convergence of national experiences with respect to the spirit, purpose and form of law.

Li agreed with Aristotle on the content of the 'rule of law' as justice without appetition, based upon the equal application of the principles of law without regard for privilege or political office. Li was often more open to foreign concepts and experience than many in the legal community who are more focused on the elevation of Chinese characteristics in the law's modern development. Although rigorously opposed to feudalism as antithetical to rational culture, he saw some positive elements in China's tradition of Legalism. Moreover, he issued a *caveat* to the effect that it would be irrational for countries to copy indiscriminately each other's experience without paying due attention to legitimate indigenous differences.

The advent of 'running the country according to law and establishing a socialist rule-of-law country' has precipitated a flood of writings in Chinese jurisprudence relating to the Jiang Zemin speech of 12 September 1997.[69] Zhang Chunshen and A Xi of the NPC Law Committee, for example, wrote in *Zhongguo faxue* (Chinese Legal Science) that this speech had moved beyond Deng's famous 16-character formulation to focus attention on the relationship between the rule of law and the

38   *Law and Justice in China's New Marketplace*

'institutionalization and legalization of democracy'.[70] The venerable jurist, Sun Guohua and his colleague, Huang Wenyi, from the Jilin University faculty of law, claimed that the Party was still needed to ensure the development of the rule of law, but that Jiang's formulation signified a 'major change in the way the party exercises its leadership'.[71]

As has already been noted with respect to Zhang Zhende and Gao Daohui, there is internal controversy on the extent of Deng Xiaoping's theoretical commitment to the rule of law and the degree to which the post-Deng leadership has brought forth a fundamentally new interpretation of that term's contents. A great deal of this interpretation has highlighted the inner connotations of Jiang's September 12th phraseology: 'Ruling the country by law is the basic strategy employed by the Party in leading the people in running the country.' The underlying notion in the following quotation of Jiang Zemin (author's italics), does bear some resemblance to the wording of Deng's 1978 exposition on entwining 'legalization' and 'democratization':

> Ruling the country by law means that the broad masses . . . participate, under the leadership of the Party and in accordance with the Constitution . . . participate in one way or another and through all possible channels in managing state affairs . . . and that *socialist democracy is gradually institutionalized and codified so that such institutions and laws will not change with changes in the leadership or changes in the views or focus of attention of any leader.*[72]

On the basis of the recommendation of a Party constitutional amendment group headed by Li Peng, the CCP Central Committee sent a proposal on 22 January 1999 to the NPC, asking that Jiang's 15th Party Congress formulation on the rule of law be inserted as a new paragraph into amended Article 5 of the State Constitution.[73] This amendment, along with several others, was passed with great fanfare on 15 March 1999. As a new strategy of governance it was one of what the NPC deputies referred to as the 'three ones', namely 'one theory' (Deng Xiaoping Theory), 'one stage' (a protracted primary stage of socialism) and 'one strategy'.[74]

Xinhua reporters put a positive spin on this amendment for foreign consumption stating:

> This declares to the world that socialist China which is building itself into a country under the rule of law will, first of all, govern and build the country in accordance with the constitution. This is to institu-

tionalize all power belonging to the people, the people being the masters of the country, the interests of the people being above everything else, and democracy in the state system as well as socialism with Chinese characteristics.[75]

Much of the commentary underlined the need for everyone in the Party to comply with the state constitution; however, the Party's commitment to 'democratic legal work' and the rule of law is not likely to convince China's critics in the West of its best intentions. Such support, however, is politically important in so far as it encourages China's legal reformers to move further into 'forbidden areas'.

Apart from this, the rule of law's growing theoretical relation to the market has sparked a series of cognate controversies over the relative ordering of, and the relationships between, the different values of law as these relate to justice and efficiency. These debates have encompassed several related questions on ownership and distribution in an increasingly 'contractual society', on the relative efficacy of private and public law, as well as on social stability and the new internal significance of legislated human rights and the appropriate legal recognition and protection of rights and interests within a rapidly changing society.

Judicial justice in the new marketplace

There is one final angle from which the 'rule of law' debate can be viewed. 'The socialist market economy is a rule of law economy' relates to the correlation of procedural and social justice. While in China's legal community there always has been a keen ideological interest in the nature of distributive justice as integral to the aforementioned 'interior and external correlations' of the legal and social systems mentioned above, there has been a lot less focus on the values of law as they relate to due process. The emphasis on the latter was historically obscured as a result of a much stronger focus on a particular interpretation of the law's 'efficiency'. The Party endorsed the law's 'flexibility', (*linghuoxing*) as a virtue which facilitated social control and the 'comprehensive management of public order'. This also accounted for the historical pre-eminence of the criminal law among the departments of law.

The 'efficiency' of law as it related to public order and security went unquestioned in Chinese jurisprudence.[76] To serve the public good apparently the state needed the criminal law's flexibility of 'combining severe punishment with leniency'. This flexibility had justified an open-ended use of analogy, *leitui*, in order to deal with the spread and changing nature of crime. It was assumed that any particular combination of severity and leniency would be dictated in immediate policy understanding of crime at a particular point in society's development. Later supporting argument for legal reform critiqued this exclusive focus on the value of order. Chen Zexian, for example, argued for criminal law revision in the light of the new market needed to protect citizens' rights: 'People's understanding is no longer limited to "criminal law as a means of proletarian dictatorship", and now law is seen as playing a multiple function in maintaining social security, stability and progress, in the state's macro-adjustment of the market economy, *and in the effective protection of citizen's lawful rights and interests.*'[77]

The reform argument also distinguished between the spurious nature of 'ruling the people with law' (*yifa zhi min*) as an outcome of the Maoist tendency towards the 'rule of man' and 'rule of law' as it relates to the new circumstances of the market economy. Zhang Zhende, for example, castigated Mao's focus on the 'instrumental values' of the law in the following discussion of the essential purposes of legal reform:

> The target of reform is the old system. [Reform must] . . . change the old legal system which focused only on the instrumental values of law, on order, and on 'rule the people with law', and [it must] establish a new systemic civilization, at the core of which is the rule of law, and which is rooted in the market mechanism and unites substantive justice [*shizhi zhengyi*] with formal justice [*xingshi zhengyi*] and can effectively restrict and rationally exercise public power.[78]

Contemporaneous with the new focus on rights and interest formation, the related subscription to 'human rights' and the fashioning of integrated systems of social and legal protection, there has been a growing focus on the necessity of procedural law. This focus has also become part of the complex interplay of 'localization' and 'internationalization'. The new human rights focus was deployed in reform argument for procedural rationality in a time of international exchange and the growing market relations in Chinese society.

Since 1995, the NPC has passed several major new laws on lawyers, judges and police and the procuratorate. These initial steps culminated in a major revision to the administrative law and criminal law of procedure in 1996 and a wholesale revision of the criminal law itself in 1997. This trend was immediately rationalized in relation to 'the market economy is a rule of law economy'. Under the latter, the traditional argument for flexibility in law in order to meet the changing needs of social control could no longer retain any validity. In their direct relation to the socialist market economy, the 1996–97 revisions represented a symbolic break with a tradition, which had accentuated flexibility to deal with the political necessities of class struggle, counterrevolution and social control.

'Flexibility' was replaced with a reinforced subscription to *nullem crimen, sine lege; nulla poena, sine lege* (there can be no crime without a law; and there can be no punishment without a law). A key drafter of the Criminal Law of Procedure and one of China's leading authorities on the subject, Cui Min, indicated in a June 1998 interview with the authors at the Public Security University in Beijing that the latest round of procedural revisions represents a major break with the past. This reform had, in his mind, accomplished two mutually related purposes, namely, to guarantee the enforcement of new substantive law and to establish the independent value of procedural law.[79]

Cui's generally optimistic assessment had to a certain extent been confirmed in Jonathan Hecht's earlier report to the American Lawyers Committee for Human Rights. Despite some serious reservations, Hecht believed that the 1996 changes to criminal procedural law had definitely broken new ground with respect to the role of defence counsel, legal aid and trial procedures. He was prepared to argue: 'Still, the 1996 NPC Decision demonstrates that China has begun to reorient its basic approach to criminal justice away from a dominant preoccupation with social control toward a somewhat greater concern for the protection of defendant's rights.'[80]

Cui Min believed that the revision balanced the need to punish crime with the need to protect human rights. Moreover, he immediately attributed the new status of procedural law to the coalescing of three large factors, namely, international human rights discussion, China's own changing historical and political circumstances and the advent of the market economy. However, as will be discussed in Chapter 5, the market has not only accentuated the importance of the efficiency of law in terms of the procedural protection of rights, but the growth of the market has been accompanied by the proliferation of new categories of economic crime. This has reinforced the political argument for the use of law as a means of achieving social control in a time of instability. However, this argument incorporated a new relation between social stability and the protection of rights and interests. Obviously, the values of order, peace and security can push jurisprudence in a number of different directions. In any societal context the interpretative prioritization of the law's values is necessarily political, and the market alone may not guarantee a consistent development of judicial justice. Legal reformers have tried to influence the revision process so as to extend the procedural protection of the rights and interests of suspects and victims as these have to be weighed in the balance with the general public interest in peace and order. They recently failed to modify the extent of the criminal law categories allowing the death penalty, and thus far they have succeeded only in limiting the application of such law through the indirect means of a new internal circular. There has been both success and failure. The notion of procedural independence from politics and privilege has been given greater priority in the context both of the market and the need for a reliable mechanism to deal with corruption.

Legal reformers have, however, claimed a victory in terms of the 1996–97 confirmation of the importance of comprehensive stipulation of the law. The latter was vetted in open opposition to analogy which had previously rationalized state instrumentalism on the grounds of efficiency and flexibility. However, the increasing identification of the law's values and purposes with the requirements of the marketplace has not automatically guaranteed a progressive expansion of judicial justice in all parts of the revised criminal procedural and criminal laws. Focus on market development and social stability justified a radical expansion of the criminal law's provisions on 'economic crime'. The state could hardly keep up with the changing nature of such crime in the marketplace and this expansion simply internalized some of the more backward-looking decisions of the early 1980s NPC Standing Committee on severe punishment and the death penalty. Even while new and important subscription was made in terms of 'no punishment without a law', there was, in some parts of the newly revised law, an awkward fit between the punishment and the crime.

At the same time as the top leadership had instinctively grabbed on to 'interest' as a basis for popular recognition of the fair mediation offered in law in the uncertain context of the market, the same leadership dismissed reform arguments which challenged the popular belief in capital punishment. In the light of intense political focus on corruption at the heart of the regime itself, 'severe punishment' seemed politically necessary, especially given the spectacular spread of corruption in the market economy. Capital punishment, for example, was believed to be an 'effective deterrent', but in addition capital punishment was politically necessary to 'assuage the masses'.

All of the above argument suggests unevenness in the jurispurdential development of the law's response to the values of the market economy.

Key issues

With respect to contemporary Chinese legal reform and the prospects for the emergence of a 'rule of law', the Chinese criminal law specialist, Stanley Lubman, once said that we may have 'to imagine the unimaginable'.[81] It would seem that the 'unimaginable' is already upon us. Mao Zedong once mused that social development, in all of its gloriously rich contradictions, is like a Hunanese sandal which takes its own shape in the making. Although jurisprudence is transitional, like society itself, its conceptual contours are coming into focus as it works its way through new market relations and the adjustment of rights and interests. The nature of jurisprudence is under discussion as scholars increasingly advocate the 'pluralization' of jurisprudence. The accelerated development of the market has significantly impacted the internal formal discussion of the rule of law as that concept is distinguished from 'legal system' and is presumed to entail the supremacy of the law and equality before the law.

However, even as jurisprudence turns away from the past assumptions of state instrumentalism, it has had to deal with the rise and fall of subjective rights and interests in the marketplace. There is no reason to expect an easy consensus on how to solve the 'value problem' in a context of tremendous social change. Perhaps the policy on the market has created opportunity for jurists to advocate the rule of law and the formal expansion of rights, but to what extent is this rule of law subordinated to what one scholar called 'fashionable and mechanistic policy interpretation'? And to what extent is the pluralization of jurisprudence just a convenient rationalization for the failure to agree on an appropriate balance of values?

The jurists in their attack on state instrumentalism have often called for the law's separation from the state. At the same time, they have called upon the state to support the development and enforcement of human rights law so as to modify the socially unacceptable consequences of market competition. The law becomes a handy and even rational tool by which to reinforce social stability on the basis of protecting rights and interests. Through its distributive and judicial justice it is expected to provide an efficient basis for stability in the uncertain context of rapid economic change and related polarization of society. On the other hand, are the essential 'values' of the law always in rational alignment? How will these values ultimately receive coherent prioritization? Can procedural law act to support substantive law while remaining independently aloof from it? Given China's prevailing political circumstances, what role should be assigned to the state's processes in defining these values? As suggested here, the market has acted politically as a driver in favour of formal recognition of the rule of law and human rights, but the existence of the market, itself, has not consistently guaranteed social and judicial justice.

At the same time as law is celebrated for its support of market efficiency, there is concern that the law demonstrate its superiority over politics in objectively exhibiting its independence from subjective interests. Apparently, the 'supremacy of law' requires such independence even as the 'rule of law' is, itself, at least partially justified in its contributions to 'the readjustment of interests'. The law's own 'efficiency' requires predictable outcomes on the basis of impartial and dispassionate mediation of competing interests. Given the focus on efficiency and the intensity of the politics associated with market outcomes, is justice likely to be blind? What are the implications for the dignity and authority of law in the marketplace?

Some of these problems of logical consistency immediately arise even with the apparently progressive notion of 'pluralized jurisprudence'. The transition from a planned to a market economy requires that the law adapt to the new plurality of subjects as interests. The multiplication of equal subjects before the law, of course, progressively modifies or diminishes the state's position in society at the same time as there is a call for the state to take an active role in society to insure that justice is available to those most in need. Not only does the market help generate opportunity for the formal legal expansion of the rights of nonstate newly emerging interests, but politically and theoretically it has sharpened the focus on 'small government, big society'. But in China's complex and somewhat distressed circumstances of transition to the marketplace is an activist state needed to ensure the success of the 'rule of law' and the expanded protection of human rights?

'Pluralized jurisprudence', in addition to its essential notion of the plurality of subjects before the law, conveyed in the Chinese as *liyi zhuti duoyuanhua*, may also take on a political connotation of 'democratization'. While the law's independence from the state is emphasized in the current 'third stage', jurists apparently still need clear Party sanction to move forward. Reacting to 'unified jurisprudence', some jurists may see jurisprudential debate as an opportune forum for competing viewpoints on the prioritization of the law's essential 'values'. The more conservative Marxist jurists, on the other hand, see what they would term the 'pluralization of ideology' lurking in the 'pluralization of interests'.[82]

Quite apart from any political anxiety over the potential for compulsive ideological disorder within jurisprudence, there is the issue of legal modernization. The market wants the rational coherence and predictability of law as an independent authority. In the context of such an extraordinary transition in the economy, the law's own efficiency in terms of defining the correlation of rights and interests and providing clear rules and legal understandings as to the resolution of conflict would seem to be especially important. Ambiguity or the lack of conceptual resolution on vital questions like 'ownership rights' would, for example, pose a monumental headache to those earnestly seeking to consolidate private, as distinguished from public, law.

A note on the organization of this book

The largely untold story of China's newly emerging jurisprudence is truly fascinating, and the following chapters will begin to tell this story, paying particular attention to contributions from increasingly influential reform jurists. Based on extensive reading of Chinese law journals, as well as discussions with many of China's most senior jurists, these chapters will expand on this introductory chapter in order to give an interior glimpse into the developing controversies which are shaping contemporary jurisprudence as it responds to the new demands of China's marketplace.

Chapter 2 explores contemporary rights and interests formation as it specifically relates to social justice and procedural protection for women, children, the handicapped and the elderly. These sectors have been tied together in a coordinated legislative strategy for the social and legal protection of their specific human rights. The influence of international experience and human rights debate is particularly evident with respect to the emergence of this 'special grouping' (*teshu qunti*), wherein the notion of 'rights and interests' has become most prominent in the articulation of contemporary law governing family relations in the era of the market. Law on women's rights and interests, for example, has moved away beyond the concerns of the revised marriage law of 1980.

Jurisprudence is probing new issues of equal opportunity for employment and education in specific response to the difficult transition to the market, and it is addressing changing patterns of social distress concerning family violence, child labour, prostitution, and sexual harassment. To many jurists working in these socially and politically sensitive areas, the protection of rights and interests immediately requires active state support. As for the enforcement of this special grouping of rights, jurists are not always prepared to accept the logic of short-term postponement of such rights for the sake of a market-based strategy based upon efficiency before justice. At the same time as jurists are looking for ways to protect rights, many politicians and scholars are increasingly concerned about the market economy's negative impact on family values. To what extent is the emphasis on the social and legal protection of rights consistent with institutionalized morality and the state's own interest in 'socialist spiritual civilization'? The 'special grouping of rights and interests' is pivotal to the analysis of jurist debate concerning 'rights and interests' formation and the interpretation of justice as it relates to values concerning equality, due process, public order and fairness.

Chapter 3, 'Justice and Efficiency in Contractual Labour Relations', refocuses on the issue of social justice but with special reference to the emergence of contract labour in the transition from a planned to a socialist market economy. Under the old planned economy, while the working class was formally part of the revolutionary vanguard in the people's democratic dictatorship, there was a paradoxically weak development of labour legislation. Professor Shi Tanjing, of the CASS Institute of Law, an eminent authority on the subject, gave the authors his own personal opinion as to why. The position of labour was, in his view, simply taken for granted by the CCP leadership. The nature of the socialist state self-evidently guaranteed the worker's position in society. Indeed, for a long time, the benefits of state enterprise workers were the envy of the rest of the general population.

However, with the advent of the socialist market economy, a variety of different types of enterprise began to emerge, and the conditions of labour began to change radically as the structures of planned economy deteriorated in a new competitive context. The inability of retiring workers to receive their pensions on time has already reached the proportions of a national crisis.[83] Soaring lay-offs are seen by many observers as disguised unemployment which will adversely affect the social order. The housing allocations provided by work units, or *danwei* are no longer guaranteed. At a time when social insurance has yet to be put in place, many workers are suffering the consequences of downsizing in state enterprises.

After years of slow progress, in 1994, the draft labour law was rushed to the NPCSC for approval. The situation was believed to be too urgent for approval to await the full session of the NPC in March 1995. As was the case with much of the legislation concerning the 'special grouping' of rights and interests, the new labour law highlighted rights and interests in its title, and debate concerning the protection of labour was similarly influenced by the wider discourse on human rights.

The progress towards 'ownership rights' and the reform of state enterprise is regarded by many observers as the key to regime stability, and indeed the law's relation to social stability in the area of labour rights and interests has become a new domestic legislative priority. To what extent can law compensate the worker for a significant loss in political and policy status? Under new law, to what extent does the worker have the ability to achieve procedural protection and remedy against the excessive demands of market efficiency? This chapter's analysis delves into jurists' debates over the transition to new contract relationships in law between workers and management with regard to the balancing of those values of the law which relate to efficiency, social justice and judicial justice.

The content of **Chapter 4**, 'Sorting out Property and Ownership Rights in Law', is closely related to that of Chapter 3. Chapter 4, however, it focuses more closely on what is probably the most woolly, and yet most politically contentious area of market-based jurisprudence. 'Public ownership' has been 'sacred'. It has enjoyed pre-eminence both in law and in legal theory. The 1980s reform efforts to revitalize state enterprise through a scheme of 'separation of ownership and management' failed. Successive calls for the 'clarification of property rights' has not resulted in the development of a coherent theory of ownership in law.

Among jurists, and apparently between jurists and economists, there is a complex terminological battle over the key distinction between 'property rights' and 'ownership rights'. This chapter analyses the internal jurist debates on an issue which fundamentally reflects the way in which socialism is distinguished from capitalism.

Chapter 5 analyses the new prospects for judicial justice. It explores the underlying reasoning for, and the change in direction of, procedural or judicial justice as it has adapted to the priorities of market reform. Some jurists stress the synthesis of the rational form of law and its substance, whereas others argue in a more familiar Weberian vein that procedural law should be viewed as separate from, but equal to, substantive law.

The national debate on human rights and the intense policy focus on the market and international economic exchange have helped to strengthen what was hitherto the weak sister of the criminal law. Criminal procedural law was the mere extension of criminal law, which received enormous political priority in terms of the state's focus on social control. Again, there is a question of how subjective interests will be placed in the scales of blindfolded Justice along with the public inter-

48 *Law and Justice in China's New Marketplace*

est in social stability. This chapter highlights the internal arguments for a more comprehensive and separate criminal procedural law, paying particular attention to theoretical debate over the balance of individual and social interests in the pursuit of judicial justice.

The shift in the strategic development of both the criminal law and the criminal law of procedure, away from 'flexibility', and the opportune state resort to analogy towards the comprehensive stipulation of law, is generally reflected in all the departments of law. While revision in the area of 'economic crime' has not always responded to human rights objection to 'severe punishment', jurist debate has clarified that the earlier approach of 1979, namely, 'general stipulations are better than specific ones', *yi cu bu yi xi*, is inappropriate to China's new market context. This old approach, based on general stipulation, gave more exclusive priority to collective rather than individual interests, and the dynamics of the market apparently require the specific elaboration of all of the categories of crime and the comprehensive and independent procedural reinforcement of the substantive purposes of the criminal law.[84]

Chapter 6 identifies and analyses the principles of contemporary Chinese jurisprudence, placing them within the explicit range of scholarly and political controversy concerning the 'balance of values' in the law's response to the market economy. The analysis reviews the extent to which these principles form a coherent strategy facilitating the current transition to the market economy on the basis of rational legal culture. The final chapter will examine the internal contradictions of China's new market jurisprudence and sum up the related trends within legal reform as these highlight controversy surrounding human rights and judicial justice. It will also examine the contents of 'the market economy is a rule-of-law economy' and 'running the country according to law and creating a socialist rule of law country', placing the development of related jurisprudence within the overall controversy surrounding the potential creation of civil society and the changing State–Society relationship in China.

2
The 'Special Grouping' of the Human Rights of Women, Children, Handicapped and Elderly

Chinese jurisprudence constitutes a discourse on what is justice, and the transition to the 'socialist market' has posed an essential question of social justice in law. How will the law, as a predicate facilitating new market relationships, respond to the 'rights and interests' of the most vulnerable sectors of society in a policy context which synthesizes justice with efficiency? The 1990s sequence of legislated human rights and its supporting jurisprudence formally established the 'special grouping' (*teshu qunti*), of the rights and interests of women, children, the handicapped and elderly. This chapter describes and analyses the contents of this particular grouping. The latter is placed within the jurist consideration of changes in society and the related weighting of justice and efficiency in the new marketplace.

The 'special grouping' has received a surprisingly high political priority in the context of the elimination of class-based strategies and policies and the transition from a planned to a 'socialist' market economy. This high priority was assigned despite a very strong political reaction against absolute egalitarianism as expressed in 'all eating from a common pot'. Whether or not the new emphasis on 'getting rich' is turning out to be as 'glorious' as it has been touted, efficiency has rarely been placed in direct antithesis to distributive justice and equality rights. Efficiency has been placed within a 'balance of values' which also responds to the 'Chinese socialist' preference for social justice and stability. There is a new political focus on the protection of human rights categories as part of a strategy to ensure social stability as it is thought to be rooted in social justice. At the same time, there is a renewed interest in the use of law to facilitate institutionalized morality in a time of societal distress.

Legislation on rights and interests came about largely as a response to economic reform policy focusing on production increase through competition. An essential corollary of such a policy is the reduction of the social welfare costs of state enterprise through a more diversified sharing of responsibilities for welfare across the state and society. Any uninhibited emphasis on the 'liberation of productive forces' has been qualified in policy and law highlighting the protection of the rights and interests of the most vulnerable sectors of society.

In various reports to the Party, Jiang has professed fidelity to Deng's 'three favourable directions', *sange youli yu*, calling for the contemporaneous liberation of productive forces with the elimination of polarization and the achievement of common prosperity.[1] Jiang reportedly expressed to US Senator Max Baucus a keen interest in Franklin D. Roosevelt's new deal strategy for alleviating the traumatic consequences of runaway capitalism.[2] However, in the pathbreaking 14th Party Congress of October 1992, Jiang referred to the difficulties contingent upon everyone reaching common prosperity at the same time: 'Socialism does not mean poverty. As it is impossible to become prosperous simultaneously, we must allow and encourage some areas and people to become well-off first, with a view to bringing along more and more areas and people and achieving the goal of common prosperity step by step.'[3]

'Step by step' might suggest some form of timed triage of human rights enjoyment, or a casual tolerance for the prioritized enjoyment of human rights. The February 1994 report on China's implementation of the Nairobi strategies acknowledged that, even though China is part of the Asia-Pacific Region – a region where economic development was until recently on the upswing – there are still 'problems'. The report explained: 'The problems facing China are insufficient funds and materials that can be used directly for women's participation in production and the phenomenon of occupational barriers in the course of economic transition.'[4] The June 1994 'white paper' on the status of women reiterated: 'China is a developing country. Owing to the constraints of social development and the influence of old concepts, the condition of Chinese women is still not wholly satisfactory.'[5] Within the normative context of such development, Chinese politics is likely to witness future battles over the state's legal responsibility for the entrenching of rights and interests vis-à-vis the increase in social inequalities as a result of economic reform.

While the Chinese viewpoint has stressed that the opportunity for human rights enhancement is somewhat circumscribed by the opportunities for development, the related scope of the law's application is steadily expanding. Jiang Zemin, for example, told the 15th Party Congress on 12 September 1997: 'China needs to develop diverse forms of ownership with public ownership in the dominant position; and third any form of ownership that meets the criterion of the "three favorables" can and should be utilized to serve socialism.'[6] Jiang has signalled that the social responsibility for 'common prosperity' will have to encompass support for the economically vulnerable sectors of society across the multiple forms of ownership in the economy. In other words, the special group of rights *should be* materialized in not only the public, but also the private sector of the economy.

The dialectical balancing of these 'favourables' is likely to become even more significant in the light of the explicit incorporation of Deng Xiaoping Theory into an amendment made to Chapter 12 of the 1982 State Constitution in 15 March 1998.[7] The problems inherent in the practical extension of the law's scope, however, are manifold particularly as they relate to the special grouping of rights and the protection of workers as discussed in Chapter 3.

Chinese policy, law and jurisprudence have self-consciously conformed to Deng's 'three favourable directions'. Party policy has conceded that 'common prosperity' is unlikely to be simultaneous. On the other hand, even given the need for greater levels of productivity in China's developing economy, there is a political reluctance to subscribe to an overt trade-off of equality rights for the material gains associated with economic growth based upon market competition. Both the formal definition of political priorities and the related NPC agenda for a special grouping of rights have rejected the well-known human rights–development tradeoff – about which Jack Donnelly and others have warned. In particular, Donnelly criticized the following viewpoint:

> Furthermore, the exercise of many human rights, both economic, social, and cultural, and civil and political interferes with or slows the rate of economic growth and development. Therefore, it has been regularly argued that in the interest of both human rights and development . . . human rights must be temporarily suspended.[8]

US human rights analysis has repeatedly charged the Chinese with 'cultural relativism', and some observers have also suggested that the Chinese government has made disingenuous use of developmental priorities in order to thwart the development of political and civil rights.[9]

For the sake of contrast, this view might be placed alongside Li Buyun's view that economic reform is a driver for progressive change in the relationship between state and society. In addition, Chinese analysis has issued many reminders to the effect that China's level of development, prevailing cultural norms, social understandings and resources are in fact all legitimately part of any authentic materialization of Chinese human rights objectives.

Indeed, the lack of resources is a fundamental problem in achieving human rights improvement on the basis of a 'step by step' approach. The official view argues that the number of poor declined from 250 to 67 million between 1978 and 1995; however, alternative World bank figures based upon a lower threshold of 'poverty', contend that currently the poor actually number 300 million.[10] In any case, these figures were largely concerned with food, shelter and clothing. In addition to these basic rights of subsistence, there are the issues surrounding social benefits in the context of market competition.

China's transitional social security system is described as 'multilayered'. New old age and unemployment insurance schemes are supposed to develop initially in the cities. Support for the rural aged '. . . will be shouldered chiefly by their families and supplemented by community assistance'.[11] Such policy challenges the renewed emphasis on improving the status of rural women and casts doubt on the new legislated commitments to provide a wider range of state-sponsored services to women and children. However, apart from these issues of social benefits – such as unemployment insurance, medical insurance and old age pensions – a new series of laws addressed problems of market transition relating to the fair enjoyment of property rights and equal access to employment opportunities.

The 1990s emergence of a 'special grouping of rights' requires serious analysis for at least three important reasons. In the first place, it is within this grouping that the new jurisprudence on the correlation of rights and interests has achieved its greatest salience in law and jurisprudence. Secondly, related analysis helps explain the complex dimensions of the state's role in the socialist 'rule of law economy'. There is conflicting opinion as to whether it is better to shrink the state or to actively use the state to consolidate 'authentic' human rights. Thirdly, the special grouping of rights have been central to the developing national debate in legal circles concerning the essential understanding of 'human rights'. This debate has been increasingly informed by comparative legal experience and legislation, as well as by the international relations of human rights advocacy.

The new salience of 'rights and interests'

The 1990s NPC legislative agenda has reflected the paradigm shift from 'classes' to 'interests', but the latter are still in an euphemistic state of indeterminate 'pluralization'. Interests are undergoing a formative metamorphosis and do not have the same immediate coherence as classes. Party reformers and critics of the Party believe that the law must respond to new subjective social needs through the readjustment of rights and interests but the Party itself has yet to endorse a particular and comprehensive theory which sets out the definitive composition of contemporary society.

There is an ongoing search throughout China's legal community for an explanation of how the state ought to foster the equitable adjustment of interests (*liyi tiaozheng*), within the context of the changing dimensions of China's society, political culture and economy. In facilitating the socialist market, the state may well have to shrink relative to society, but at the same time the state is called upon to facilitate social stability on the basis of a fair 'adjustment of interests'. There is related controversy in the West over the potential development of 'civil society' in China.[12] Some scholars argue that markets naturally generate 'civil society', but there is a lack of agreement as to the extent to which China's 'socialist' market actually conforms to the requirements of capitalism. Others anticipate the possible metamorphosis of the traditional authoritarian state into some form of soft corporatism and consultative authoritarianism. In China, there is related adaptation to Marx's originally critical writings on 'civil society'. On the other hand, the advocates of civil law have pushed hard to consolidate the distinction between public and private law.

The key correlation of rights with interests in the new generation of law on the rights of women, children, the handicapped and the elderly was politically deliberate.[13] Although some scholars have argued that 'rights' implicitly include interests, 'rights' generally form a smaller circle of legally stipulated content within a bigger circle of ideal social relations. 'Interests' were referenced only episodically in pre-1978 legal theory, but since then, 'interests', within these two overlapping circles, have been used to reinforce 'rights' vis-à-vis 'obligations'. In the post-class context of economic reform, Party leaders liked to refer to 'interests', as they were presumed to be readily understood by the masses, that is, the general public. What is more, the focus on 'interests' addressed the anxieties of those sectors of society who were concerned about the immediate consequences of market competition and related societal change.

Within the so-called 'third stage' of jurisprudence, 'interests' were explored with reference to new understandings of the individual and collective association in changing society. Sun Xiaoxia, for example, discussed 'social interests' as broadly conceived 'public social interests' which transcend 'class', in political science, and 'group', in sociology.[14] On the other hand, recent emphasis on 'group', *qunti*, in contrast to 'collective', *jiti*, is sometimes used to stress the pluralism of interests in society as distinguished from the collective harmony of society's constituent elements.[15]

On one level, one might expect that Marxists would adjust instinctively to a notion of rights anchored in differing social, if not class, interests. At least the attempt to understand law in relation to the composition of society would seem familiar; however, senior conservative Marxist legal theorists, such as Zhang Guangbo and Gong Pixiang, have bitterly opposed the emergence of a 'pluralized jurisprudence' in its challenge to the *a priori* relevance of 'obligations' and to the state's 'objective' understanding of the composition of society.[16] Their revisionist colleagues have, on the other hand, welcomed the elaboration of a plurality of groups in society as fully consistent with the advent of a socialist market.

'Group interest', as distinguished from 'collective interest', is acquiring a positive connotation of common interests shared by individuals. Luo Mingda and He Hangzhou described 'interests' as integral with the individual's human needs and social reality. These authors drew contemporaneously on western philosophy and Marx's interpretation of 'civil society'. Their 'interests' were defined as 'subjectively determined and pursued'. Despite their inherently subjective character, these interests were carefully distinguished from anything that could be termed 'selfishness'.[17] The latter was not construed – as in the economic philosophy of Adam Smith – to be an unintended force which strengthens the economy. The individual was separated out theoretically from the excesses of individualism. However, if the positive, subjective dimensions of new societal interests are acquiring a greater degree of legitimacy in politics and law, there is still the question of whether the liberation of interests will explicitly challenge the ascriptive dimensions of traditional political culture as well as contemporary institutionalized morality.

Moreover, there is always the danger that the state co-opts interests in a politically self-interested prioritization of reconstructed rights as part of an expanding soft corporatism. Chapter 1 of this book, for example, discussed Tong Zhiwei's grand theory of 'socio-rights'. Tong's critics took him to task for moving in the direction of such corporatism. Tong sought to re-establish the jurisprudence of 'rights and obligations' as the mainstream theory of law. In addition, he defined rights, *quan*, so as to include both the sum of the legal rights of individuals and the power which belongs to public institutions.[18] Tong's theory both transcended the limitations of class analysis and conformed to the Party's own refurbished view of the unity of state and society. His theory also drew intellectually from a tradition of dialectical materialism in that it understood all interests as 'expressions of wealth in socioeconomic relationships'. In addition, the Tong theory attracted criticism for its indiscriminate bundling together of individual interests, public interests and the 'spontaneous interests of society'.[19]

Conservative Party opinion feared the political implications of 'rights and interests' and the consequent modification of the state's legal positivism. Even the supposedly more 'enlightened' state constitution of 1954 had highlighted 'rights and obligations' in its third chapter. Article 94 required that the state 'pay special attention to the physical and mental development of young people'. Article 96 insisted that women should enjoy 'equal rights with men in all spheres – political, economic, cultural, social and domestic'; however, these rights were developed within the prevailing synthesis of rights and obligations. There was a single fleeting reference in Article 98 to the 'just rights and interests', *zhengdang quanli he liyi*, of overseas Chinese.[20] These rights and interests passed much later into law in 7 September 1990 with the NPC approval of 'The Law of the PRC on the Protection of the Rights and Interests of Returned Overseas Chinese and the Family Members of Overseas Chinese'.[21]

Article 1 of the 1950 Marriage Law referred briefly to the 'protection of the lawful interests of women and children' and to the 'interests of the child', in the Article 20 context of divorce.[22] Its third chapter, on the other hand, was entitled: 'The Rights and Obligations of Husband and Wife'. In contrast, the 1980 Marriage Law placed Chapter 3 under a new heading, 'Family Relations', and directly incorporated a new and suggestive language into Article 2, which proclaimed: 'The lawful rights and interests of women, children and the aged are protected.'[23] Article 48 of the state constitution of 1982 gave a new constitutional blessing to 'women's rights and interests'.

Article 18 of the 1982 constitution also offered to protect the 'lawful rights and interests' of foreign enterprise. A similar emphasis was explicit in the wording of Article 33 regarding the 'lawful rights and interests' of foreigners within China's sovereign jurisdiction. All such 'rights and interests', however, were outlined either in the first chapter on general principles, or in the second chapter, which reiterated the unity of rights and obligations.[24]

56 *Law and Justice in China's New Marketplace*

In 1988, 'rights and interests' figured in the controversy over the legal definition and protection of private enterprise. Article 11 of the 1982 State Constitution had referenced the state's protection of the 'legal rights and profits of the private economy'. Article 1 of the 1988 'Interim Regulations on Private Enterprises of the People's Republic of China' elaborated more significantly on 'protecting the lawful rights and interests of private enterprise'. Chapter 4, however, returned to the 'Rights and Obligations of Private Enterprise'. Article 4 reacted against worker exploitation when it emphasized: '... the employees' lawful rights and interests are protected by national law', but Article 30 stopped short of a legally required introduction of social insurance for workers.[25] The issue surfaced more extensively in the mid-1990s debates over the new labour law and social security law as discussed more fully in Chapter 3 of this book.

'Rights and interests' acquired greater theoretical status after Tiananmen Square in a fresh round of debate over the societal implications of economic reform and a related flurry of law-making. Anxiety over the possible revocation of the 1986 General Principles of Civil Law proved to be premature. In fact, the civil law was reinforced with the 9 April 1991 promulgation of the Law of Civil Procedure of the PRC. The advocates of legal reform triumphantly proclaimed that this law enhanced 'subject equality' before the courts and extended 'women's rights and obligations in civil lawsuits'.[26]

The focus on 'protection of women's lawful rights and interests', *baozhang funude hefa quanyi*, was integral to the post-Tiananmen human rights debates. The orthodox view of 'unity of rights and obligations', *quanli yiwu xiang tongyi*, was challenged in the expanded advocacy of equality rights. The conventional dialectic in the law texts, 'rights are but obligations and obligations, rights' was criticized as a phony 'unity' sacrificing 'rights' to overweening state power.[27]

'Rights and interests' steadily gained ground in the context of unprecedented national debate on human rights, and the readjustment of interests has been justified in relation to the Party's open door and economic reform policies and the need for social stability. 'Rights and interests' have been assigned in legislative instalments, not only to women and children, minors and the aged, but also to the handicapped, workers, Overseas Chinese, private households and private entrepreneurs.

Interests were deliberately associated with rights so as to strengthen rights politically and legally, but 'interests' did not have the same obvious counterpart in 'obligations'. Whereas rights were a strict matter of immediate stipulation and enforcement, 'interests' encompassed the nebulous content of stated ideals and socialization.[28] Politicians, lawmakers and jurists have not yet agreed on the extent to which interests should be judged in relation to competition (as opposed to harmony). There is no universally applied social justice criterion, but there is a great deal of debate over the relative priorities of efficiency and social justice.[29]

As a result, 'interests' are, at bottom, profoundly political. They involve the legislated prioritization of specific interests in relation to the state's definition of social justice and the related distribution of declining state resources. While open door and economic reform considerations may dictate greater focus on the protection of rights and interests, Party leaders find it difficult to resist a utilitarian distribution of state resources that is based on the prioritization of those newly emerging interests which make the most immediate contributions to the economy. This may conflict with the Party's commitment to 'common prosperity'.

Social and legal guarantees and the changing role of the state

The theoretical and legislative development of a special grouping of rights has raised the issue of whether the state is part of the problem or part of the solution to the formation and enjoyment of authentic human rights. As was discussed in Chapter 1, a new rights orientation challenged the past tendency of the state to maximize obligations to the state at the expense of the rights of individuals and autonomous social organization. The linkage of rights with interests was partly designed to compensate for past 'obligational fundamentalism'. This might imply the contraction of state authority and the development of the law's autonomy vis-à-vis the state. On the other hand, in the light of weak legal consciousness in society and in the context of the transition to the market economy, many legal reformers are prepared to support a new role for an activist state in legally guaranteeing the rights and interests of the most vulnerable sectors of society.

The current emphasis on a complete legal system is pursued in tandem with a state-sponsored social activism based on an updated mass-line organizational strategy. In the past, such strategy had often contradicted the formal legal response to change at the same time as obligations took obvious precedence over rights. US Professors Hung Dahchiu and Shao-chuan Leng, for example, saw swings of the pendulum between the 'jural' (formal) and 'societal' (informal) models of

China's post-1949 political modernization. These models accentuated the difference between the consolidation of impersonal codified rules and political socialization reinforced by 'extrajudicial apparatuses'.[30] Now the issue is whether the state can play a progressive role in support of entwined legal and social protection of subjective rights and interests.

The qualitative distinctions between the past and present mass-line are worth keeping in mind. The early 1950s mass-line politics encompassed large-scale class struggle which attempted to engineer societal and behavioural change through the mobilization of an entire network of interconnected social agencies and mass associations. In the early 1950s implementation of the first marriage law, for example, this approach self-consciously featured 'unified Party leadership' towards the achievement of a 'general call' to bring about sweeping social change. Currently, mass-line strategies regarding policy formation and public education in policy and law still exist, but there is no longer violent large-scale class struggle. The Party is self-acknowledged to be undergoing a 'crisis of faith' and 'unified Party leadership' has been rejected as monolithic.

New law relating to the special constituencies served by the various mass associations would seem to involve a greater active participation in consultative partnership in the drafting of specific provisions. The All-China Women's Federation (WF), for example, has only enjoyed politically qualified autonomy in its role to serve as a mobilizing agent for policy education and information transmission, but under the April 1992 women's law, the association acquired a legally recognized responsibility to help provide the social guarantees necessary for the protection of women's rights and interests. There is a spectrum of opinion within the WF over its agenda and strategy. Moreover, the way in which such responsibility is exercised is likely to vary with the changing politics of state funding and public apathy towards the Party state. As the pluralization of opinion occurs within the WF itself, and as the Party weakens, there may be greater opportunities 'to struggle autonomously for group-defined interests'.[31]

The 1990s legislation, rather than referring to 'civil society', endorsed a revised conception of the relation between 'state and society', *guojia he shehui*. The state is formally required to provide for the stipulated constitutional and civil law protection of rights and interests, but it is also expected to reinforce a system of social protection, *shehui baozhang zhidu*. The latter is to guarantee the practical enjoyment of these rights and interests through broadly based education and directed social activism.

In November 1991, in the first so-called 'white paper' on human rights accepted the legitimacy of human rights terminology. China's legislative strategy for social progress and family development focused on the creation of a 'complete legal system' which was legally designed to protect 'rights and interests' in law. At the same time, subsequent laws included deliberate reference to perfecting the system of social protection. The strategy for the legal and social protection of rights and interests seems to have been folded into an updated organizational approach featuring state-sponsored education, social control and activism.[32]

The white paper announced the state's intent to provide 'guarantees in terms of system, laws and the material means for the realization of human rights'. Subsequent legislation was considered part of a larger effort throughout society to help shape societal attitudes favourable to the development of human rights. The law could help clarify and entrench new standards, but it was also assumed that rights could only develop out of social reality and authentic consciousness. 'Legal rights', *fading quanli*, were theoretically distinguished from the 'actual rights', *shiyou quanli*, which were entrenched in social consciousness and practice. Moreover, social protection and activism were critical to the expanding practical enjoyment of those rights which had already been set out in the law.[33]

The 1990s human rights legislation, featuring the correlation of rights and interests, presumed that the best way to insure the enjoyment of these rights and interests is through the development of moral education and the related benchmarking of such rights and interests in the precise stipulations of law. New law encompassed explicit reference to integrated social and legal protection, and specific articles featured a hard and soft law distinction between what 'should' (*yingdang*) be done and what 'must' (*bixu*) be done. Both were presumed to carry formal legal responsibility. 'Must', however, requires immediate compliance with the specific stipulations of law whereas 'should' allows for more timed compliance with legally validated goals as the appropriate conditions in society become more favourable.[34]

In the 29 August 1996 'Law on Protecting the Rights and Interests of the Elderly', Article 3, for example, reads like a set of overarching objectives from a human rights charter requiring the coordination of social efforts, public education and the staged allocation of state resources:

> The state and society *should* adopt measures to perfect the social guarantee system for the elderly; gradually improve the elderly's living conditions, health, and conditions for participating in social

development; and ensure that the elderly get support and assistance, can get medical care, can continue to contribute to society, can continue to study, and can enjoy their lives.[35]

While 'should' invokes the social dimensions of public awareness, education and behaviour, it is directly incorporated into the law's provisions and is formally a matter of law. As law, the use of 'should', however, is less definite in its definition of what constitutes timely and acceptable compliance to the law.

While there is a legislative trend requiring that the state responds to justice, there is also a qualifying trend calling for the contraction of the state's responsibilities in favour of socially organized solutions and new individual consciousness and responsibility. This alternative emphasis is explicit in the exploration of the state–society relationship in terms of 'small government, big society' (*xiao zhengfu, da shehui*), based upon the widely acclaimed Hainan model for economic development and social security. This model represents a particular perspective on existing processes accentuating the Party's separation from government, and the state's separation from the management of enterprise. The model presumes both that government is a sub-system of society and that the state–society relationship must reflect a principle of inverse proportionality in that the stronger the state's control functions become the weaker the processes of self-management and self-organization within society. Also, according to this logic, the self-determining individual must take some shared responsibility together with the state and collective organization to establish a multi-tiered approach for the provision of social benefits.[36]

Legislated equality has not meant the deployment of new levels of centrally controlled funding to provide universal access to services and benefits. 'Big society' means more individual and associational participation in the achievement of social justice, less exclusive stress on state enterprise responsibilities in a competitive economic environment; it also means a very great political concern for social stability in what is acknowledged as the morally stressful circumstances of accelerated economic growth.

As argued in Chapter 1, there is a 'value problem' in emerging jurisprudence which informs the role of the state in the market context. The expectations of the state vis-à-vis society are not always consistent. The advocates of Hainan-style economic reform, for example, want to downsize the state and to enhance social and individual responsibilities. On the other hand, some legal reformers want to enhance the state's role in the creation and legally enforced enjoyment of human rights. The latter, in light of their perceived realities of a generally weak legal consciousness in society and the lack of practice in exercising the rights of citizenship, are often willing to justify the direct role of the state as an agent which actively creates the appropriate social conditions, political consciousness and legal guarantees to ensure the popular enjoyment, or 'authentication' of human rights.

The Party has reacted against the past experience of the over-centralized state and command economy, but it has not necessarily eschewed the ideal unity of state and society. The Party is still quite prepared to use the law to establish what it regards as the culturally valid norms of Chinese family life. In its attempt to shore up the Chinese family vis-à-vis new trends in juvenile delinquency, sexual harassment, third party interference in marriages, rape in marriage, the abuse of children and the elderly, and so on, the law sometimes appears to serve as a component of the state's mass-line project to insure conformity with the norms which the state assigns to society. The law's substantive function is explicit in the social justice implications of the 'special grouping of rights'. The state must protect rights and interests according to law. At the same time, the state has, since the late 1970s, attempted to create a networking of mass associations and formal institutions so as to achieve normative social control, or the 'comprehensive management of public order' (*shehui zhi'an zonghe zhili*).[37]

This mass-line emphasis on the state's active involvement conflicts not only with the organizational assumptions underlying the Hainan model, but also with optimistic western assumption highlighting the ready adaptation to civil society in China. Even while the Party has contemplated the qualified separation of party and state in the economy, it often prefers to deal with contemporary social dilemmas of interest adjustment through the same united front tactics of cooptation which originate in CCP organizational history. That having been said, the increasing complexity of the state–mass association relationship requires nuanced analysis. Within any given regime there is a likely relationship between law and social values, and the NPC legislation on rights and interests has tried to express a positive association of state and society in the legal protection of 'rights and interests'.

'Internationalization' and the 'special grouping' of rights

The issue of social values and the state's role in the normative development of rights and interests has to be placed within the context of self-conscious adaptation to 'internationalization'. The special grouping of rights was conveyed in new law which responds not only to a rational principle of 'localization', *bentuhua*, meaning the law's sensitive adaptation to the underlying values and understandings of China's distinctive society and political culture, but also to a learning process, dubbed 'internationalization'. As discussed in Chapter 1, the latter synthesizes the 'interior' and 'exterior correlations' of jurisprudence. Within this synthesis, Chinese human rights law becomes part of 'the international developmental process in law in which the particular legal systems of each country in the world, approximate more closely and coming together in convergence in order to take shape in mutual interdependence and linkage'.[38]

Recent legal trends in China have stressed the importance of a culturally nuanced understanding of family relations. This 'localization' has, however, to be weighed in the scales of analysis along with the extensive adaptation, on the part of China's jurists and law-makers, to comparative foreign legal experience in dealing with unfamiliar social phenomena such as family violence, sexual harassment in the workplace and the manipulation of the property rights of elders.

The new legislative agenda aimed at entrenching a special grouping of rights developed in tandem with China's tentative participation in international human rights discourse. The State Council's November 1991 'white paper' recognized the applicability of 'human rights' terminology to China. This provided the basis for pivotal new rights legislation for women and children.[39] Internal controversy and, ultimately, legislation was contemporaneous with new diplomatic offensives, particularly in the area of women's and children's human rights, which eventually resulted in the hosting of the UN Fourth World Conference of Women (FWCW) in September 1995.

The Chinese have become part of an ever-widening circle of international relations over the role of the state and the importance of international and domestic social activism in the advancement of human rights. The continuing importance of social activism was recently stressed by one of China's leading comparative law experts, Beijing Professor Shen Zongling. Shen, for example, cited the integration of law with social activism in the development of western feminist jurisprudence. While recognizing the international relevance of western theory concerning 'equality rights' and 'special rights', he noted that legal methods can either advance or detract from the cause of gender equality. He believed that western feminist jurisprudence had played an important role in the consolidation of legislation and in the judicial response to women's rights, but he added that this was not simply a matter of law as advanced by a specific group of feminist legal experts, for, more importantly, the law had developed within the 1960s/1970s matrix of social movements in the western developed countries.[40]

The correlation of law and politically sponsored socialization was specifically addressed in Article 3 of the UN Convention on the Elimination of All Forms of Discrimination Against Women which referred to the need for 'activism'. Governments were urged not only to pass laws against discrimination, they were to foster 'all appropriate measures' in the advancement of women. The latter assumed the modification of social and cultural patterns of conduct as a matter of public education.

Paul McKenzie has discussed how the UN Convention on the Elimination of all Forms of Discrimination Against Women projects an 'activism' which presumes that the right to sexual equality 'transcends the political and civil realm'. McKenzie found a parallel rejection in Chinese activism which militates against preconceived Western public–private distinctions: 'However, insofar as this activism dispenses with the public–private distinction, the Convention might be more acceptable to China than to a western democracy adhering to the notion that certain realms are beyond the legitimate purview of government influence.'[41]

While the public–private law distinction is a hot area of contemporary debate, Chinese mass associations are acquiring more explicit legal responsibility for both the legal and social protection of specific 'rights and interests'. Legislation assumes some form of unity of state and society, and it has expanded mass associational legal and organizational responsibilities within entwined systems of legal and social protection of rights. Point number 20 of the Beijing Declaration, on the other hand, specifically endorsed '. . . the participation and contribution of all actors of *civil society* (original italics), particularly women's groups and networks and other non-governmental organizations and community-based organizations with full respect for their autonomy . . .'.[42]

In 1980, China was one of the first group of countries to endorse the 1979 UN Convention on the Elimination of All Forms of Discrimination against Women. The latter's emphasis on special rights received favourable attention in Chinese jurisprudence. In 1985, the final year of the UN decade on women, a new law on the rights and interests of Chinese women was first proposed by the Chinese Women's Federation. In 1989, China was one of the co-sponsoring countries which had participated in the drafting of the UN Convention on the Rights of Children. Also, in April 1989, the Special Group for Women and Children of the Committee for Internal and Judicial Affairs of the National

People's Congress (NPC) was charged with the coordination of a related legislative agenda.

In 1990, China made its first bid to host the 1995 UN Women's Conference. That same year, the Working Committee on Woman and Children was established within the State Council to coordinate all the related government departments and mass associations. The Committee's membership represented a cross section of appointees from judicial organs and related line ministries. More recently, it set up its administrative headquarters within the new offices of the WF, and it has focused especially on issues originating with economic reform such as maternity benefits and the terms of layoff and the condition of women in the workplace.

Although the overall organizational thrust of reform in the area of women's and children's rights might be described as top down, conceptual elements of recent national legislation were inspired by early to late-1980s provincial regulations for the protection of the rights and interests of women and children.[43] In March 1991, the Chinese government signed both the World Declaration on the Survival, Protection and Development of Children and the related action plan. The April 1996 white paper on the status of China's children subsequently reported: 'The Chinese nation has long cultivated the traditional virtues of "bringing along the young" and "loving the young"'. And it linked the open door and economic reform policies to the internal move to place children's programming on to the 'social, scientific and legal tracks'.[44]

The State Council Work Committee formally assumed responsibility for departmental implementation of both the February 1992 National Program of Action for Child Development in the 1990s and the April 1992 Law on the Protection of Women's Rights and Interests. The orientation towards action and the comprehensiveness of the latter was regarded as pivotal to China's 1980 treaty commitment to the elimination of gender discrimination and to the honouring of the Nairobi forward-looking strategies.[45]

The new women's law was the subject of a mass publicity campaign which purportedly integrated a legal education process with specific projects dealing with literacy, technical education, maternal health care and the issues of prostitution and increasing the rate of girls' enrolment in the rural elementary school system.[46] While new law has tended to enhance the legal responsibilities of mass associations and may eventually impact on the autonomy of these associations, the integration of legal and social activist approaches has conveniently conformed with the Party's understanding of 'comprehensive management of public order'.

Chen Muhua, as vice-chairperson of the NPC Standing Committee, participated in the drafting of the new law. Prior to convening the FWFW, Chen, as the new president of the WF, joined other NPC Standing Committee members in a high profile fact-finding tour of the hinterland of Yunnan province and the Guangxi–Zhuang Autonomous region to assess the problems in enforcing the new law in rural national minority areas.[47]

The State Council's Work Committee nationally coordinated public education exercises which brought the Committee together with the CCP Central Committee Propaganda Department, the Ministry of Justice and the WF. In the light of the thematic emphasis of the UN FWCW on pragmatic state action, the State Council committee assumed responsibility for the implementation of the 7 August 1995 'An Outline of Chinese Women's Development 1995–2000', many provisions of which presaged the Beijing Declaration and Action Program.[48]

Just before the formal opening of the FWCW, Chen Muhua, head of the Chinese delegation, and president of the conference, claimed that the convocation of the conference in Beijing '... is a full confirmation of the tremendous achievements of China's burgeoning women's liberation movement'. Chen highlighted new domestic legislation and drew on a wealth of internal and international statistics to conclude that China's women's liberation movement '... demonstrates that China's human rights situation has fundamentally changed'.[49]

At the FWCW welcoming ceremony, President Jiang Zemin proudly claimed that the Chinese government '... has always regarded gender equality as an important measurement of civility'. Jiang focused on women as 'promoters of social development' who make 'a special contribution to the reproduction of the human race'.[50] The international media, however, headlined the subsequent remarks of Hillary Rodham Clinton who raised outstanding criticisms of female infanticide, forced sterilization and abortion. Her reference to inadequate non-governmental participation at Huairou was a pointed criticism of Chinese organizational deficiencies.[51]

Chen Muhua defended China's recent record citing the 7 August 1995 'Outline of Chinese Women's Development (1995–2000)' and reiterating the importance of a 'complete legal system' which would synthesize provisions scattered across the various departments of Chinese law, such as constitutional, civil, economic and administrative law, so as to protect women's rights and interests across the entire spectrum of state and social activity. Chen underlined the importance of the expanded inter-departmental cross-referencing of related provisions of the Marriage Law (1980), Election Law, Inheritance Law (1985), Mandatory Education Law (1986), Procedural Law on Civil Affairs (1991), Labour Law (1994) and The PRC Law on Protecting Women's Rights and Interests (1992).

Whatever one may say about the Chinese human rights performance, the issue of human rights within China itself has become internationalized, and the related creation of a special grouping of human rights has been informed by the attempt to balance 'localization' and 'internationalization'. Within the legal system and judicial process, the degree of western influence and ideas has never been greater, even as the Chinese have sought to consolidate a culturally distinctive view of the family in the context of the stresses and strains of the transition to the market economy. At one and the same time, the state is required to protect rights and interests and to maintain prevailing social values within an essentially family-orientated society.

The handicapped in the 'special grouping' of rights

The 1990 PRC Law on the Protection of the Disabled took five years to draft. It represented the first instalment in the 1990s special grouping of rights.[52] Its 9 chapters and 54 articles stipulated the legal responsibilities of state and society for the rehabilitation, education, employment, cultural life, welfare and environment of China's estimated 51.64 million handicapped.

While 'rights' were not entwined with 'interests' in this law's title, Article 1 of the 'General Principles' gave new legislative priority to the 'legitimate rights and interests of handicapped people'. The China Federation of Associations of Handicapped People was referenced under Article 8, as an agency which 'undertakes assignments the government entrusts to it', but there was a deliberately holistic organizational focus in this law's articles which featured the shared moral responsibilities of 'state and society'.

This sharing of organizational responsibility was conveyed in terms of 'should' rather than 'must'. Article 6 was amended by the Law Committee of the NPC to include the following wording, which referred to ongoing work based upon inter-governmental agreement:

> The State Council and the people's governments at the provincial, autonomous regional, and municipal levels *should* take measures and coordinate with pertinent departments to carry out the work con-

cerning the handicapped. The specific agencies to handle the work are to be decided by the State Council and the people's governments at the provincial, autonomous, regional and municipal levels.[53]

The state assumed the responsibility for ensuring employment opportunity, but the law in Article 28 specified a seemingly federal approach to the provision of employment which 'combines centralization and decentralization'.

Article 7, in an uninhibited display of legislative idealism, appealed to the people in society as a whole to manifest a 'socialist humanitarian spirit' towards the handicapped. The *Renmin ribao* (People's Daily) commentary, noting that the handicapped were falling behind social and economic development, emphasized that the new law was 'a law with Chinese characteristics'. It acclaimed the 'deep love' of the families of handicapped people; and at the same time hailed the law as 'a practical step taken by China to safeguard human rights and respond to the UN 'Worldwide Action Program on the Handicapped'.[54] This co-ordinated 'state and society' approach incorporated political notions of 'self-reliance and community initiative'[55] which neatly coincided with the reasoning underlying the Hainan model's approach to social welfare.

Article 1 featured the law's underlying philosophy of equality, participation and co-enjoyment of equal rights, and it incorporated a policy preference for rehabilitation through special education and equal opportunity, which included quotas for the recruitment and hiring of the handicapped within state departments. The NPC Law Committee also added the following emphasis to Article 11: 'The prevention of disabilities should be carried out in a systematic manner and leadership over the work strengthened.'[56]

'Obligation' was referenced only twice in Articles 9 and 10. These articles stressed that legal supporters and guardians have obligations to ensure the rights and interests of the handicapped in their care, and that at the same time the handicapped have obligations to 'follow public order, and respect public codes of ethics'. Article 10 directly offered the following charter-like moral instruction: 'Handicapped people should be optimistic, respect themselves, have confidence in themselves, improve themselves, rely on themselves and contribute to socialist construction.'

This 'state and society' approach suggested an updated soft corporatist strategy. The latter still presumed the state's leading role in ensuring ideological leadership over the charitable support of the handicapped, but it also presumed a new dimension of micro-management and rational sharing of welfare functions. Theoretically, there was a strong new emphasis on 'rights and interests' as the law on the handicapped was developed from within an unfolding domestic human rights debate which readily drew on international comparative experience and ideas.

In 1987, the NPC's Standing Committee endorsed the 1983 ILO Convention Concerning the Vocational Rehabilitation and Employment of Disabled Persons. This was followed in March 1988 with the creation of the Federation of Handicapped Peoples Associations. Deng Xiaoping's handicapped son, Pufang, took a leadership role at the Federation. Neither the ensuing funding scandal of Deng Pufang nor the unfolding of events of Tiananmen Square delayed the NPC Standing Committee approval of the new law in 28 December 1990. The Chinese authorities moved ahead of the full sitting of the NPC in the following spring. The new law was widely proclaimed as China's strategic response to the UN World Programme of Action Concerning the Handicapped, and it was cited as China's contribution to the UN Decade for the Handicapped, 1983–92.[57]

The rights and interests of women and children

Until very recently, children's issues have, more often than not, been treated as incidental to the wider western scholarly literature on the changing Chinese family. On the other hand, there is already in place a strong and discrete scholarly literature on Chinese women's issues which has critically weighed Party policy in light of the promise of socialism to liberate women from the bonds of Chinese patriarchal society.[58] Many authors such as Elizabeth Croll, Margery Wolf, Judith Stacey, Kay Johnson, Deborah Davis, Margaret Woo, Ellen Judd, Gail Hershatter, and others have laid the groundwork for the ongoing study of the debilitating effects of contemporary economic reform on gender equality and family life.

Throughout the 1990s' response to the formation of 'human rights' and the market stress on family values and social stability, there was a deliberate convergence of mutually reinforcing laws relating to the 'rights and interests' of women and children. Indeed, the latter have been deliberately packaged together in the law texts and in the cross-references of the NPC's legislative agenda. The focus on interests in the law on children anticipated the even greater prioritization of interests in relation to rights in the PRC Law on Protecting Women's Rights and Interests. It was not as extensive as the 1990s law on women and the elderly since it did not need to address the key issue of employment opportunity which had significantly informed other laws in the same 'special grouping'.[59]

The PRC Law on the Protection of Minors (1991) was acclaimed as the centrepiece of a new programme enhancing children's 'rights and interests'. While the Chinese tradition had been very wary of the state's direct involvement in intimate family issues, the September 1991 law on minors proclaimed that '. . . the protection of children is now within the scope of law'.[60] Protection, in this case, emphasized the importance of the 'comprehensive moral, intellectual and physical development of minors'. Protection was very closely tied to education, which was construed as the generally coordinated responsibility of 'state, society, schools, and families'.[61] Article 5 announced in a similar vein: 'All organizations and individuals have the right to practice dissuasion against or take action to stop behaviours of infringing upon the legitimate rights and interests of minors, or to lodge reports or accusations to the departments concerned.'[62]

The PRC Law on Protecting Women's Rights and Interests was also widely acclaimed as key legislation. Articles 2 and 3 of this law perhaps best expressed the related strategy of the 'perfecting of a system of social protection'.[63] Related responsibility was to be shared 'by the whole society'. The December 1995 'white paper', 'The Progress of Human Rights in China', reiterated the importance of both the social and legal guarantees of rights and cited the law's new provisions on the respective responsibilities of family, school, society and judicial institutions.

Subsequently, the April 1996 State Council white paper on the status of China's children featured the 'comparatively complete provisions' of new law citing the integration of the state constitution, criminal law, and civil law with the Marriage Law (1980), Education Laws (1986 and 1995), Law on the Disabled (1990), the Law on the Protection of Minors (1991), the Law on Protection of Women's Rights and Interests (1992), Law on Maternal and Infant Care (1994), Law on the Prevention and Control of Infectious Diseases (1989) and the Law on Adoption (1991).

The fast-tracking of children's and women's legislation reflects a particular view on the readjustment of interest which draws upon specific domestic and international political factors. The sense of domestic urgency should not be overlooked in an exclusive focus on the efficacy of foreign human rights pressure. The Party leadership has become increasingly anxious over social stability and regime survival. The latter is tied to the prolonged impact of the Cultural Revolution on family relations and values and to the proliferation of inequities in the contemporary 'socialist market'. The Cultural Revolution is widely believed to have precipitated a decline in Chinese family values, which has more recently resulted in increasing domestic violence and juvenile delinquency. Chinese post-Cultural Revolution analysis was contemporaneous with the Nairobi Conference focus on an international crisis of domestic violence, and – especially since the Cultural Revolution – Chinese analysis has focused on juvenile delinquency as a rising component in the overall crime rate.[64]

China's legal scholars have emphasized an unprecedented rise in family violence, human trafficking, prostitution, child labour, infanticide and drug-related crime. The regime is ideologically in decline, and the logic of economic reform seems at times to encourage a separation of society from the state. On the other hand, if the Party leadership does indeed act as a 'public patriarchy', its legislative strategy for 'rights and interests' has highlighted a new mix of protection and social control. In the case of key legislation on women and children, there has been a dual emphasis on the clarification of legal responsibility and a concomitant appeal for social activism. These laws subscribed to an inclusive coordination of legal and moral responsibilities cutting across the state, society, family and individual.

Protecting minors' rights and interests

Given the Chinese self-perception on 'loving the young', Party leaders were not surprisingly outraged by western 'fabrications' of child abuse in China. The April 1996 white paper, for example, responded to the specific allegations of the British television programmes of 14 June 1995 and 9 January 1996 concerning the 'dying rooms' in Hubei and Guangdong welfare homes, and the related allegations of a Human Rights Watch/Asia report of 7 June 1996 concerning the institutional abuse and starvation of Chinese orphans in Shanghai.

The white paper detailing the situation of Chinese children starts with statistics culled from the UN's basic indexes in the 1996 *State of the World's Children Report* to demonstrate the general improvement in the life of children. It noted that in 1994, in five unidentified developing countries, the mortality rate for children was 101/1000 and 56/1000 in East Asia and the Pacific regions and 43/1000 in the PRC. Taking the data for 1980–94, the white paper contended that, while children of low weight constituted an average of 35 per cent of their respective cohorts in the developing world, this figure dropped to 23 per cent for East Asia and the Pacific and to 17 per cent for China. These findings, however, do not directly refute the following conclusion of Professor Kay Johnson: 'Nowhere is the tenacious Chinese preference for sons more obvious than in China's orphanages.'[65]

Domestic legislation on the protection of minors' 'rights and interests' originates in a synthesis of domestic and international concerns regarding the effects of the Cultural Revolution and economic reform on family life and Chinese co-sponsorship of the UN Convention on Children's Rights. Internal legislative development professed to integrate the UN guidelines with China's 'actual situation'. New law accordingly enhanced the powers of the state to intervene within the family to protect the rights of children.[66]

The Chinese interpretation of the 'actual situation' is analytically interesting. As juvenile crime has become an increasing political concern, the state has formalized the rights of minors vis-à-vis their parents and has generalized the subjective dimensions of their own independent interests even while formally subscribing to the Chinese tradition of 'loving children'. The proper nurturing of children has become a matter of law. Specific discrimination against female minors and handicapped minors and the drowning of infants were dealt with in Chapter 2 (Family Protection) of the new law on minors. In Article 12, the failure of guardians or parents to provide adequate protection could result in the suspension of parental rights under Article 16 of the General Rules of the Civil Law.[67]

Even as the law has become more 'complete', and as it intervenes more directly into family matters, the NPC's legislative strategy has drawn upon those remedial elements of mass-line thinking and community organization, emphasizing education and reform over the punitive dimensions of the criminal law. The formal subscription to 'the principle of relying mainly on education while making punishment secondary' is striking in that the 'comprehensive management of public order' was originally conceptualized in the Party's June 1979 response to the Post-Cultural Revolution rise in juvenile delinquency.[68] As indicated in Chapter 5, this sharply contrasts with the situation in the field of economic crime where such 'management' encompassed 'severe crackdown' and an internationally criticized application of new categories for the imposition of the death penalty.[69]

Formal policy on juvenile crime has diverged from the general historical focus on deterrence and the punitive dimensions of the criminal law, but the state has, by traditional standards, intervened aggressively into areas of parental responsibility and action in favour of the protection of minors as independent rights-bearing subjects before the law. Under the NPC Law Committee's revisions to Article 12 of the 4 September 1991 Law of the PRC on the Protection of Minors, offspring acquired the right to sue parents for failing to uphold parental duties or for infringing the 'legitimate' rights of minors.[70] A similar conceptual recognition of the possible adversarial relation between parent and child in law had been dealt with in the earlier 1986 law on education. Under the latter's stipulations, minors were required to attend school for nine years, and it provided for the suspension of the 'right of guardianship' in cases of 'infringement' whereby parents prematurely suspended a minor's education for the purposes of 'child labour'. Article 17 of the 1992 law on women's rights and interests made particular specification relating to gender: 'Parents or other guardians are obligated to ensure that female children or juveniles receive compulsory education.'[71]

The law on minors also incorporated an entire chapter on 'school protection' which outlined a wide range of school and teacher responsibilities with regard to minors' 'rights and interests'. For example, under Article 13 of Chapter 3, the schools '... are to comprehensively implement the state's educational principles and give moral, intellectual, physical, aesthetic, and labor education to students as well as giving guidance to their social life and giving them knowledge about puberty'.

The September 4th law was woolly in its generalities as to what 'should' be done. While it represented a charter-like statement setting out standards of behaviour and related social activism, it was supposed to stipulate clearly legal responsibilities which would contribute to the effective enforcement of law. Parental duties were, for example, widely interpreted in Article 10:

> Parents or other guardians are to use healthy thoughts, good conduct, and proper methods to educate minors, guide minors to engage in activities good for their physical and mental health, prevent and stop minors from smoking, indulging in alcoholic drinking, roaming about, gambling, taking drugs, and prostitution.

The above wording was actually toned down in the NPC revision process, but the draft insisted that parents were legally bound to stop their teenagers from 'roaming about' (*liudang*). In this case, the law lapsed into a semi-traditional form of admonishment, and a morally conceived parental mentoring was subsumed within the wider dimensions of 'comprehensive management of public order' calling for the active relation of courts and community associations.[72]

The need for protection of 'rights and interests' was recognized as self-evident, but the new law also sponsored social control through education and reform. Article 5 treated parents as only one set of a very wide range of responsible parties. The protection of minors' 'rights and interests' was construed as a '... common duty [*gong tong zeren*] for state organs, armed forces, political parties, social organizations, enterprises, institutions, mass organizations of self-management at the grassroots level in urban and rural areas, guardians of minors, and other adult citizens'. This Article generally supported the informal conventions of neighbourhood mediation and intervention.

Articles 3, 5 and 36 highlighted the same inclusive organizational relationship of 'state, society, schools, and families'. Xi Jieying, a member of the NPC group responsible for the affairs of young people, commented on how the September 4th Law reflected the four related agencies of protection encompassing the family, school, society and judicial process.[73] In this view, the problem of 'rights and interests' violation was both legal and social in nature. The new law called for formal legal action in deliberate coordination with community associations and schools and education and propaganda so as to challenge 'prevailing habits and social traditions'.[74]

The law synthesized rights protection and state-controlled social networking. Article 15, for example, served notice that teaching staff of schools and kindergartens '... are to respect the human dignity of minors, and must not carry out corporal punishments in obvious or disguised forms against underage students and children...'. The September 4th Law, itself, did not stipulate what is included under 'disguised form of corporal punishment', *bianxiang tifa*, and it did not list specific sanctions. However, Article 52 strictly cited any person's criminal liability for the infringement of personal or other legitimate rights of minors with explicit reference to Article 182 of the Criminal law detailing criminal punishment for the abuse of minors by family members.[75]

The new law addressed contemporary societal pressure on the Chinese family. While Chinese crime rates remain extraordinarily low by international standards, the perceived potential for abuse, juvenile delinquency and family violence has become a politically hot concern. In a context of dramatic value change, the new materialism of the socialist market has strained familial relationships. Child labour is acknowledged to be a pressing social problem requiring strong legal action, but China's political leaders are also concerned about the way in which Cultural Revolutionary 'leftist' excesses had harmed family life. There were, for example, many distressing cases where minors were forced to bear false witness against their 'capitalist roader' parents. Casual writings such as personal letters and diaries were used in vicious trumped-up accusations against family members. In response, Article 31 declared: 'No organization or individual is allowed to conceal or ruin the letters of minors.'

74   *Law and Justice in China's New Marketplace*

   While the September 4th Law gave new precedence to the protection of 'rights and interests', the 29 December 1991 'Adoption Law of the People's Republic of China' was cast from within a stronger reference to the orthodox 'unity of rights and obligations'. Article 1 referred to safeguarding the 'rights' of all parties involved in adoption. Article 2 stated: 'An adoption shall benefit the rearing and growth of an adopted minor and shall follow the principle of equality and voluntariness. It may not violate social morals.' The latter were not detailed, but Article 3 inveighs against the use of adoption as a means of escaping family planning obligations. When compared to the September 4th law, the protective provisions of the adoption law made more reference to obligations and less reference to 'rights and interests'.[76]

Assessing the law on the rights and interests of women

The new correlation of rights and interests received its greatest endorsement in the April 1992 Law on the Protection of the Rights and Interests of Women. This law is considered to have semi-constitutional status.[77] Moreover, its drafting acquired tremendous political priority in light of China's preparations for the UN FWCW. The April 1992 law's development of 'rights and interests' moved progressively beyond the more limited association of rights with obligations in the 1950 and 1980 Marriage Laws. In terms of contemporary jurisprudence, the 'objects' of this law relate to 'the sum of the legal standards regulating social relations between the sexes and the relations directly related to women's rights and interests'.[78]

   Article 1 of the first Marriage Law (1950) briefly referred to the 'protection of the lawful interests of women and children'. Article 2 of the 1980 Marriage Law stated: 'The lawful rights and interests of women, children and the aged are protected.' However, this language was then developed from within the syntax of 'rights and obligations' whereas the 1990s legislative strategy independently featured 'rights and interests'.

   China's official February 1994 report on the Nairobi strategies later described the 3 April 1992 Law as 'an embodiment of China's commitment to the Convention on the Elimination of All Forms of Discrimination Against Women'.[79] As in the earlier law on minors, the notion of 'protection', *baohu*, was incorporated into the title of the law itself. This title signalled the ascendance of 'rights and interests' terminology. With the exception of Article 6, encouraging women to 'fulfill obligations prescribed by law', the 'unity of rights and obligations' was hardly referenced. The legal nomenclature reflected both an attempt to prioritize rights in the light of the past violations of rights and reluctance to consolidate and expand these rights.[80]

The new law addressed growing internal political frustration over the erosion of women's opportunities for employment and education in the increasingly competitive context of economic reform. Commenting on Chapter 4's provisions on the right to work, NPC reformers reiterated that women accounted for 70 per cent of the urban jobless and 70 per cent of the estimated 180 million illiterate people in contemporary Chinese society.

The June 1994 'white paper' later claimed that the 3 April 1992 Law provided 'an operational legal basis for enforcement of the law'. Seventy-five per cent of the 54 articles detailed the consequences and the legal responsibilities for infringements.[81] While this law may have represented a significant step forward, official commentary at the time of the FWCW acknowledged that the enforcement of the law was still in an 'initial stage' and that the state would have to commit much more resources over the long term to insure full implementation.[82] Again, resource allocation related to the law's distinction between 'must' and 'should'.

At the time of the original drafting in March 1992, the NPC Law Committee debated revisions which revealed an interesting controversy on how rights and interests are organizationally sustained in society. Some reformers were impatient with the WF's lack of leadership. There was even a suggestion that women's associations be disbanded at all levels.[83] This was a challenge to the traditions of Party leadership and the mass line. The same issue of course later informed the international controversy over the organization of the UN FWCW. An unsigned letter of a Chinese Conference participant alleged that China's WF is a 'branch of the Chinese government' and an 'obstacle to equality and freedom' in that it pre-empted 'real non-governmental groups' from attending the conference.[84]

The adoption of 'rights and interests' in the 3 April 1992 law supposedly conveyed the regime's new commitment to legal and social action in dealing with the inequities originating in economic reform. The NPC Law Committee obliquely responded to criticisms of the WF's traditional mass-line approach by including new wording in Article 3. This amendment referred to the specific responsibilities of the state organ's social and mass organizations, but it also stressed that these responsibilities had to be 'shared by the whole of society'.[85]

The April 1992 law envisaged a seamless division of labour between 'state and society' so as to guarantee the social protection of rights on the widest possible basis of legal and social action. This approach was explored in a *Renmin ribao* editorial exhortation to women to take up the task of materializing the principles stated in the new law:

> The work of protecting women's rights and interest involves various social aspects, and its progress depends on the endeavors of the entire society. Hence, it calls for society to show concern for and give support and help to the implementation of the 'Law on Protecting Women's Rights and Interests,' and create a favorable social environment.... According to their own limits of authority, various relevant departments in society must perform their obligations of protecting the rights and interests as stipulated by the law; have a division of labor with individual responsibilities; coordinate with each other; and employ various administrative, economic, and legal means to bring their activities into line and exercise an overall control so as to ensure the implementation of the 'Law on Protecting Women's Rights and Interests'.[86]

If Article 3 introduced a qualified element of compromise, Article 5 underlined the 'supporting roles' of the Trade Unions and Youth Leagues and reaffirmed the WF's primary role in representing and safeguarding women's rights and interests.

Article 12 re-focused on women's participation in political life and stressed that women's federations at all levels 'may recommend' women cadres to positions in state institutions and enterprise. Article 10 was deliberately vague in its commitment to the promotion of women's cadres. It referred only to the need for 'adequate numbers of women's delegates'. China's 1994 response to the Nairobi strategies more specifically offered to keep the election of women's deputies at all levels above 20 per cent.[87] At that time women accounted for 21.03 per cent of the NPC deputies and 12.3 per cent of the NPC Standing Committee whereas 14 per cent of the deputies of the Chinese People's Political Consultative Conference and 9.2 per cent of the membership of the CPPCC's National Committee were women.[88]

Professor Stanley Rosen's analysis of women's participation in political life suggests that, in comparison with current reform era, the previous Cultural Revolution period encompassed greater change in the real rates of political participation through 'state mandated official quotas'. Rosen ambivalently concluded that the current reform era has not only created the opportunity for a revival of traditional prejudices, but it has weakened the state's institutional ability to advance the cause of women's liberation:

Reform led to the decline of women's status in some areas and the rise of some elements of civil society in other aspects. Put another way, the most salient question has been the relationship between modernization and government intervention in promoting women's participation. As [Women's Federation] leaders have suggested, 'women's liberation' will improve along with the development of the productive forces.... However, a decision to rely solely on the market, with a concomitant reduction of state intervention, seems likely to lead to less, rather than more participation in social life by Chinese women, at least in the short term.[89]

Participation in the actual formal congressional structures of power would have been difficult in the context of unbridled Cultural Revolutionary class struggle, and Rosen's comparatively positive view of the impact of the Cultural Revolution on rates of political participation does not address some of the concerns expressed by Chinese observers. Han Henan of the Beijing Women's College, for example, has argued that women's political participation from the Anti-Rightist Movement through to the end of the Cultural Revolution was seriously hindered in the united front context of democratic party politics where they had previously achieved significant leadership position. On the other hand, Han suggested that in the 1990s more women intellectuals and professionals were acquiring top government positions.[90]

The specific issue of a legislated quota system within the state congressional system arose at the time of the drafting of the new 1992 women's law. Those who expressed concern that the shortage of women candidates might present an obstacle to the local election process thwarted or at least delayed the stipulation of a precise quota for gender-based congressional representation. The NPC Law Committee concluded that the level of participation would vary from place to place; however, subsequent provincial attempts to implement the new law followed along two different tracks. Some provinces fixed the proportion of women deputies while others preferred to stipulate a fixed proportion of women candidates. The latter response was apparently inspired by fear over whether failure to ensure a fixed proportion of deputies might nullify the election process.[91]

Responding to international censure, Chinese officials have often stressed the redeeming nature of the April 1992 law on women's rights and interests; however, there has also been internal criticism which argues that this law is already in need of further development. Ma Yinan, of the Beijing University Law Faculty, made a compelling case for revision, emphasizing the urgent need for clearer stipulation of legally defined responsibilities for those who violate the law's provisions. Ma wanted to extend the scope of the application of legal responsibility. Noting that administrative disciplinary measures only apply to state or collective enterprise, she observed that the law's scope did not readily correspond with the realities of the market economy. Apparently, the denigration of human rights was especially serious within private, joint and foreign-owned enterprise all of which lie outside the reach of state disciplinary procedures.

Ma also urged revision to Article 50 which presumes that the workplace violations of rights and interests can be effectively taken up by the leadership of the work unit or 'higher authority'. In Ma's view, there is no clear understanding of who constitutes higher authority. What is more, the Law of Administrative Procedure makes it almost impossible to appeal to the people's courts to start administrative procedures against either the victim's work unit or an undefined higher authority for failure to take disciplinary action against those who had violated the 1992 law.[92] Even if the law was clear on this point, this still begs the question as to whether state administrative discipline is an optimal method for dealing with official failure to apply the law against public functionaries.

Jurists now highlight the connection between the April 1992 law and the wider stipulation of related laws in the civil, constitutional, criminal, criminal procedural and administrative spheres. Commenting not only on the importance of the 1992 law, but also on the significance of its cross-referencing with law in other departments, Li Mingshun conceived of new women's law in terms of 'readjustment of the social relationships between the genders, as formulated or approved by the state' and the construction of the scope and content of these relations in law 'affirming the legal position of women and protecting women's rights and interests'.[93]

The 1992 law targeted workplace discrimination relating to pregnancy and maternity leaves, salary and benefit inequities, housing subsidies, etc.; however, the subsequent FWCW helped generate a new interest in the idea of a nationwide system of maternity insurance.[94] Articles 56–65 of the 1994 Labour Law provided new protection for female minors in the workplace. In addition, Article 59 emphasized biological differences in work abilities. Female workers were prohibited from taking up physically demanding labour such as working in mine shafts; and Article 60 made provision for sheltering women in their menstrual period from low temperatures and cold water.[95]

Specific issues of prostitution and the abduction and sale of women and children had already been raised in two earlier decisions of the Seventh NPC on 4 September 1991. The latter's provisions attempted to fill in the blanks left by the Criminal Law of 1979. The 1979 law mentioned kidnapping, but this was not specific to the kidnapping of women, and the 1991 NPC decision stipulated the selling and kidnapping of women as two separate crimes.[96] The 1991 decision in effect proposed a wider attack on the social network sustaining prostitution, stipulating heavier criminal penalties as well as increasing the time of 'mandatory corrective legal and moral education'.[97]

Provisions on abduction and kidnapping subjected state personnel to criminal prosecution for failure to act in the protection of women and children. Articles 1, 2, 6, 7 and 8 targeted the personnel in the hotel, food and drink, cultural, entertainment and transport industries [i.e. taxi drivers] who could be charged with 'organizing others for prostitution', or 'assisting others for prostitution'. The extended notion of criminal liability for networking at the same time reflected a renewed emphasis on the 'comprehensive management of public order' and the human rights concern for legal protection of rights and interests.

The original Criminal Law of 1979 had included in Article 182 stipulated punishment of not more than two years of fixed-term imprisonment for the crime of seriously abusing family members. The 1992 Law, in Chapter 4 on the rights of the person, briefly addressed the issue of violence and abuse of women and girls. The issue was not flagged as a priority in the 1992 law, but the FWCW facilitated new domestic interest in the subject. The issue of family violence has been researched by local institutes, and the municipality of Changsha and the province of Hunan have been engaged in devising related regulations. According to one of the drafters of the Hunanese regulations, Chen Mingxia, law regarding family violence is more likely to start locally and slowly move towards the accumulation of national experience resulting in central legislation. Although there is presently a lack of political consensus on the extent of the problem of family violence, Professor Chen also emphasized that such violence was more prevalent in the countryside than in the urban centres.[98] The 1997 revised criminal law, however, did not assign an immediate priority to changing the original provisions of 1979 on the abuse of family members.

The 1992 law on women's rights and interests was supposed to make the existing set of laws more complete, but it did not refer to 'sexual harassment', *xing saorao*. Arguably, an April 1992 stipulation in this matter would have been weak given the lack of backup in the Criminal

Law. As a stopgap, some jurists were prepared to endorse a creative, but overly generalized adaptation to 'hooliganism', as it is referenced in Article 160. This placed the 'humiliation of women' in the unlikely context of the instigation of brawls and public disorder. Critics, however, countered that this irresolute adaptation of a catchall category diverges from the overall pattern of comprehensive stipulation in the reform of the criminal law.

During a Hong Kong meeting of American and PRC experts prior to the FWCW, there was an exchange of opinion on family violence. PRC scholars evinced interest in American law dealing with rape within marriage. They acknowledged that 'sexual harassment' in China's work and learning environments would eventually have to be addressed. Zhang Xianyu's report of the discussion noted that while 'sexual harassment' was first defined by a US federal court in 1975, the terminology was only two or three years old in China, and that it was still under study. Zhang did, however, state the case for the development of new law on 'sexual harassment', as opposed to adaptation to the existing category of 'hooliganism'.

The issue is sensitive in that it highlights basic differences between western and Chinese society. Also, the integration of revision to the 1992 women's law with cognate revision to the provisions of criminal and civil law is an ongoing prospect. There is argument, however, that such new law has to build upon local experience such as in the 1994 Beijing municipal regulations which tentatively responded to corresponding elements of sexual harassment. Timing is critically important. Issues like domestic violence and sexual harassment were not on the table at the drafting of the 1992 law, but these issues began to receive new attention in 1993 during the build up to the FWCW.[99] Subsequent Chinese analysis largely agreed with the 'guiding principles' adopted at the FWCW. These principles defined three categories of violence against women, including domestic violence such as battery, family sexual abuse, rape within marriage, the drowning of female infants; and public violence including sexual harassment, sexual slavery and forced prostitution; and the third category, wartime rape.[100]

The 1997 Criminal Law revision gingerly took a step forward into this contentious arena. Whereas Article 160 of the original 1979 criminal law mentioned the humiliation of women in an enumeration of instances of 'hooliganism' (*liumang zui*), the 1997 Article 237 provided the following expanded stipulation: 'Whoever, by violence, coercion or other means, forces, molests, or humiliates a woman is to be sentenced to not more than five years of fixed-term imprisonment or criminal detention.' The new stipulation developed further a category of crime relating to the deliberate attempt to destroy women's reputation through defamation and false charges.

The same article referenced the earlier article's emphasis on related unlawful assembly, but it also added a new reference to child molestation. Furthermore, the 1997 revision of the criminal law, while it held over clauses 1 and 2 of the older 1979 Article 139 on rape, added a third clause to the new Article 236 incorporating concrete indicators which could be used to measure more effectively the seriousness of the circumstances of rape cases.[101] The same revision paid special attention to the stipulation of crime and punishment relating to the involvement of underaged girls in prostitution.

While these issues have not yet received sustained attention in western research, 'The Maternal, Infant Health Care Law' of 27 October 1994 ignited a firestorm of international human rights protest. The Chinese Minister of Health, Chen Minzhang, informed the media that the December 1993 draft was rewritten in the wake of international outcry over references to 'eugenics' and 'inferior births'.[102] Chen commented that while international criticism had exclusively focused on an unclear translation of *yousheng*, as 'eugenics', the government was keenly interested in the special rights of mothers and was seeking a coordinated legal and political approach to questions concerning rural female infanticide which would draw together specific provisions of a more complete set of laws on minors and women.

The Chairman of the NPC Law Committee, Xue Ju, discussed how the Committee had crafted a stronger wording against the practice of female infanticide and the inappropriate use of technology, such as ultrasound, in the illegal gender identification of the fetus.[103] Vice-Chairwoman of the NPC Committee on Education, Science, Culture and Public Health, Hao Yichun, added that the improper use of ultrasound technology was rare, but that the law still had to act to arrest any possible spread in the future use of such technology in society.[104]

Much of the above new law sought to balance the social and legal protection of rights with the integrity of social values within the normative context of family relations. One of the internal arguments against the relevance of 'civil society' in China promotes a 'rule of law' which not only facilitates the market but also facilitates the integrity of Chinese culture and society. While the reform proponents of civil law have focused on the equal enjoyment of rights in society, the advocates both of institutionalized morality and of the social and the legal protection of rights and interests have supported the definition and comprehensive imposition of legally stated standards of social behaviour.

The issue of just how the law might be deployed to support gender equality came up in 1995 when the people's court of Xinjin County, Sichuan, voided the village regulations of Shucai village for discrimination against women who had married non-villagers. Writing in one of the most widely recognized law journals, *Zhongguo faxue* (Chinese Legal Science), Yu Min hailed the court's decision as an application of the 'theory of direct effect of the constitution'. The latter's stipulation of gender equality was immediately applicable as compared to the staged introduction of evolving civil law principles concerning 'public order' and 'good customs'. In Yu's view, the 'theory of indirect effect of the constitution', as applied in Japan and Taiwan, would give inappropriate priority to the civil law's indirect handling of inequality. In short, some form of progressive state was needed to sustain social justice in the competitive context of the socialist market.

Yu's argument for just state intervention through the direct application of constitutional law drew on three related conclusions. Yu bluntly stated (1) that the reality is China does not have a full market economy requiring the 'complete separation of political state and civil society'; (2) that in the villages, ascriptive status is a palpable social reality which conflicts with the abstract notion of natural person as defined in civil law; and (3) that a current reliance on the Constitution's provisions for equality was likely to achieve a more effective result in light of the lack of legal foundation for such cases in either the civil or administrative law.[105]

Alternatively, even given their different points of development, both constitutional law and civil law might be deployed contemporaneously in the quest for social progress. This would seem to support the WF approach based upon a 'complete legal system'; however, Yu's opposition of 'direct effect' and 'indirect effect' suggests the inherent difficulties of a legislative strategy, which incorporates state-sponsored social activism with the legal orientation of the marketplace. The latter wants the state to shrink before society while the developmental concerns of social justice underline the importance of the activist state in providing for social stability, based upon the integrity of the family and the fresh redistribution of interests.

Revisiting the marriage law: rights protection and institutionalized morality

The normative issue of the law's relationship to morality in the advent of market economics is especially evident in recent controversy over the 'jurisprudence of domestic relations' and the imminent revision to the 1980 Marriage Law. Whereas women's law on rights and interests took as its 'objects' the rights and interests that originate with the social relations between the sexes, the 'objects' of the marriage law relate to the sum of the legal standards regulating the beginning and ending of marriage and familial relationships. As such, this law covers the personal and property relationships of the marriage including those between husband, wife, children and close family relatives.[106]

The salience of related family law has been confirmed in prevailing opinion, which argues that although the 1986 General Principles of Civil Law defined marriage law as part of the civil law, new family law is acquiring a relatively independent and discrete status.[107] Mounting political concern relates to the doubling in the 1990s of the 1980s divorce rate and the growing tendency of couples to live together out of wedlock. In addition, there is a growing focus on the need for extended stipulation in the law regarding the custody and proper support of children after divorce. Such crucial issues focused attention on the relative efficacy of law in upholding society's morality as it is interpreted by the state. Those seeking the marriage law's revision have stressed the need for much more extensive detail in the law's stipulation in self-conscious departure from past tendencies to adapt the law's general observations to specific cases. In ideology and theory this was the difference between 'showing-examples-ism' (*lishizhuyi*) and 'using general principles-ism' (*gaikuazhuyi*).[108] In this respect, it is important to recognize that emphasis on greater stipulation does not always exclusively support rights protection from an individual perspective. In fact, the latter may be rolled into a preferred institutionalized morality.

There is currently an external policy push for more detailed stipulation of the marriage law in relation to the societal complications of contemporary market reforms for family life. The existing law is criticized for its lack of adequate provision to ensure that legal responsibilities are honoured in practice. The content of the original Article 180 of the 1979 Criminal Law which dealt with crimes of 'impairing marriage' (*fanghai hunyin*), including bigamy, was shifted in the 1997 criminal law revision from the section, 'Crimes Disrupting Marriage and the Family' to the section, 'Crimes Infringing on the Rights of the Person and the Democratic Rights of Citizens' to emphasize the protection of women's personal rights in the context of marriage and also to give the law 'scientific' precision.[109]

As market materialism impacts on the family, divorce rates are apparently soaring. Many in legal circles are concerned about the loss of a sense of responsibility on the part of marriage partners and an upward trend in domestic violence. Yu Jing, in her recommendations for revision of the marriage law complained about the traditional cultural persistence of 'pan-moralism' (*fan daode zhuyi*), the contemporary tendency in law, preferring 'rough outlines to detailed rules' (*yi cu bu yi xi*) and the anachronistic oversimplification of Chapter 5 of the 1980 Marriage Law which provides inadequate regulation in cases of the law's violation. Without updated and well stipulated laws in the new socialist market context, she contended that 'young mistresses' (*xiao mi*) and 'concubines' (*er nai*) are challenging the foundations of marriage and social morality. Yu advocated more stipulated punishments against third-party interference and the protection of the personal and property rights of women and children. She also called for the legal definition of the rights and obligations of engagement as the latter was creating new opportunities for mercenary and arranged marriage as well as the engagement of young children for the sake of parental gains.[110] In Yu's view, the law's intervention into family relationships was necessary in light of popular relapse back into 'feudal morality'.

Also, the legal concept of 'divorce' has become the subject of intense controversy. According to Yang Dawen, of the Faculty of Law, People's University and Ma Yinan, Department of Law, Beijing University, related 1990s controversy can be summed up with reference to three specific viewpoints on how to draw the line between divorce freedom and reckless divorce. There is the *status quo* position of scholars and jurists who see no reason to change the grounds for divorce, as they are happily rooted in Marxist theory and several decades of correct juridical practice. Secondly, there are those who maintain that the law, as it exclusively focuses on 'the breakdown of affection' (*ganqing polie*), or 'alienationism' (*fenliezhuyi*), is losing its ability to protect family life and marital relations in the context of economic reform. This view asserts the legal importance of the 'unity of affection and obligation' in divorce law.

The third view, which is the mainstream one, distinguishes between 'breakdown of affection' and 'breakdown of the marriage' (*hunyin polie*). This view rests upon several points of argument. First of all, the 'breakdown of marriage' is the rising trend in comparative national legal experience. Secondly, the communication of affection is conceptually only one component of three such components defining the substantive nature of a marital relationship. Communication of affection relates to spiritual life, but the other two components focus on sexual and material life, hence this view expands the notion of breakdown to cover all three components.

The advocates of revision to the marriage law are primarily concerned about reckless divorce and its consequences for the rights and interests of women and children. They are also concerned about the lack of clarity in law as to invalid marriage and the law's lack of response to adulterous cohabitation. They propose to regulate more strictly both consensual divorce through administrative procedure and juridical divorce as promulgated by the people's court. On balance, this view gives greater, although not exclusive, priority to the protection of family life rather than to the individual's freedom to choose divorce.

Pro-revisionists focus on the law's careful discrimination between the innocent victims of marital breakdown and the party allegedly at fault. When the innocent party suffers from the consequences of a partner's adultery, then, they would propose that the restriction on divorce be relaxed in favour of the innocent party and that a consequent property settlement be skewed with 60 per cent of jointly acquired property going to the innocent party.[111]

The issue of property rights in the family has received self-conscious attention in the light of the influence of the new market economy on the family; for example, Zhang Qinmian and Wang Shengluan, of the Chinese Women's College, recently explained:

> No matter whether in the cities, or in the villages, the emergence of variegated economic relationships, such as contracts entered into by individuals or by families, partnerships, individual business and private enterprise, has transformed the family into a principal component of the socialist economy. Family property has greatly increased not only in its quantity and value but also with regard to its [new] range of sources. People have, therefore, to realize their property rights. A couple can hardly accept as the basis of adjustment of the property relations of husband and wife a singular regulation of jointly acquired property. Instead, they will demand a differentiation of the categories and amount of personal property depending upon the relationship between its source and the individual and demand the improvement of the contractual property system so as to protect personal property rights.[112]

The advent of the market economy focused public and legal attention on inequities within the family as an evolving socio-economic unit. There is a new focus on personal rights and personal property rights, but the market has also generated a challenge to social stability and familial mores which has resulted in a call for the state's intervention through law to insure the integrity of the family.

While pro-revisionists want to improve upon the law's clarity and detailed regulation of divorce, they have also sought to inject a new flexibility into the law regarding the guardianship of children after divorce. Article 29 of the 1980 Marriage Law had stipulated that the relationship between parents and children cannot be terminated subsequent to their parent's divorce, but often custody was interpreted in such a way as to divest the non-domiciled parent from his or her rights of guardianship. The latter included a wide range of involvement with children's rights and interests, relating, for example to the supervision of property, education and correction. Apparently, in practice, this related particularly to the exclusion of the mother's rights of guardianship over son(s) who resided with their father.

Pro-revisionists slotted foreign legislative experience into three categories based upon the principles of single parent custody, shared custody and recognition of both principles of single and shared custody. Current opinion tends to favour the third principle of 'combining unilateral and bilateral guardianship' as this allows for greater flexibility in dealing with the complications of career change, health, mobility and remarriage and is deemed as 'in the best interest of the children'.[113]

Marriage law revision has generated a new focus in jurisprudence on domestic relations and related protection of personal rights and personal property rights, but the market has also generated a challenge to social stability and familial mores, which has resulted in a focus on the state's intervention through law to insure the integrity of the family.

The law of protecting the rights and interests of the elderly

The 26 August 1996 Law on Protecting the Rights and Interests of the Elderly, like the earlier women's law, featured the protection of 'rights and interests' in its title. Like the law on children and the proposed revision to the marriage law, its 6 chapters and 50 articles placed great stress on the importance of family values.[114] This law paralleled the approach taken in the law on children, women and the handicapped in that it explicitly endorsed a combined state and society approach. This approach has been justified with reference to China's hard developmental and demographic realities. Currently, there are nearly 100 million people over the age of 60, but this 9 per cent of the population total is expected to rise sharply by 2025 to 19.8, which is 6.1 per cent higher that the world old-age people ratio of 13.7 per cent.[115]

Article 3 of the 26 August 1996 law stipulated: 'The state and society should adopt measures to perfect the social guarantee system for the elderly....' Even before the NPC promulgated this law, the State Council in June 1991 subscribed to a new rationality of burden sharing in the field of old age insurance, moving from the planned economy focus on the sole responsibility of government or enterprise to combined payment by the government, subsidies by enterprises and individual bank deposits.[116] This policy viewpoint was invoked in the 1996 law's reference to the 'common responsibilities of society'.[117]

A report on the Hainan model has argued for a multi-layered strategy which incorporates a new notion of individual 'obligation' and furthers an 'organic' combination of fairness and efficiency, hence the following optimistic conclusion:

> It is entirely possible to organically combine fairness and efficiency with both aspects taken care of. For instance, the method of combining the issue of pensions with paying for the insurance brings together rights and obligations, and is both equal and efficient. So long as fairness and efficiency are not forced together, but organically combined, both mechanisms, fairness and efficiency, can play their role at the same time.[118]

This organic, or pragmatic, approach presupposed that while individuals would generally assume some future responsibility for the socialization of insurance, old-age care in the rural areas would gradually move away 'from care by children to care by society'. The following recommendation perhaps reveals an underlying 'organic' synthesis:

> One way to realize [old-age care] is to establish security shareholding banks, based on self-willingness; an other way is to continue to advocate that young people should provide for their elderly, to hold back the speed of dismissing the role of families for taking care of the old as a result of commercial economy and [the] rise of nuclear families....[119]

Article 5 of the new law on the elderly paralleled Article 6 of the 1990 law on the rights and interests of the handicapped in that it presumed that governments at all levels would act in coordination to increase resource allocations to support the elderly. Again 'the common responsibility of all of society' was referenced in Article 6. Article 9 affirmed that the handicapped would themselves carry out their legally required 'obligations'.

Perhaps the most concrete emphasis on 'obligation', however, came in the stipulation of family support in Chapter 2. The law herein was predisposed to upholding traditional family responsibility towards the elderly. In Article 11, 'supporters', referring either to the children of the elderly or 'other people who bear the supporting duties according to law', were told that they 'should properly arrange housing for the elderly, and must nor force the elderly to move to housing with inferior conditions'. What is more, Article 15 stated that even if 'supporters' were to give up their rights to inheritance, this would not obviate their legal obligations to their elders, who in the event of supporters failing to discharge their duties would have the right to demand support payments. In addition, Article 18 stated that 'supporters' had no right to interfere in the divorce, remarriage or post-marriage life of the elderly. Once again the law was to create a level playing field and this meant giving priority to the rights and interests of the weaker party.

The law also reflected an ongoing political perspective on the positive role which the elderly can play in maintaining the integrity of community life. This 'organic' state–society approach obviously coincided with the renewed strategic emphasis on the 'comprehensive management of public order'. Article 41 not only stressed how the elderly might impart their scientific and professional knowledge to their communities, but how they might continue with their voluntary assistance in local neighbourhood mediation and 'collectivist education'. As was the case in the women's law, there was also an obvious concern to address malicious social circumstances of abuse and character assassination. Article 46 stipulated:

> People who use violence or other methods to openly humiliate the elderly or slander the elderly by cooking up false stories or maltreat the elderly should be punished according to public security management rules if the cases are not too serious, and should be brought to justice for their criminal responsibilities if they are found to be offending the criminal law.

In sum, the 26 August 1996 law protecting the rights and interests of the elderly closely paralleled earlier law setting out the common philosophical and organizational features of the 'special grouping of rights'. Related legislation confirmed an attempt to protect rights and to achieve social stability in the new market context through a 'state and society' approach requiring a newly revised strategy of using the law to achieve an apparently 'organic' materialization of efficiency and justice.

Conclusion

In the current era of unprecedented subscription to market principles, competing domestic and international perspectives push simultaneously for the expansion and the contraction of the state within Chinese society. Yu Min's point was well taken. China does not yet have a fully fledged 'civil society'. The Party has rejected the latter, focusing alternatively on its own notional unity of Chinese state and society. At the same time, the state has been required to define and stipulate the protection of new rights and interests; it is also required to intervene in the non-traditional regulation of domestic relations in order to ensure an institutionalized morality predicated in specifically Chinese family values. Contemporary legislation has attempted to create new social protection law which cuts across the standard divide between public and private law.

While legislation has taken up the cause of 'rights and interests', it has done so without the benefit of a fully established jurisprudence clarifying the contemporary composition of Chinese society and the related legislative criteria for the adjustment of rights to interests. However, while 'class' has become a theoretical anachronism, law and jurisprudence are still focusing on social justice. Rights have become more important than obligations, and the latter are undergoing a process of redefinition.

In a time of profound axiological crisis, the Party is struggling with the competing aspects of a contradiction. On the one hand, the Party seeks to maintain social control, and, on the other, the Party is promoting the legal and social protection of newly defined 'rights and interests'. The 1990s legislative strategy for rights protection was rationalized in 'third stage' jurisprudence. Legislation regarding women and children might still be construed as part of an evolving Chinese corporatist charter of rights. While there is a growing focus on the law's autonomy, the legal system still remains integral to the 'comprehensive management of public order'. Ironically or not, it is the Party's own interest in the latter which has provided legal reformers with their most powerful justification for the protection of rights.

However, it would be too simple to dismiss the new special grouping of rights as an exercise in formalism, cultural relativism and specious human rights diplomacy which has no practical significance. The

Chinese do not pass legislation just so that they can fool their foreign critics. In many important respects, the related sequence of rights and interests legislation represents a new level of formal development which builds upon increasing reference to international legal experience and which originates in a changing ideological conception of the Chinese state–society continuum. Moreover, despite such an extraordinary policy focus on efficiency in the marketplace, the new vocabulary on rights and interests has, nevertheless, acquired unprecedented political priority.

On one level, this suggests the new political strength of the reform perspective on the relevance of 'human rights' categories. Even as the conceptualization of 'rights and interests' has been defined in Chinese socialist terms, formal legal thinking and legislation have also been profoundly affected by western concepts and values. Paradoxically, as the state attempted to make room for relatively autonomous actors in the 'socialist market', it is also focused on the need to shore up Chinese family values. In a time of significant regime decline, the new 'special grouping of rights' was conceived during national debate on 'human rights'. This may help to explain the contradictory mix of legal and social protection in the 1990s legislation.

The contradictions of contemporary society and politics are magnified in this legislation. While the punitive direction of criminal law have been modified to deal with juvenile delinquency, the state, in response to recognized problems of abuse, has moved directly into areas of parental responsibility that were traditionally closed to legal remedy. The law has comprehensively focused on what should be, and what must be done. At the same time as the proponents of gender equality have sought to strengthen the constitutional law's direct interventions into rural society, there has been a renewed focus on the familial dimensions of civil law, The attempt to entwine the new civil procedure law and the PRC Law on the Protection of Women's Rights and Interests is ongoing.

The advocates of the special grouping of rights have highlighted the importance of a complete legal system which systematically reinforces the wider cross-referencing of constitutional, administrative, criminal, civil and economic laws dealing with rights and interests protection across a continuous spectrum of social and legal guarantees. At times this comprehensiveness has singled out the importance of protecting the rights of the individual. The Hainan model assigned new emphasis to the self-determining individual who must undertake obligations in law as a matter of self-respect. At other times the same move to the law's comprehensiveness has synthesized the individual's rights within the context of familial relationships. In other words, the protection of the individual has often been centred in the protection of the family itself. The new theme of protection as it relates to the state–society strategy is also interesting in its attempt to endow related mass associations with a more explicitly legal persona. Mass associations are now involved in a transitional process of budgetary politics, and the legislative sanction of interests is not unrelated to their guaranteed access to the state's resources. At the moment these associations provide the most important institutionalized basis for social activism as it relates to entwined social and legal guarantees of rights and interests.

Even as the state tries to impose itself on society, it is being pulled in a number of contradictory directions. Even as the state contracts its sphere of public administrative competence, there is increasing demand for public law which supports both social justice and the 'fresh readjustment and distribution of interests'. As the state contracts it has committed itself to provide a wider cross-referencing of laws within a 'complete legal system'. At the same time the state appears to be elaborating a corporatist strategy which 'organically' seeks to make the individual self-determining with a new strategy of shared social responsibilities.

As early as 1986 when the new General Principles of the Civil Law of the PRC were first promulgated, legislators and law professors commented favourably on how these principles constituted a victory for the cause of 'subject equality' vis-à-vis the historically regressive tendencies of the arbitrary state which sacrificed the individual and the plurality of interests to the requirements of economic planning. However, at the same time, there were reservations over the direct incorporation of the marriage law into the department of civil law. Some reformers contended that this would insinuate principles of commodity economy into family relations and that this would further diminish the educational function of the marriage law.[120] The household has in fact become a well defined socio-economic unit in law. The current debate on revision to the marriage law suggests the extent to which reformers are prepared to rely on a presumably progressive state actively to protect the integrity of the family vis-à-vis the changing nature of domestic relationships in the market economy.

Clearly, there is an increasing focus on the materialistic denigration of family relations. The recent debate over the prioritization of constitutional as distinct from civil law remedies raises the difficult question as to what degree of a top-down state approach to social activism is needed to protect 'rights and interests' in China's transitional circumstances. The dangers of an exclusive reliance on state-sponsored constitutional development were explicit in Tong Zhiwei's theory of 'socio-economic rights'. However, this has not stopped some reformers from arguing that a 'socialist rule of law state' requires inspired positive state action so as to ensure that the protection of rights and interests rests upon a balanced approach to efficiency and fairness.

The special grouping of rights has raised the vexing, but genuinely important, question as to what are the best practical socially and legally appropriate means for protecting the rights and interests of the economically and socially vulnerable sectors of society in the contemporary circumstances of China's transition to the 'socialist market'. Related 1990s law and jurisprudence reflects the regime's Chinese ideological and political cultural preferences, but at the same time it has constituted an unexpectedly complex response to Western influence and human rights thinking.

3
Justice and Efficiency in Contractual Labour Relations

Recent labour legislation highlights the tension between justice and efficiency in Chinese jurisprudence. This tension originates with competing institutional and ideological trends. Legal reformers are increasingly focusing on 'big society', if not 'civil society'. In this context, jurist debate over the drafting of labour law has highlighted the protection of worker rights and interests, contract equality, enhanced mediation and dispute settlement mechanisms, the devolution of labour discipline to enterprise and the cultural shift from 'administrative labour relations' to 'legalized labour relations'.

Along this same continuum of politics, jurisprudence and law, there is a growing opinion to the effect that labour law, in its intimate relation to social justice, is different from civil law. While some reformers might emphasize that the civil law has a lot to do with justice in terms of establishing subject equality before the law and the autonomy of the rights bearing individual vis-à-vis the state, this opinion emphasizes that labour law *per se* must encourage a 'progressive' state activism so as to guarantee social justice and the protection of the human rights of workers.

The 1994 Labour Law (hereinafter 1994 LL) is the centrepiece of what has been until recently a surprisingly underdeveloped 'socialist' labour law. Its modernizing task is to legalize the entire labour management process from establishing to terminating employment or labour relations, so as to promote economic efficiency. But, for many Chinese legal scholars, labour management efficiency cannot be achieved without maintaining justice and fairness in labour relations. As generally discussed in Chapter 1, social justice is part of the 'balance of values' needed to consolidate the market economy on the basis of the rule of law. The current rationale for the rule of law also includes a political emphasis on 'market order'.[1] China's jurists are often in agreement with political leaders who believe that social justice forms the very foundation for social stability as is thus the necessary condition for the success of market reform.

Clearly, the recent concern of legal experts with the notion of social justice in the labour process originates with the introduction and the radical expansion of private enterprises in the past decade and with the recent structural reform of state enterprise. These reforms have already contradicted the Maoist three-tiered interests structure and the harmonious labour relations which were lauded under the old planned economy.

Contemporary labour law has been greatly influenced by policy perspective concerning China's transition to the 'socialist market'. The rate and quality of related socio-economic change has always been deliberately benchmarked in Chinese constitutional law which pointedly records the prevailing ideas on labour and capital in relation to what is a self-declared ideological understanding of the structures of distribution and ownership in society. The recent history of constitutional amendment tells the story of transition from the planned to market economy and highlights some of the substantive issues concerning the rights and interests of workers.

The 1988 revision to the 1982 State Constitution merely tolerated the existence of private ownership as a 'supplement' to the legally dominant form of public ownership. The 1993 amendment virtually abolished the central planned economy in favour of building a 'socialist market economy'. The state constitutional amendments of mid-March 1999 included the elevation of private economy as an 'important component' of the socialist market economy. Jiang Zemin's thinking on distribution was sanctioned in the following addition to Article 6:

> In the initial stage of socialism, the country shall uphold the basic economic system in which the public ownership is dominant and diverse forms of ownership develop side by side, and it shall uphold the distribution system with distribution according to work remaining dominant and a variety of modes of distribution coexisting.

This dual complexity of pluralized ownership and distribution conflicted with the simplicity of Article 6 of the 1982 State Constitution which originally stated: 'The system of socialist public ownership supersedes the system of exploitation of man by man; it applies the principle of "from each according to his ability, to each according to his work"'.² Under Jiang Zemin, the Party has given greater priority to efficiency, and the essential reference points of distribution have been revised to give newly weighted recognition to inputs such as capital, resources and technology.

In a further attempt to clarify the substance of the 'socialist market' the following phraseology was incorporated into Article 11: 'The state shall protect the legitimate rights and interests of the non-public sector comprising self-employed and private businesses, and shall exercise guidance, supervision, and management over this sector.'³ Previously, legal theory paid little attention to the fundamental differences in interests between individual workers, enterprises and society since the workers were the masters both of the enterprises and society. Labour relations between individual workers and these enterprises were ideologically construed as part of a harmonious unity demonstrating the superiority of socialism over capitalism.

Currently, there is a more complicated mix of public and private economy, and, in the context of deepening economic reform, there is a greater potential for uneven enjoyment of worker rights and access to the benefits. Moreover, while enterprise has acquired a new ability to recruit, and may dismiss workers for failing to meet their contractual obligations, workers are now free to choose their jobs. In the uncertain context of the disappearing planned economy, law has acquired a more extended and explicit responsibility for the mediation of essentially new disputes between labour and management. Suddenly labour law has become a much more significant medium by which to understand the defined rights and interests of the workers.

While the workers, as 'proletarians', have lost high political privilege and guaranteed lifelong employment, they have acquired new legally defined 'rights'. Whether the law can, in fact, compensate them for their loss of status is an inherently political question. As suggested in Chapter 1, Chinese analysis is moving beyond the 'will of the ruling class', but it has not yet conceded the worker's loss of 'master' status. Sun Xiuping, Director of the Hainan Institute for Reform and Development, for example, explained the basic connotations of this status as follows:

> The relationship between the employer and the employees is set through labor laws and contract. This is not in contradiction to workers as the masters, which will be embodied chiefly through the right and duty of the citizen. It is essential to do away with the concept of life-long, fixed employment and develop the concept of market mechanism and labor market all over society, in order to

revitalize enterprises and increase productivity and economic end-results.[4]

Sun made a virtue out of the uncertainties of the labour market, arguing that the past notion that the labour force 'belongs to the state or public' conflicts with the worker's contemporary rights of self-determination:

> It is imperative to change the concept that the labor force 'belongs to the state or public' into one that is possessed by the laborer himself. In the past highly concentrated planning economy with unified employment and assignment, people often said that once you got through the public institutions' doorsteps you became a man of the state. In fact, it was not a socialist idea, nor did it conform to Marxist basic theory, but somehow it, in practice, became the source of eating in the state's . . . iron rice bowl. Socialism should provide laborers with more choices of jobs than capitalism . . .[5]

Concepts such as 'the structure of pluralized interests' and 'pluralized labour relations' attempted to capture the ebb and flow of new contract labour relations. While the 1999 amendment to the State Constitution still referred to public ownership as 'dominant', it granted reinforced legal status to 'other modes of ownership'. The 'structure of pluralized interest' recognized that in private and foreign enterprise there is a newly emerging social and political relationship between capital and labour. Workers and management in these ownership systems would not necessarily share the same interests as was the case in state enterprise in the past.

As suggested in the preceding chapters, the correlation of rights with interests originated with the regime's political attempts to offset public anxiety over the unpredictable social consequences of accelerated economic growth. Seizing the initiative, reform-minded jurists demanded a new generation of labour legislation. They contended that workers ought to have their own legitimate rights and interests, independent from enterprise, especially in the private and mixed ownership sectors. Given new opportunity for disputes between workers and enterprise, workers' rights and interests had to have the benefit of the wide stipulation in new law.

Contemporary jurisprudence is weighing labour management efficiency in the scales of justice along with values associated with social stability and the cognate emphasis on the protection of the rights and interests of workers. The latter's association with the regime priorities of social stability may have served to give more it precedence than it might otherwise have in the light of the strong political focus on efficiency.

The 'rule of law' debate has sparked controversy over the extent to which the state must play an activist role in supporting new institutional and association adjustment in law as a means of mediating conflict. Chapter 2 provided examples of state organized legal and social protection of a 'special grouping' of rights for women, children, handicapped, and the elderly. On the other hand, the notion of 'small government, big society' has featured the distinction between public and private law and has encouraged the market to take over from the state plan and enterprise in providing for a new diversified mechanism of social security. Mao must be spinning in his Tiananmen Square mausoleum, but labour really has become a commodity!

The 1982 State Constitution stipulated that labourers have rights to obtain material assistance from the state and society when they are old, ill, or disabled.[6] But, in the reform era, the Party, in the hope of balancing social justice and efficiency, has given much greater formal recognition to the legal and social protection of workers' rights and interests. Jiang Zemin, in his report to the CCP 15th National Party Congress in 1997, stated that the reforms in distribution need to adhere to the principles that '... efficiency is primary, justice and fairness secondary; at the same time, social stability must be maintained'.[7]

Even while justice is seen as critical to social stability, prevailing economic priorities in the context of the transition from the planned to the market economy have been designed to negate the 'three irons system'. This prioritization has targeted the 'iron chair' for permanently employed government cadres, the 'iron rice bowl', meaning lifelong employment for enterprise workers and the 'iron salary' referring to formulae for increasing salary on the exclusive basis of seniority.[8] The irrelevance of class in these assumptions is particularly obvious. The workers have their very own 'iron rice bowl', just as the hated bureaucrats have an 'iron chair'. Mao, again, must be spinning in his Tiananmen Square mausoleum. The 'masters' are now told they should not expect to eat from an 'iron rice bowl'. Premier Zhu Rongji bluntly instructed the workers that they will have to 'change their job concept' so as to deal with the changing realities of the labour market:

> guide workers to change their job concept so that as many laid-off workers as possible can find jobs again. When laid-off workers are re-

employed, they should sever labor relations with their original enterprises. Those who fail to find new jobs after three years of unemployment should also sever labour relations with their original enterprises and apply for their unemployment insurance funds at social security institutions.[9]

The workers can no longer count on their vanguard status. Given this loss of status, legal protection has suddenly become very pressing. Chinese jurists have responded to this internal dilemma of Chinese socialism with emphasis on labour legislation requiring state intervention in order to enforce industrial standards and to protect workers' rights and interests. In this way, labour law, as compared to civil law, reflects a different orientation towards the state's role in the achievement of social justice.

The 'balance of values' in the evolving jurisprudence of rights and interests has to be put in the context of reform which has already profoundly altered ownership and distribution structures. One of China's leading jurists, Li Buyun, observes that law should reflect social values and mediate social relations which are fundamentally 'interests relations' (*liyi guanxi*). One of the essential functions of law is to mediate the interest relations among the state, collectives and individuals.[10] Prevailing social values become important criteria by which the interest relations are readjusted.

What are the values that should be embedded in law under the new 'socialist' market economy? Wang Jiafu, the former Head of the Institute of Law of the CASS, has argued that such values include the principles of maintaining social justice, protecting the vulnerable, and balancing interests among the state, collectives and individuals.[11] Under market competition, labour has been explicitly identified as vulnerable. Compared to their counterparts in large enterprise, individual labourers are in an isolated and economically disadvantaged position. Ideally, the law is expected to succour the weak and to restrain the powerful. For such purposes, an important component of a 'rule of law economy' (*fazhi jingji*) is social legislation which plays a central role in regulating the market. The purpose of social legislation is to protect labourers, the old, the unemployed, the disabled and the vulnerable. The social legislation includes labour law, and laws on social insurance and security.[12]

As was discussed in Chapter 1, Chinese jurisprudence, in synthesizing the rule of law with the socialist market, has run up against a 'value problem', highlighting the difficulties associated with the relative weighting of justice and efficiency. As was suggested in Chapter 2, the correlation of these priorities relates to the conceptual formation and actual enjoyment of human rights through the enforcement of law. Furthermore, with the dismantling of the planned economy and the benefits strategy associated with it, there have been attempts to reconfigure social guarantees. The workers have a new 'self-determining' and diversified approach of shared obligation which substitutes law for administration. This approach features principles such as 'first establish the rules and then handle affairs' (*xian li guiju hou banshi*) and 'use law to administer' (*yi fa xingzheng*).[13] Law in this approach would standardize both rights and obligations. As Li Buyun would have it, this is a self-conscious matter of adaptation to modern 'rational legal culture'.

While the CCP leadership has not endorsed western 'civil society', there has been a related focus on the relationship between state and society which promises to have a major influence on the development of labour relations. The issue can be seen most clearly in the growing advocacy of 'small government, big society' (*xiao zhengfu da shehui*). In practice this Hainan strategy meant 'rational sharing' and the diversification of the insurable base of benefits and social security so as to move away from the exclusive emphasis on state enterprise responsibility and to share the burdens of cost with individual workers and collective funding agents in the creation of new insurance programmes. Theoretically, this strategy synthesizes justice and efficiency in a rational 'unification of obligations, rights and interests'.

In his advocacy for reform of the unemployment and industrial injury insurance systems, for example, Sun Xiuping advocated three specific principles, which invoked Deng Xiaoping's 'three favourable directions'. Sun argued for a minimal and basic insurance, which would guarantee the life of the worker during a period of lost income. Secondly, he advocated the 'unity of rights and obligations' on the basis of 'what is reimbursed is linked with what is insured'. Thirdly, Sun endorsed the 'unity of fairness and efficiency' which would sustain the basic life of the unemployed and injured while 'promoting the competition and rational flow of the labor force'.[14] Sun located these principles in the new market context. Moreover, he claimed that the planned economy had irrationally separated rights from obligations. Sun conscripted obligations in the shift from big government to big society.

Under the pressure of accelerated economic reform, there has been an extraordinary readiness to review the comparative labour law experience in the developed economies for purposes of distilling those aspects of law most appropriate to the circumstances of China's 'socialist market'. This amounts to self-conscious 'internationalization' or 'transplantation'. Wang Jiafu advanced a twofold reasoning for 'transplantation'. He argued that through the discriminating adaptation to foreign experience China could quickly absorb all the relevant legislative experience accumulated by the developed countries in the past centuries since there are recognized common concerns and regularities of the market economies in different countries. Secondly, such transplantation would rebound to China's credit within the international economic community resulting in a new appreciation of China's secure environment for international investment. Wang felt that he could make this claim and at the same time advise against the blind copying of western law without due consideration of China's specific realities.[15]

In fact, the actual drafting process of the 1994 LL was hailed as an instance of successful and appropriately nuanced transplantation. According to Ren Fushan, at the Capital Economy and Trade University, Beijing, the drafting of the 1994 LL, and the subsequent detailed rules and regulations for its implementation, drew extensively on the experience of international conventions in many areas. These included the minimum wage system, pay equity, the system of working hours, prohibition from hiring minors, employment promotion policies, employment discrimination, establishment of a social security system, and industrial standards.[16] Similarly, Professor Wang Quanxing, of the South China Politics and Law University, highlighted the relation between the 1994 LL's stipulated protection of worker rights and interests with the international human rights movement.[17]

Paradoxically, this 'transplantation' was contemporaneous with growing reformer anxiety over the inequitable impact of 'globalization' on Chinese workers. The urgent need for protection of China's domestic workforce was constantly aired in early 1990s press coverage revealing the legal system's failure to address adequately the conditions of work in foreign-funded and privately-run enterprise, particularly overseas Chinese-funded enterprise. Publicized abuses of workers' rights and interests included forced overtime, arbitrary deductions against worker salary, firing employees at will and depriving workers of their basic personal freedoms. One report even indicated that an enterprise had stipulated that the time for a meal could not exceed 10 minutes and that workers must not go to the toilet when on duty. Many of the enterprises totally disregarded labour safety and forced their employees to work with an excessive workload in an adverse environment of intolerable noise and dust. As a result, industrial accidents occurred frequently.[18] In some cases, the labour abuses resulted in strikes, physical injury, and even destruction of equipment by angry workers.[19]

Despite the obvious fact that such patterns of worker abuses also relate to foreign and private enterprise, it has as yet received only intermittent attention in the foreign monitoring of Chinese human rights performance. At any rate, Josephs suggests that the provisions of the 1994 LL on working conditions and benefits are largely a response to these domestically publicized reports of worker abuse.[20] This chapter specifically explores the key theoretical issues concerning the value problem in Chinese jurisprudence, highlighting the notions of social justice, efficiency and rights protection, as these informed jurist debate over the drafting of the pathbreaking 1994 LL.

The paradox in CCP labour law history

The labour law, in 1949–92, was surprisingly weak and disparate. It was broader than it was deep. According to Professor Guan Huai, of the Chinese People's University, and Wang Quanxing, of the Southern Chinese Law and Politics University, labour laws, in a broad sense, included not only labour legislation passed by the NPC, but also various regulations issued by the State Council or the Ministry of Labour. These regulations are legally binding given that they are consistent with the State Constitution and the law promulgated by the NPC.[21]

There is also a plethora of local regulations issued within the local people's congressional system. Moreover, international labour conventions, signed by the PRC, are also regarded as part of Chinese labour law, although it is not clear how such conventions should be enforced in legal practice.[22] In terms of its substantive content, Chinese labour law is slotted into four categories: laws on adjusting and regulating labour relations, such as laws and regulations on individual labour contract and collective labour contract; laws on the participation of workers in enterprise management and on labour dispute settlement; laws on labour standards and on labour protection in general; and laws on the implementation of labour law.[23]

The shallow depth and uneven detail of the contents of these categories of law and regulation were the by-products of politics. In the early 1950s new democracy and transition to socialism, the private sector played a fairly important role in revitalizing a national economy that was basically on the verge of collapse due to the pre-1949 cycle of civil and international war fought on Chinese soil. During this period, some significant pieces of labour legislation were passed so as to regulate labour relations and to protect the workers from private enterprise exploitation. These included the 1950 PRC Trade Union Law, the 1951 PRC Labour Insurance Law, the 1949 Regulations on Collective Contract between Workers and Capital, and the 1950 Regulations on Procedures for Labour Dispute Settlement. These laws and regulations may serve as historical footnotes to the era of planned economy, but today they have little relevance to the labour problems characterizing the transition to the 'socialist market'.

The 1950s laws and regulations were enacted to facilitate regime consolidation. They were politically designed to reduce and eventually to eliminate the private economy. In contrast, the labour laws and regulations of the late 1980s to the present reflect a growing recognition of the self-standing legal status of private enterprise. After the Socialist Economic Reconstruction Movement of the earlier 1950s, China issued only a small number of labour-related laws and regulations primarily concerned with job assignment, wages, retirement and labour discipline. Particularly after the Great Leap Forward and with the advent of Cultural Revolution, there was a runaway class struggle resulting in legal nihilism and the absolute idealization of labour harmony within state enterprise.

After 1986, a series of labour regulations were issued by the State Council and the Ministry of Labour challenging the 'iron rice bowl' employment system in the state enterprise by introducing the labour contract system and regulations concerning settlement of labour disputes. Nevertheless, until 1992, the increase in labour legislation was still largely confined to the piecemeal improvement of the existing labour system within the framework of an increasingly transitional planned economy. The labour law and regulations during this period were fitfully enacted to solve the immediate problems occasioned by economic reforms. Such a piecemeal legislative approach, according to Professor Guan Huai, resulted in conflicts between various labour regulations. The *ad hoc* and incremental character of the law reflected the lack of clear guiding principles in the law-making process. In addition, regulations often became quickly dated in the light of the uncertainties of reform policies, particularly before 1992.[24]

Labour law in the 'socialist market'

The initiation of the socialist market economy reform in 1992-93 heralded a new generation of labour law. As early as 1979, the Labour Bureau under the State Council had begun to organize a group of labour law experts to draft a comprehensive labour law. However, before 1992 little progress was made due to a lack of resolve on the disposition of the planned economy. Then, as indicated earlier, the constitution was amended to support the socialist market in 1993. The same year the Party approved a momentous decision on the establishment of the 'socialist market'. The way was suddenly cleared for an immediate passage of a labour law based upon new underlying principles.[25] For Chinese labour law experts, the 1994 LL is the most important piece of labour legislation. It was adopted at the 8th Session of the Standing Committee of the 8th National People's Congress on 5 July 1994 and went into effect on 1 January 1995. Chinese legal scholars have regarded the 1994 LL as 'the fundamental labour law' (*laodongfade jiben fa*).[26] This law absorbed all prior-1994 reforms in labour concepts and system. Hilary K. Josephs, an America-based Chinese labour law expert, has argued that the 1994 LL represents:

> the culmination of approximately four decades of debate and revision.... The law is a summary of basic principles drawn from an extensive body of existing administrative regulations. It lends an importance to workers rights which they did not have previously and demonstrates a conscious effort of the Chinese government to bring its system of labour law and industrial relations into closer compliance with international standards.[27]

The 1994 LL built upon the past, but its underlying theory represented more than simple continuity. It provided a fundamentally new direction and framework for the subsequent labour legislation. Since its promulgation, the State Council and Ministry of Labour have issued a plethora of Regulations, Notices, and Provisions to facilitate its implementation.[28] The 1994 LL serves as a litmus test in our understanding of the effect of new jurisprudence on labour legislation during the transition to the socialist market.

The most frequently researched question in Chinese jurisprudence is what are the fundamental principles of a law? For Chinese legal scholars, fundamental principles of a law not only reveal the essence of the legislation, but also serve as a guide for the law's implementation. In the past, Chinese law was often deliberately general. Its flexibility was extolled. Its general character and simple language were characterized as being easier to understand by the masses. Mass-line perspective emphasized the importance of the law's popularization. More recently, however, jurists have focused on how the lack of substantive detail gives rise to the inefficient and inconsistent enforcement of the law.

After December 1978, economic reform advanced vigorously but there was little legislative experience to fall back on. For Chinese scholars, to improve stability and continuity in law enforcement and subsequent law making, the accurate understanding of the principles of a law became essential. Despite persisting political ambiguity over what these fundamental principles ought to be, jurists openly debate the principles of labour law. The 1994 LL provided a clear statement of fundamental principles,[29] but even then China's legal scholars did not give it their unanimous acceptance. Instead, they were vigoroused developing a number of different principles in official law school textbooks. This suggests both increasing liberalization of legal research as well as the *de facto* tendency towards 'pluralized jurisprudence'.

Jurists differed on the relevance of the 1982 State Constitutional provisions on labour. One group of scholars argued that the constitution served as the basis for the principles of the 1994 LL. They thought that the 1994 LL was enacted merely to flesh out existing constitutional guidelines concerning labour relations.[30] The problem with this approach is that the 1982 State Constitution itself no longer accurately reflected China's social reality. As discussed above, China's economic and social structures have undergone rapid transformation since 1982. This resulted in basic amendments to the constitution in 1999 eulogizing Deng Xiaoping's contribution to socialism with Chinese characteristics and outlining the protracted nature of the primary stage of socialism, the new importance of private ownership and the changing principles of distribution.[31]

Other scholars creatively stressed the importance of China's reality as equally important as the 1982 State Constitution for deriving the fundamental principles of the 1994 LL. Professor Guo Jie of the Northwest Chinese Politics and Law College argued that the 1994 LL judicially balanced competing interests in labour relations. He listed four dialectical combinations. These synthesized (1) the protection of rights and interests of labour with consideration of the interests of employers; (2) distribution according to labour with social assistance; (3) competition between equal subjects in the labour market with protection of special labour groups including female workers, minors, the disabled, minority ethnic workers, and former military personnel; and autonomy in the labour market with state intervention.[32]

Li Boyong, the Minister of Labour, in his official explanation of the 1994 LL to the Standing Committee of the NPC, reviewed four guiding principles which he believed had informed the drafting of the 1994 LL: the protection of the rights and interest of labour; expediting the development of the production forces; the regulation of the labour market; and the convergence with international convention while at the same time respecting China's own realities.[33]

In its adaptation to a market system of employment, the 1994 LL incorporated a strong new emphasis on the protection of worker 'rights and interests'. Professor Guo Jie argued that such an emphasis was critical in the light of the workers' comparatively disadvantaged position vis-à-vis employers in their access to resources. The labour law was designed to maintain equal status in law between employers and the employed and to prevent the former from taking advantage of the latter. Guo noted frankly that employers in a market economy will pursue a maximum profit often at the expense of rights and the interests of labour. Moreover, the rights and interests of employers had been earlier stipulated in laws concerning enterprises, such as 'The Provisions for Transforming the Management Mechanisms in Publicly Owned Industrial Enterprise'. Employers had gained various rights in regard to the hiring and dismissal of their employees and the payment of wages. Guo, therefore, called upon the state to redress the worker–employer balance and to define and limit closely the power of employers so as to prevent worker abuse.[34]

From state-imposed obligation to rights protection in the 1994 LL

The 1994 LL and subsequent labour legislation highlighted the state's new legal responsibilities regarding labour relations. Chinese legal scholars define labour law as laws regulating labour relations between workers and employers. For Chinese legal scholars, it is important to define the concept of labour relations, and these relations are specifically discussed with reference to the subject (*zhuti*) and the object (*keti*). For them, the labour relations consist of rights and obligations relations (*quanliguanxi he yiwuguanxi*) between workers and employers who are the two subjects of labour relations.

The configuration of 'the objects of labour relations', has resulted in controversy. Scholars have squared off in their support for 'labour object theory' (*laodongli shuo*) and 'theory on principal and supplementary objects' (*jingben keti yu fuzu keti shuo*). The former suggested that the object of the labour relations is concerned with labour, not with labourers. This theory argued that in labour law, all rights and obligations are therefore concerned with labour, including the use, preservation and transition of labour.[35]

The latter, however, divided the objects of labour relations into primary and secondary categories. The principal category highlighted labour activities, while the supplementary category featured the conditions under which labour activities are carried out. The conditions were stipulated as wages, fringe benefits, labour protection, and so on.[36] Therefore, rights and obligations in labour relations were associated with labour activities and conditions. Guo Jie criticized this labour object theory for its separation of labour from the actual labourers. The principle and supplementary object theory was considered superior in that it accounted for the co-existence of multiple objects in labour relations.[37]

Labour relations are classified into administrative labour relations (*laodong xingzheng*) and legal labour relations (*falu guanxi*). The former are primarily about the relations between the government administrative departments and employers or employing units. The latter focus on the contractual undertakings of both employers and employees. For Professor Li Jingsen, of the Chinese People's University, and Professor Wang Cangsuo, of the Chinese University of Political Science and Law, labour relations in law are especially meaningful as these relations are based on consultation and consensus between the parties and have equal subject status. In such relations, the employers may exercise their autonomy in deciding how to use labour, but the employees are free to choose whom they will work for. As these labour relations are regulated by law they are presumably more predictable and efficient. In contrast, the administrative labour relations constituted a tightly controlled and hierarchical form of the labour relations under the planned economy.

One of the important purposes of the economic reform since the early 1980s was to clarify the administrative power of the government organizations, and consequently to reduce administrative control over the labour process. Professors Li and Wang observed that in the context of the market economic reform, the 1994 LL profoundly transformed labour relations. These relations have become 'legalized'. Administrative control over these relations has been reduced, and the interpretation of labour law as 'labour administrative law' has become irrelevant.[38]

Although market labour relations are concerned with both rights and obligations of employers and workers, the 1994 LL gave more priority to the protection of rights and interests of workers than to their obligations. Employee rights were mainly stipulated in Article 3 of the 1994 LL. They included rights to employment and free career choice, the rights to compensation, rest, and vacation, the right to a safe and sanitary working environment, the right to vocational training, social security and assistance rights, the right to mediation and arbitration and 'other rights according to law' such as trade union membership. At the same time, many other specific rights were stipulated with respect to disputes settlement, individual labour contract, and collective labour contract. Legal protection of rights and interests of labour in the 1994 LL were reinforced in the stipulation of employer obligations regarding working hours, minimum wage, the payment of labour insurance, and so on.

Although the Hainan model for economic reform focused new attention on individual obligation as part of a diversified 'rational sharing' of the burdens of social welfare and benefits, the 1994 LL lacked detailed substantive provisions on worker obligations. The law merely mentioned that labour has obligations to fulfil their assigned tasks, to observe safety regulations and to improve their technical skills. The 1994 LL did not absorb past regulations on labour discipline such as the 1982 'Rules for Rewarding and Punishing Workers' and the 1986 'The Provisional Regulations on the Dismissal of Workers Who Violate Disciplinary Measures in the State-Owned Enterprises'. Instead, the law stipulated that within the law's guidelines it is the employers' obligation to develop clear rules and regulations by which workers fulfil their obligations.[39]

This stipulation did coincide with the Hainan model's requirements in its confirmed departure from past practice where labour discipline was centrally controlled through government-issued rules and regulations. In the past, labour discipline was rooted in the symbiotic purposes of social control and efficiency in production. Under the 1994 LL, the responsibility for worker discipline shifted from the state to enterprise, but in this case 'efficiency' was tied to the key notion of lawful contract.

In their understated analysis, People's Supreme Court (SPC) experts, Liang Shuwen and Hui Luming, claimed that this shift was largely the result of the technical requirements of legislation. As the Chinese economy underwent rapid transformation, the constant implementation of new reform policies led to the emergence of new economic systems and new concerns in labour relations. Labour legislation initially reacted by offering guidelines rather than detailed stipulations to regulate labour relations.

In recent years, this legislative approach has been attacked for its overly general orientation, its failure to provide predictability and for inconsistent law enforcement. Liang and Hui, however, suggested that employers were in a better position to take into account the specific characteristics of their enterprises so as to provide detailed rules and regulations concerning worker discipline. Article 4 of the 1994 LL may in fact play an important role in encouraging employers to provide specificities in disciplining labour, something which government rules and regulations had often failed to do in the past.[40]

Liang and Hui also suggested that work rules and regulations developed by employers are important extensions of labour law.[41] Indeed, such rules and regulations have become important bases for adjudication in the labour disputes settlement process. Legally, this represents significant development towards legalization of labour discipline. But in practice, this transformation may negatively impact upon the protection of workers' rights and interests since Article 4 of 1994 LL stated that employers 'should' (*yingdang*) not 'must' (*bixu*) provide such work rules or regulations. Without either employer or state disciplinary regulations, there is the potential for labour abuse. In fact, a large number of labour disputes recorded were due to either the absence or ambiguity of the work rules and regulations. One must also consider whether or not the devolution of obligation to employers supports the 'self-determination' of the worker and the equality of employers and employees.

Critics have suggested that many such rules and regulations are inconsistent with state laws. However, in many situations, it is difficult to tell whether certain work rules are contradictory to state laws since the state laws, themselves, are not detailed enough to allow the courts to make an effective judgment. In fact, government organizations, including the Ministry of Labour, the State Council, and the All China Federation of Trade Unions (ACFTU), have recognized difficulties in enforcement due to the abstract nature of the 1994 LL. These organizations have been intimately involved in vetting the supporting detail to implement the various provisions of the 1994 LL.

The shift in responsibility for the regulation of worker discipline confirms jurist argument that one of the most important legislative intents of the 1994 LL was to protect rights and interests of workers, as contrasted with the imposition of obligations on labour in the command economy of the past. Possibly this can be taken as evidence suggesting a developing shift in Chinese legal theory of function of law from primarily enforcing social control to balancing social control with the protection of rights and interests.

Li Buyun has commented on the related issue of rights versus obligations in law in his essay attached to Wang Jiafu's 1997 Zhongnanhai lecture. Li argued that legal relations are concerned with both legal rights and obligations but that the legal protection of rights has priority over the imposition of the obligations. The essence and value of the law are intertwined with its protection of the rights, although the rights cannot be realized without the enforcement of obligations. However, the protection of rights is the very purpose of law, while legally stipulated obligations only serve to strengthen the protection of the rights.[42] This focus on protection has been explicitly rationalized with reference to the importance of social stability in the context of market transition.

Professor Shi Tanjing of the Institute of Law of the CASS, a key drafter of the 1994 LL, informed the authors that after 15 years and 30 drafts, the new labour law was rushed to the NPC Standing Committee for fast-track approval. With the acceleration of economic reform, the Party leadership reacted swiftly to the potential spread of labour abuse and unrest. The prospect of serious social instability was often cited by legal scholars and trade union officials to urge the Party leaders to protect rights and interests of workers. Such protection was integral to the drafting of the 1994 LL. The *Gongren ribao* (Workers' Daily), the official organ of the ACFTU, authoritatively commented that the content and intention of the 1994 LL hinged on the protection and readjustment of those rights and interests of workers which had been compromised during market reform.[43]

Several jurists have optimistically contended that the 1994 LL reconciled the economic reform focus on efficiency with a strong new emphasis on the protection of worker rights and interests. Professor Gu Jie, of the Northwest Chinese Political and Law College, saw a positive connection between new rights protection and production efficiency.[44] In his very optimistic analysis, Professor Guan Huai claimed that the 1994 LL was intended to reform the four most critical aspects of Chinese labour management system. The 1994 LL sought to establish an employment system that would introduce labour competition based on rational labour mobility and the principle of 'survival of the fittest'. Secondly, the wage distribution system had to adapt to the principles of distribution based on 'efficiency as primary and fairness as supplementary'. Thirdly, the 1994 LL required that the government establish a social security system; and finally, the direct control of government deparments over labour management was modified in favour of indirect control as exercised by the enterprises themselves.[45]

Assessing the shift to contract labour

The introduction of the labour contract system is the key feature of the self-proclaimed 1994 LL dual approach to labour efficiency and the protection of the rights and interests. The late Gordon White explored the critical ramifications of this shift in the following way:

> it heralds considerable change in the socio-economic position of China's state industrial workers and in their relations with managerial superiors. The issue engages established interests and embodies a redistribution of social power among social strata; it is therefore an

interesting area in which to explore the politics of Chinese economic reform and nature of the Chinese policy process.[46]

As noted in this chapter's introduction, some Chinese jurists stressed that labour, unlike civil, law encourages the state's legitimate intervention into labour relations in order to achieve social justice. R.H. Folsom and J.H. Minan offered a somewhat different perspective on this:

> Chinese contract is a civil law concept based on the principle of equality, voluntariness, and mutual benefit. Consequently, the labour contract will result in not only promoting labour efficiency, but also the development of mechanisms to guarantee workers' right and interests under their contracts and to prevent enterprises from abusing their considerable regulatory powers.[47]

Without doubt, contract, whether or not its origins are traced to civil or labour law, has seminal relevance to labour law. It has become the key to understanding 'pluralized' labour relations within the 'socialist' market economy. During the early 1950s new democratic phase of the 'New China', an employment contract system (*laodong hetongzhi*) was deployed in the context of mixed economy. After 1958, the remnants of this system were gradually replaced by a ironclad employment system, characterized by a highly centralized labour management with total control over the distribution of labour resources. The employment process was basically controlled by the government's labour and personnel bureaus.

Under this late 1950s' regime, the labour contract system was applied only to temporary and seasonal workers. It was simply assumed that the permanent employment system played a positive role in securing a badly needed labour force, in reducing unemployment and stabilizing social order. There was, of course, a major change in attitude in the post-1978 reform period. The permanent employment system came under attack for its inflexibility in adjusting to the changing supply and demand of the enterprises for labour. Enterprise could neither dismiss workers whose skills were no longer required nor hire those whose skills were most needed.

After 1980, the government attempted to reintroduce the contract system in various forms of enterprises so as to qualify, if not eliminate, the 'three irons' labour system.[48] The 1994 LL devotes a section of 20 articles to the various requirements of employment labour contract.[49] Since the 1994 LL's promulgation, the State Council and Ministry of

Labour have issued several series of regulations detailing the implementation of contract.[50] The reintroduction of the labour contract system provoked fierce opposition. Fearing that contract might transform the 'masters' of society into 'hired labour', critics charged that the new employment system was essentially capitalist in nature.[51]

Professor Guan Huai reminded anyone who would listen of the fundamental differences between the capitalist and socialist contract systems. In the first place, unlike the capitalist system, the socialist labour contract system features public ownership. Secondly, labour is not a commodity under the socialist labour system. Evidently such conventional differentiation was too sanguine. For one thing, it has been officially recognized that China now has multiple systems of ownership under the mainstay of public ownership. Currently, the most extensive application of the labour contract is in the private and foreign investment sectors.[52] Secondly, while there has been no formal pronouncement on whether labour under the socialist market system is a commodity, the practical purpose of the current economy reform is clearly to establish a labour market that allows allowing labour competition. Essentially, this transforms labour into a commodity. Liang Shuwen and Hui Luming have no qualms in arguing that, on the contrary, the past difficulties in labour management were chiefly due to the fact that 'labour' was not treated as a commodity and thus could not be separated from 'a labourer'.[53]

For jurists and legal scholars, the introduction of the labour contract system has profound implications. The labour contract legalizes employment relations between individual labourers and employers by folding the rights, obligations and responsibilities of both parties into a legal contract. As labour relations are extremely complicated and vary across different economic sectors and enterprises, one might expect that a premium would be placed on flexibility; however, contract provided a opportunity for employers and employees to express their legal rights and mutual obligations in the formation of new labour relations.

Law reformers have identified the several important functions of the labour contract system. In their view, contract can eliminate the inefficiencies of the permanent employment system, promote labour mobility and create a rational labour market, while eliminating the status difference between workers and party officials. Under the planned economy, one's wage level, fringe benefits, and certain privileges were associated with his/her political status and rank, not with his/her job position. In the event of transfer to a different position, the privileges attached to a person's particular status would simply be transferred to the new workplace. The contract system on the other hand ignored personal status and attached a wage level and benefits to the particular job position. In this sense, this system threatened the privileged political classes by encouraging free competition for job positions without giving due consideration to personal status.[54]

The new contract system also promised a reduction in labour disputes. In the past, labour relations were established through administrative orders according to government regulations, policies and the Ministry of Labour's Notes which were often extremely vague in their explication of the rights and obligations of the parties involved. This documentation failed to provide clear guidelines for determining which disputes could be rightfully settled.

Ideally, with the explicit expression of rights and obligations of the parties in the contract, the parties are eager to fulfil their obligations to avoid breach of contract. At the same time, in the case where a dispute does occur, it can be easily settled since the labour contract normally provides clear guidelines for mediation or/and an arbitration to settle the dispute.

According to Shi Tanjing, because of the absence of labour contracts, government departments were unable to determine the proper responsibilities of employers and management in the event of harm caused to workers' rights and interests. Shi believed that contracts would clearly provide a check against the abuses of workers' rights and interests.[55]

Chen Wenyuan, law professor of Chinese University of Politics and Law, Beijing, also emphasized that the clear requirements as set out in the labour contract would benefit both labourers and enterprises as it combines both rights and interests, as well as the obligation of labourers and enterprises. Contract was hailed as the new panacea in the state's search for social stability.[56]

State guarantees of contractual equality

The 1994 LL prohibits employment without a labour contract, and it also defines the procedures for validating the contract and stipulating and penalties for the breach of the same contract.[57] Chinese legal scholars believe that through such a requirement the state can formally define labour relations and integrate labour relations as part of the legal system.[58] This provides the state with a legal foundation for protecting workers' legitimate rights and interests.[59] A labour contract must explicitly spell out all important employment conditions and conditions for terminating the contract.[60]

According to Article 18, the contract must include the following clauses: time limit of the labour contract; work content; labour protection and conditions; remuneration; disciplinary regulations; conditions for terminating labour contract; obligations in the event of contract violation. At the same time, the law also stipulates that a valid labour contract cannot contravene state laws and administrative regulations. The significance of these requirements is that legally they limit the power of the management and allow for an impartial third party to resolve the conflicts through a formal system of disputes settlement.

Article 17 of the 1994 LL states that the formation of a valid contract must follow four principles, namely, equality, voluntary participation, agreement through consultation and legality. 'Equality' requires that the employers or employing units and labourers should form an individual labour contract on the basis of equality. It specifies that the two contracting parties have equal status in law and that they have equal opportunity and power to negotiate their rights and interests in the formation of a labour contract. These articulated principles assumed the vulnerability of labour, particularly in the contemporary context of rising employment. The principles of equality and voluntary consensus were thought to be mutually reinforcing as there can be no voluntary consensus without equal status.

The principle of voluntary participation confirms that the terms or particulars of the contract would be subject to the will of both parties; therefore, neither party could force the other to accept particular terms, nor could a third party interfere in settling the terms of contract. Article 19 of the 1994 LL stated that a labour contract is invalid if it is formed on the basis of force, threat or fraud. To assist the implementation of the 1994 LL, many key words relating to labour contract were defined in the Notices and Explanations subsequently issued by central ministries, especially the Ministry of Labour. The definitions of 'threat' and 'fraud' conformed with those set out in the 1986 General Principles of Civil Law (GPCL).

'Threat' implies behaviour forcing or coercing a party to accept terms against her/his will through threatening property damage, physical harm, or harm to personal or family reputation. 'Fraud' means to induce another party to agree to certain terms through providing false information, or by concealing the facts from the other party. The 'principle of consultation' obviously affirmed the need for legitimate mutuality in consultation. Any resulting invalidation of a contract necessitated adjudication either by labour dispute arbitration committee or by the people's court.[61]

These principles of the 1994 LL converged with those of the 1986 GPCL.[62] Chinese jurisprudence, however, carefully avoided a wholesale equation of employment relations with civil law relations. Unlike the case in the civil law sphere, the state retained the right to intervene in the formation of labour contract and in the overall process of forming employment relations. The 'principle of legality' emphasized that contract would necessarily conform with state laws and regulations. According to Professor Shi, this principle incorporated three components, lawful subjects, lawful content, and the lawful method of forming contract. The 'lawful subject' (*hefa zhuti*) of a labour contract refers to the legally recognized condition of employment. The 1994 LL did not treat this extensively. With respect to the issue of protecting minors, as discussed in Chapter 2, it did indicate under Article 15 that minors under 16 years old are not qualified to be employed. The expert opinion of the relevant working group within the Supreme Court Opinion has stipulated that student workers are not required to enter into a labour contract. Such employment is considered to be part-time, and is not construed as legal employment between an employer and employee. This left a gap in the system of protection designed to further the rights and interests of children.

Although reformers have focused on the efficiencies which result from getting rid of the 'three irons', there has been very little initiative in clearing up the confusion surrounding the legal status of enterprise cadres such as Party secretaries, management and technical personnel or trade union chairmen. Again, related Supreme Court opinion has claimed that the 1994 LL intentionally eliminated the difference in status between the cadre and labourers and subsumed them under a single category of labourers (*laodongzhe*). This presumed that the cadres would enter into contract negotiations to secure their own rights. Nevertheless, the practice continues in state-owned enterprise, where the cadres form labour contracts with the superior department in charge, instead of with their own enterprises. On the other hand, the trade union cadres became an important exception to this practical rule. They were allowed to enter directly into labour contract with their respective enterprises. Increasingly, contract is assigning status to position rather than to the person, and the trade union cadres are themselves seeking the protection of contract.[63]

According to Article 19 of the 1994 LL, the rights and interests of the contracting parties is placed along a supposedly flexible spectrum distinguishing between legally required terms, governing the time limit of contract, work content, labour protection and conditions, remuneration, labour discipline, contract termination, labour disputes and obligations in the context of breach of contract, and the specific contractual terms of reference, settled in employee/employer negotiation. Although the 1994 LL permits independent negotiation of the latter category of contract terms, it insists that these additional terms of reference are expected to conform to labour law and regulation such as set out in Articles 14 and 15 of the 1994 LL itself.[64] Professor Shi regarded such state intervention as necessary to the protection of worker rights and interests. He therefore argued that the orientation of labour law is basically different from that of the civil law.[65]

Termination of contract labour relations

The termination of contract labour relations is a key political issue with respect to the transition from the planned to the market economy and the protection of rights and interests within a newly forming labour market. Article 41 of the 1982 State Constitution proclaimed that citizens have the right and obligation to work. The new contract system, however, assumes that the lawful termination of employment may be deemed economically rational. This, of course, has a direct bearing on the welfare of the worker who for so long had enjoyed 'mastery' in labour relations.

The notion of contract labour relations inherently favours a principle of enterprise efficiency. For reasons of productivity which was presumably weighted down by the 'three irons system', enterprise had to acquire in law the ability to make independent decisions on the hiring and firing of workers so as to deal effectively with market conditions. Not surprisingly, this trend has been linked to an increasing trend in labour disputes. In fact nine out of the 106 articles of the 1994 LL were devoted to issues concerning the termination of contract.

According to Gu Angran, Chairman of the Legal System Working Committee of the NPC, the 1994 LL provisions on dismissals were designed to achieve a balance of values. These provisions offered to improve managerial efficiency by allowing the employer to dismiss redundant and unqualified workers, but they also offered enhanced stipulations against employer abuse of the terms of dismissal. Worker rights and interests were highlighted in the explicit clarification of the conditions and procedures for dismissal, and in compensation for dismissal.[66] Articles 23 and 24 allowed normal termination at the time of the contract's expiry, or by mutual agreement. The 1994 LL also hedged unilateral employer dismissal which was classified into three categories, fault dismissal, no-fault dismissal and dismissal due to changing economic conditions.

'Fault dismissal' occurs under four possible circumstances. In the first place, the law tolerates dismissal if a worker is proven unqualified during the probationary period of employment. The law itself, however, did not provide a working universal standard which meaningfully distinguished between a 'qualified' and 'unqualified' worker in every workplace. Moreover, the 1994 LL did not remedy the past situation where foreign enterprise generally exploited similar provisions in the law to dismiss workers. Secondly, the law allows dismissal for serious violation of enterprise labour discipline.

Gu Angran has pointed out that many of the disciplinary rules of 'three capital' enterprises are in conflict with state laws and regulations. Article 25 (2) of the 1994 LL did not define 'serious violation of labour discipline'. To compensate for this, Liang Shuwen and Hui Luming tried to find related stipulations in two related State Council regulations,[67] namely, 'The 1982 Rules concerning Rewards and Punishments of Enterprise Workers' and 'The 1986 Provisional Regulations Concerning Dismissal of Workers in the State-Owned Enterprises Violating Disciplinary Rules'.

These regulations referenced 'serious violation of labour discipline' but they did not offer sufficient clarity in law. In terms of actual legal convention, such serious violation included absenteeism, frequent lateness, leaving work early and slow downs that seriously impaired normal production and working order. However this kind of State Council regulation antedated the 'socialist market' and did not fit well with private enterprise.

Thirdly, 'fault dismissal' was countenanced in cases where workers were found guilty either of serious dereliction of duty, or 'practicing graft or corruption' (*yingsi wubi*) that causes great losses to the enterprise's interests. Fourthly, Article 25 dismissal could be initiated as a result of worker violation of the criminal law. 'Fault dismissal' in each of the four cases was rationalized so as to improve the quality of the work force and enterprise productivity. Such provision did not, therefore, entail employer responsibility for worker compensation.

In contrast, the three instances of no-fault dismissal did envisage compensation. Such dismissal is sanctioned if, after the end of a medical treatment for illness or injuries outside the workplace, the worker is unable to perform either originally assigned duties or the revised duties. Secondly, such dismissal was allowed if the worker is found to be incompetent after remedial training or job reassignment. Liang Shuwen and Hui Luming, for example, defined 'incompetency', based on the worker failure to oblige the contract job description and the amount and nature of the contracted responsibilities.

The third rationale for dismissal was potentially the most controversial. 'No-fault' dismissal permissively responded to market changes allowing dismissal in response to 'change in objective conditions' (*keguan qingkuang bianhua*). Dismissal, in other words, could be lawfully precipitated in the light of a drastic change in the conditions in which the contract was originally premised and the failure of the contracting parties to negotiate remedial measures responding to these specific conditions.[68]

Within such change, Liang Shuwen and Hui Luming included enterprise relocation, amalgamation and redirection of the development of enterprise. This particular understanding of 'no-fault' has understandably attracted a great deal of attention as it basically affects the balance between the contracting parties. In this case, the scales of jurisprudence have often been tipped in favour of justice over efficiency. Article 28 of the 1994 LL accordingly stressed the importance of worker compensation. Liang Shuwen and Hui Luming may have attempted to qualify the thrust of the 1994 LL when they attached a reservation to no-fault dismissal precluding compensation in specific cases relating to change in taxation, natural disaster, war and economic adjustment.[69]

With particular reference to economic adjustment, Article 27 of the 1994 LL deliberately stipulated dismissal due to economic conditions in the following way:

> An employer can also terminate a labour contract during the period of legal readjustment because of near bankruptcy or because the enterprise faces serious difficulties in production and operations. However, the employer is legally required to explain [enterprise] conditions to the trade union or the entire staff members and workers three months in advance and to submit a [related] report to the relevant labour administrative department.[70]

This category of dismissal obviously approximates the concept of dismissal for redundancy in Western labour law.

According to Gu Angran, the NPCSC faced a dilemma in its review of the draft 1994 LL. On the one hand, it recognized the importance in permitting enterprises to dismiss workers for redundancy in order to revive deeply indebted state-owned enterprise. On the other, the NPCSC feared that massive dismissal for redundancy would precipitate serious social unrest. In response, the NPCSC inserted in Article 27 (2), phraseology requiring that state enterprise give priority to rehiring workers within a six month period after layoff.[71]

The effective application of this redundancy principle in Article 27 required further clarification of 'in the period of legal adjustment' and 'in serious difficulties in production and operations'. The Ministry of

Labour's 1994 September Explanations to the 1994 attempted to clarify 'the period of legal adjustment' in the stipulations of the PRC Bankruptcy Law and the Law of Civil Procedure. Article 2 of the Ministry of Labour's November 1994 'The Regulations of Enterprise Dismissal due to Economic Conditions' indicated that 'the period of legal adjustment' would be confirmed in a notice of the people's court.

Dismissal for redundancy also required legal confirmation of 'serious difficulties in production and operations'. Both the Ministry of Labour Explanation of the 1994 LL Article 27 and the related Article 2 of the November 1994 regulations governing dismissals in enterprise, suggested that this condition would best be defined by local government. However, Articles 4 and 5 of the November 1994 regulations made it clear that dismissal for redundancy would require the support both of the trade union concerned and of the employees.

The issue is clearly related to government concern about potential social unrest. Both the trade union and the local department of labour bureau can make suggestions to the employer about the dismissal and compensation payment for redundancy. Such suggestions, however, can be ignored since the employer has autonomous power to decide on the use of dismissal for redundancy within the law.

In this instance, the 1994 LL and related regulations emphasize upholding the autonomy of enterprise in the hiring and dismissal of workers so as to promote management efficiency. At the same time, the law's provisions attempted to respond to the 'special group of rights' discussed in Chapter 2. An enterprise's resort to redundancy is qualified with reference to the disabled or workers with occupational disease, hospitalized workers, and female workers who are in pregnancy or in maternity, and with reference to 'other cases according to law'. The latter terminology applies to no-fault dismissal and represents a resort to a principle of flexibility, which leaves open the possibility of future legislation.

The scale of compensation was set out in companion regulations by the Ministry of Labour in December 1994. Article 9 of the 'Methods of Economic Compensation for Breach and Termination of the Labour Contract' confirmed that those workers dismissed for no-fault redundancy would be entitled to a month of salary for every year worked in the enterprise. Article 30 of the 1994 LL swung from efficiency towards justice in making provision for resort to either arbitration or to the people's court in instances of formal grievance stemming from dismissal.

There were further attempts to qualify unilateral dismissal under Articles 26 and 27 of the 1994 LL. These articles precluded dismissal on four grounds. Workers with occupational disease or work-related injury were not to be dismissed. Nor were workers undergoing medical treatment for illness or injury. These articles also backed up the women's law in that employers were ordered not to dismiss pregnant or nursing mothers. A fourth proviso referred to 'other circumstances' as provided by law and administrative regulation.

In addition, under Articles 24, 26 and 27, employers are instructed to pay compensation to the workers involved in contract terminations.[72] All the legally imposed limitations on an employer's ability to terminate a labour contract confirm the new emphasis in labour law on the protection of rights and interests of workers. Workers, on the other hand, can terminate a labour contract unilaterally with 30 days' notice during their probationary period, or in response to employer threats and illegal limitation of worker freedom, or in cases where the employer has failed either to pay wages or to provide appropriate working conditions as specified in the provisions of the labour contract.[73]

This still leaves open the very critical question as to what happens when a contract is breached? It can be breached by an employer, or an employee, or both. The consequences of breach of the labour contract provided in Articles 89–102 of the 1994 LL are primarily monetary. The details concerning compensation were outlined in 1994–95 in two sets of Ministry of Labour regulations, 'The Methods of Economic Compensation for the Breach and Termination of Labour Contract' and 'The Methods of Economic Compensation for the Violation of the Provisions for Labour Contract in the 1994 LL'. The former clearly stipulated that compensation would be paid to those workers who did not receive their wages on time. But these regulations focused primarily on economic compensation concerning termination of the contract. The second set of regulations set out more specific procedure for the calculation of compensation and referenced breach of contract by both the employers and the employees.[74]

The trade union's role in the new era of collective agreement

As indicated in Chapter 2, the protection of rights and interests, as it concerns social justice in China's new marketplace, has formally integrated the complementary facets of legal and social protection. The market naturally generates competition, but policy has stressed the enhanced importance of legal mediation to insure fairness in the labour management process. How then does Chinese jurisprudence deal with social tensions and the requirements of collective bargaining in the new market context? Surprisingly, the right to strike has only received intermittent support in the modern history of Chinese socialism. Priority was placed on social stability, and worker–management solidarity – in the harmonious unity of state and society – was simply assumed.

What role is assigned to the trade union in the context of the new legal emphasis on 'rights and interests'? According to government officials, the 1994 LL sought to encompass non-publicly owned enterprise under the legal provisions of collective agreement.[75] Liang Shuwen and Hui Luming have argued that the collective agreement system creates opportunities for labourers in an enterprise – especially in a private owned enterprise – to act as a whole so as to balance unevenly distributed resources between individual labourers and employer. This balancing would enable labour to negotiate with employer on a fair and equal basis so as to secure their interests. As an individual labour contract, a collective agreement is also an extension of labour law in that it details, as well as customizes, the general provisions in the 1994 LL. Chen Wenyuan has also argued that the collective contract can supplement the law's provisions on the protection of the rights and interests of labourers in areas where the labour law may not be comprehensive.[76]

Liang Shuwen and Hui Luming have claimed that the collective agreement system enhances the legalization of labour management as well as reduces labour disputes. Shi Tanjing, in his explanation of how the collective agreement system enhances the protection of worker rights and interests, highlighted the connection between the provisions for collective agreement and individual labour contract. He particularly supported the remedial nature of Article 35 of the 1994 LL which states:

> a collective contract concluded between an enterprise and its staff members and workers according to law is legally binding. Labour conditions and labour remuneration in labour contracts concluded between individual workers and an enterprise shall not be lower than the standards prescribed in a collective labour contract.

Within a collective contract, individual labourers can avoid unfair management practices through their participation in the process of making a labour contract. The provision allowing the trade union to reach a collective agreement with the management indicates that the 1994 LL gave labourers the legal right to defend their own interests.[77] Professor Shi, however, was disappointed that the 1994 LL failed to provide a new chapter on collective agreement as he had originally proposed. The latter was detailed in only three articles, Articles 33–35. This reflected some disagreement among the drafters as to the usefulness of the collective agreement in labour management. Inadequate stipulation soon resulted in problems of implementation, and the Ministry of Labour quickly stepped in with its December 1994 'Regulations on Collective Agreement' detailing the process of negotiating a collective agreement.

Compared to the provisions on collective agreement, in the 1950 and 1992 Trade Union Laws, the 1994 LL took a major step forward in its emphasis on the protection of the rights and interests of labour. The 1950 and 1992 content of collective agreement was limited narrowly to the worker participation in enterprise management. Article 33 of the 1994 LL allowed trade union representatives greater discretion to bargain with management on more meaningful issues, including compensation, hours of work, days off, vacation, labour safety and sanitation, insurance and welfare benefits.

Worker participation in enterprise management was reiterated in Article 8 of Chapter 1 of the 1994 LL; however, this stipulation was so general that many questioned its practical value. Guan Huai, for example, appealed for a more effective law to guarantee democratic participation in enterprise management.[78] Such emphasis conforms with the contemporary focus on the relationship between democracy and the rule of law in the context of accelerated economic reform.

In addition, the ACFTU, in the face of opposition from the State Economic Planning Commission, had lobbied hard for the passage of the 1994 LL.[79] Subsequent to the latter's adoption, Xue Zhaojun, vice-president of the Federation, told the NPCSC that the unions would have to shift their emphasis to the protection of worker rights and interests and that union branches would have to undergo a structural transformation. The latter were to be transformed from government departments to the 'homes of the workers'.[80]

The ACFTU continued to push for appropriate legal development. In 1995, on its own cognizance, it issued 'The Provisional Methods of Trade Union Participation in Equal Consultation for the Signing of Collective Agreements' which addressed three new issue areas including dismissal for redundancy, vocational training, and 'other items' agreed upon by two parties. Legally, this addition was not a revision to the 1994 LL. The ACFTU's 'methods', however, are likely to have political significance in the growing context of state enterprise reform, spreading redundancy and worker unrest.

The stipulation of collective agreement touched on two other major areas of concern. The first relates to the situation where either there is failure to reach a collective agreement or there is a dispute over the enforcement of a mutually concluded agreement. The second concerns a technical question of contract legitimacy. A contract becomes legally binding at the time of signing; however, its validity is subject to subsequent confirmation by the labour disputes arbitration commission or the people's court. Under 1994 LL Article 34 the collective agreement can take effect only if the local labour department raises no objection within 15 days after receiving the related documentation. This indeterminacy suggests a persisting cautious attitude in the state's response to the possible consequences of industrial action.

Much to the disappointment of prominent legal reformers such as Shi Tanjing and Chen Wenyuan, the 1994 LL did not affirm the workers' right to strike. Chen, for example, argued that the balance of power between trade union and the management had to be adjusted in favour of the weaker party, the trade union, so as to insure equality in negotiations. This balance was central to the protection of worker rights and interests.[81] This certainly is a familiar viewpoint in the West. Steven Anderman, for example, argued with specific reference to British Labour Law:

> it has long been recognized that without a credible threat of demanding industrial action there is little assurance that management will be willing to engage in meaningful negotiation with trade union representatives over disputed issues of management decision making and meaningful collective bargaining has been accepted albeit, grudgingly at times, as a necessary method of determining wage levels in a decentralized way as well as the basis of a measure of industrial democracy in working life.[82]

At discrete points in time Chinese constitutional law explicitly endorsed the right to strike. Both Article 20 of the 1975 and Article 45 of the 1978 State Constitutions listed the right to strike as one of a series of key civil rights. These constitutional articles were informed by the 'leftist' Party line of 'continuing the dictatorship of the proletariat', and the support of the right to strike was explicit in the politics of Cultural Revolutionary class struggle. As time went on, however, the Party leadership and even Mao, himself, more generally preferred to deal with worker agitation or 'contradictions among the people' on the basis of Yan'an rectification practices. The senior leadership has often associated strikes with 'disturbances' which challenge 'correct ideas' under democratic centralism.[83] At any rate, the official, unlike the unofficial, right to strike has seldom been exercised by the trade unions.

Paradoxically, it was in the period of economic reform that the right to strike was deleted from the 1982 State Constitution in response to the political prioritization assigned to social and political stability. Folsom and Minan have interpreted the deletion as an indicator of Party's adverse reaction to the Polish solidarity movement and consequent demise of the Communist regime in Poland.[84] In China, workers' strikes have always been regarded as political rather than economic phenomena. But in the transition to the socialist market, there has been a dramatic incidence of unofficial strikes in both private and state enterprise.[85] There has been a contemporaneous increase in jurist support for the official right to strike, as the last resort for workers to express their grievances concerning immediate economic issues.

Local government has often tolerated illegal strikes partly because the circumstances were aggravated by the illegal conduct of employers, and partly because the local government feared that strong repression of striking workers would result in more radical worker uprisings. Shi Tanjing, in a 12 June 1998 interview with the authors, indicated that the NPCSC is now seriously reconsidering the legalization of the right to strike. Although Professor Shi had advocated the inclusion of this right into the draft 1994 LL, in 1998 he seemed to anticipate a watering down of this right and was, therefore, inclined to wait for a less qualified wording.

Shan Dongshan, a University of Suzhou law professor, has pointed out some of the most serious related difficulties which have arisen in the context of economic reform. According to Article 33 of the 1994 LL, a collective contract has to be signed by a trade union or the representative selected by the staff members and workers, but, in reality, the trade unions are not themselves fully developed in terms of membership and their exercise of legal functions, especially in the private enterprise context. By 1996, only 10 per cent of the non-state owned enterprise had trade unions.

In the contemporary shift to 'big society' there is a complicated evolution of mass organization, some of which is ignoring the long-established bonds of state supervision. The trade union had for a long time been one of the purest examples of state-controlled corporatism; however, the unions have had to cope with the internal organizational and political implications of the transition to the market economy. Frequently, the managers of state enterprise have enjoyed trade union membership, and the trade union itself was treated as a financially dependent department of state enterprise.

The salaries of full-time union workers are normally paid by employers in both private and state-owned enterprises. Recent Gansu provincial legislation on the wages of union workers in foreign invested enterprise is a case in point. The regulation stipulated that in foreign invested enterprises, the wages, bonuses, and welfare benefits of the full-time president and vice president of the trade union, as well as full-time union workers, will be paid by enterprise.[86]

Professor Shen has argued that the first step towards truly effective collective agreement is to develop independent trade unions in enterprises, the members of which must have full financial responsibility for their own organization. Shen wanted to exclude the managers from trade membership on the basis of a new principle of trade union autonomy. In his view, the trade union in the context of economic reform would necessarily become a separate interest group which would maintain a reasonable independence from management so as to be able to represent and negotiate with management on the behalf of labour and its interests.[87]

While some advocates have stressed the importance of the labour law as an extension of state activism in the cause of social justice, the labour law has steadily moved towards the legal recognition of trade union autonomy. When taken together, the 1992 Trade Union Law, the 1994 LL, and regulations such as the ACFTU's August 1995 'The Provisional Methods of Trade Union Participation in Equal Consultation and in Signing Collective Agreements' and 'The Provisional Methods of Trade Union Participation in Labour Disputes Settlement', suggest a modest trend towards recognition of trade union autonomy and the legal protection of rights and interests through clear and detailed description of legitimate union interaction with management, the Party and government.

The protection of rights and interests has become part of the 'core mission of the party', but the trade union has a long way to go in terms of achieving its full autonomy.[88] A certain amount of autonomy in the context of the market has been rationalized as an effective guarantee of worker rights and interests.[89] The official organ of labour, the *Gongren ribao*, attempted to negotiate the conflicting parameters of legal change and organizational response with an updated mass-line strategy:

> accepting party leadership conscientiously is not the same thing as simply toeing the party line. Faced with a host of new circumstances and new problems in the market economy, trade unions will hardly

be able to develop and may even run the risk of divorcing themselves from the masses, which will threaten their very survival, if they take leave of their independence and initiative, if they cease to be innovative, and if they fail to balance their accountability to the authorities above with their responsibility to the masses.[90]

Even before the issue of trade union autonomy can be addressed there has to be a trade union. To the dismay of the ACFTU, much of the private or foreign enterprises and township enterprises have yet to set up trade unions so as to get on with the task of protecting workers' rights and interests.[91]

The government is increasingly focusing on 'three-capital' enterprises out of its concern for social stability. It has recognized that trade unions can help maintain stable labour relationships and reduce labour disputes and that labour relationships are more stable in foreign enterprises that have trade unions. According to government officials, in 1995, 99.8 per cent of the foreign enterprises in the Shekou Industrial Zone of Shenzhen, Guangdong Province, established trade unions and have resolved 99.2 per cent of labour disputes in the enterprises, with no need to resort to lawsuits.[92] In addition, the state has a political and organizational preference for the legal formation of trade unions that can address the spread of illegal unions and radical industrial action.[93]

The state has had to cope with the increasing societal ambiguity of market reform. It runs the risk of the protection of rights and interests getting in the way of labour management efficiency. On the other hand, the Party has often responded positively to argument to the effect that rights and interests protection promotes social stability. The trade union is an important actor in this unfolding story of social justice and stability, but then so is the newly developing disputes settlement mechanism.

Social justice and the labour dispute settlement system

Labour disputes settlement is a key component of 'efficient' labour management. Chinese legal scholars and government officials have gradually come to recognize that the occurrence of labour disputes in both the individual and collective setting are unavoidable. The importance of the dispute settlement mechanism lies in its provision of a new channel through which workers can redress their grievances. The labour law textbooks all contend that the disputes settlement mechanism in the 1994 LL was designed to promote both justice and efficiency in labour management.

Apparently, this mechanism serves three self-evident interrelated purposes. It protects lawful rights and interests of labour; it resolves conflicts between employees and employers so as to promote economic efficiency; and it reduces labour disputes and promotes stable labour relations. The protection function is based on the system's ability to reduce the absolute power and control of the management over their workforce. Professor Josephs has pointed out that the significance of the new system of labour dispute settlement rests with its ability to protect individual rights against encroachment by the state, enterprise, or by fellow citizens. Also, the new system is predicated in the important theoretical assumption that conflicts do indeed arise between the state, enterprise, and workers in the process of employment.[94]

The first formal labour disputes settlement system was established in 1949, but, for the most part, it was limited to private enterprise. After the transition to socialism it was abolished. The workers under socialism had become the undisputed 'masters' of enterprise. In 1956–86, an informal system called 'people visiting' system (*renmin laifang zhidu*) was in operation. This system, however, was unable to contribute effectively to the timely settlement of serious disputes in the post-1978 era of economic reform. The promulgation of 'The 1987 Provisional Regulations of Labour Disputes Settlement in State-Owned Enterprises' represented the first step into a new era of dispute settlement.[95]

There has recently been an unprecedented rise in labour disputes over individual and collective contracts. Professor Guan Huai has explained that this trend is closely associated with 'pluralization of labour relations' and the co-existence of private and public economy. In private enterprise, labour relations are theoretically antagonistic since the workers no longer work for themselves. State enterprise labour relations are comparatively more harmonious,[96] but increasing autonomy in these enterprises in the areas such as hiring, dismissal and wage distribution has apparently given rise to worker conflict with management.

After 1987, the state authorities became increasingly concerned about the escalating instances of labour disputes. This resulted in a new generation of stipulated regulation such as 'The 1993 Regulations for Labour Dispute Settlement in Enterprise'. According to Professor Guan, there was a growing public awareness of the pluralization of interests associated with diversified labour relations. The public interest in justice and fairness was apparent in the proliferation of cases relating to compensation and unemployment insurance. Guan also highlighted public concern over the greater increase in the disputes in foreign and private enterprises as compared to state and collective enterprises, particularly in light of the profit margins of the 'three-capital' enterprises.[97]

In response to the disadvantaged resource position of the workers, as compared to management, the 1994 LL sought to even the playing field through the stipulation of a new labour disputes mechanism which was to operate on the basis of the principles of legality, impartiality and timeliness.[98] The jurisprudential emphasis on impartiality (*gongzheng yuanze*) is noteworthy, given the fact that labour disputes also involve state enterprise. The Maoist 'structure of interests' had, in practice, assumed the priorities of state and collective interests vis-à-vis individual interests. In Mao's day, justice was presumed. The contemporary reference to 'impartiality' placed the individual on the same legal footing as state enterprise as legal persons.

The new law and regulation based upon the 1994 LL, 'The Regulations of Labour Dispute Settlement in Enterprise', 'The Provisional Methods of Trade Union Participation in Labour Disputes Settlement', expect that the parties to a dispute will seek mediation, arbitration, or file a suit at the court according to law.[99] Once disputes occur, the parties are urged to refer their case to a labour disputes mediation committee within their respective enterprise. This committee is an official mass organization.[100] However, Donald Clarke has observed that 'Chinese dispute resolution procedure, especially mediation, have been perhaps the single feature of the Chinese legal system most extensively studied in the West'.[101] And mediation is an extra-judicial method, which is not legally binding. Mediation has been a long-established practice in China, and even in the context of a growing emphasis on formal adjudication, Chinese jurists are favourably disposed towards the further development of such informal methods as the basis of a uniquely Chinese strategy of social protection for worker rights and interests.[102]

In fact, the parties to a dispute are required to submit to mediation before they can proceed to either arbitration or adjudication in the people's courts. According to the law, the mediation committee consists of at least two worker representatives, as well as one representative from the management and the trade union, and it is chaired by a third trade union member.[103] Under Article 10, 'The PRC Regulations of Labour Dispute Settlement in Enterprise', issued by the State Council in July 1993, a 30-day time limit is imposed upon the Committee.

In the event that the disputing parties resort to an arbitration committee, this committee operates as an impartial administrative and judicial organ, which works independently of government offices. This process is highly regulated.[104] The majority of cases are adjudicated by either full-time or part-time certified arbitrators who are professionals or semi-professionals and include law professors, lawyers, trade union workers and labour administrators. This semi-professional arbitration process represents a significant improvement over the past dispute settlement process which relied heavily on administrative orders and on personnel.

Nevertheless, Josephs has questioned the independence of the contemporary arbitration committee. She suggests that the labour dispute arbitration committee may be partial to the interests of enterprise management since it is chaired by the labour administrative department which is immediately superior to the enterprise.[105] This may be true, especially in the cases where the management has a good relationship with the local labour administrative department.

The decision of an arbitration committee has to be based on majority opinion. As for the formation of such a three-member committee, the chief arbitrator is appointed by the chairperson of the arbitration committee, and the other two members by the two parties to the dispute. The independence of the arbitration process is emphasized, but the arbitration committee can override the arbitration tribunal's decisions in complicated or difficult disputes.

If the parties cannot agree upon an arbitration ruling, they have the final option of filing suit at a people's court within 15 days.[106] A report from the High People's Court of the City of Shanghai indicates that the civil law courts at all levels have been taking the responsibility for adjudicating labour disputes. The cases dealt with by the courts were concerned primarily with compensation in private enterprises and wrongful dismissal, medical insurance, fringe benefits, especially those related to housing, compensation, and unemployment insurance in state-owned enterprises.

The 1994 LL requires adjudication by an arbitration committee prior to the filing of a suit before the people's court. But in practice, this has not always been closely followed. The Shanghai High People's Court indicates that the civil courts at all levels in the city adjudicated many cases before they were heard by the arbitration committees. The relatively small number of qualified arbitrators in the Shanghai area could not cope with their huge caseload, and major disputes required immediate attention in order to prevent their spinning out of control. This pattern is in keeping with past utilitarism emphasizing timeliness over methodical settlement procedure.

The same prevailing emphasis on substance over procedure is revealed in the decision-making by judicial personnel. The Shanghai report suggests that if an employer violated labour-related laws in both substance and procedure, the court would rule against the employer's decision. On the other hand, if the employer's decision was consistent with substance of the law, but violated procedural law, the court might well rule to maintain the employer's decision. Two closely related conclusions might be drawn from this. First, in adjudicating labour disputes, substance can override procedure. Secondly, this implies that justice and fairness are still mainly concerned with substance of law, and not procedure. This pattern, however, conflicts, with the ascending primacy of procedure in the developing criteria of judicial justice, as detailed in Chapter 5.[107]

Changing principles of wage distribution

Those changed with dispute settlement have to deal with very hot issues over what is a fair wage. In order to facilitate the related provisions of the 1994 LL, some provincial people's congresses have passed enabling regulations which have set out in detail procedures for organizing mediation and arbitration committees, one such being 'The Hainan Provisions on Labour Disputes'.[108] The notion of justice and efficiency is seminal to the recent reform in the wage distribution system. In the reform era, the essence of the old administratively centralized wage distribution system has been roundly discredited as 'egalitarianism', and wages have been progressively linked with worker performance.[109] The 1994 LL incorporated a post-1985 series of State Council and Ministry of Labour regulations into a new set of laws governing wage distribution, wage levels and minimum wage.

The 1994 LL stipulated two fundamental principles of wage distribution, namely, 'distribution according to work' and 'equal pay for equal work'. According to Professor Guan, these two principles are fundamental to the socialist system. As mentioned in the introduction to this chapter, the Party leadership sanctioned a revised notion of distribution which was confirmed by constitutional amendment in 1999. Even prior to this amending process, reforms had precipitated changes to the interpretation of the conventional principles of distribution.

Liang Shuwen and Hui Luming have argued that 'the basic implication of the principle of distribution according to work is that wages shall be distributed according to both quality and quantity of work or product'.[110] In the past, 'work' was apparently misconstrued as simply 'showing up for work'. The quality and quantity of work played little role in determining wage distribution. This situation led to unacceptable 'egalitarianism' in wage distribution. Liang and Hui have argued that the emerging principle of distribution based on both quality and quantity of work will promote efficiency.

In its concern for efficiency, the 1994 LL reflected the underlying premise of the 'small government, big society' strategy. Article 47 reduced the central government's role in the determination of wages and delegated such responsibility to state enterprise, which was under instruction to compete with other forms of economic organization on the basis of its independent management of profits and losses. As Professor Guan has indicated, state enterprise was previously an 'administrative appendage of the government which maintained tight budgetary control over wage distribution methods and wage levels'.[111] There is still a residual element of central paternalism. State enterprise does not have complete autonomy, but it has acquired the ability to link the total budget on wage distribution to enterprise performance. Increases in average wage levels are forbidden to rise above the rate of production increase.[112]

In its concern for social justice the 1994 LL also deals with the minimum wage issue. Taking into account the differentials across regional economies, the 1994 LL provides a relatively clear formula for calculating the minimum wage.[113] The law also responds to common complaints about delay in the payment of wages with the explicit stipulation of a monthly wage.[114] These stipulations reveal the law drafters' intent to balance market efficiency and rights and interests protection. To enhance the protection of worker rights and interests, one-third of the 1994 LL, or 40 articles across six chapters, provided detailed stipulations on many important issues, such as working hours, vacation time, wages, labour safety, sanitation in the workplace, special protection for female workers and working minors, job training and social insurance and welfare. These stipulations provide a 'floor' with respect to the provision of such benefits.

Social insurance in the scales of efficiency and justice

Deng Xiaoping's original 'three favourables' qualified the primacy of efficiency in that the liberation of productive forces within the social structures of the economy had to be accompanied by state programming which would work to avoid societal polarization. This is why the issue of converting to a market economy and the related re-structuring of state enterprise has always been contemporaneous with national policy-level insistence on the creation of newly devised social insurance schemes to serve as a 'safety net' or 'shock absorber'. In 1995 alone about 20 million state enterprise workers lost their jobs.[115] Such job loss and worker distress has often preceded the full development of new schemes.

The PRC's first social insurance program was established in the early 1950s, but it covered only the workers in the state enterprise. Responding to the new mix of public and private enterprise, the 1994 LL looked forward to new social insurance programming which would also cover all of the workers in the 'three capital' enterprises.[116] In addition, Article 73 called for the protection of the retired, elderly, sick, injured, disabled, unemployed and female workers with child. Under a new system of 'rational shared responsibility' enterprise was no longer exclusively responsible for the costs of benefits.[117] Article 72, in particular, confirmed the new system of conjoint responsibility which was alternatively designed to foster 'self-sponsored insurance consciousness on the part of individuals' who were expected to work with government and enterprise in the creation of new insurance, based upon diversified funding.

On the other hand, stipulated reference to 'collective welfare' (*jiti fuli*) indicated the transitory nature of the evolving social security system. Such stipulation was at odds with the economic reform emphasis on the conversion of state enterprise into competitive and efficient economic agents. Economic policy had focused on the exclusive and costly burden of state enterprise provision of an extraordinary range of benefits and services including housing, dining, bath halls, daycare centres, medical services, recreational facilities, taking care of retired and the sick, and so on. This pattern of state enterprise reliance was now seen as in conflict with the 'big society' and was criticized as 'enterprises running society' (*qiye banshi shehui*).

Hu Xiaoyi, the Head of Social Insurance Department under the Ministry of Labour, defensively glossed the contradictory stipulations of the 1994 LL. Hu emphasized the long-term and gradual conversion to shared responsibility systems. State enterprise would need time to transform their operational mechanisms, and time would also be needed to create new programming to take up the slack left by transforming state enterprises. In other words, social insurance is a work in progress; 'should' is more conditional than 'must'. The layoffs can continue while experiments with more broadly based social security programming continues. As the law, it both extols good intentions and plays for time, caught as it has been, between the old and new systems.[118]

Justice and equality in the scope of the 1994 Labour Law

Labour law and jurisprudence more generally have affirmed the equal enjoyment of rights and interests. Aspects of this were raised in detail in Chapter 2. Newly revised law recognizes 'special labour subjects groups' (*teshu laodongzhe qunti*), including female labour, minors, the disabled, minority nationalities and military veterans. The purpose of this special protection is to 'adjust' for their disadvantaged positions.[119] There are, however, other important dimensions relating to the scope in the enjoyment of human rights and the principle of equality in the application of labour law.

In his remarks, Professor Guo Jie noted the past exclusive application of labour law in relation to specific types of enterprise. According to Guo, the 1994 LL set out a new direction. The earlier 1986 'Provisional Regulations on Contract Labour System in State-Owned Enterprise' only applied to the workers in the state-owned enterprise, and 'The Regulations Concerning Labour Management in Sino-Foreign Joint Enterprises' were similarly specific. Guo warned that labour legislation might, in its own categorization, foster inadvertent disparities in the legal standing of workers located in different types of enterprise.

In the era of planned economy, this pattern had been accentuated as the result of the co-existence of two labour management systems in state enterprise. The managerial and technical personnel were managed by the personnel department at various levels whereas ordinary workers were controlled by the labour department. The 1994 LL addressed this tendency insisting on the application of the law in relation to workers in all types of enterprise.[120] At the same time, the scope of the 1994 LL was expanded in Article 2 so as to include the individual household economy and the parts of public institutions and government organizations which had not been previously included.

Subsequent regulation, however, qualified Article 2. The 11 August 1995 Ministry of Labour 'Opinion Concerning Several Issues in the Implementation of "The 1994 Labour Law"' asserted that the 1994 LL was not meant to cover five specific groups: state functionaries and other personnel who held similar positions in state and party organization; rural workers, with the exception of workers in township enterprise; migrant workers in the cities and rural workers involved in business or commerce; military personnel; and domestic workers who are covered under civil law.[121]

This unevenness in the law's scope attracted significant criticism. During the drafting of the law, labour law experts recognized the fact that labourers may be associated with different legal entities, and they offered two perspectives on who should be protected under the law. Some argued that the law should protect all labourers in enterprises, institutions, government organizations, and mass associations and other hiring units.

Perhaps borrowing loosely from class analysis, others freely subscribed to a differentiated categorization of workers. In this view the law should apply more exclusively to workers in enterprise as the labour relations in government organizations, institutions, and other mass associations are essentially of a 'non-antagonistic' nature. In other words, there is no fundamental conflict of interest in the public sector, and hence government functionaries and military personnel need not be subject to the 1994 LL. This second viewpoint acknowledged that the workers in 'three capital' enterprises would need protection as their relations with management were indeed 'antagonistic'.[122]

Gu Angran, Chairman of the Legal System Working Committee of the NPC, in his lecture to court personnel, explained that the 1994 LL was not drafted to apply to government personnel because the relationship between such personnel and the state is legally different from that between employees and employers in enterprise. Gu emphasized that enterprise workers have the same legal status as their employers. Their relations are civil law relations based upon contract. However, the relationship between state functionaries and the government, and between other personnel such as teachers, medical doctors and researchers and public institutions, are administrative relationships regulated by administrative law. The state as such cannot enter into contract with its employees.

Actually, the 1994 LL was for the most part concerned with the protection and management of contract labour. At the CASS Institute of Law, Shi Tanjing argued yet another point. In his view, the 1994 LL could not apply to the labourer who works as a family member within a family-based production unit.[123] But the scope of the 1994 LL did include the following two specific constituencies, as indicated in Article 2: '... this law is applicable to the enterprises and individual economic organizations (hereafter referred to as employing units) within the territory of the People's Republic of China, as well as to the workers who have formed a labour relationship with them'.

Secondly, it indicated: 'This law is also applicable to the workers who have established a labour contract relationship with state organs, institutions, and social organizations.' In effect, the subjects of the 1994 LL might legally include labourers in enterprises and individual economic organizations (*geti jingji zuzhi*) regardless of whether or not these workers had actually signed a contract, together with those workers in public institutions who had actually signed contracts.

The controversy over the law's scope and the related issue of social justice did not end with the drafting of the 1994 LL. Chen Wenyuan has pointed out that Article 2 is still problematic as it left out many who are most in need of protection. For instance, the law does not yet apply to the unemployed, to whom many stipulations of the law, such as the newly outlined social assistance programme, are designed to protect.

As already indicated, some rural labourers are covered under the law; however, the 11 August 1995 'Opinion' cast doubt on the legal status of significant sectors of the rural working population. Moreover, the Labour Ministry's September 1995 'The Regulations concerning Employment Registration', reflected a serious urban bias in the state planning for social security. Under these regulations only the urban unemployed are qualified to register in the local employment registration office, and consequently may receive unemployment insurance.[124]

Migrant rural labourers are subject to well-known discrimination in the cities. In rural China, there has always been a rural labour surplus originating in the poor ratio of population to arable farmland. Under the planned economy, the city registration (*chengshi hukou*) system prevented rural workers from flowing into cities to seek permanent employment. Economic reform encouraged rural labour mobility. Since the latter half of the 1980s, a large number of rural surplus labourers from central and western China have poured into the country's prosperous coastal areas to seek employment.[125] Up to 1994, about 50 million rural labourers have migrated to the large and medium-size cities. A 1996 report warned that rural migrant labourers flowing into cities could reach as many as 214 million.[126] This unprecedented rural labour migration has already created severe social tension between rural labour and the urban unemployed.

Municipalities, often with the support of central regulation, have acted to curtail migrant worker access to social services; meanwhile, urban crime rates are climbing. In her recent study of the 'floating population', Dorothy Solinger noted that not only had the state failed to provide security and sustenance to the rural migrants, who were treated as 'foreigners' or 'second class citizens', but the migrants' presence in the cities challenged the norms of community and politicized the official allocation of public goods.[127]

In recent years, some urban areas experienced a steady rise in the percentage of crimes committed by rural migrants in terms of all types of crimes, including rape and violent property crime.[128] City authorities in Beijing and Shanghai adopted regulations to prevent rural migrant labourers from seeking jobs in their cities. The Beijing municipal regulations imposed strict limitations on the inward bound movement of rural labourers so as to protect Beijing's unemployed and redundant workers.[129] Similarly, in Shanghai, the city requires migrant labourers to obtain a work permit before starting work.[130] Municipal policy rests on the principle, 'the city resident has priority over the rural migrant, the local resident has priority over the outsider'. Some local governments, such as that of the city of Qingdao, have even provided financial incentives to enterprise for employing local residents.[131]

Discriminatory local regulation was episodically reinforced by the central government itself. For instance, the November 1994 Ministry of Labour's 'The Provisional Regulations on Rural Labour Seeking Employment Outside One's Home Province' gave local labour priority over rural labour in the assignment of jobs. Article 12 of these 'Regulations' restricted rural labour mobility by stipulating that rural labour shall not be employed unless they obtain permits and pay registration fees to migrate in order to seek employment outside their native provinces. Article 11 assigned the local authorities unlimited power to refuse issuing such permits. Rural migrant labour can only obtain the necessary permit if they happen to possess certain employable skills, are free of legal obligations and meet all of the criteria established by local government.

Such restriction has encouraged a pattern of avoidance as rural workers migrate without the appropriate documentation and reside in the cities without any legal protection as subjects under the 1994 LL. Without legal status, this segment of the working population lacks access to the newly initiated social insurance programming including unemployment insurance, disability insurance, old age insurance, works' compensation insurance and maternity insurance.

Chinese legal scholars have often criticized local protectionism, decrying it as being in contradiction with the market reform to promote equal opportunity employment, labour mobility and justice and fairness in competition. Lin Zhe, of the Institute of Law, Shanghai Social Sciences Academy, however, bluntly justified local employment protectionism with reference to local government responsibility for the maintenance of social stability and the support of local residents. The latter, he noted, contributed more to local social and economic wealth, as compared to the rural migrants.[132] In other words, the enjoyment of human rights is correlated with specific contribution to the economy.

Obviously, there are many contradictions developing within legal circles and within law that originate with controversy over the responsibilities of government for the regulation of the new labour market. The 11 August 1995 'Opinion' adopted an enlightened interpretation of the 1994 LL in that it suggested the latter ought to apply to rural labourers who are working in cities, but its internal provisions did not always conform with this general purpose. State policy has proved ambivalent on the issue. Central regulation has acted to restrict surplus rural labourers from working in the major cities where unemployment rates are already high. On the other hand, the government has called for the rational flow of labour in accordance with market conditions and has planned for 'the orderly trans-regional migration of rural labourer'. According to the requirements of this 'orderly' migration, before going elsewhere to work, each rural worker has to obtain a permit from his own local government supplying detail as to current employment, as well as a certificate from the local government of his intended destination.[133]

The urban worker benefits most from the 1994 LL. This may well reflect the fact that the Chinese government has always tended to take urban workers more seriously both politically and economically. Although Mao had once surrounded the cities with the countryside, ideology has steadfastly presumed the importance of the proletariat in the urban context of large-scale production. In addition, the government was politically wary of the concentration of temporary rural workers in the cities.

In contrast, while recently there has been serious unrest in some rural areas, rural labourers are more interested in protecting their existing interests and are also more widely dispersed. They are less likely to unite themselves in favour of drastic social change. Moreover, the ACFTU, although it has actively supported labour law legislation to protect worker rights and interests, has a possible urban bias in its organizational structures.[134]

Conclusion

The above discussion of jurisprudence, law and politics, as they relate to the protection of worker rights and interests in the new market context of pluralized ownership and distribution, certainly suggests the need for keeping an accurate ledger of all of the implications and contradictions of legal reform. Chinese law is caught in the transition between an old and a new system.

Jurisprudence has tried to juggle efficiency and social justice while economic reform policy has focused on the elimination of the 'three irons system'. Guaranteed employment is a thing of the past. The workers' master status is an anachronism. Labour is a commodity. In the context of 'pluralized labour relations', the 1994 LL, nonetheless, represents a self-consciously new approach both in terms of the legal protection of rights and in the use of law as distinct from the application of administrative *fiat* which is primarily concerned with state-imposed obligation.

While conservative jurists fear the spiralling consequences of 'rights fundamentalism', those reformers who have invested in the development of labour law have accentuated the difference between civil and labour law, as well as the importance of an activist state that defends worker rights and interests through the creation, in law, of a level playing field for the lawful exercise of contractual rights and interests.

Although reference to contract highlights the importance of subject equality under the civil law, and reform strategy such as 'small government, big society' has also emphasized the self-determination and the obligations of the individual within the rational sharing of responsibilities for social insurance, the advocates of labour law have attempted to carve out a role for the state in the name of social justice. This disposition is, of course, reinforced in an explicit political motivation which values labour peace in the context of the societal uncertainties generated in economic reform.

There has been unprecedented legislation giving conceptually new and forceful emphasis to the protection of worker rights and interests in an era of contract negotiation. The jurists and scholars, however, are well aware of the shortcomings of contemporary labour law legislation and enforcement. The issues have been sincerely articulated with eloquent reference to the 'balance of values' in law; however, if the importance of achieving an appropriate scope, guaranteeing equal enjoyment of rights and interests throughout the entire working population has been duly noted, rights formation and practice has often been correlated with the utilitarian necessities of efficiency and production. The market is creating new wealth; however, even on the supposedly rationally shared basis of the Hainan model, resources are still not sufficient to provide universal access to social services throughout China's vast rural areas. In practice, human rights are being parcelled out in instalments, and the law, in a transitional society, is in a state of transition itself.

4
Sorting out Property and Ownership Rights in Law

In his defence of labour vis-à-vis the inequalities of property, the fiery French anarchist, Pierre Joseph Proudhon, attacked property as incompatible with justice, and pronounced, 'Property is theft!'[1] Rejecting counterpoint that property is legitimately anchored in civil law, Proudhon contended that law, in the final analysis, is essentially disingenuous social convention which masks the harsh injustice of capitalist society. Marx later elaborated on a similar theme of the oppression of living labour by dead capital. While disagreeing with Proudhon's general theory, Marx was just as blunt: '... the theory of the Communists may be summed up in the single sentence: Abolition of private property'.[2] Marx also claimed that under capitalism the real economic position of labour and capital '... is no concern of the law'. For Marx, there was no real equality between capital and labour in contract law to begin with, and it is what happens 'behind legal curtains' that is really important.[3]

Under such an assumption, law in the capitalist context becomes a convenient rationale for social injustice. What then becomes of law in China's unprecedented transition to a 'socialist market', wherein classes – if not the will of the ruling class – have been superseded by newly emerging interests? How does law 'readjust' such interests and how does property fit into newly 'pluralized ownership'? One could well argue that it is essential to China's socio-economic development and also to the related enjoyment of human rights that Chinese politicians and jurists strongly support the appropriate clarification in law of ownership and/or property rights. In fact, however, Chinese jurisprudence has not been able to go beyond 'groping for rocks on the riverbed'. Property law is one of the most confusing and disappointing chapters of contemporary legal development as it relates to the creation of a 'rule of law economy'.

A former Attorney General of the US, Edwin Meese III, once lectured senior Chinese jurists on the importance of the conveyance of property in the context of the rule of law. He came directly to the point: 'For Americans, therefore, property rights are fundamental human rights.'[4] Given the comparatively ambivalent normative context of the transition to the 'socialist market', how will the law now treat ownership? To a great extent, Chinese jurists have tried to tap the assumptions of the familiar Continental civil law tradition. In addition – and this is perhaps unexpected and paradoxical – the political debate on property and ownership has been greatly influenced by co-opted 'American' notions of property.

While there have been a steady stream of singular theoretical initiatives in the area of ownership, jurisprudence still has no grand theory on the subject. As discussed in Chapter 3, public and private ownership in law has been premised in the Party's theoretical distinction between socialism and capitalism. The Chinese ideological concept of 'ownership system' (*suoyouzhi*) or the 'system of the ownership of the means of production' (*shengchan ziliao suoyouzhi*) originated with Marx's theory on productive relations and this has been a continuing source of theoretical obfuscation.[5]

During the Cultural Revolution (1966–76), there was radical objection to residual 'bourgeois right', as well as a sharp reiteration of the dominant position of 'ownership by the whole people'. The 'gang of four's' theory on 'continued revolution under the dictatorship of the proletariat' raged against 'capitalist restoration' and the 'theory of the dying out of class'. They looked forward to the day when all of the means of production would be converted into 'the common property of the whole society'. Their provocative theory presumed that the 'superstructure', or the politics of productive relations, had been allegedly misappropriated by a generation of Party leaders who used their political power to convert pubicly owned property into their own private interests.[6]

In 27 June 1981, the Party passed a seminal resolution on Party history, which conclusively repudiated Cultural Revolutionary radicalism based on the 'leftist thesis' originating in 'class struggle as the key link'. The Resolution announced that 'the system of exploitation of man by man has been eliminated'.[7] Those jurists trained in the Continental law tradition aspired, in the mid-1980s context of the open door and economic reform, to extricate the civil law concept of ownership from the ideological notion of ownership system.

A series of related legal concepts were vetted in jurist debates of the 1980s and 1990s. In 1979, 'operational management rights' first appeared in the State Council 'Regulations concerning the Further Expansion of the Operational and Management Rights of State Enterprise'. This confirmed the trend towards separating state enterprise from state administration, and it required the separation of management and ownership responsibilities. The term, operational management rights (*jingying quan*) was subsequently incorporated into Article 16 of the 1982 State Constitution as well as into Article 82 of the 1986 General Principles of Civil Law (GPCL).

'Ownership rights' (*suoyou quan*) were legally conceived in Article 71 of the GPCL, and these were encapsulated in the rights to possess, use, benefit from and dispose of one's own property. 'Property rights' (*caichan quan*), on the other hand, were referenced in Section 1 of Chapter 5 of the GPCL, but while these rights enjoyed later policy salience, they have not been clearly recognized in law. As state enterprise began to acquire status as a 'legal person', the policy notion, 'ownership rights of a legal person' (*faren suoyou quan*) was formulated. This notion was featured for the first time in a 1986 legal conference organized under the auspices of the Shanghai municipal Party organization, and then it was subsequently highlighted in a 1987 law conference hosted by the CASS Institute of Law in Beijing.[8] This notion has received widespread support since 1997, but it has still to be developed as a formal concept within the law itself.

The legal and policy focus on ownership and property continued through the 1980s and into the 1990s. There was a brief period, just after the Tiananmen Square Incident in 4 June 1989, when the ideological focus on the 'socialist public ownership system' seemed to acquire renewed salience. In October 1989, for example, the *Renmin ribao* (People's Daily), editorialized on the substantive content of worker-peasant leadership of the state with reference to the following familiar assumption: 'First, this is demonstrated in our socialist public ownership system over the means of production. All workers and peasants as a class entity jointly possess the most important wealth, namely, the means of production.'[9]

With the 1993 triumph of 'Southern Tour Theory', 'the liberation of productive forces' and the advent of the 'socialist market', class struggle was no longer relevant. It was superseded in a pluralization of interests. A new labour market emerged. Even capital became a legitmate criterion within the socialist market's system of distribution. 'Property rights of legal person' (*faren chan quan*) first appeared in the 1993 Decision of the 3rd Plenary Session of the 14th National Party Congress, and the same year it was entrenched in Article 4 of the PRC Company Law.

How meaningful are the substantive distinctions between 'ownership' and 'property rights' and 'ownership rights of legal person' and 'property rights of legal person'? For almost 20 years there has been deliberate ambiguity in related jurisprudence. Possibly, this is nothing more than making a virtue out of necessity. The well-known US professor of Chinese Marxist intellectual history, Maurice Meisner, referred specifically to peasant demands for the legal freedom to buy and sell property and suggested that there is an implicit political genius in the ambiguity of contemporary law and policy on ownership: 'Thus far, however, the post-Mao regime has been successful in avoiding the politically explosive question of formal ownership without undermining the functionally capitalist character of the reformed economic system.'[10]

Edward Steinfeld, an MIT management professor, has carried out a more recent study of the 'corporate governance failure' of Chinese state enterprise reform and the constraining factors of economic behaviour; he has, however, questioned the contemporary focus on property/ownership rights in law, enterprise autonomy and economic 'liberalization'. He is doubtful as to whether the new emphasis on rights can, in and of itself, reverse the deteriorating position of state enterprise in support of the social good. Moreover, Steinfeld introduced a very different perspective on the ambiguity of contemporary enterprise reform:

> No matter which way they run, [Chinese] policy makers now face grim choices. The key state-sector reforms have been deferred for so long that it makes actual implementation all the more difficult and painful. If decisive action is taken, millions of workers over a very short period of time stand to lose their jobs, their health care benefits, and their pensions. Yet, if no action is taken, China stands to cripple not only its modern industrial sector, but also its entire financial system. The nation's economic policy makers are, in the crudest sense, 'damned if they do and damned if they don't.[11]

While the following analysis focuses on formal points of law and legal theory, Steinfeld's caution is well worth pondering. There are going to be tremendous social and economic costs whether the Chinese persist in political ambiguity or opt for legal predictability and a full-scale adaptation to ownership rights. Expansion of civil law subject equality and the transfer of the state's 'ownership rights' to state enterprise could well precipitate a basic regime change. On the other hand, it is hard to imagine a genuine development of a 'rule of law economy' in the long-term context of confusion over ownership.

This chapter's discussion largely confines itself to the formal analysis of China's little known contemporary jurisprudence of property rights and ownership in political context.[12] It details and assesses complicated, if not arcane, jurist debates over the evolving terms of reference governing property and ownership in state enterprise, township enterprise and private enterprise. The issues raised originate with the politically inspired bifurcation of 'property' and 'ownership rights'.

In the attempt to deal with the legacy of the 'ownership system', Chinese jurisprudence has repeatedly contemplated the 'clarification of property rights'. This clarification has had at least two important policy implications. First of all, civil law clarification has expanded the scope of the protection of property rights so as to deal with the rights of the state, the collective and the individual.[13] Jiang Zemin endorsed 'clarifying property rights' as a fundamental matter of property rights protection in his 1997 speech to the 15th National Party Congress. He stated that '[we] need to perfect the property legal system, and to protect the lawful rights and interests of various forms of enterprises and fair competition . . .'.[14]

In an earlier 1995 lecture to the senior Party leadership, Wang Jiafu had emphasized the importance of the equal protection of the property rights of both the state and the individual in civil law. The new market economy, in his view, was established on the understanding that all the economic entities, including the state, legal persons, and natural persons, enjoy subject equality before the law. Wang related the clarification of property rights to the stability of property relationships as these underwrite the foundation of economic efficiency and the acquisition of new wealth through market-based productivity.[15] Huang Sujian, a CASS expert on property rights, agreed that clarified property relations are the prerequisite for the development of a socialist market economy. He too concluded that the market economy is 'a rule of law economy' which can only operate on the basis of clearly defined relations between property rights and obligations.[16]

The second major implication of the clarification of property rights derived from a powerful policy focus on efficiency requiring significantly improved management responsibilities within enterprise. In the early 1980s, the separation of government from the management of state enterprise was viewed as critical to the raising of the languishing levels of enterprise productivity and efficiency. 'Separating ownership from operational management rights' (*suoyouquan yu jingyingquan fenli*) was sanctioned by the 1984 3rd Plenary Session of the 12th National Party Congress in an ill-fated bid to convert state enterprise into a legal entity responsible for its own profits and losses. Enterprise operational rights in their relation to state-owned property were subsequently stipulated in Article 82 of the General Principles of Civil Law of the People's Republic of China (GPCL) in 1986.[17] The GPCL, however, did not clearly define such operational rights with the result that there was ensuing great debate over the nature of these rights and the appropriate legal relationship between the state and state enterprise.

Property versus ownership rights in the state's relation to state enterprise

The need for clarification has been especially critical in the state enterprise sector as the status of this sector is closely tied to the legitimacy of 'socialism with Chinese characteristics'. The critical 1993 CCP decision on the establishment of a 'socialist market economic structure' still referred to 'taking the publicly owned sector as the mainstay', but it anticipated the 'simultaneous development of all economic sectors', the 'transformation' of state enterprise and the clear legal definition of the property rights and obligations of state enterprise.[18]

Indeed, the pluralism of newly emerging interests and the related focus on the protection of rights and interests now reflects a multi-dimensional mix of public and private ownership. Notwithstanding Meisner's understanding of the virtues of ambiguity, the political salience of ownership has been inversely correlated with legislative vacillation and terminological confusion in the law that governs the transition to the socialist market. The frequent urgings of the political leadership to achieve the clarification of 'property rights' has only served as an awkward reminder of persisting confusion in the definition of the basic terms of ownership.

Within the context of the restructuring of state enterprise, China's economists have, at least momentarily, moved ahead of the jurists in getting the Party leadership to focus rather exclusively on market efficiency. Economists, such as Li Yining of Beijing University and Wu Jinglian, have been very impressed by property law in the common law tradition which allows for a fractioning of ownership into variegated 'property rights', particularly as this fractioning is highlighted in the American economics literature. In contrast, Chinese jurists are more interested in the more familiar legal notion of 'ownership' in the Continental civil law tradition.

Drawing on western comparative property law studies, Chen Jianfu observed that indeed the notion of 'ownership' is central to property law in the Continental legal tradition which treats ownership as the absolute control or the fullest rights over a thing. This tradition emphasizes the principle of 'unity of powers contained in ownership [which] mean[s] that totality of all ownership powers cannot be split into various kinds and vested with different persons; but only the totality of powers as a whole can be transfered'.[19] In short, the critical issue concerning property in this tradition is 'who owns the property'.

Exclusive and undivided ownership may have served well the past social and political system of China which was so firmly anchored in the predominance of public ownership. The problem with this legal tradition, as Chen points out, is that the legal position of the person who exercises ownership rights, but does not own the property, remains undetermined. In contrast, property law under the common law tradition is more friendly towards the division of the rights of ownership. Property law in this tradition focuses on possession, entailing the relative, rather than the absolute, entitlement to the property. The ownership can be fractioned. It follows that different persons can all own some interests in the same property.

This tradition seemed tailor-made for dealing with the problems of separating ownership and management in Chinese state–state enterprise ownership relations. In this tradition, the question of who owns the property is less pressing and there is a focus on the efficient management of property.[20] This system of property is, however, more consistent with the common law institution of trust. Property law under the Continental tradition alternatively features the legal clarity of property relationships by emphasizing the totality of ownership. At any rate it is easy to pin down what the comparative advantages of efficiency and legal clarity are in any given national context.

In China, there has been a great deal of political debate over the separation of ownership and management in state enterprise and the related issues of efficiency and legal clarity. The CCP has been very concerned to make state enterprise competitive, and it has repeatedly underscored the importance of 'clarifying property rights'. On the other hand, there is a great concern to protect and conserve publicly owned assets, and the legal system has generally evolved out of modified civil law assumptions which drew wholesale from Soviet legal experience. Party leaders appear to be conflicted over the degree to which ownership rights can be divided. The great debate among Chinese jurists on the ownership rights of the state enterprise in the 1990s is largely a result of the demand of political leadership for both legal clarity and the efficient management of economic organization.

China's top leaders have often stated that state-owned enterprise is the 'pillar' or 'backbone' of the socialist economy. In 1996, after almost two-decades of reform, Jiang Zemin, who had himself repeatedly called for the clarification of property rights, reluctantly conceded that the past state enterprise reform was a failure. He stated that '... difficult issues left over from the old structure – such as changing enterprise operating mechanism, separating enterprise management from government administration, establishing a social security system, the excessive debts of enterprises, and enterprises operating social welfare undertakings – have not been fundamentally resolved'.[21]

Chinese jurists have not hesitated to trace the lack of legal clarity to political confusion over state and state enterprise property relationships. For many, state ownership of the enterprises implied 'everyone owns, but no-one takes care of it'. The top party leadership agreed. However, while the Party sought to 'clarify property' rights so as to foster enterprise efficiency, it has tried to evade the political consequences associated with the outright dismantling of state ownership of state enterprise.

In his response to 'clarifying property rights', Professor Huang Sujian of CASS raised a series of difficult practical issues. For instance, in theory, all state-owned enterprises belong to the central government. But, given formally recognized differences of interest between the central and local governments, some local governments suggested that some of the enterprises ought to be designated as local state-owned enterprises in so far as these enterprises had been initially funded by provinces, cities, districts and counties. In addition, some enterprises had never received state investment and were instead developed on the basis of loans. Some jurists have argued that such assets should be designated as employee-owned, while others have claimed that the state should have the ownership in light of the preferential treatment in state loans and tax exemption which helped grow such enterprises in the first place. There has been very little law to help sort this out.[22]

More generally the jurist debates of the mid-1980s centred on the understanding of the two key concepts, namely, property ownership rights (*caichan suoyou quan*) and operational management rights (*jingying quan*), and the relationship between the two.[23] In 1997, the concept of 'property rights' (*caichan quan*), appeared in Party leadership statements and became increasingly important. There are differing theoretical interpretations of the legal connotations of operational management rights and their relationship to ownership rights.

For leading advocates of the civil law, such as Jiang Ping and Kang Deguan, at the Chinese University of Law and Politics, operational management rights connoted 'right of possession' (*zhanyou quan*). Possession implied only that enterprise would enjoy 'relative ownership' (*xiangdui suoyou quan*) over enterprise property. Zhang Kaiguo added that the right of operational management consists of both the right to use and of usufruct. In this view, the state has no right either to participate in management activities or to the benefit from the enterprise.

Zhao Wanyi went further, suggesting that the state possesses 'ownership in name only' over the enterprise, while the enterprise enjoys the actual 'power and function' (*quan neng*) of ownership. Here, Zhao refers to the state's ownership as 'legal ownership' (*falu suoyou quan*) as distinguished from the enterprise's 'economic ownership' (*jingji suoyou quan*) which includes the right of operational management. Other legal experts, including Liang Huixing, argued that the ownership right, possessed by the state, is 'ultimate ownership' (*zhongji suoyou quan*), and that state enterprise has the 'ownership right of legal person' (*faren suoyou quan*).[24]

Elaborating on his reasons why state enterprise needs to have some form of ownership right, Liu Shujun pointed to the emergence of diversified interests within the public ownership domain. Liu treated the state and the state-owned enterprise as separate entities with independent interests. To realize state interests and to protect state property rights, the state needs to acquire ownership rights over the enterprise. At the same time, state enterprises have their individual respective interests due to differences in their management and production conditions. To realize and protect their own independent interests, the enterprises also needed ownership rights over their property. Such rights enable enterprise to become an autonomous participant in economic activities and to enjoy civil law rights and interests and to be liable.[25]

Liu divided state ownership rights into macro and micro components, assigning macro ownership to the state, and micro ownership to enterprise. The latter included the possession, use and disposal of property. It also included an operational management right which seemed to allow enterprise to override the wishes of the state. Conceptually, however, this operational management right is part of the state's macro 'ownership rights'. Once the state transfers enterprise property to an enterprise, the state still retains the right to profit and the right to approve property ownership transfer. However, the state loses the right to intervene in enterprise activities such as production, the raising of capital, marketing and the distribution of profits.[26]

These theories revealed competing nuances, but there was also a common jurist concern – that state enterprise possess at least partial ownership of the enterprise property in order to achieve full enterprise autonomy and economic efficiency. Party leaders such as Li Peng, on the other hand, never intended to compromise on the state's sole ownership over the enterprises. The inability to clarify operational management rights confounded the property relationships between the state and the state-owned enterprise, and this situation became obvious in the early 1990s.

While endorsing the separation of enterprise from government administrative control, the 1993 Party decision on the socialist market dropped the earlier reference to operational management rights, preferring instead to use the term 'property rights of legal person' (*faren chan quan*). This use was duly incorporated into the 1993 Company Law and the 1994 State Council's 'Regulations on Supervision of State Enterprise Property'. This usage also failed to clarify property relationships. In fact, it became a new source of confusion as there was no clear definition of the term in the 1993 Company Law and its supporting documents and regulations. Article 4 of the Company Law stipulated that an enterprise, as a corporation, enjoys 'property rights of legal person'. Articles 27–29 of the Regulations on the Supervision of State-owned Enterprise Property provided that the state-owned enterprise has the 'property right of legal person', including the right to dispose of enterprise property. The government and its administrative organizations could not dispose of any form of property, while enterprise, as a legal person, had to shoulder new civil law liabilities.

The source of confusion surrounding the concept 'property rights of legal person' mainly originated with the advent of 'property rights'. In Chinese, the latter is often expressed as '*caichan quan*', or in its shortened version as '*chan quan*'. It was first mentioned, but not clearly defined in Chapter 5 of the 1986 GPCL. Professor Zhang Guangxing, of CASS Institute of Law, has pointed out that 'property right' originated with the Anglo-American, as opposed to the Continental legal tradition.[27] Indeed, members of the Institute of Law had strenuously argued for an alternative focus on 'ownership right'.

Jiang Zemin, however, endorsed the 'property' rather than the 'ownership rights of enterprise legal person'. In his 1997 report to the 15th National Party Congress, Jiang emphasized that state enterprises reform would be premised in the principle of 'clarification of property rights' (*minque chan quan*), the clarification of rights and obligations, and the separation of government from enterprise and scientific management'.[28]

Professor Shi Jichun, of the Chinese People's University, criticized the inherent ambiguity of the term, 'property rights', claiming that it obfuscated state and state enterprise property relations and exacerbated the downward spiral in the loss of state assets. In successive attempts at clarification, the State Council has, since 1992, issued a series of regulations, ordinances, and rules, including 'The Rules of Supervision and Management of State Enterprise Property', 'The Methods of Evaluation of State Property' and 'The Methods of Registering State Enterprise Property Rights'.

Interpretation of 'property rights' has proliferated under 'pluralized jurisprudence'. For instance, Wu Jinglan considers property rights as ownership rights, while others regard property rights as equivalent to the 'rights in things' (*wu quan*) which is further broken down into the 'rights in things belonging to oneself' (*ziwu quan*) and 'rights in things that belong to others' (*tawuquan*). Technically, only the 'rights in things' entail ownership rights. Wang Hejian, however, has suggested that in law property rights ought to constitute a 'system of rights' (*quanli tixi*), including not only ownership of tangible property, but also intellectual property rights, obligatory or creditor's right, and other related rights.[29]

For some scholars, the essence of 'property rights' is in fact ownership rights, but the Party leadership's preference for this term originated with political sensitivity over the uncertain implications of the relationship between ownership system (*suoyou zhi*) and ownership rights (*suoyou quan*). Again, the former is a key ideological construct, while the latter concerns the legal concept of ownership right, as expressed in 'property relationships' (*caichan guanxi*) between civil law subjects under the GPCL.

Following the GPCL logic, ownership rights include four constituent rights over property, the right of possession (*zhanyou quan*), the right to use (*shiyong quan*), the right to benefits or usufruct (*shouyi quan*), and the right to dispose of property (*chufen quan*).[30] For those jurists who want to consolidate the Continental law tradition, ownership rights have to be placed in the context of 'the right in things', and 'ownership rights' are mostly concerned with tangible property.[31] In the contemporary Chinese political economy literature, the ownership system (*suoyou zhi*) is divided into private and public, and this reiterates the difference between the capitalist and socialist systems.[32] Chinese legal scholarship has had to tread very carefully to avoid any appearance of counterposing ownership rights to the dominance of public ownership as the mainstay of the economy.

Despite the lack of agreement over the definition of 'property rights', in 1993, the Party leadership decided to adopt 'a modern enterprise system' requiring the separation of state and enterprise and the corresponding restructuring of state enterprise. Starting from 1995, such a policy was actively implemented in practice.

The priority of efficiency in the reform of state enterprise

Although the Party has acknowledged that the state and state enterprise may have different interests, justice and efficiency have not been synthesized in the policy and law on state enterprise reform. At least on the surface, theoretical development with respect to property, particularly when compared to Chapter 3's discussion of labour law, reveals a curious diffidence towards the balance of values in jurisprudence. A more exclusive emphasis was placed on efficiency as critical to the survival of the public nature of the national economy. While social justice as it expressly relates to public ownership has not been as well articulated, there has also been a lack of adaptation to 'ownership' as distinct from 'property rights'. This suggests that social justice remains a very important political concern despite the lack of explicit reference to the 'balance of values' in the jurisprudence of ownership relationships.

Since the beginning of market reform, there has been a growing diversification in the systems of ownership; China's state enterprise, however, continues to be critically important in national and regional politics. After nearly two decades of reform, the problem of the low efficiency and productivity of state enterprise has not been fundamentally solved. In the following commentary, Gao Shangquan and Chi Fulin of the China Institute for Reform and Development, Hainan, frankly pointed to the lack of genuine enterprise autonomy from state control as the key issue. They concluded:

> the more than a decade of reform aimed at removing government interference in enterprise management activities has not achieved its expected goals. The status of enterprise as a legal person has not been clearly defined, the property relationships among various parties concerned have not been straightened out. Deep contradictions between the new market economy and the old planned economic system have created difficulties in the reform.[33]

In order to separate enterprise and government and to change the operational mechanism of enterprise, the Third Plenary Session of the 14th CPC Central Committee in 1993 endorsed 'a modern enterprise system'.[34] The latter was distinguished in its five essential characteristics. Enterprise has to have clearly demarcated property rights. This characteristic, however, presumed that the ownership of state assets in a particular enterprise would still belong to the state whereas enterprise would shoulder civil law obligations with respect to the 'property right of legal person'. Secondly, and most unlikely, enterprise was presumed to operate independently. This operation entailed responsibility for investment, profits and losses. Thirdly, the investors were to enjoy rights and interests and to assume any liability in proportion to the value of their investment. Fourthly, the enterprise was presumed to operate on the basis of market supply and demand for the purposes of promoting production efficiency and obtaining profits. Finally, an enterprise was expected to deploy scientific management and to adjust the relationships among owners, managers and workers and to establish a management mechanism that encouraged initiative and self-regulation.[35]

The joint stock enterprise system has been identified as one of the major forms of enterprise organization under this 'modern enterprise system'. Chinese experiment in the corporate conversion of state enterprise began with the late 1970's creation of sino-foreign joint ventures. Related regulation was provided by the State Economic System Reform Commission, which issued several documents in 1992, including 'The Methods for Formation of Pilot Joint Stock Enterprise', 'An Opinion on Standards of the Joint Stock Limited Liability Company' and 'An Opinion on the Standards of the Limited Liability Company'. In 1993, the 3rd Plenum of the 14th National Party Congress officially initiated the process of legally incorporating state enterprise. From 1997, the Party leadership became increasingly enthusiastic in transforming state enterprise into joint stock or limited liability companies in the name of greater and greater efficiency.

Chen Jianfu of La Trobe University has pointed out that the joint stock system is regarded by many in China as a disguised attempt to reform not only the operating mechanism for invigorating state-owned enterprises, but also the socialist public ownership system. Even those who treat investment merely as a managerial mechanism, believe that the implementation of a share system would eventually change the structure of ownership in China. This perceived 'change of colour' in the ownership system precipitated strong ideological opposition.[36]

Jiang Zemin's speech to the 15th National Party Congress addressed several sensitive theoretical issues on the modern enterprise system. He explicitly stated that public ownership would naturally take on multiple forms in its realization. The joint-stock system was treated as a form of capital combination for modern enterprise. In his view, the nature of enterprise ownership would not be determined by the form of the enterprise, but rather it would derive from the identities of the investors. Jiang seemed to obscure the underlying ideological issue of ownership when he indicated, '. . . we cannot say in general terms that the joint-stock system is public or private; what counts here is who has the shareholding power over the shares'.[37] Jiang outlined a standardized corporate system for large and mediumsized state enterprises. A handful of state enterprises for special products and services (such as the military and financial industries) were to be transformed into whole state-owned corporations. Other enterprises were criticized for conversion to limited liability companies or shareholding companies in order to absorb institutional, individual and foreign business investments as well as inter-enterprise stock participation.

State enterprise was slotted into two categories of corporate structure. Enterprise, with the state as sole investor, was distinguished from mixed ownership enterprise with both state and private investors. The former implied 100 per cent state ownership while the latter required that the state have at least 51 per cent of the shares in order to have the controlling interest in the company. In this way, the government hoped to restructure state enterprise ownership for the purpose of efficiency, but, at the same time, the dominant position of public ownership in the national economy was to be preserved.[38] As for small state enterprises, the government proposed a variety of measures – including reorganization, association, merger, leasing, contracting, shareholding cooperatives or sale. This differentiated approach, based on enterprise size, was formulated as *'zhu da fang xiao'*, grasping the big, while enlivening the small.[39]

The 1993 PRC Company Law defined a limited liability company as one in which the investors would assume responsibility for their company proportionate to their contributions and the company would assume responsibility for its liability with all its assets. By comparison, in a joint-stock or shareholding company, the company's entire capital is divided into equal-value shares which will be purchased by the general public. Therefore, a joint-stock company pools its capital through public issuance of stocks. In contrast, a limited liability company raises its capital through private investment, by issuing shares. Shareholders in a joint-stock company assume responsibility for the company proportionate to the shares they hold; and the company assumes responsibility for its liabilities with all its assets. In either case, the investors or shareholders of a company, as contributors to its capital stock, are entitled to owners' asset returns and the rights of major decision-making and choice of managers, in proportion to the size of their contributions. The company is entitled to the entirety of the legal person's rights to the property constituted by shareholders' investments, and it enjoys civil rights and assumes civil responsibility.

Property rights versus ownership rights of legal person

The 1993 Company Law was promulgated in the context of evolving jurist controversy over the relative legal merits of the 'property rights of legal person' as compared to the 'ownership rights of legal person'. The drafting of the 1993 law provided the context for debate on the property relationship between the corporate company and the state. Article 4 stated that '... a corporate company has the property right of legal person over all enterprise property invested by the shareholders. The state has ownership rights over state assets in the company'. The government adopted the joint-stock corporate system intending to achieve clarified property relations and well-defined responsibilities. However, this article did not obviate the ensuing confusion. There was no clear answer to the question, what is the meaning of 'the property right of the corporate legal person'. In response to growing interest in 'property right' there has been new focus on the legal protection of property, as well as the importance of promoting efficiency, but the law has yet to clarify the relationship between the state's ownership right and the property rights of the corporate legal person.

It seemed obvious to the economist, Yuan Mu, that the property rights of legal person would have three preconditions. First of all, the rights and interests of the owner must be ensured. Secondly, the enterprise's independent operation must be ensured, and thirdly the investor and the enterprise must each assume limited liability. Yuan's scheme did not, however, require that state enterprise have ownership over the state invested assets in the enterprise.[40]

For many of China's legal experts, the term 'property rights of legal person' remains a source of considerable frustration. No doubt, this is a critically important term in describing enterprise obligations. The term, itself, however, did not come with clearly stipulated corporate rights and obligations regarding state property. It is not clear to what extent the state can act as an owner of enterprise assets. There are two fundamental issues that need first to be clarified in this context before achieving clarified property rights. What is the meaning of property rights of a corporate enterprise legal person? Secondly, who has the ownership rights over corporate property?

At least three major theories have sprung up to explicate the meaning of the property rights of enterprise legal person. Some jurists claimed that since 'property right' means ownership right, the property right of a legal person is equivalent to the ownership right of the enterprise. A second interpretation contended that the property rights of an enterprise legal person differs from both the operational management right of enterprise and the ownership right of an enterprise legal person. The operational management rights apparently entail a specific set of inclusive rights, which flow from ownership rights. In contrast, the property rights of the enterprise legal person can help differentiate enterprise as an independent legal person from other civil law subjects in terms of their rights and obligations in relation to enterprise property. Such rights would include rights related to ownership right, intellectual property right, the creditor's right, and the right to profits. Kong Xiangjun, a post-doctoral researcher at the Chinese People's University, suggests that this interpretation coincides with the understandings of the 3rd Plenum of the 14th National Party Congress.[41]

A third group of jurists narrowly argued that the property rights of the enterprise legal person are the same as the operational management rights of enterprise. The property rights here do not imply that an enterprise owns the enterprise property. It only means that the enterprise has rights to possess, utilize and dispose of such property according to law. These rights are not equal to ownership rights. Concerning the practical implications of ownership rights in the protection of state property, Xie Cichang of the National State Property Management Bureau under the State Council argued that the essence of the property rights of a legal person lies in the operational management rights. By granting property rights of a legal person to the enterprise, the state has divested itself of the responsibility for routine management activities, but the state still retains a qualifying residual legal interest in the protection of the rights and interests of the state property.[42]

Professor Shi Jichun, of the Chinese People's University, partly endorsed Xie's argument, suggesting that the property rights of a legal person is concerned with the right for disposal of the property, and not with ownership. This interpretation treats disposal as a functional right derived from ownership rights. In fact, it was this interpretation which was adopted in the 1994 'Rules of Supervision and Management of State Enterprise Property', issued by the State Council. The latter still constitute the most authoritative interpretation of the term, 'property right of legal person'.[43]

However, Kong Xiangjun was convinced that there are indeed fundamental differences between operational management rights and property rights of an enterprise legal person. Unlike the latter, the former failed to include the right to profits. Secondly, the property right of a legal person precluded the state from being liable for the debt of the enterprise, while the operational right anticipated just such liability. Thirdly, the 'operational management right of enterprise' defined the respective rights and obligations of the state and state enterprise, while the 'property right of legal person' defined the appropriate relation between an enterprise legal person and enterprise property, as well as defining other civil law rights and interests.[44]

'Property right of legal person' strained under the weight of proliferating interpretation. Kong, however, endorsed the term in so far as it represented a progressive step beyond the notion of the operational management right of enterprise in describing the relation between the state and the publicly owned property of state enterprise. The drafters of the Resolution of the 3rd Plenum of the 14th National Party Congress encountered controversy over how to define and express the property rights of enterprise.

Deliberations over the content of 'property right of an enterprise legal person' revealed two major considerations. Although the 1986 General Principles had stipulated operational management right of enterprise (*jingying quan*), as an independent civil law right, in reality, such rights had often been interpreted as traditional administrative rights. Secondly, the alternative term 'ownership right of a legal person' was deliberately not used so as avoid any impression that the state was handing over its ownership rights to state enterprise. The 'property right of an enterprise legal person' amounted to a compromise between operational management right and the ownership right of enterprise legal person.[45] Moreover, according to Wang Chuang and Zhang Han of CASS, the current use of the property rights of legal person confirmed the apparently precocious influence of Chinese economists on the lawmakers.[46]

In Kong Xiangjun's optimistic reading, however, the 'property right of legal person' could well serve as a transitional concept which would eventually be replaced by the 'ownership right of enterprise legal person'. In this view, 'property right' was an elastic concept which could encompass an expedient variety of interpretations. At the same time, the 1994 'Rules of Supervision and Management of State Enterprise Property' defined the property rights of an enterprise legal person by allowing such a legal person to control enterprise property without state intervention. This definition promised enterprise the essence of ownership rights, that is, the independent control (*zhipei*) over things.

Even so, Kong still attempted to qualify the content of the 'ownership right of legal person'. In his view, this right did not encompass ultimate ownership over the property. Apparently this right constituted an intermediate ownership right for the purpose of maximizing the profits or interests of shareholders or investors. Shareholders and investors would ultimately enjoy the interest accruing to their investment through their rights to stock or shares. The ownership right of a legal person is then treated as an extension of a shareholder's ownership right over his or her investment. Kong, nevertheless, persisted in his civil law assumption that 'ownership right of a legal person' rather than the 'property right of a legal person' would better clarify the legal property relationship between the state and state enterprise.[47]

At the Chinese University of Law and Politics, Kang Deguan reiterated that attempts to avoid explicit equivalence between the property rights of legal person and the ownership rights of legal person originated with confusion between the concept of ownership (*suoyou quan*) in law, and ownership system (*suoyou zhi*) in political economy. He argued that the changes in ownership rights should not be equivalent to changes in the ownership system. For many, including senior Party leaders, the protection of state property and the maintenance of state ownership are the most important issue in any discussion of rights clarification. This issue simply would not go away. But for Kang and his colleagues, the autonomy of enterprise is critical to the rational development of enterprise operations and to increases in production through efficiency. Also, in their view, the state's loss of property originates in the lack of enterprise efficiency.[48]

Zhang Guangxing tried to force his way out of this labyrinth. He declared that Jiang Zemin's report to the 15th Party National Congress, September 12, 1997, provided a new basis in law for interpreting the 'property rights of a legal person' as the ownership rights of a legal person. He reasoned that this follows from the situation whereby there are many shareholding systems in which the state does not own enterprise but does own some shares in enterprise. Zhang limited the state's right of ownership to the ownership of specific shares in specific enterprise, but he reserved the right of ownership to enterprise. This attempt to obviate terminological confusion generated yet another round of related controversy over the legal position of shareholders in corporate enterprise.

At least three major theories developed in response to questions concerning corporate enterprise ownership and the appropriate relationship between companies and their shareholders. The proponents of 'corporate enterprise ownership theory' pushed the debate to its outermost limits, assigning corporate enterprise ownership over enterprise property. Wang Jianping, of Eastern China Normal University, for example, concluded that corporate enterprise is a legal person which acts as an independent civil law subject and has accordingly to be assigned corporate enterprise rights to use, right to benefit from, and to dispose of enterprise property. In this 'liberal' ownership theory, corporate enterprise's ownership over all of its property is a prerequisite for the enterprise to be an independent subject with civil law rights, obligations and liabilities.[49]

The influential Director of the CASS Institute of Law, Wang Jiafu, endorsed this 'liberal' theory and urged that the Party leadership to abandon its predisposition favouring enterprise property rights. The latter theory had clearly given the state ownership rights over enterprise property, and enterprise was left with only operational management rights. This theory was invented by Soviet legal scholars in 1940s to implement the planned economy. According to Wang, it was an unacceptable anachronism incapable of facilitating a rational relationship between the state and state enterprise in the market context. Wang contended that the recognition of the ownership of a legal person was vital to the performance of enterprise as a true subject of the market.

Wang Jiafu was not convinced by those who argued that enterprise could enjoy the property rights of legal person while the state would still enjoy ownership over either state enterprise or enterprise where the state served as sole investor. Wang concluded that while the state would enjoy ownership rights over its shares, the enterprise itself, in its status as legal person, would enjoy the ownership rights of legal person. The state, as shareholder, would only have the rights originating with its shares, and the state's liabilities would be limited to the size of its shareholding. Such shareholding enterprise would have an independent legal personality and a material basis for independent management activities. It would be responsible for its own profits and losses based on its entire property. The ownership right of a legal person, in other words, would not determine the public or private nature of such enterprise.[50]

An alternative theory, 'shareholder ownership theory', contended that the enterprise would have the right to dispose of property, while the shareholders would enjoy extensive rights of ownership. A shareholding company is merely a means to pool capital, while the ownership of the capital rests with shareholders. Critics of this theory point out that shareholders could not have ownership rights over an enterprise as a whole. They could only have ownership over the shares embodied by share certificates. This argument transformed shareholders' ownership over their shares into the debt of the company to shareholders. For the proponents of this theory, shareholders are strangely only interested in the value of the shares, and not in control over the management and decision-making process of the company.[51]

Wang Jiangpin has argued that, in practice, shareholders' ownership theory conflicted with the reform emphasis on economic efficiency. He reasoned that if a shareholder is the owner of an enterprise, the corporate company cannot be an independent civil law subject in economic activities, especially in the cases where the state is the shareholder. Wang questioned the validity of policy that 'the person or legal entity who invests in an enterprise shall have ownership of the enterprise'. If shareholders own the enterprise property, the corporate legal person will not be able to own the same property, as one thing cannot be owned by two different owners.

A third theory glossed over Wang's last point and billed itself as a compromise between the first two theories. This theory was, predictably enough, dubbed 'joint ownership theory', or 'dual ownership theory'. It argued that both shareholders and corporate enterprises have ownership over the enterprise, but in the end it endorsed the qualification that enterprise could only enjoy a 'secondary' ownership, namely the ownership right of a legal person. This theory derived from the ownership theory of English–American legal tradition highlighting the possession and disposition of property. For many Chinese jurists, however, such theory lacks clear definition of ownership and confuses concepts of 'ownership' (*suoyou quan*) with 'rights in things'.

At bottom, this debate has been about whether the state owns corporate enterprise with the state as a sole investor. For Wang Jianping, the state does not risk the loss of its property if it complies with the ownership of an enterprise legal person. In this view the reason why the state lost property in the past had to do with the lack of an actual owner who could be counted upon to take on a clear responsibility for the caring of enterprise assets.[52]

For Shi Jichun, such corporate ownership theory is in fact utterly problematic in its confusion of ownership with the 'power and function of ownership' (*suoyou quan quannong*). This theory in effect deprived corporate enterprise of ownership and lodged it with the shareholders. The enterprise was given powers and functions, but not ownership, *per se*. Shi reminded his colleagues that the existence of an enterprise, as a legal person, does not depend upon its possession of ownership of the enterprise. Civil Law allows for the existence of an independent legal personality, even under the conditions where a legal person does not own any property.[53] Shi's colleagues, however, replied that the power and function of the ownership cannot really be separated out from the ownership as ownership is itself an unlimited right in things.[54] Shi countered that, as shareholders possess the ownership, enterprise legal person cannot possess the same property. Therefore, the prevailing legal concept, 'property right of a legal person' cannot be equal to the 'ownership right of a legal person' in a corporate system.[55] A recent consensus formed among jurists supports enterprise ownership theory. Although senior Party leaders may be reluctant to admit it, there seems to be no easy way out of the present predicament calling for the actual separation of state and state enterprise. Politically, compromise over state ownership may mean less risk compared to the risk involved in stopping the reform of state enterprise at a time when increasingly large numbers of workers are 'off duty' (*xiagang*) or 'waiting to return to their positions' (*daigang*).

Kong Xiangjun bluntly outlined the Party's current dilemma. In his view, Party policy failed to solve the problem of enterprise efficiency, and this failure originated with the lack of a forthright approach to state ownership in law. The lack of clarification sponsored a series of problems relating to the lack of enterprise autonomy and the selective enterprise responsibility for profits as distinct from losses. Kong warned that the contemporary issues surrounding shareholding and the failure to grant ownership to enterprise could well result in a unprecedented political and economic disaster.[56]

Liu Shujun uses property and ownership rights interchangeably. For her, the formal assignment of ownership rights to corporate enterprise, however, does not, in and of itself, provide a complete solution to the present predicament. The state must still find a way to guarantee that appropriate care is taken of its investment in enterprise. She takes a close look at corporations formed entirely with state investment. Liu drew attention to the crucial question, who shall act as the representative of state ownership over the investment of the state. She then answered that the state might control its investment through an intermediary property management organization (*zhongjie jigou*).

Granted, the state, as a shareholder would not be allowed to intervene directly into enterprise operations even when it happened to hold the majority of the company's shares, but still the state could influence company operations and the decision-making process through the shareholders' meeting and by performing shareholder responsibilities. At the same time, Liu recommended the creation of multiple ownership enterprise which would join state ownership together with collective and private ownership. In her view, this 'mixed ownership' (*hunhe chan quan*) and the 'pluralization of enterprise ownership' (*qiye chan quan duoyuanhua*) would promote the efficiency of state owned enterprise.[57]

The economist, Yin Wenquan, also endorsed pluralized ownership. Yin observed that it is important to use all kinds of means to change state ownership over large volumes of assets into other forms of ownership of a public nature. The most important matter in this respect is to have institutional shareholding and inter-enterprise shareholding.[58] Some jurists wanted to go further to impose limits on the formation of the shareholding company on the exclusive basis of state investment. They contended that sole state investment contradicts one of the central purposes of current reform, namely, separating enterprise and government. This situation threatened to leave the door wide open for the 'state legal person' (*guojia faren*) and its property management appointees to abuse power. Others have raised the question as to the legality of the state's position as exclusive shareholder in light of the basic assumptions of subject equality in civil law.[59]

The legal relationship between the state and state enterprise in the context of the modern enterprise system is necessarily complicated by the politics of regime legitimacy and survival. More than anything else, this explains the confusing terminology of property and ownership rights discussed at length above. Low productivity has given a political edge to efficiency. Reform jurists, trained in the Continental tradition, are frustrated by the apparent confusion generated by economists who in their benighted ignorance of jurisprudence have apparently bandied about the term 'property rights'. The Party leadership has so far not been prepared to accept jurist assurances that the granting of ownership rights to enterprise would not constitute the privatization of enterprise. While justice has not been well articulated in the contemporary theory over the property and ownership rights of the legal person, obviously the issue of justice underlies the contemporary politics and law on the subject of state ownership.

Efficiency and justice in the reform of township enterprise

Classical Chinese Communist theory on socialism has over many years formally distinguished between 'socialist ownership by the whole people' (*shehuizhuyi quan min suoyou zhi*), 'socialist collective ownership of the working masses' (*shehuizhuyi laodong qunzhong jiti suoyou zhi*) and 'individual ownership under the socialist system' (*shehuizhuyi zhidu xia de geren suoyou zhi*).[60] If one were to go looking for justice on the basis of the assumptions underlying this terminology, one might expect to find its more explicit expression in state enterprise. Somewhat counterintuitively, justice has figured more prominently in the discussion and development of township enterprise reform which is formally, if not always practically, part of the 'socialist collective ownership of the working masses', recognized in Article 8 of the 1982 State Constitution.

China's collective economy, as it is officially an integral part of the structure of publicly owned economy, is also undergoing a drastic transformation highlighting the need for clarified property relations and economic efficiency. Collective enterprises have suffered from the same maladies as state enterprise, such as excessive indebtedness, backward equipment and technical conditions, and poor management. But, unlike in the case of the large- and medium-sized state enterprise, the state has shown less interest in these enterprises and has made little related investment. At the same time, it has been extremely difficult for collective enterprise to obtain adequate funding from banks to transform into joint-stock or limited liability companies.

In theory, the ownership of collective enterprise property belongs to the collectives or working people of the enterprises concerned. But both in law and practice, the individual subject of ownership rights has yet to be clearly identified, and this situation has occasioned a series of management problems. Chen Jianfu takes a close look of this issue from a civil law perspective. He points out:

> In dealing with property rights relations under civil law, it is maintained that there must be a specific organization or individuals in which property rights are vested. In the case of collective enterprises, the concept of 'working people as a collective' is no more clear than the concept of 'the whole people' as in the case of SOEs [i.e. state owned enterprises]. Therefore, property rights relations in collective enterprises are in no way clearer than those in SOEs.[61]

Chen indicates that Chinese scholars rightly observed that all the controversies surrounding property rights and ownership rights in SOEs are equally relevant to collective enterprise.[62]

For Louis Putterman, collective enterprises are indeed part of state property. Putterman stated:

> Chinese collective ownership was fictitious, with state and Party exercising real control over the management of 'collective' assets, and the distribution of proceeds from their sale generally proscribed. ... But even in the reform era the property of townships and village has remained under the control of local officials, so it makes more sense to think of 'rural collective property' as rural local government property.[63]

Not surprisingly, collective enterprise reform has focused on the clarification of property relationships and the related separation of collective enterprise from the state, so as to better protect enterprise workers' property rights and to establish more efficient management systems. Many scholars and jurists have argued that the joint-stock and limited liability systems which are being tested in the state-owned sector may not be particularly appropriate to the reform of township enterprise. Simply, collective enterprise was originally created to promote mutual cooperation as well as to increase productivity and profits. Values such as mutual assistance, equality and justice among the workers with respect to risk taking and the distribution of enterprise profits seems to have better survived the transition to the socialist market in the collective ownership context of township enterprise. The strong political reaction against 'absolute egalitarianism' appears to have centreed more on state enterprise rather than township enterprise where law and policy self-consciously drew on more robust rural cooperative values.

A great deal of perspective on the current reform of collective enterprise can be gleaned from an examination of the emergence, in the transitional market economy, of a new rural form of enterprise system – the shareholding cooperative system. This enterprise form has also been used within urban collective enterprise and small state-owned enterprise.[64] Arguably, the most dynamic aspect of the rural collective economy has been the township enterprise. Many of these enterprises developed out of the 1980s and early 1990s household cooperative contract system. For instance, in 1993, the output of township enterprises accounted for 35 per cent of GNP, and 71 per cent of all rural gross output values. Deng Xiaoping once praised the rapid development of township enterprise as an unexpected 'new force [that] suddenly [came] to the fore' and he placed such enterprise alongside large and medium state enterprise as one of the three major advantages in the building of socialism with Chinese characteristics.[65]

Nevertheless, in recent years, township enterprise has declined in output at the same time as local government has intervened more intensively in its operations. Shi Xiaoyi of the Township Enterprise Economic Research Institute of the Ministry of Agriculture observed that in recent years township enterprises have devolved into 'rural administrative appendages'. In some cases, these enterprises are completely controlled by township governments. Some local government treat township enterprises as 'money trees'.[66] Chen Jiangguang and Pan Libing's investigation of township enterprise in 15 provinces and regions noted a growing shift of financial burdens from local government to township enterprises. In some areas, the enterprises have incurred as many as 204 financial obligations to local government departments. This situation makes it impossible for such enterprises to effectively adapt to market competition.[67]

The lack of enterprise independence can be partially attributed to the failure to define properly the property relationships between the enterprise and local government and within enterprises. Shi Xiaoyi calls township enterprises 'a sort of cadre or government economy' in which every villager or worker has a share, but no one takes responsibility. Originally, such enterprise may have been organized on the basis of clan identity and private connections, but these factors have apparently turned negative in that they have undermined rational management practices in the enterprise employment system.[68]

Chinese scholars have looked for a solution to downward spiral in the relationship between township enterprise and local government. The recent restructuring of township enterprise ownership has featured a 'shareholding cooperative system' (*gufen hezuo zhi*). Scholarly advocates have suggested that, unlike joint-stock and limited liability system, this enterprise form is a true modern enterprise system with Chinese characteristics. It purportedly synthesizes a mix of traditional cooperativization with the modern shareholding system in its adherence to a principle of 'shared investment, shared profits, and shared risks'. Li Dewei of the State Administration of Industry and Commerce Research Centre has, in fact, identified this system as 'shared economy'.[69] This system also subscribes to a 'balance of values' which calls for equality and justice in distribution and the protection of the rights and interest of workers.

Shao Bingren, Vice-Minister of the State Commission for Reconstructuring Economy, indicated that by the end of 1996, there were more than 4 million shareholding cooperative enterprises in China of which more than 3 million were situated in rural China. This shareholding cooperation system was first invented in rural China in the early 1980s with the policy intention to absorb rural surplus labour. The rural population's long experience with various forms of cooperativization since 1950 may have popularly predisposed those with cooperative experience to adapt to 'shareholding cooperation'.

The latter first appeared in the Central Committee's Internal Document no. 1 in January, 1985. This document provided an initial basis for regulation, which was then expanded in the 1990 Ministry of Agriculture's 'The Provisional Regulations on Peasant's Shareholding Cooperative Enterprises'. This new corporate personality was then endorsed in the famous 1993 Party decision on establishing the 'socialist market'. The decision required that '... township enterprise should perfect their contractual management responsibility system, develop the shareholding cooperative system, and conduct innovations in the property rights system and [related] operational methods'.[70]

This new shareholding cooperative system has apparently 'blazed' a new trail. It emphasizes the importance of harmony in capital–labour relations and features work as the key principle of distribution. At the same time, this system deliberately assimilates the latest trends in international enterprise system development such as 'shared economy' through profit sharing, and employee stock equity plans. In Li Dewei's official research opinion, the adoption of this particular form related to its compatibility with the dominant position of public ownership and its adaptation to the protection of the rights and interests of workers.[71]

Whether or not the working nature of this new form of shareholding is more public than private remains controversial. A variety of forms have emerged, but there is still inadequate national legislation regulating shareholding cooperative enterprise. What new shareholding regulation there is, has, however, subscribed explicitly to the unity of capital and labour. Unlike in the typical shareholding company where shares are made up mainly of capital, the shareholding cooperative enterprise converts into shares a diversified range of production factors, including capital, equipment, technology, and, perhaps most importantly, labour. Under this system, the distribution of profits is according to work and capital.

The shareholding cooperative system has commonalties with both shareholding and cooperative enterprises, but at the same time it is different. According to Li Dewei and law scholar, Gu Gongyun, cooperative enterprise and the shareholding system correspond to different stages of enterprise development. The former is a historical form, which assumed the large-scale efficiencies of voluntary worker organization. The status of capital was conditioned by participation in labour. The worker could only contribute capital on the basis of personal labour input into the cooperative. In contrast, the shareholding system, as manifest in either the joint-stock or limited liability company format, is expressly designed to pool capital, not labour. Indeed, this new system has not always required direct participation by labour.[72]

For Li Dewei, past cooperative enterprise had its flaws. While it presumed the inherent justice of distribution according to work, it precluded the 'efficient' capital inflow from private investment. This served as a drag on the expansion and productivity of cooperative enterprise. While the new form of shareholding qualified the conventional ideological relation between labour and capital, it provided for expanded utilization of public capital. On the other hand, the deployment of the latter was still qualified in explicit reference to cooperative justice. The shareholding cooperative system featured both shareholding and cooperative elements.

In terms of the shareholding components, the enterprise assets could be divided into shares, purchased by either workers or non-workers. The percentage of shares owned determined the level of participation in enterprise decision making. The distribution of profits now took into account both capital contributions and labour inputs. A certain proportion of profits was reserved for distribution according to labour.

The introduction of the shareholding cooperative system was supposed to solve a number of problems affecting the reform of township and other collective enterprise. Li Dewei and Vice-Minister Shao believed that the emergence and development of the shareholding cooperative system would effectively 'clarify' the property rights of enterprise in the crucial context of the induction of previously state-owned and collective assets into a modern enterprise system.[73] The 1997 State Economic System Reform Commission's 'Guiding Opinion Concerning Development of Shareholding Cooperative Enterprises in Urban Areas', claimed that this form of enterprise organization would meet the relevant criteria of a modern enterprise system. These criteria included the clear demarcation of property rights, the explicit definition of rights and obligations, the separation of enterprise management from government departments and the adoption of scientific management techniques.[74]

The new shareholding cooperative enterprise recognizes three forms of equity, including: employee shares purchased by enterprise employees; enterprise collective shares, owned jointly by employees and enterprise, some of which were converted from the assets of former collective enterprise during restructuring; and shares purchased by outside investors, including community shares, rural collective shares, social organization shares, and foreign capital shares. This enterprise constitutes a pluralized ownership structure and addresses the confusion in ownership rights and obligations associated with old rural collective enterprise. By pluralizing the ownership structure, industry was invited to utilize diversified capital resources.

A second major reform to the shareholding cooperative system sought to remedy the declining status of enterprise workers by converting labour into capital shares. In this way, the workers were given newly devised access to enterprise decision-making. This new style of decision-

Property and Ownership Rights 165

making was designed to pre-empt potential conflict between labour and capital by emphasizing a qualified principle of distribution according to work and capital. According to Shao, the shareholding cooperative system recognized the subordination of capital to labour cooperation and assumed that enterprise profits are for the most part generated by employees through their labour.

Presumably the utilization of capital, not only from workers in an enterprise, but also from outside of the enterprise, would allow shareholding cooperative enterprise to maintain long-term production efficiency. The principle of 'shared investment, shared return, and shared risk' was designed to stimulate the initiative of both workers and owners. This principle was squared with efficiency and with a focus self-regulating management mechanisms, requiring responsibility for both profits and losses.

In recent years, this system was widely used to revitalize urban collective enterprise. The State Economic System Reform Commission's 1997 guiding opinion successfully promoted the transformation of the collective enterprise and small state-owned enterprises in urban areas into such cooperative enterprise; however, this system has not been introduced as a standardized form in law. Some scholars have cautiously commended the shareholding cooperative enterprise as a transitional form which may provide the experimental basis for a standard shareholding company in the future.

Both Shao and Li argued that this system responds to important social values and to China's particular social and economic conditions. At least on the surface, there is no full-scale ideological surrender to the private dimensions of the market in that the rationale for the shareholding cooperative has been brought within the developing assumptions of a more diversified socialist public ownership. Moreover, there does not appear to be significant pressure on the political left to convert the collective form of public ownership into ownership wholly owned by the people.[75]

As with most areas of ownership reform, these key theoretical issues remain unresolved and have increasingly been the subject of debate within the legal community. Again, notwithstanding any allowance for creative ambiguity, there is a range of opinion on shareholding and the nature of collective enterprise and collective economy. State Commission Vice-Minister Shao has addressed the controversy over the creation of community or village shares in the formation of shareholding cooperative enterprise. In his view, in cases where related state or collective enterprises pre-existed the new shareholding cooperatives, the introduction of employee collective equity through the recognition of community shares seemed rational and appropriate. In the absence of any link with pre-existing enterprise, Shao rejected the creation of community shares.[76]

Ma Yuejin of the Overseas Chinese University went beyond this question of issuing shares to draw attention to the problem that the contemporary collective shares suffer from the same deficiencies as the old style collective enterprises in that they too lack appropriate clarification in law as 'subjects' of ownership. Ma warned that this lack of clarification had encouraged local government administrative interference with enterprise operations.[77]

Scholars and government officials are divided on the question of whether enterprise shares should be distributed equally among employees. Currently, in most cases, managers hold more shares than ordinary employees. With the issuing of new shares after the distribution of the yearly dividend, management control creeps upward as shares wind up in the hands of fewer and fewer shareholders. Scholars have claimed that this pattern of relative concentration has both advantages and disadvantages. Some have supported a politically correct middle road which avoids a corrective lapse back into egalitarianism, but which also stresses that share distribution ought to reinforce the role of employees as 'masters' and arouse their enthusiasm.

There is also the familiar issue of whether the state should hold a certain percentage of the shares. Some analysts suggest that in the case where a small state-owned enterprise has been restructured into a shareholding cooperative enterprise, state shares are no longer necessary. The state-owned assets of the restructured enterprises can simply be disposed of through sale or leasing, as in the case of land. In this way the state can rationally exit from such enterprise. This view stresses that such a disposition is in fact consistent with the state's rights and interests and benefits the state by relieving it of a heavy burden. At the same time, it should enhance the vitality of enterprise. The 1997 guiding opinion on urban shareholding enterprise mentioned above envisaged the issue of workers' collective shares, state shares, legal person shares, as well as individual worker shares. This left the enterprise investors, however, in an effective position to decide upon the final distribution of shares.[78]

The new shareholding cooperative system addresses some of the outstanding issues which stalled the systematic clarification of enterprise property rights, but there is obvious controversy within China's legal circles as to the exact legal nature of the shareholding cooperative enterprise. Some have already conceded outright that it is private in nature.

Others have contended that it is collective in name, but private in reality. In the official view of Vice-Minister Shao, the shareholding cooperative enterprise belongs to the collective economy. The law scholar, Gu Gongyun, has stated candidly that such a classification would indeed amount to what Maurice Meisner has called creative ambiguity. In other words, Shao's classification is for the purpose of easing leftist political pressure on the system so that it can continue to exist and develop. For him, the whole debate is meaningless as the classification of enterprise system based on the 'ownership system' will only limit, and not help to develop the enterprise system.[79] This ambiguity is apparent in the 1997 guiding opinion on urban shareholding cooperatives as it assumes that the new form belongs to the collective economy.[80] In the same opinion, however, Article 13, suggests that the ownership of a shareholding cooperative enterprise should belong to its investors.

Since the early 1990s, the notion of collective ownership underwent considerable changes. In the past, the property of a collective enterprise was owned collectively by all of the enterprise workers or community. It could not be divided up even after the disintegration of the enterprise. Historically, there was an obvious clarity in the requirement that a certain proportion of profits would be earmarked for worker salaries based upon the simple principle of 'each according to his [or her] work'. The 1991 Regulations on City Collective Enterprises changed the rules by allowing for individual investment in the form of shares in collective enterprises as long as the collective assets were maintained at the level of 51 per cent or more of the total enterprise assets. As discussed in Chapter 3, the principle of distribution was modified to include an additional recognition of capital input, so that distribution may now take account of investment in enterprise shares.[81]

The apparently innocuous identification of the collective nature of shareholding cooperative enterprises has certainly served well the ideological constraints of official policy governing the restructuring of public ownership in rural China. Whether or not this is a matter of convenient political fiction, by supporting the collective dimensions of public ownership, it supports the viewpoint that public ownership is still the 'mainstay' of the economy.[82]

Over two decades of economic reform, the collective economy has steadily expanded its share of the total value of the gross domestic product; the share of state owned enterprise on the other hand has plummeted. This pattern within the twofold dimensions of public ownership has reversed the singular 'socialist' course of progressive public ownership by the whole people, as anticipated by the 'gang of four'. Moreover, the rural collective economy has been severely eroded over the past 20 years during the period of experimentation with household responsibility systems.

According to Han Yuanqin of the Agriculture Economics Institute of Chinese Academy of Agroscience, in practice, the rural collective economy includes both general and specific components. The general component includes all forms of a rural cooperative economy such as a rural community cooperative economy, all specialized agricultural collective economies, and supply and marketing, and credit and consumers' cooperatives which are currently under reform. The specific component of the rural collective economy includes a cooperative economy based on the old people's commune system – such as the household responsibility operating system – which is considered to be a system of dual operation, integrating centralization with decentralization. This form of production organization is also called 'community cooperative economic organization'.[83]

Han observed that the specific components of the rural collective economy are actually broad ranging. These may include community cooperative economic organization in industrial fields, such as production operations, manufacturing and sales, technical services, and capital financing of all rural industries. Such organizations, however, lack a set of clear standards. There are many operating problems, which make it difficult for them to perform any cooperative function. The dual operation system, associated with the household responsibility system, was established by replacing the old 'inefficient' people's commune system without at the same time privatizing land. It still presumes the public ownership of the basic means of production, such as land, but it is also focused on the economic decision-making of the peasant household. It assumes the smooth operation of the household management responsibility system. It presumably stimulates both collective and peasant household initiative, thus expanding the scope of extensive agriculture, and developing a diversified economy.

The operation of this dual operating system has increasingly become the subject of controversy.[84] Jiang Zemin's 1997 report to the 15th National Party Congress responded with a policy synthesis that asserted that public ownership would remain in a dominant position, while legal reform would increasingly facilitate the simultaneous development of forms of non-public ownership. Jiang instructed the Party:

> upholding the dominant position of public ownership is both a basic principle of socialism and a hallmark of China's socialist market

economy. This principle must be adhered to throughout the entire course of reform, opening, and modernization. Only by ensuring the dominant position of public economy can we prevent polarization and become rich together. If we waver at all, if we do anything to abolish the dominant position of public ownership, we will go astray from the socialist direction.[85]

The declared purpose of the current ownership restructuring is not to eliminate the dominant role of public ownership economy; however, within the formal context of policy, ideology and law there is a newly declared opportunity to redefine the collective dimensions of public ownership so as to achieve a presumably improved balance of efficiency and justice in the transition to the 'socialist market'.

New perspectives on private ownership and property

Prior to the inception of economic reform in 1978, Chinese socialism largely focused on the ideological contradiction between labour and capital and the progressive expansion of public ownership. While the private economy was sometimes tolerated, it was not always legally protected. If it was allowed at all, private ownership was presumed to be a temporary aberration which could be made to serve the interests of the public economy as the 'mainstay' of the national economy. However, in the reform era, private property is more than an expedient stopgap. It is acquiring a more autonomous legal persona while at the same time there is a growing diversification in the forms of public ownership – all of this proclaimed in the name of greater efficiency.

Economic reform has focused political attention on the restructuring of enterprise ownership, and this restructuring has already altered the characteristics of the traditional public ownership economy in a fundamental way. Experimental restructuring of the ownership system of state enterprises has opened the door to the development of a new range of non-state-owned options, including collective, individual owned, private, and foreign-run enterprises, while maintaining the public ownership system in a dominant position of the national economy.

The public ownership economy still broadly consists of the state-owned and collective economies. In the past these two forms were presumed to exist only in pure form. Neither could converge with private elements. The current reform has sometimes tolerated and even supported such convergence. Both corporate enterprise and the new forms of collective enterprises with minority investment from private individuals have been conveniently assigned to the publicly owned sector.

At the same time, private ownership has acquired new legal status, as 'an important component of the socialist market economy'. The 1982 State Constitution had stipulated that 'the basis of the socialist economic system of the People's Republic of China is socialist public ownership of the means of production, namely, ownership by the whole people and collective ownership by the working people'.[86] Individual or private economy was cited, but there was no accompanying definition. In addition, Article 11 required that the individual economy should be guided, assisted, and supervised by state administration. The private economy was described as a mere complement to the socialist public ownership economy. Private ownership was classified into two categories, namely, ownership of materials for consumption in everyday life, and ownership of the means of production. The former included personal incomes, savings, houses and household furniture. The 'private' plots in rural China were not privately owned. Legally, they belonged to the collectives and the state. Peasants only had a right of use, as distinguished from ownership rights.

According to influential scholars of civil law such as Tong Rou, Wang Liming and Ma Zunju, the ownership of the means of production in rural China covered two distinct components: the means of production required to operate both individual industrial and commercial households (*geti gongshang hu*) and rural management responsibility contract households (*nongcun geti jingying chenbao hu*); and capital investment in private enterprise.[87]

CASS Institute of Law Professor Zhang Guanxing explained to the authors that before the economic reform, private ownership referred exclusively to the ownership of the materials for everyday consumption. Such ownership could not include the ownership of the means of production. The term, 'private property', rather than 'private ownership' was used when referring to daily items of consumption. After the economic reform and the implementation of the open door policy, 'private ownership' was used in routine reference to the three capital enterprises (*sanzi qiye*), including enterprise with 100 per cent foreign investment, joint venture with foreign and Chinese partners, and joint cooperative enterprise.[88]

Unlike a foreign–Chinese joint venture, the joint cooperative enterprise is typically a short-term arrangement based on a contract negotiated between the two parties. This form of enterprise was created particularly to accommodate overseas Chinese investment, mainly from Hong Kong and Taiwan. It maxmimized 'relationships', *guanxi*, but it did not acquire legal person status. The joint venture, on the other hand, was formally set up as a legal person and regulated under the 1979 Law on Sino-foreign Joint Ventures for the purposes of attracting capital and technology.[89] The joint venture must go through a strict approval process, and hence there is less opportunity for disputes.

In the early to mid-1980s, private enterprise emerged, and policy acknowledged three types of capital, but law still did not recognize private ownership, *per se*. The 'private' element was in legal theory merely a supplement to the public economy. The three types of capital constituted 'private property', but they were not accorded 'private ownership' in law. Professor Zhang pointed out that this purposeful distinction between private ownership and property originated in Soviet civil law theory.[90] 'Ownership' was exclusive to the state sector. 'Ownership right' could only be expressed through the ownership system as a distinctive form of political economy. The type of ownership system determined the type of ownership right.

'Private property right' (*siren zaichan quan*), was regarded as an exception to 'ownership' and its limited parameters related only to consumption in everyday life. In legal theory, such private plots were not important in terms of the whole of the economic system. The state condescended to protect private property rights as part of its strategy to guarantee popular subsistence levels. Later, when large-scale private enterprise emerged, this too was regarded as an appendage to 'public ownership'. However, the government had to contend with the blurring of the lines between collective and private enterprise. It imposed registration limitations on private enterprise so as to pre-empt its classification as collective enterprise. Improper classification of private, as collective enterprise, had become problematic in that the former had misappropriated the concessionary benefits of collective enterprise. Professor Zhang confirmed the spread of this 'red hat' phenomenon.

Such fraudulent registration, however, resulted in controversy over the real nature of such enterprises and helped produce a new political focus on the importance of 'clarifying property rights'. This issue was implied in Jiang Zemin's plaintive references to 'clarifying property rights' and has proven very difficult to resolve. Such clarification involves at least two major concerns, namely the disposition of the originally invested capital and the remedial ability to differentiate when private enterprise, masquerading as collective enterprise, misappropriates collective enterprise advantages relating to the use of workers, the borrowing of money from the banks, more favourable taxation and usage of land. If the emphasis was to be placed on who put in the original capital, then how was policy and law to respond to the growth in capital which originated with the preferential advantages of a 'red hat'?

Secondly, there were many cases where entrepreneurs used public money to establish a 'red hat' enterprise for purposes of speculation in housing and land. They would use work-unit money, promising to pay it back. This was done on the notorious basis of personal relations. From the point of view of popular opinion, it looked and smelled like corruption, but as long as it was reported, it was considered legal. Sometimes, in the case of a successful business venture, the borrower would return the money to the work units. Sometimes, in the case of business failure, for example, the lender would fail to repay the money owed. A few years ago this was a common problem as there was no legal redress in cases where there was a failure to return enterprise monies.

The revised 1997 PRC Criminal Law deliberately attempted to stop the blatant misappropriation of state enterprise funding. Article 384 of the 1997 Criminal Law treats such behaviour as criminal conduct punishable with 6 months to 5-year imprisonment if the amount of the fund involved is largely for the purpose of a business venture or if there is a failure to return the fund after three months. The lack of applicable law before 1997 may be partly explained by the political influence of leadership offspring, or 'princelings', who were sometimes heavily involved in such schemes.

Private enterprise received new, but qualified recognition in law as the result of the State Council's 1988 promulgation of the 'PRC Provisional Regulations on Private Enterprises'.[91] Article 2 defined 'private enterprise' as economic organization 'whose assets are owned by individuals and which have eight or more employees and are intended to be profit-making enterprises'. Article 3 reiterated prevailing wisdom to the effect that while the state was obligated to protect the 'rights and interests of private enterprises', the 'private economy complements the socialist public ownership economy'. According to Article 5, private enterprise could come in three different forms, sole proprietorship, partnership and limited liability enterprises.

The forward looking 1994 Sichuan Provincial 'Regulations on the Management of Private Enterprises' elaborated on these types of private enterprises and other important details regarding the development of private enterprises.[92] These regulations assigned private enterprise a higher status in the national economy than was provided for in the 1982 State Constitution. Article 4 stated that '... private enterprises are an integral part of the socialist market economy....' The regulations also granted private enterprises a series of rights that were currently enjoyed by state-owned or collective enterprises, such as applying for legal person status, hiring other enterprises (including state enterprises) to engage in production and business activities on their behalf, and participating in property transfer and enterprise mergers.

The October 1997 15th Party Congress formally recognized the ownership of private property. The Congress also pledged that the law would protect non-public ownership. This was a substantive departure. The 1986 GPCL had reiterated the conventional position that state property rights are sacred, but that the state would merely endeavour to protect private property. While Tong Rou and his colleagues at the Chinese People's University have argued the GPCL provided equal protection for civil law subjects, these principles did not proclaim the equal status of public and non-public ownership.[93]

Chen Jianfu has researched the sources and consequences of the unequal treatment of the different ownership sectors, and he concluded:

> In fact, the Chinese socialist politico-economic system presents some fundamental barriers to the implementation and realization of such fundamental private law principles as equality and universality. Essentially, the upholding of socialist public ownership as a sacred principle of socialism inherently leads to discrimination against any economy based on other forms of ownership than public ownership, and hence, discrimination against economic activities by sectors of the economy other than the state one.... One of the consequences of upholding this discriminatory politico-economic system and the exercise of state ownership rights by the state and administrative authorities is that public law and private law are often fused and difficult to distinguish from each other in the PRC.[94]

In the candid opinion of CASS Professor Zhang Guangxing, many important issues still need to be resolved before one might expect to see a new 'law on rights in things' (*wu quan fa*) which assigns an unequivocal equality to public and private ownership in the socialist market economy.

The 15th National Party Congress made a number of important breakthroughs in economic policy which moved some of these issues beyond the more limited understandings of the 1982 State Constitution. The Congress endorsed a diversity of ownership forms. Many legal experts welcomed this as an unprecedented commitment.[95] Article 6 of the 1982 State Constitution had affirmed that the 'socialist public ownership of means of production means ownership by the whole people and collective ownership'. Jiang Zemin's latest elaboration on the ownership theory has included the state-owned and collective sectors of the mixed ownership system as part of the public ownership system, and this is apparently a creative extension of the original concept of public ownership. Jiang Zemin's report to the Congress redefined the status of the non-public ownership economic sector by suggesting 'the non-public ownership economy is an important component of the socialist market economy'. The non-public ownership economy was legitimized as a self-standing part of the national economy.[96]

The 1999 constitutional revision used, for the first time, the term, 'ownership' to describe the private possession of the means of production. This would certainly have been a vile heresy in Mao's day. Article 14 of the revision stated that 'in the initial stage of socialism, the state adheres to a basic economic system in which public ownership is in a dominant position, while allowing simultaneous development of non-public ownership economy'. At the same time, the revision assigned the non-public ownership economy a higher status, it also stressed the protection of lawful rights and interests of non-public economies, although it was silent on whether such protection was equivalent to that which was guaranteed to the public ownership economy.

Socialist market reform is transforming China's ownership structure in a fundamental way. The non-public ownership economy has acquired new constitutional status. Private law, such as the 1986 GPCL and the relevant regulations for its application, has been gradually introduced so as to replace the state's administrative function in regulating property relationships and the ownership of the means of production.[97] Chinese legal scholars view such a transition as integral to the general trend of reform in establishing 'a small government and a big society'. Under the planned economy, it was taken for granted that the interests of society as a whole had to be placed above the interests of individual. Under the Soviet influence, the civil law was nothing more than an adjunct of public law. In the reform era, the civil law is emerging as an independent area of private law chiefly concerned with the rights and interests of individuals, as equal subjects before the law.

The significance of increasing the importance of civil law in economic life is that civil law, as private law, does not automatically underwrite the unity of state and society. Also, the new jurisprudential aspects of civil law have helped sponsor a 'rights fundamentalism', designed to provide the individual with contractual freedom, equality, and the lawful protection of rights and interests.[98] In his Zhongnanhai lectures, Wang Jiafu argued that the civil law, as a private law, is a basic law under the socialist market economy. It is concerned chiefly with the economic and property relationships between equal subjects in the market. This law reflects important principles of the market, including voluntarism, equality, justice, and self-responsibility for profits and losses.[99] Most importantly, it provides for equal protection under the law.[100]

The current metamorphosis of state and collective enterprise into shareholding companies and shareholding cooperative enterprises has important implications for civil law. In the past, property under civil law was slotted into rigid public and private categories and private property, while it was tolerated, lacked essential status in law. The corporatization of state enterprise has placed new emphasis on the need to protect equally public and private property. With pluralized ownership, there is less acceptance of the subordinate status of private ownership in the national economy and growing pressure on jurisprudence to come up with a new 'balance of values'.

Conclusion

'Seeking the truth from the facts' has fostered an errant experimentalism which has turned into a form of purgatory for jurists who want resolution on the key issue of 'property' versus 'ownership' rights. Too often the former analysis suggests a notorious correlation between a vacillating politics and opportune semantics in legal theory and law. Politics dictates a convenient ambiguity; it does not welcome integrated jurisprudence. Indeed, it has alternatively fostered a quixotic legal terminology which is euphemistically credited as 'pluralized jurisprudence' dealing with 'pluralized ownership'. In this case, however, pluralism masks the failure to create a well-integrated jurisprudence which definitively sets out the fundamental principles of ownership on the coherent basis of a widely accepted single legal tradition.

Jurisprudence is teetering, along with politics, on the see-saw of China's developmental experiment in market economics. Politics, law and ideology are all newly impressed with the importance of efficiency, but if there is a lack of explicit reference to the balance of values as it pertains to the legal consolidation of 'ownership rights', there is also a lack of political will to resolve the underlying issue of the state's relation to state enterprise. Efficiency might require the radical reduction of state ownership to make state enterprise competitive, but the wholesale elimination of the state's 'ultimate ownership' in a time of spreading corruption could also eliminate the state's opportunities to promote actively principles of social justice, vis-à-vis the anticipated inequalities of private ownership.

Reacting against 'absolute egalitarianism', the CCP embraced efficiency. The economists' fascination with American notions of property reinforced the Party's rush to efficiency while at the same time 'property rights' ironically offered the Party an opportunity to cling to its conventional notion of political economy. The jurists, for their part, were frustrated by the economists who ignorantly capitalized on Dengist experimentalism, at the expense of what they saw as the solid legal notion of indivisible ownership in civil law. 'American' efficiency, based on the convenient fractioning of property rights, was ironically conscripted in the cause to pre-empt the granting of unqualified ownership rights to state enterprise. The Party wants the efficiency of the marketplace in order to acquire the legitimacy which comes with ever-increasing production, but it does not want to run the risk of perceived social injustice which would inevitably follow hard upon the loss of publicly owned assets. Hence, there is general legal confusion.

While they can often agree that state enterprise needs more than operational management rights in order to compete in a market economy, jurists cannot agree on the essential connotations of the 'property rights of legal person'. Some would simply pretend that property rights are ownership rights, while others demand the Party confirm outright the legal superiority of ownership rights.

The restructuring of the key relationship between the state and state enterprise forms a large part of the story, but there are other parts. While there is a frustrating ambivalence in the 'pluralization' of the state sector, there are other indications of substantive change. Policy, legal theory and ideology have, for example, recently combined to underwrite the new constitutional status of private ownership as an 'important component' of the national socialist market economy. Secondly, in new shareholding collective enterprise, there is an explicit synthesis of justice and efficiency in the revised balance of labour and capital.

At times the boundaries separating the public and private dimensions of new shareholding enterprise have been deliberately blurred. The 'red hat' phenomenon obscured the legal and practical distinctions between collective and private enterprise. Also, policy and law have sometimes preferred the formal diversification of public ownership to the permissive expansion of distinct forms of private ownership. If property is no longer 'theft' in a society experiencing the rise of 'legitimate' new private and public interests, it is still not clear who has the definitively clarified ownership rights over separated and mixed public and private property.

This lack of clarity in jurisprudence and law, as it has been deliberately fostered in the politics and policy of the sort described earlier by Maurice Meisner, raises serious questions about the prospects for the genuine development of a new 'rule of law economy' in the transition to China's 'socialist market'. Where does efficiency truly lie in this developmental predicament? The socially painful dilemma of what to do with public property is at the centre of China's market reform, and yet the essential superiority of the 'rule of law' is often presumed to lie in the creation of an independent and meaningful framework of clear and widely accepted impersonal rules which deliberately structure subject equality in law.

5
Balancing Society and the Individual in Judicial Justice

The importance of reviewing Chinese criminal law and supporting legal discourse, so as to identify and confirm the meanings which the Chinese attach to their newly emerging legal concepts, is obvious.[1] Professor Jonathan Hecht is one commentator who has noted the importance of monitoring and evaluating the Chinese criminal law system so as to create 'a base of knowledge about Chinese law and practice from which to promote China's compliance with international norms'.[2] Western evaluation has often critiqued Chinese 'state instrumentalism' and 'legal positivism'.[3] The current transition in Chinese politics has generated controversy over two related questions. How best to describe the essential nature of the contemporary Chinese state: as, for example, 'mature totalitarianism', 'consultative authoritarianism' or 'fragmented authoritarianism'? And is the contemporary trend more towards civil society or state corporatism? This chapter's analysis asks a third, but obviously related, question. How does change to the underlying principles of the criminal law system factor into contemporary regime change, as the jurisprudential axis of the criminal law shifts from class struggle to market reform?

In his analysis of the early consequences of Tiananmen Square, Professor Jerome Cohen noted that China's leaders '. . . while ruthlessly manipulating the nation's public law and criminal justice systems to maintain themselves in power, have sought to contain the fallout from their actions by preserving the role of law in promoting economic growth, international business cooperation, and social stability'.[4] This might suggest that post-Tiananmen legal development has followed along two separate tracks of socio-political control and market reform, but the reference to ruthless manipulation does not capture the new balancing of societal and individual rights and interests in the 1996–97 qualitative revisions to the criminal procedural and criminal laws. This chapter's analysis will explore the internal reasoning which currently supports the reconceptualization of judicial justice and will address how the Party's changing focus on social stability squares with the new emphasis on the protection of citizen's rights and interests.

In their fear of spreading corruption, precipitous value change and regime instability, China's Party leaders have refocused on the stabilizing function of criminal law. At the same time, they have endorsed a new emphasis on the procedural protection of citizens involved in the criminal law process. Many of China's most senior jurists and lawmakers regard the related revisions to the PRC's Criminal Procedural Law and the Criminal Law in 1996 and 1997 as having systemic significance in the evolution of China's rule of law. In the past, the criminal law in particular enjoyed a pre-eminent status within the legal system in the light of its contribution to social order as understood by the political authorities. Today, the law of criminal procedure is acquiring a new status vis-à-vis the criminal law and together these laws enjoy pre-eminence by virtue of their contribution not only to social order, but also to the protection of rights and interests. The 1996 and 1997 revisions, taken together, suggest the makings of at least a partial paradigm shift in that they not only reiterated the purpose of social control, but also gave new precedence to basic personal freedoms. At least in formal terms, there is a new balancing of the law's purposes.

This reference to a reconstructed balance deserves appropriate recognition, as it constitutes a departure from the exclusive pattern of past state instrumentalism. The shift from an unqualified focus on crime control to a balance of reconceptualized control with the protection of rights and interests of individuals within the criminal process is no small achievement, as the 1979 Criminal Law (1979 CL) and Criminal Procedure Law (1979 CPL) were clearly enacted for the purposes of punishing 'criminal elements' and struggling against 'counterrevolutionaries.'

After many failed drafts, the PRC's first Criminal Law and Criminal Procedure Law were passed by the 2nd Session of the 5th National People Congress in 1 July 1979 and implemented on 1 January 1980. The 1979 CL and CPL reinstated the 1954 Constitution's reference to 'equality before the law'. It promised new levels of protection for those who had suffered from the arbitrary persecution of the Cultural Revolutionary class struggle; but the 1979 CL and CPL, while recognizing the past excesses of class struggle, still incorporated the Party's modified assumptions concerning politics, the law and the continuing relevance of class struggle.

The 1979 CL and 1979 CPL were designed to pre-empt runaway class struggle, convulsive mass mobilizations and the proliferating false accusations of extremist politics, but these laws still had to contend with the occasional class enemies of socialism. The Cultural Revolution had politically confirmed that even the country's most powerful leaders needed legal protection vis-à-vis the violent extremes of leadership change and class struggle. The class enemy was reduced in its size and theoretical significance. However, while there was a great push to codify law and to make legal principles clear, 'class' remained at the heart of the criminal law. If the 1979 CPL brought back 'equality before the law',[5] Article 2 of the 1979 CL re-affirmed that the criminal law was still an important tool of the state in the continuing struggle against counterrevolution.

There was a desperate need to re-establish social order and political unity after a decade of near civil war conditions. In this context of rebuilding state structures, which had collapsed under the weight of random large-scale class struggle, there was a renewed state instrumentalism. At the same, there was a new appreciation of the importance of the law's contribution to the modern process of institutionalization. In short, law offered an attractive institutional predictability when compared to the extremes of continuing leadership struggle. The 1979 CL reflected a new and important political understanding of the dangers of indiscriminate charges of counterrevolution in the context of leadership struggle, but the notion of counterrevolution was modified rather than negated.[6] At the time, the promulgation of new codified criminal law and criminal procedure law was widely hailed as a significant step forward in the development of Chinese law. Internationally, these two laws attracted the reserved, but nonetheless positive, interest of western legal experts, who had detected an incipient trend towards legal form and predictability.[7]

The retention of 'class' in the 1979 CL dictated a politically distinctive approach to the development and application of the criminal law. There was, for example, open subscription to 'flexibility' (*linghuoxing*) as a guiding principle in both the general and specific provisions of the law. Jurists and NPC law-makers subscribed to the principle of 'flexibility' as necessary to social control and the state's adaptation to the changing and uneven spatial and societal circumstances within China's vast territory and population.[8] For the same reason, analogy was vetted as a legitimate part of the state's response to the changing nature of crime.

In the absence of specifically stipulated categories of crime, the state authorities often charged suspects of crimes which they flexibly construed as being similar in nature to those actually on the books. This conflicted with western understandings of *nullum crimen sine lege; nulla poena sine lege* (no crime without a law; and no punishment without a law), as an essentially rational matter of natural justice within modern legal culture. In the politics of 1979, however, inconsistent legal terminology and the deliberately vague stipulation of the elements of specific crime and the incomplete classification of crime were tolerated, as they were consciously correlated with the preconceived prerequisites of social and political order.

The persisting emphasis on social control through law may also help explain the apparently paradoxical expansion in the categories of capital punishment in the transition to a commodity economy. These categories proliferated even as the argument was made for the law's predictability in market relations and the need for greater procedural protection vis-à-vis the arbitrary nature of class struggle. Subsequent mid-1990s internal criticism of this outstanding tension was later partly rationalized with reference to the inexperience of China's law-makers at that time.[9]

In the 1990s the entire conceptual edifice of the 1979 CL unravelled. The difficulties in the enforcement of vaguely stipulated law became increasingly obvious as economic reform gave rise to an extraordinarily complex proliferation of economic crime. A *Renmin ribao* commentary, welcoming the 1997 revision of the criminal law, candidly acknowledged the shortcomings of the 1979 CL, observing that '... because in past criminal codes there were either no stipulations at all, or very loose stipulations without specific language about many criminal offenses, in reality it has been hardly possible to claim that there are laws to abide by in all cases'.[10]

Over the past several years, Chinese scholars have increasingly articulated the fundamental relevance of legal procedure to the evolving notion of a 'rule of law' in a socialist state. Chen Guangzhong and Zheng Xu recently wrote that the last 20 years of development in criminal procedural law could be cast in two related stages from 1978 to 1992 and from 1993 onwards. The second stage was initiated at the 14th National Party Congress which established the socialist market economy and was consolidated at the 15th National Party Congress which brought forward the strategy, 'running the country according to law and creating a socialist rule of law country'. Chen and Zheng are convinced that the current purpose of legal reform is 'to realize judicial justice, which is a basic requirement in a civilized society, and without which, there can be no social justice'.[11]

Cui Min, one of the senior drafters of criminal procedural law, similarly indicated to the present authors that the two central elements of the rule of law are justice and due process (*gongzheng he youxu*). In his view, Jiang Zemin's newly endorsed principle of 'running a country according to the law' means to do things according to procedure.[12] This was not the case when the 1979 Criminal Procedure Law was enacted. Based on Chinese legal theory at the time, criminal procedure law reflected all of the innate characteristics of criminal law. The former did not have its own self-standing purpose. It was expressly treated as an appendage to criminal law. Zhang Zipei of the Chinese University of Politics and Law, Beijing, and his colleagues, in the 1982 edition of official Chinese criminal procedure law textbook, for example, argued that the relationship between a criminal law and criminal procedure law ought to be viewed as the relationship between methods and tasks (*fangfa yu renwu*) or between substance and form (*neirong yu xingshi*).

According to this conventional reasoning, the criminal law is much more concerned with the substance, while a procedural criminal law provides the form through which substance is expressed. It also follows that substantive criminal law is concerned with the determination and punishment of crime, while criminal law procedure merely facilitates the application of the substantive content of the criminal law.[13] In line with this theory, the characteristics of class analysis and the necessity of 'flexibility' in the 1979 CL governed the internal requirements of the 1979 CPL.

This prioritization of substantive over procedural criminal law was well established in the imperial legal tradition. Shen Jiaban, an eminent Qing jurist, explained that the criminal law's substance was closely associated with procedural criminal law. However, the former acted as 'substance' (*ti*), while the latter was relegated to 'form' (*yong*). This constituted a philosophical ordering of substance over form, even though substance could not be expressed without form.[14]

CASS Institute of Law Professor Fu Kuaizhi confirmed in an interview that this traditional subordination of form to substance passed into the post-1949 development of Chinese criminal and criminal procedural law,[15] but Professor Fu emphasized that this mainstream theory had been more recently superseded by theory alternately referred to as either 'independent purposes theory (*duli jiazhi shuo*), or 'dual purposes theory' (*shuangchong jiazhi shuo*). This theory affirms that criminal pro-

Judicial Justice 183

cedure law has to emphasize its own independent purpose as well as that of the criminal law.

The subordination to and integration of criminal procedural law with criminal law was seriously challenged in the late 1980s' Chinese debate on human rights. In 1985, Professor Chen Guangzhang of the Chinese University of Politics and Law in Beijing, a leading criminal procedural law expert, who had participated in the drafting of the 1979 CPL, was one of the first to suggest that, in addition to providing procedural guidance for enforcement of criminal law, the criminal procedure law should also be used to protect human rights in the criminal justice process. This suggestion provided the formative basis for the development of the dual purposes theory.[16] Wang Minyuan, a new generation jurist at the CASS Institute of Law, later helped to consolidate this theory. He argued that although the criminal procedural law would have to dovetail with the criminal law, it could also substantively respond to the need for judicial justice and the related protection of human rights in the criminal law.[17]

In recent years, the theory of dual purposes has been widely accepted, and it played a key role in the revision to the 1979 CPL. The acceptance of this theory is closely associated with two important conceptual changes in criminal procedure studies among Chinese procedural law experts. The first conceptual change is associated with the concept of procedural justice, while the second relates to the evaluation of procedural efficiency. In the past, procedural efficiency was measured exclusively in terms of the law's effectiveness in punishing crime. This exclusiveness was modified in the 1996 CPL revision which newly highlighted the notion of 'due process'. As for the reference to efficiency, Zhang Lingjie, of the CASS Institute of Law, has argued that efficient procedure has to meet three specific criteria. First, procedure is to provide protection of the rights and interests of the individual involved in criminal proceedings. Second, the procedure must be adequately operationalized. And, finally, it should be cost efficient. In sum, the determination and punishment of crime could not stand as the sole criterion of procedural efficiency.[18]

Procedural justice has become a critical priority in recent legal discourse. Many scholars contend that it is central to the rule of law. Procedural justice forms an independent purpose of procedure law, and it is through actualization of procedural justice that human rights protection is achieved in criminal process. According to Mao Guohui of the Changsha College of Politics, Hunan, procedural justice encompasses four distinct elements: equal status among the parties involved in criminal process, such as judicial institutions and the accused; balanced rights and duties between the parties; democratic principles in various proceedings; and rationalized procedures. In Professor Mao's reform view, it is more important for criminal procedure law to achieve procedural justice in criminal process than it is for such law to service the substantive criminal law in achieving the successful determination and punishment of crime. In effect, Mao put the protection of individual rights and interests ahead of the protection of society.

This may have amounted to Hobson's choice, but, in debate, scholars often felt compelled to choose between 'society fundamentalism' (*shehui benweizhuyi*) and 'rights fundamentalism' (*quanli benweizhuyi*). On the other hand, the fact that scholars would actually consider placing procedural justice ahead of the criminal law punishment of crime, suggested a new development in legal thinking. In the past, the law's purpose was to deter crime through educating the criminal and the public on the punitive dimensions of the law. Mao Guohui, however, focused alternatively on the development of procedure protecting the rights and interests of the individual in the judicial process. Procedural criminal law then becomes not only the means by which to resolve conflict but it also acts as the guarantor of basic human rights.[19]

Many Chinese jurists recognize the inherent tension between pursuing procedural justice to protect rights and interests of the individual and punishing crime to protect the interests of society in criminal process. And of course there is potentially a positive relation between the social need for order and the individual's enjoyment of rights. However, Zuo Weimin paralleled Herbert Packer's typology of criminal process,[20] classifying criminal procedure law in both the Continental and Common Law legal systems into two models, the crime control model and the rights protection model. Zuo anticipated conflict between these models, and he concluded that criminal procedure law ought to try to balance out their competing purposes.[21]

Song Yinghui, of the Chinese University of Politics and Law, added that overemphasis on either purpose would negate the legal order, if not the rule of law itself. Balancing the purposes of criminal procedure in crime control and rights protection, has, therefore, to be actualized through the careful structuring of criminal procedures. This includes a series of interlocking balances dealing with the relations between judicial institutions and the relations between the accused and victims in society. Song also addressed the balance between procedural justice and procedural efficiency when he called for a balancing of the interests of state and society and the interests of the individual.[22]

Li Fuyan, of the People's Procuratorate of Fushan, Guangdong, and his colleagues, further suggested that this last crucial balance between society and the individual required the limitation of state powers, particularly of its judicial powers. They reasoned that imposing limitations on judicial power of the state is not to deny the interests of society as a whole, but rather to prevent an imbalance in rights and interests protection between society and the individual. However, inconsistently, Li and his colleagues also acknowledged that in some cases where state secrets are involved, the interests of society can override rights and interests of the individual.[23]

Such a viewpoint has called for the balancing of rights and interests (*liyi quanheng yuanze*) between the society and the individual in criminal procedure legislation. However, Song Yinghui warned that in specific stages of the criminal process, the judiciary has been forced to choose between competing interests. In his view, the criteria used to balance the competing interests are directly related to purposes of criminal procedure. Song saw the latter operating at three distinct levels.

The first level concerns the interests of society and the security of the state; the second consolidates the integrity of the legal procedure system through the development of specific regulations concerning, for example, the right to counsel. The third level, which immediately derives from the second, expressly concerns the status of the individual. Song's own balancing subscribed to the protection of society's interests as fundamental, but at the same time he rejected any antithesis between society's interests and individual human rights. He stressed that in specific cases individual and social interest may be compatible and also that the protection of lawful interests of the accused is necessary to the integrity of the state's legal system.[24] For many Chinese jurists, however, there is currently an imbalance which has to be redressed through compensating weight assigned to human rights protection and the reinforced guarantee of the individual's procedural rights in the criminal process. This early to mid 1990s discourse had a profound influence on the revision of the 1979 CPL.

The 'Resolution on Amending the PRC Criminal Procedure Law' was passed by the 4th Session of the 8th National People's Congress on 17 March 1996 and took effect on 1 January 1997. Chinese legal scholars regard this revision as a 'milestone' in criminal justice reform.[25] This revision, although it was seminal, was not comprehensive. According to Professor Cui Min, of the Chinese Public Security University, who actively participated in the entire process of the revision, the revision intended only to address several critical procedural concerns in criminal process. These included issues concerning coercive measures, the role of the defense counsel in criminal proceedings, the role of the people's procuratorates in determining guilt or innocence, and the stipulation of trial proceedings. The revision made 143 changes, added 62 articles, deleted 2 articles, and consequently, increased the total number articles from 164 to 225. According to Cui's own authoritative study, the most important feature of the revision related to its new emphasis on the protection of human rights.[26] Xiao Yang, the Minister of Justice, drew virtually the same conclusion:

> The recent amendment of the Criminal Procedure Law has... scientifically embodied the dialectical relationship between punishment of crime and protection of citizen's rights. What needs to be specially pointed out is that this amendment conforms to international practices and commonly observed judicial principles; and therefore proves beneficial to a strict enforcement of the law, to the protection of human rights, and to our efforts to reinforce our international cooperation and struggle in the fields of jurisdiction and human rights.[27]

The 1996 revision marked a major change of course, and Cui Min, in his detailed explanation to the authors, traced this change to the Party's desire for linkage with the international community, the developing perspective on the implications of the Cultural Revolutionary experience and the transition to the socialist market. The lessons of the Cultural Revolution had convinced many scholars of the importance of procedure and this viewpoint resulted in a focus on the balancing of interests within criminal law processes.

According to Cui Min's account, the revision process officially began in October 1993. From the very beginning, almost every article that came under review for revision was controversial, and, inevitably, controversy originated with the innate tension between the protection of human rights and the punishment of crime in criminal procedure. Many Chinese jurists believed that the false and unjust charges and punishments of the Cultural Revolution were especially heinous in the context of a lack of stable procedure, and that the 1979 CPL was primarily designed to facilitate the accurate application of the criminal law.[28]

In discussing the general principles underlying the proposed revision to the 1979 CPL, Gu Angran, Chairman of the Legal System Working Committee of the NPC, referred to existing twin emphases on crime control and rights protection in 1979 CPL. Article 2 of the 1979 CPL had stipulated that 'the task of the Criminal Procedure Law of the People's Republic of China are to guarantee the accurate and timely clarification of the facts of crime, to apply the law correctly, to punish criminal elements, to safeguard innocent people from criminal prosecution . . .'.[29] Referring to the proliferation of new types of crime in the context of economic reform, some jurists, especially those in the public security organs and the people's procuratorates, placed greater stress on the strengthening of the punishment of crime in the revision. Zhang Qiong, Vice-President of the Supreme People's Procuratorate (SPP), for example, insisted that the revision focused on punishment and strict law enforcement. He warned his colleagues not to adopt blindly the failings of the capitalist criminal procedure system. Unqualified adaptation, he said, would eventually destroy China's own political system.[30]

Disregarding Zhang's cautionary tale, many legal scholars continued to argue that the 1979 CPL had overemphasized the punishment of crime at the expense of rights protection. They noted, for example, that 'innocent people' in Article 2 did not include criminal suspects and the accused. Rather, it was used to refer only to the victims, the innocent and the general public. There was no procedural protection of rights and interests of the criminal suspects and the accused. It followed that the revision had to redress the imbalance between crime control and human rights protection.[31]

In October 1993, Professor Chen Guangzhong was asked by The NPC Legal Work Committee to organize a research team, which was mandated to propose draft revisions to the 1979 CPL. The draft, which was completed in June 1994, formed the basis for the 1996 revision. Chen's draft gave new precedence to human rights protection. He agreed that rising rates of crime were becoming problematic, but he, nonetheless, focused on the imbalance of social control and rights protection. The draft outlined four key aspects of rights protection. The law had self-consciously to protect the lawful rights of general public. This aspect duly required emphasis on criminal law punishment. Secondly, the law had to prevent the prosecution of innocent people. Thirdly, the law had to guarantee the procedural rights of the various parties involved in criminal justice process, especially defendants. Finally, Chen required that the law punish the guilty based on a lawful procedure, reliable facts and adequate sentences.

Professor Chen also emphasized that the revisions should further rationalize (*kexuehua*) and democratize (*minzhuhua*) the criminal procedure system. For him, rationalization and democratization meant to further separate the functions of judicial institutions, to incorporate the principle of judicial independence and presumption of innocence into the criminal procedure, to strengthen the protection of rights and interests of the criminal suspects and the accused, and to prevent governmental abuse of coercive measures.[32]

Wang Hanbin, a venerable law-maker and chair of the NPC's legal work committee, personally lauded the approved CPL revisions as a major achievement in 'running the country according to law'. Reflecting prevailing jurist opinion, he underscored the protection of citizen's rights and interests as the key feature of the revision. Hence 'fighting crime' was balanced anew with the protection of citizen's rights and interests. These emphases were not only correlated with a stronger focus on the efficient and fair handling of cases, but more broadly with 'the development of socialist democracy and legal institutions'. Wang candidly admitted that implementation would be difficult in the light of so many years of resistant customary practice. In his view, implementation was in effect a matter of 'changing our concepts, both in the ideological realm and in practical work'.[33]

The approved draft of the revisions did not incorporate all of the legal experts' suggestions, but those that survived the vicissitudes of the political process were of such qualitative magnitude as to suggest a major change of course within the criminal law process. Harvard Professor Jonathan Hecht, for example, has concluded that '. . . the 1996 NPC Decision demonstrates that China has begun to reorient its basic approach to criminal justice away from a dominant preoccupation with social control toward a somewhat greater concern for the protection of defendants' right'.[34]

The balance of interests in the revised CPL

With the significant exception of Jonathan Hecht's report to the US Lawyers Committee for Human Rights, Western scholarly analysis of internal jurist debate – as it has related to the balance in Chinese criminal procedural law – is surprisingly limited in its scope and volume. The following section identifies the 1996 revisions to the original articles of the 1979 CPL, particularly as they relate to the protection of the rights and interests of the individual. The substance of the revision process, of course, was not exclusively legal in nature and the debates among jurists and judicial personnel are outlined and analysed with specific reference to politics and the influence of NPC law-makers.[35]

The CPL and the administrative measure, 'custody for investigation'

The 1979 CPL incorporated five different forms of pre-trial coercive measures, including compulsory summons (*junchuan*), 'obtaining a guarantor and awaiting trial' (*qubao houshen*), 'living at home under surveillance' (*jianshi juzhu*), 'detention' (*juliu*) and 'arrest' (*daibu*).[36] Detention and arrest constituted two of the most severe forms of pretrial coercive measure as they result in the deprivation of personal freedom. The 1979 CPL, however, responded to the specific excesses of the Cultural Revolution, hence it gave new emphasis to the protection of personal freedom. The law laid out the conditions delimiting public security powers of arrest. The latter were required to obtain a warrant either from a people's procuratorate, or a people's court.[37] The legal prerequisite for an arrest became: '. . . the principal facts of whose crime have been clearly established through investigation and whose minimum possible sentence would amount to a fixed-term imprisonment'.[38] Similarly, Article 41 clearly spelled out seven specific situations permitting the detention of suspects.

Moreover, the law required that the family or work unit of the detained be notified within 24 hours of the reasons for and place of detention of a family member.[39] Under the 1979 CPL, public security could interrogate the detainee within 24 hours following detention. They could detain a suspect for up to three days, and in exceptional cases for up to seven.[40] Thereafter, a people's procuratorate must either sanction the detention or order the release of the detainee within three days. For the police and prosecutors, these standards for arrest and the newly stipulated short time frame for pre-trial detention threatened to frustrate their efforts in punishing criminals. Many jurists also regarded the conditions for an arrest as impractical.[41] As a result, public security sought to circumvent the 1979 CPL requirements and resorted to a previously widespread administrative coercive measure, 'custody for investigation' (*shourong shencha*). This measure was never incorporated into the 1979 CPL itself. 'Custody for investigation' was an excellent example of systemic, if not principled, flexibility. It was first used as an administrative coercive measure in 1961 for the purpose of preventing the rural population from freely migrating into the cities. During the anti-crime campaigns in the 1970s and 1980s, it was used extensively to detain all forms of criminal suspects.

Cui Min reported that during that period, as many as 70 to 80 per cent of all detainees were arrested and detained through 'custody for investigation'.⁴² In 1985 to 1993, the Ministry of Public Security recognized the extensive abuse of 'custody for investigation' and issued five official notices curtailing its application, but these failed to contain the situation. For many Chinese legal experts, this irregular police power violated Article 37 of the 1982 Constitution which clearly stipulated that only people's courts and people's procuratorates have the right to approve arrest or detention.

Long before the revision process, jurists had already suggested that the NPC eliminate such deviant administrative practice in order to protect human rights. But the powerful Ministry of Public Security was able to block NPC revision. The Ministry politically relied on a law and order theme, claiming: '[custody for investigation] is an indispensable means for public security organs to maintain social security and to crack down upon criminals. Especially under current circumstances of reform and opening up, in order to maintain social stability, this method must be continuously used and must not be abandoned'.⁴³

For their part, the law-makers sought to balance the competing demands of the jurists and the Ministry. On the one hand, the NPC eliminated police resort to 'custody for investigation'. Since 'custody for investigation' was never a CPL-sanctioned coercive measure; its elimination was not mentioned in the 1996 CPL revision. But accompanying NPC documentation explicitly indicated that 'custody for investigation' would no longer be tolerated. On the other hand, the NPC accommodated the Ministry of Public Security by means of a trade-off, lowering the standards for arrest. Article 60 of the revised CPL replaced the original 1979 wording in Article 40, 'principal facts of crime are clarified', with the conveniently loose formulation, 'there is evidence to prove the facts of the crime'. At the same time, Sections 6 and 7 of Article 41 of the 1979 CPL were reworded in the new 1996 Article 61 to update the description of two categories of person who were of particular interest to the public security and procuratorial authorities. These two categories of persons now included those who fail to provide the authorities with details of their true identity and those suspected of going 'from place to place committing crimes, or who repeatedly committed crimes' or 'ganged up with others to commit crimes'.⁴⁴

Cui Min confirmed that the revision to Article 61 was part of the package deal for the elimination of 'custody for investigation'. These two groups of persons were originally subjects under the administrative practice of 'custody for investigation'. The second of these two groups was singled out for expressed legal attention in that the particular period for detention in this case was extended from the original 7 to 30 days.⁴⁵

During the revision process, opposition to this extension surfaced. Opponents argued that 30 days far exceeded internationally accepted standards. The proponents of revision replied, pointing to China's large population and territory. The hoary argument for 'flexibility' was resuscitated in response to the new problem of widespread transience in the context of the 'open door' and economic reform.

Arguably, growing transience had created a new criminal dynamic which taxed the patience and resources of those responsible for criminal investigation, and the extension in Article 61 was rationalized as a catch-up measure in dealing with this new pattern of alleged societal deviance.[46] While Professor Cui Min emphasized the importance of procedurally protecting rights and interests, he too leaned in favour of Article 61's extended detention period. He explained to the present authors that unidentified detainees had seriously disrupted the progress of criminal investigation, and he gave the example of migratory drug smugglers from Burma who had frequently refused to provide true identification to the Chinese authorities.[47] Cui, himself, was very reluctant to release such alleged criminals from detention without knowing who they were.

Some Chinese scholars were not entirely happy with the relaxed requirements for arrest and detention in as much as these particular revisions seemed to place investigative priorities ahead of the protection of citizen's rights. On the other hand, they seemed ready to recognize the legitimacy of the NPC's strategy for compromise. The latter seemed particularly realistic especially as public sentiment was significantly aligned with the Ministry of Public Security, and the compromise deal offered a way out of the long-standing impasse over 'custody for investigation'. Indeed, the extensive resort to the latter had become something of an international human rights embarrassment.[48]

In his review of these changes, Harvard Professor Jonathan Hecht gave the Chinese a mixed but somewhat favourable review when he stated:

> overall, then, the provisions of the 1996 Decision relating to pretrial detention show some movement toward greater protection of the rights of suspected criminals. The elimination of 'shelter and investigation' means one less 'legal' way for the police to avoid altogether the time periods, procedural requirements, and supervisory mechanisms contained in the CPL ... While these are welcome steps, in other respects the 1996 NPC Decision actually weakens restrictions on the use and length of pre-trial detention.[49]

'Presumption of innocence' and 'exemption from prosecution'

A similar balancing approach was evident in the NPC response to one of the most controversial issues in the history of making Chinese criminal procedure law – the presumption of innocence (*wuzui tuiding*). Since the 1950s there has been a internal debate about whether Chinese criminal procedure law should embrace this fundamental principle,[50] and, not surprisingly, this issue was featured in discussion leading to the 1996 CPL revision.

Those opposed insisted that the Chinese principle of 'taking facts as the basis and the law as the yardstick' (*yi shishi wei genju yi falu wei zhunsheng*) was reliably scientific and value-free in its underlying orientation. This principle was specifically sanctioned in Deng Xiaoping's 'seeking the truth from the facts', and it was extolled as superior to the presumption of innocence in as much as it was construed as equally concerned with the fair treatment of the innocent as well as the punishment of the guilty.[51] The retentionists argued that the switch to 'presumption of innocence' would result in criminals evading punishment whereas the current principle, 'taking the facts as the basis and the law as the yardstick', would still protect the rights and interests of both suspects and accused.

The proponents of the 'presumption of innocence', however, pointed to its extensive adoption in international law as well as its confirmation in Article 87 of the Basic Law of Hong Kong, which the NPC itself had promulgated in 4 April 1990.[52] They claimed that this principle provided enhanced procedural protection for human rights since it assumes the pre-trial innocence of criminal suspects and the accused and grants them various procedural rights, including the right to counsel.[53]

Lu Zhongya argued rather ingeniously that the essentially scientific assumption of 'presumption of innocence' had already been captured in the Chinese formulation, 'taking facts as the basis and the law as the yardstick'. Lu opined:

> [the principle of] 'taking the facts as the basis and the law as the criterion' ... demands that, in handling cases, the judge use objective facts instead of subjective imagination and presumption to determine the case and to measure the punishment. In various criminal proceedings, such as investigation, prosecution, and adjudication, evidence is invariably used to ascertain the facts of the case. Emphasis must be placed on evidence, and credence should not be readily given to oral statement. It is on this basis that sentences are rendered according to law. The presumption of innocence principle opposes

the use of subjective arbitration to replace authentic and conclusive evidence. It seeks to use valid evidence, unimpeachable testimony and sufficient defense to ensure that the judgment is substantial and truthful. Therefore, it can be said that 'taking the facts as the basis and law as the criterion' is related to and not contradictory with the presumption of innocence principle in its original legislative intention.[54]

CASS Institute of Law Professor Wang Minyuan, however, begged to differ. Highlighting the difference between the two principles, he concluded forthrightly that the Chinese principle is inferior in its focus on protection and that presumption of innocence represents a step forward in the conceptual development of modern criminal justice. Wang argued that the Chinese principle came with an inappropriate historical baggage. It pursued the truth so as to punish the criminal without emphasizing judicial justice. It revealed a legalist or utilitarian bias towards 'rule by law'. In contrast, he believed that the new concept underwrote a series of rational methods and deliberate procedures focusing on the procedural protection of the defendant.[55]

Cui Min observed that there was no clear winner in this debate as the NPC once again preferred to compromise. Article 6 of the revision endorsed 'taking the facts as the basis and the law as the yardstick'.[56] On the other hand, the NPC incorporated into the CPL some important components of the principle of presumption of innocence. For instance, Section 3 of Article 162 stipulated that 'when the evidence proving guilt is insufficient and the defendant cannot be found guilty, a verdict of innocent shall be given on the grounds the charge of crime cannot be established'. This stipulation has important practical implications as it allowed the judicial authorities to close the books on cases where there was insufficient evidence to convict.

Similarly, Article 12 of the 1996 CPL stipulated that 'no one shall be pronounced guilty without a verdict pronounced by a people's court according to the law'. Some legal experts believed that this stipulation converged with the presumption of innocence.[57] Indeed, this trend was reinforced in the move to eliminate 'exemption from prosecution' (*mianyu qusu*). The latter was justified in the self-conscious emphasis on the principle, 'no guilt without trial'. However, Hecht has suggested that Article 12 may not be as significant as some Chinese scholars would like to think. He concluded: '[Article 12 says] nothing about the burden of proof, standard of guilt, or any other issue commonly associated with the presumption of innocence. It should be seen rather as a straightforward statement of functional responsibility: only a court – and no other individual or institution — can determine guilt'.[58] He was also dubious about the overall effect of the revision when he stated: '[it] failed to achieve a clear-cut resolution of the issue at the heart of the presumption of innocence: the burden of proof. The essence of the presumption is giving the defendant the benefit of the doubt'.[59]

The issue of whether China has already adopted the presumption of innocence is important. The revision moved in a new direction. Eliminating 'exemption from prosecution' is a significant step forward toward protection of rights and interests of the individual in practice. Article 101 of the 1979 CPL stipulated that '. . . in cases where, according to the provisions of the Criminal Law, it is not necessary to impose a sentence of criminal punishment or an exemption from criminal punishment may be granted, a people's procuratorate may grant exemption from prosecution'.[60]

Indeed, 'exemption from prosecution' acted as a guilty verdict without punishment. Furthermore, it was often extolled in the past as an application of the state's policy of 'combining punishment with leniency'. The major problem with this system is that this verdict is determined not through a court trial, but by the procuratorate. It violated the principle of 'no guilt without a trial' and it inhibited new procedural focus on the rights to counsel and appeal of the accused. In recent years, this procedure was extensively abused by lower level procuratorates to mitigate improperly the corruption of local officials.

The deletion of 'exemption of prosecution' ran into serious opposition from the SPP. The SPP argued that 'exemption from prosecution' was a genuinely Chinese creation and that it had served well as a powerful weapon in cracking down on crime and maintaining social order. At the same time, this system was consistent with the principle of cost efficiency in criminal process.[61]

Although the NPC did not adopt the principle of the presumption of innocence as one of the guiding principles of the criminal procedure, the revisions attempted to accommodate the jurists in so far as they made greater reference to 'no guilt without a trial' and to the protection of the rights and interests of the accused. Bureaucratic politics cut across the legislative process in as much as judicial institutions such as the public security organs and people's procuratorates adopted a dedicated practical stance which stressed their intrinsic institutional functions of punishing crime and protecting society as a whole. On the other hand, the jurists attempted to deploy procedural law to limit the power of state judicial institutions and to curtail their participation in human rights abuses. Revisions concerning the right to counsel and open trial proceedings revealed the same tension between the jurists and the security and procuratorial authorities.

Expanded right to counsel and open trial proceedings

The 1979 CPL stipulated that a defendant may have a defence counsel for his/her defense. The court was to appoint a defence counsel in the event of procuratorial involvement.[62] The law also required that compulsory appointment of defence counsel would apply in any case where a defendant is deaf, dumb or a dependent juvenile. Drawing upon massline convention, this law also made alternative provision for a layman to serve as a defence counsel.[63] However, it gave priority to lawyers, granting them privileged access to the case materials of the procuratorate.[64] According to the 1979 CPL, the defence counsel on the basis of the facts and the law may present materials and opinions proving the defendant's innocence or the minor nature of the crime.

However, the 1979 CL allowed several limitations concerning defendant's right to counsel. The defendant's right to counsel was only enjoyed during trial proceedings, and not in the criminal or pre-trial proceedings. The defendant had to face the pre-trial investigation process without legal assistance. At the same time, defence lawyers were handicapped in that they did not have adequate time to prepare the defence. The courts were to provide notification of impending trial proceedings only seven days before the trial date. Only at this point, could the accused actually appoint a defender.[65]

Furthermore, the 2 September 1983 'Decision of NPCSC regarding the Procedure for Rapid Adjudication of Cases Involving Criminal Elements Who Seriously Endanger Public Security' further shortened this preparation period in serious cases, such as rape, robbery, homicide, causing explosions, and other serious endangerment to public security. In these cases, defence counsel had less than seven days to prepare the defence. It is also well known that courts did not take the defence counsel's job seriously. In fact, in most cases, court verdicts were determined before the trial. This situation is self-consciously described in the Chinese as 'decide first, trial later' (*xianding, houshen*).

To protect rights and interests of defendants, jurists strongly suggested that defence counsel shall be allowed to provide legal assistance and protect defendants' procedural rights in the investigation stage of the criminal process. Both public security organizations and people's procuratorates questioned such a suggestion by arguing that lawyers' earlier entry to criminal process might put their criminal investigation into jeopardy. As in other instances, the NPC adopted a position in the middle of the two opposing arguments. On the one hand, the revision advances a suspect's right to counsel to the day when the case materials are delivered to the procuratorate. The 1996 CPL stipulates that a people's procuratorate must inform the suspect of his right to counsel within three days of receiving the case materials.[66] At the same time, the revision stipulates that the court should appoint a defence counsel in cases where a suspect may be sentenced to death.[67]

The revision moved in a new, but qualified direction towards the protection of the rights and interests of suspects, but at the same time, NPC law-makers were obviously sensitive to the claims of the procuratorial and security authorities. The latter were expressly concerned about what they perceived to be the undue interference of defence counsel, especially those counsellors who happened to be the relatives of the accused, in the appropriate conduct of criminal investigations. The revision gave the investigating authorities the right to be present at the meetings of counsel and the defendant. In cases involving 'state secrets', the defendant had to get public security or procuratorate permission to engage and meet with a defence counsel.[68]

This explicitly statist perspective on law and order may well invoke the traditional bias against the lawyer as a shameless 'litigation stick'. Long Zhongzhi and Zuo Weimin, for example, partly attributed support for the police presence at lawyer–client meetings to popular scepticism concerning the qualifications of lawyers and their lack of a code of professional conduct.[69] It is not surprising that Jonathan Hecht saw the NPC's compromising approach as a mixture of success and failure. While impressed with the new pre-trial involvement of lawyers in the criminal process, Hecht was very disappointed with the limitations imposed on the grounds of 'state secrets'.[70]

Nevertheless, the revised right to counsel has to be placed within the overall reform of trial proceedings. To actualize the right to counsel, the NPC had substantively to overhaul the latter. According to the 1979 CPL, the basic level adjudication of cases had to be conducted by a collegial panel composed of one judge and two people's assessors. In addition, the court proceedings were thrown open to the public and correspondents were to be allowed coverage of the proceedings.[71] In the West, one of the important purposes of having open trial proceedings is to give the public the opportunity to observe whether the accused is fairly dealt with and, if need be, justly condemned. But in the Chinese case, the open trial under the 1979 CPL was created for the purpose of realizing the people's rights to be 'masters in their own court and to participate in state administration'. Trial activities were placed under the people's supervision.[72] At the same time, it was believed that open trial performed an uplifting educational role in society.

In recent years, Chinese jurists increasingly recognized that the problem with the 1979 CPL trial system was that trials invariably ended in guilty verdicts.[73] In effect, the court ideologically confirmed that the power of state had been properly exercised by the security and procuratorial authorities. 'Decide first, trial later' had reduced trial proceedings to meaningless formality. Defence counsel had no real opportunity to present arguments relating to case materials from the defence point of view, and hence the CPL right to counsel had been vitiated in bureaucratic self-justification and the perennial search for public order.

Jurists were quick to point out that the root of the problem lay in Article 108 of the CPL. The logical distinctions within this article's wording had reinforced 'decide first, trial later'. Article 108 presumed a specific pattern of decision-making. The people's court would invariably conduct a review of a case in which a public prosecution had been initiated. Once the facts of a crime were established and the evidence was presented in its entirety, the court would try the case in open session and adjudicate. In the unlikely case where the principal facts had not been clarified, the court could return the case to the procuratorate for additional investigation. In the event that there was no need for a criminal sentence, the court would require the procuratorate to withdraw the case.

This provision presumed that before trial the court would already have adapted to the law's requirement, namely, that 'the facts of crime are clear and the evidence is complete'. Essentially, the court would pass a verdict at the pre-trial stage. In remedial response, on 30 November 1992, the Supreme People's Court (SPC) issued 'This SPC Opinion for Trial Proceedings of First Instance in Cases involving Public Prosecution'. This Opinion sought to enhance the defence counsel's role in the protection of the rights and interests of the accused and to shift the judges into a more neutral position between the defence counsel and procurator. The Opinion outlined a number of significant reforms, including a more generous time allowance for defence preparation, greater qualification to the 1979 emphasis on the pre-trail clarification of the facts of a crime, the granting of the defendant's right to dismiss counsel during trial and to obtain new counsel, insistence on the verdict of innocence in cases where the evidence was unclear and insufficient, the transfer of the court's power to question the defendant to the defence and prosecution, and the required presentation of live evidence instead of the procuratorate's presentation of the written record. The Opinion endorsed a series of pilot projects so as to monitor the outcomes of the SPC initiative.

These reform proposals were designed to enhance the defendant's right to a fair trial, but there was serious opposition from the SPP. Lu Fei and Dai Yuzhong of the SPP lamented the reduction of the procuratorate to the same level as the defendant and the offloading of the court's responsibility to investigate the facts and evidence to the now unhappy procuratorate. In their view, the Opinion weakened the state's power to control crime and violated the 1979 CPL. In response, they proposed a kind of bureaucratic, if not civil, disobedience. They openly urged the lower level people's procuratorates not to cooperate with the people's court in launching the pilot projects which had been featured in the Opinion. This opposition temporarily delayed the SPC process of reform.

After several years of jurist debate on the Opinion, the NPC lawmakers opted for yet another compromise. On the one hand, the 1996 revision endorsed several key components of the Opinion. First, the court's pre-trial examination of filed cases was to focus on procedural legality rather than on the complete review of the facts and evidence.[74] Second, the collegial panel was invited to issue its verdict independently. In serious cases where panel members disagreed, the adjudication panel could be consulted after the trial and not, as in the past, when consultation occurred before the trial.[75] Third, the court was instructed to issue the notification of trial to the defendant ten instead of seven days before trial.[76] Fourth, prosecutors were obliged to provide the court with 'physical' rather than 'live' evidence, as referenced in the Opinion.[77] Fifth, the courts were reminded to issue a not-guilty verdict in cases where the facts and evidence were underwhelming.[78]

In his review, Cui Min concluded that the revisions amounted to a basic change in trial proceedings. The court had dropped its customary inquisitory role to adapt a neutral position vis-à-vis the defence and procuratorate. This requirement shifted the burden of proving guilt from the court to the procuratorate.[79] The revision, however, neglected other aspects in the Opinion, those which sought to reinforce the protection of citizen's rights and interests, including the defence counsel's right to call its own witnesses and to apply for a court adjournment in order to evaluate new evidence.

Long Zhongzhi and Zuo Weimin also concluded that the 1996 revision constituted a structural shift in trial proceedings from the past reliance on the 'scientific' or 'inquisitorial method' to the 'adversarial method'.[80] This apparently galling revision placed the once mighty procuratorate on a par with the defendant so as to protect better the latter's rights and interests. Long and Zuo also calculated that the defence counsel's new right of independent investigation would have a checking effect on the public security and procuratorate who would be under a greater onus to show that they were indeed conducting a fair investigation.

Those opposed to the adversarial method raised a predictable hue and cry over the apprehended loss of procedural efficiency. They pointed out that the new system would not be able to outline the true facts and to respond to state policy requiring 'swift and heavy' punishment of serious crime. Not only would the now eviscerated procedural law free up serious criminals to carry out their evil purpose, but it would also abet inequalities among defendants in that the collection of evidence would vary with their economic conditions and the relative qualities of their defence counsels. Ordinary Chinese, they contended, would never countenance such a trial system especially in the current malignant context of spreading corruption.[81]

Certainly, the law-makers believed that there was a growing public antipathy towards criminals and widespread support for their severe punishment, and it was in this relatively hostile context that reform jurists were successful in pushing for a new balance in the criminal procedural law which would include new reference to the protection of the rights and interests of the accused. In the light of this new balance, the CPL would not longer be regarded merely as an operational guide for the administration of substantive criminal law. Also of significance was the fact that the rationale for procedural change incorporated the explicit need to protect the citizen from the excesses of state administered justice in the much abused name of social stability.

The NPC law-makers did not automatically adopt all of the suggestions of the reform jurists, but they did move away from the exclusive focus on punishment and the comprehensive maintenance of public order. Their lack of resolve on the 'presumption of innocence' has, therefore, to be weighed along with several new procedural initiatives in the related scales of justice and politics.

The process of revision revealed a complicated legislative politics implicating the Ministry of Public Security and the SPP. These authorities had had a great deal of licence as the self-appointed custodians of social stability, law and order. The NPC in effect informed these agencies that they would have to uphold more vigorously the protection of citizen's rights and interests. The 1996 revision confronted these agencies with a new balance in procedural law even at a time when there was strong public concern over the perceived loss of state control vis-à-vis proliferating new crime in the context of accelerated economic growth and unsettling reordering of values.

China's legal scholars have energetically sponsored the significance of criminal law procedure in human rights protection. The regime's desire to link China with the international community and to counter vociferous international human rights criticism gave China's legal reformers important domestic leverage over new legislation even in the face of popular discontent over rising crime rates and spreading corruption. Also, the new emphasis on procedural protection reflected new internal conceptual distinctions between individual and societal interests.

The 1996 CPL revision was part of a more general NPC trend to balance individual and society rights and interests as well as to craft a careful political compromise in its legislative priorities. The NPC, in other words, balanced both content and institutional concerns. The developing significance of rights protection within this new balance has thus far failed to attract the full attention of many scholars in the West. In 1996, Stanley Lubman, for instance, focused on the 'instrumental use of the courts as part of the state apparatus of control'.[82] He emphasized the central importance of social control without detailing the increasing demands among Chinese scholars and the related revision of the law to protect citizen's rights and interests.

The 1996 revision did not go as far as some legal experts had hoped, but it endorsed a new concept of balance, which required a stronger criminal procedural law. It clearly signalled that China's criminal process is moving away from the old predominant 'crime control model' toward the 'due process model'. According to Herbert L. Packer, the crime control model of criminal justice process stresses 'the efficient, expeditious and reliable screening and disposition of persons suspected of crime as the central value to be served by the criminal process'. In contrast, 'the due process model' focuses on the procedural protection of the dignity and autonomy of those involved in the judicial process. The criminal control model is administrative and managerial, while the due process model is adversarial and judicial'.[83]

Chinese jurists, themselves, would contend that China has moved beyond the exclusive reliance on the crime control model, but they would readily concede that it is difficult to classify the 1996 CPL in the exclusive terms of either model. Long Zhongzhi and Zuo Weimin, for example, have shown how the revision reflects the tension between the two models at the different stages of the judicial process. The revised pre-trial proceedings tilted toward the crime control model as the NPC law-makers gave priority to the efficient and expeditious investigation of crime over the protection of the rights and interests of defendants, particularly in cases involving state secrets. On the other hand, the court's inquisitorial role was qualified and due process was accentuated in the subsequent trial proceedings as the court moved into a neutral position and the defence and prosecution were given similar opportunities to present case materials and evidence.[84]

This seemingly conflicting scenario permeated the entire revision and challenged the conventional unity of the judiciary with state administration. The new conceptual balance also altered the conventional institutional balance of legal relations within the judicial process as these had traditionally presumed 'mutual cooperation and restriction' (*xianghu hezuo, xianghu zhiyue*) between the judiciary, public security and procuratorate.[85] On the one hand, the revision weakened the procuratorate's power by eliminating 'exemption for prosecution' and by placing the prosecutors on a pare with defence counsels in trial proceedings. The procuratorate complained that it was no longer in a position to exercise its right of judicial supervision over the courts as sanctioned in Article 129 of the 1982 State Constitution.

On the other hand, this loss was compensated for in other terms. The procuratorate gained in its supervisory position vis-à-vis public security in its enhanced control over the filing of a case against a suspect. However, if the revision strengthened supervision over investigation, it reduced the extent of supervision over the court's adjudication.[86] This more complex pattern of institutional qualification likely originates with the transitional nature of the CPL as it incrementally reflects the new NPC balancing strategy vis-à-vis the protection of rights and interests of society and the individual. And at least one prominent expert has suggested that the 1996 revision, while very important, is only the first stage in an extensive reform of procedural law.[87]

Indeed, the 1996 CPL left a number of unresolved issues. Bai Xiuyun, for example, pointed out that it did not address judicial independence and that the latter is crucial to the protection of citizen's rights and interests. 'Judicial independence' in China has not had the same connotations in the West.[88] There has never been the opportunity to create a 'separation of powers', but since the early 1980s there has been an interest in *'shenpan duli'* connoting the reinforcement of the independence of court proceedings vis-à-vis direct Party interference in sentencing. In this latter sense, Bai supported the autonomy of judges and the right of the accused to an independent trial.

Such a suggestion, however, runs counter to ingrained institutional bias. There has been almost no latitude for either a judge or collegial panel to reach a decision independent of interference from the adjudication committee or administrative section of the people's courts, especially in the current context where judicial activities are so dependent on local government administration for resources.[89] Bai also raised a concern over the content of Article 93 of the 1996 CPL requiring that the accused answer honestly all of the questions put. In her view this article abetted self-incrimination by denying the accused the right to silence and, moreover, the same article transferred the burden of producing evidence on to the accused and this violated the presumption of innocence.[90]

Song Yinghui's study on the comparative law of non-self-incrimination noted that this principle would be of special significance as a means of countering the exaggerated importance of confession in China's legal tradition. Song attempted to balance the societal need for truth and procedural efficiency with due process which protects the accused against forced confession. Song accordingly placed non-self-incrimination alongside a number of mutually reinforcing principles such as the equal status of the defendant, the idea of subject in criminal procedural law theory, the presumption of innocence and the burden of proof.[91] Song saw in Article 93 an excuse to reinforce the idea that the questioning of suspects is the major means of obtaining evidence and determining guilt. He regretted that, while neither the 1996 CPL, nor the 1997 CL endorsed the right to remain silent (*ziwo guizui yuanze*), they did reference the obligation to state the truth (*rushi chenshu*).[92]

Even given the detailed weakness in the 1996 revision to the CPL, this revision represented on balance a major shift in procedural law, which was self-consciously predicated in a new balancing of the rights of society and the individual. In historical terms, it was a major step forward. The political context was not entirely friendly, and Chinese legal experts still had to operate within the practical context of the power of the CCP. Even given these very real limitations, there were significant opportunities to shift the weight of the criminal process away from an exclusive preoccupation with social control towards a qualified, but newly substantive reference to the protection of rights and interests. This trend was confirmed and amplified in the extensive 1997 revision of the Criminal Law.

The changing substantive principles of Chinese criminal law

Possibly China's senior most authority on the criminal law, People's University Professor Gao Mingxuan, described the 1997 revision of the criminal law in the following terms:

The new criminal code... strengthens the protective function of the law. [As placed] in a prominent position in Chapter 1 of the General Principles, the new criminal code establishes the principles that crimes must be legally defined, that the criminal law must be equally applied to everyone, and that punishment must fit the crime. It has abolished the system of analogy in the 1979 criminal code that is contrary to the principle that crimes must be legally defined. This is the most noticeable point of revision.... The establishment of these basic criminal law principles will contribute to the preferences for the rule of law over the rule of man, equality over privilege and fairness over favouritism and fraudulent practice.[93]

Gao effusively welcomed the revision on a number of counts. He cited new emphasis on leniency for young offenders, the strengthening of the citizen's rights to appropriate self-defence, the introduction of relatively comprehensive regulations concerning the violation of basic civil rights, including personal rights, democratic rights, the right to work, property rights and rights concerning marriage and the family. Gao noted the equal application of the criminal law irrespective of the social status of the accused as well as the equal application of penalties and the rejection of 'heavy penalty-ism' (*zhongxingzhuyi*). Gao conceded that the revision was especially needed, given that the underlying systemic preference for heavy criminal law penalties to deter crime is 'deeply rooted among the people', and even judges continue to put 'their blind faith in the effect of heavy penalties'.

Indeed, the 1997 CL revision constituted a self-conscious break with tradition. It embraced a self-consciously new approach to the development of the criminal law as it adapts to changes in society with new principle and procedure and the creation of new categories of crime in order to cope with the societal impact of economic reform. In addition, it favoured more stipulated description of the components of specific crime, particularly but not exclusively in the area of economic crime. While such stipulation does not, in and of itself, guarantee a greater degree of lawful protection of rights against arbitrary state politics, the 1997 CL agreed with the 1996 CPL in its challenge to the state's 'flexible' interpretation of law in undefined areas of crime where there was a pronounced lack of exact stipulation. Moreover, the revision also reflected changes in the prioritization of class struggle, state interests and social control as the criminal law's substantive purposes were explicitly re-aligned with the policy purposes of economic reform.[94]

In a very important act of political symbolism, the revision dropped terminology relating to 'counterrevolutionary crime' and highlighted new values concerning the importance of protection of citizen rights and interests as against arbitrary politics and corrupt judicial practice. As 'class' passed into history, so did 'counterrevolution' and 'flexibility'. In its alternative subscription to the two cognate principles, *nullum crimen sine lege; nulla poena sine lege* (no crime without a law; no punishment without a law), and its corresponding rejection of analogy, the revision endorsed a major change in the principles governing the making and application of the criminal law.

Professors Donald Clarke and James Feinerman recently discussed the critical importance of criminal law noting that it '. . . it is in the realm of criminal law and human rights discourse that much of the Chinese conception of law itself is worked out'.[95] In gross political terms, the criminal law has always enjoyed a pre-eminent status within the Chinese legal system as it has served as one of the most convenient means of asserting the state's requirements for social control. The scope, organization and underlying jurisprudential assumptions of the new criminal law are, therefore, relevant to ongoing assessment of contemporary legal reform and the related struggle for the 'rule of law' in China. As was the case in the earlier CPL revision, the stipulated content of the new criminal law obviously encompasses a transitional mix of continuity and discontinuity.

In 1997, China's leaders brought the priorities of economic reform directly into the criminal law. Does such service in the cause of economic change constitute a basically new course, or are we merely dealing with a refurbished, softer variant of 'state instrumentalism'? In the light of continuing focus on social control, value change and the related changes in the nature of crime, the criminal law might still be understood as a legitimate instrument of state policy, if not as a tool of state instrumentalism. In the context of revision to the criminal procedural law, Long Zhongzhi and Zuo Wemin anticipated a mixing of the models of social control and due process. The relationship between the state and criminal law has always been placed explicitly within prevailing perspective on the state–society relationship; however, the 1997 CL is remarkable in its reiterated support for the predictable protection of non-state interests based upon reiterated and newly endorsed substantive principles such as equality before the law, 'no crime, without law' and 'no punishment without law'.

The 1997 revision highlighted the failure of the 1979 CL to respond effectively to new economic crime as well as its failure to protect adequately the rights and interests of citizens. In the early 1980s, there was only an *ad hoc* remedial approach to plug the holes in the CL 1979.

Internal circulars were initially used to remedy confusion originating in the vaguely defined provisions of 1979. There was, nonetheless, glaring inconsistency in the application of the law. In the light of increasing trends in economic crime and deteriorating social order, and in order to legitimize a series of anti-crime campaigns, the NPCSC began in 1982 to amend the 1979 CL in a piecemeal fashion. By late 1996 it had already issued a total of 22 decisions. This *ad hoc* revealed the original failure to provide proper stipulation of crime in the light of the qualitative change in the nature of crime.

For many of China's most influential legal scholars, this incrementalism insulted the integrity of the law and violated the newly cherished principle of non-retroactivity which they had fought so hard to include in the 1979 CL. For instance, the 1982 NPCSC decision on severe punishment of economic crime stipulated that crimes committed before the promulgation of the decision could be punished according to the decision. People's University criminal law professors, Zhao Bingzhi and He Xingwang reviewed the 22 NPCSC decisions of 1980–96 and concluded that the *ad hoc* amendment process had grossly violated the principle, *nullum crimen sine lege; nulla poena sine lege*. The rational fit between the nature of crime and lawful punishment had broken down in a arbitrary resort to severe punishment, and the amendments exacerbated the ambiguity inherent in the 1979 criminal law approach.

Without any hesitation, Zhao and He stated that the 1980–96 decisions contradicted the 1979 CL itself.[96] Even the Minister of Justice, Xiao Yang, agreed. In his report on the 1997 revision, he acknowledged retrospectively that the wholesale revision of the 1979 CL was 'an urgent demand of China's judicial practice'. The 1979 CL had failed to keep up with the times.[97] The lack of proper criminal law stipulation contrasted conspicuously with the more comprehensive development of economic legislation and related supplementary regulation which had rapidly developed in response to Deng Xiaoping's 'Southern Tour Theory'.[98]

In the new era of market reform, Party leaders quickly recognized the compelling utility of law in regulating the increasingly complex behaviour of a new range of economic actors in society. Although, as was confirmed in Chapter 4, there has been a lot of confusion over the terms property and ownership, it was still generally recognized that the law's predictability could no longer be automatically sacrificed on the altar of 'flexibility'. If economic reform was to succeed, economic outcomes had to be predicted with greater reference to firm legal understandings.[99] Much of this emphasized the separation of law from the state and policy, and it ran against the natural grain of Party instincts for politically dictated social control based on unreserved application of severe punishment. The fundamental purposes of law were revised to include reference to 'the market economy is a rule of law economy', *shichang jingji shi fazhi jingji*, and 'running the country according to the law and creating a socialist rule of law country' *yifa zhi guo, jianshe shehuizhuyi fazhi guo*.[100]

Chinese legal scholars repeatedly justified the comprehensive revision of the criminal law in relation to the expedient facilitation of socialist market reform. They lauded the technical legal genius of law and its capacity for the rational mediation of competing interests. They now expected the 1997 CL to transcend unpredictable political purposes. Possibly, there was more to this than a disingenuous rehabilitation of 'state instrumentalism'. Certainly, the issue of equality before the law has to be glossed with reference to the strong new emphasis on protecting the credibility of the judicial process in response to spreading corruption during economic reform. Reformers called for the criminal law protection of the newly emerged rights and interests of individual citizens and the contemporaneous limitation of the coercive power of judicial institutions.

After 1992, senior criminal law scholars disavowed the anachronistic political purposes of the 1979 CL, the main object of which was to suppress counterrevolutionary crime rather than to facilitate the new economy.[101] The underlying approach of 1979 was 'general stipulations are better than specific ones' (*yi cu bu yi xi*). This approach was condemned for its exclusive focus on collective rather than individual interests and for its dismal failure to suppress official corruption. Many critics were somewhat frustrated in their contention that the law should highlight accurate rather than 'severe' punishment.[102] Rejecting flexibility and analogy, they endorsed the specific elaboration of the categories of 'crime' based on the principles, 'no crime without law' and 'no punishment without law'.

Reference to 'socialist market economy' called for the comprehensive definition of new categories of 'crime', and the related reconsideration of the purpose, methods and principles of criminal law punishment so as to better serve the market. The provisions of the criminal law were, therefore, greatly expanded to deal with 'economic crime'. For the first time, punishment was formally, if not always practically, correlated with economic benefit, as distinct from the automatic imposition of severe penalties. Under the impact of economic reform, the criminal law was expected to consolidate 'equality before the law' and *nullum crimen sine lege; nulla poena sine lege*.[103]

The more or less progressive outlines of the 1997 revisions should not have come as a surprise.[104] They were clearly anticipated in an emerging consensus within the community of jurists and senior legal scholars.[105] Analysis, however, must also account for disturbing continuity in the areas of severe punishment and social control between the 1979 and the 1997 CL. This anomalous continuity conflicts with popular Weberian assumptions which presume the progressive development of due process in the market context, but it can be explained partly with reference to growing public antipathy towards malfeasance and the proliferation of serious economic crime. The following analysis tentatively explores the competing dimensions of criminal law development in the transition from class struggle to the 'socialist market'.

Nullum crimen sine lege and the termination of analogy

The lack of precise stipulation of crime has often been seen in the West as a statist opportunity for political manipulation of the judicial process at the expense of the rights of citizens to a fair trial. The 1979 CL, like the 1979 CPL, took new steps towards rights protection; under the 1997 revision to the CL, however, there was a pronounced subscription to protection in new emphases on *nullum crimen sine lege* and *nulla poena sine lege*. The 1997 CL retained the general structure of the 1979 CL, consisting of General and Special Provisions, but it sharply reduced the politically and ideologically loaded terminology in first two articles of the 1979 CL, which Berman and his colleagues had regarded as the most onerous features of the 1979 CL.[106] These articles had originally enshrined Marxism–Leninism Mao Zedong Thought as 'guiding ideology'.[107]

In the 1997 CL, the 1979 CL references to 'counterrevolution' and 'the cause of socialist revolution' were unceremoniously dropped. The 'system of the dictatorship of the proletariat was belatedly replaced with 'the people's democratic dictatorship and socialist system', bringing the criminal law into better alignment with the 1982 state constitution. The 1997 CL was no longer burdened with the multifaceted legally confused struggle against counterrevolution, but was instead to focus on fighting economic crime in the new era of market relations.[108]

The 1997 adaptation to *nullem crimen sine lege* hinged on the treatment of 'analogy' (*leitui*), whereby unstated categories of crime were freely extrapolated from supposedly analogous crimes which had already been fully stipulated in the law's provisions. The 1997 CL flatly rejected analogy in the name of better process and rational legal culture. The greater reliance on stipulation does not automatically guarantee a consistently progressive content in the law's specific provisions, but it was unquestionably rooted in a challenge to the abuse of open-ended and politically inspired application of general principle through analogy.

The 1979 CL had begun to place a new but certainly not exclusive emphasis upon the protection of the people from criminals. The 1997 CL reflected an even stronger perspective on the protection of the rights and interests of the people vis-à-vis the coercive dimensions of state power and judicial administration. In the past, analogy had been used extensively to buttress the interests of the state. Prior to the fashioning of the 1979 CL, analogy had been included in two earlier acts for punishing counterrevolutionaries, namely, 'Chinese Soviet Republic's Provisions for Punishing Counterrevolutionaries' (1934) and 'People's Republic of China's Provisions for Punishing Counterrevolutionaries' (1951). Subsequently, the 1979 CL significantly entrenched analogy within the criminal code.[109]

A few NPC 1979 CL drafters dared to highlight the past abuse of analogy, arguing that law based upon anological extrapolation would not provide a clear and adequate basis for public differentiation between right and wrong in the law. The repudiation of the 'gang of four's 'leftist thesis' reduced the orbit of class struggle. There was no longer a need to mobilize the instruments of the state against a rising 'new bourgeoisie', as a class generated within the ranks of the Party. However, mainstream opinion still maintained that analogy was necessary to protect socialist society from criminals and a presumed handful of residual class enemies.

Gao Mingxuan, a key participant in the 1979 CL, sponsored its retention in the light of China's huge population and territory and the extraordinary extent of China's contemporary transition. Since criminal activities would inevitably and ceaselessly change, Gao argued that the criminal law needed analogy to adapt to rapidly changing societal circumstances and the related changing categories in the nature of crime. Moreover, Gao believed that 'flexibility' (*linghuoxing*) could be synthesized with principle; hence he contended that the principle of 'no crime without a law and no punishment without a law' could be made consistent with 'flexibility' as one of five central requirements in the development of the legal system.[110]

Retention was widely criticized by Western scholars. Hungdah Chiu, for example, pointed out that the use of analogy in Article 79 of the 1979 CL undermined 'the basic spirit of "rule of law"' and subsequently conflicted with the 1982 state constitution's commitment to the rule of law.[111] During the drafting of the 1997 CL, the comparative merits of analogy and *nullum crimen sine lege* were openly debated. The advocates of retention theory (*baoliu shuo*) attempted to discredit the advocates of deletion theory (*feichu shuo*). The 'retentionists' reiterated their arguments, those which had temporarily succeeded in 1979.[112] They disingenuously claimed that the newly emerging emphasis on commodity economy placed an even greater premium on the need for analogy as new types of crime would ceaselessly proliferate together with the newly emerging opportunities for criminal activity in the marketplace. Moreover, they hailed analogy as a politically correct Chinese legal invention.[113]

In 1997, however, Gao Mingxuan switched sides, aligning with the emerging consensus in the legal community. Gao now claimed that such deletion would not create difficulties in protecting the new social and economic order. He put a new spin on flexibility while severing its odious connection with analogy. He contended that in the event of the manifestation of non-stipulated harmful social activity, the criminal law could still seek redress in special decisions. In his view, this approach had worked in dealing with economic crime activities in the recent past.[114] Gao reminded the retentionists that the most serious criminal activities had already been defined in the criminal law.

Gao drew Party attention to the fact that deletion would bring China's criminal law into a desirable alignment with accepted western norms relating to the rule of law. He did not, however, anticipate any loss in the law's practical capacity for the protection of society's interest. Perhaps somewhat defensively, he underscored the infrequent application of analogy noting that over the last 17 years the Supreme Court had approved only 73 applications of analogy.[115] Gao's argument was designed to pacify conservative Party opinion, but for the Chinese legal community as a whole, the deletion of analogy was a defining moment in the history of Chinese legal development.

Ma Kechang rushed to take advantage of the Party's latest pronouncements, arguing that the continued use of analogy in a criminal code would lead to the arbitrary determination of crime and punishment at the expense of 'running the country according to law'.[116] For Zhao Bingzhi, a rising star, and former student of Gao Mingxuan, and his co-researcher, Xiao Zhonghua, an active participant in the framing of the provisions of the 1997 CL, the use of analogy contradicted the rule of law. In their view, the 1979 CL retention of analogy proceeded from the bogus principle, 'determining crime without law'.[117] They wanted the criminal law to balance the protection of society and the protection of citizen's rights and interests. Retention in 1979 had placed the protection of society above the protection of rights and interests of individuals. On the contrary, these authors now believed that emphases on severe punishment and the limitation of the state's powers of coercion should only be used to support criminal law protection of the rights and interests of individual citizens.

To drive home their point, Zhao and Xiao warned that analogy encourages judicial institutions to intervene improperly in legislative activity. They also contended that the market economy requires a criminal law, which democratically reinforces the notion of equality before the law. This implies that the legislature should stipulate explicitly crime and punishment in law so that individuals can predict the consequences of their activities. Conversely, analogy serves to obscure the real nature of such activity, and cannot provide legal guidelines, which help support legally predictable behaviour in the market. Zhao and Xiao concluded that, in so far as the criminal law is rooted in analogy, it cannot truly facilitate the rational development of contract between the individual and the state in terms of the clarification of what behaviours are allowed and what are the desired outcomes of people's economic and social activities.[118]

Zhao Bingzhi and Xiao Zhonghua likewise challenged traditional theory on the purposes of criminal law. In the past, scholars in the legal establishment were inclined to assume a benign identity between the interests of the individual and the interests of state and society whereas Zhao and Xiao dealt with the possible clash of interests. They argued that the power of the state had to be limited so as to better protect the rights and interests of individual citizens.

Perhaps Gao Mingxuan placed himself 'on the side of the angels'. Adjusting to a groundswell of jurist opinion, he endorsed an explicit stipulation in the draft 1997 CL that 'only those committing acts clearly and explicitly stipulated as crimes under the law should be convicted and sentenced. Those committing acts which have not been defined as criminal acts in existing criminal laws should not be sentenced'.[119] The NPC incorporated similar phraseology directly into the 1997 CL.[120] Gao emphasized that entrenching *nullum crimen sine lege; nulla poena sine lege* reinforced 'running the country according to law' and demonstrated the willingness of the state to punish the criminals according to law as well as to limit the power of judicial institutions so as to protect 'human rights'.[121]

The 1997 revision altered the purposes of criminal law. The latter could no long exclusively focus on the protection of the state's overt interests; it had to balance the interests of the society and the rights and interests of the citizens vis-à-vis the power of the state's judicial institutions. The Minister of Justice, Xiao Yang, put his own gloss on this basic change when he explained:

> the principle of convicting a crime and meting out punishment according to the law has replaced reasoning by analogy. This is historical progress symbolizing an important step taken by China in 'running the country according to the law'; and it has as much epoch-making significance as the elimination of determining guilt by presumption of guilt from the criminal procedural law. This principle, which can prevent arbitrariness in convicting crime, provides a more powerful legal guarantee for citizens' personal freedoms and rights, as well as a solid legal foundation for the judicial organ to severely punish crimes and to protect people's interests according to the law.[122]

The clear rejection of 'flexibility' and the new emphasis on *nullum crimen sine lege* was also reflected in defining specific crime in a more detailed fashion in the Special Provisions other than those governing state security. The new law removed three catch-all crimes (*koudaizui*), namely, dereliction of duty, hooliganism and profiteering.[123] These provisions were dismissed as 'general and fuzzy'.[124] The 1979 CL had failed to provide adequate and clear definitions of these crimes. The interpretation and application of these provisions varied from person to person and from place to place and this ambiguity was often linked to the spread of corruption within the judicial process itself. For instance, Article 160 of the 1979 CL defined 'hooliganism' to include assembling as 'a crowd to have brawls, stir up fights and cause trouble, humiliate women, or engage in other hooligan activities undermining public order'. The more serious dimension of such crime included the undermining of 'public order'. The judicial process used this vague provision to punish the apparently social deviant behaviour that the criminal law had not clearly stipulated.

In 1984, the People's Supreme Court and People's Supreme Procuratorate had jointly issued long answers to questions concerning the application of the 1979 criminal law in dealing with cases of hooliganism. In this interior circular, 'other hooligan activities' were interpreted broadly to include new social phenomenon such as sexual harassment, orgy (i.e. excessive sexual indulgence at a wild party), homosexual behaviour with foreigners, and other presumably distasteful sexually related behaviours.¹²⁵ It seems that the interpretation of the 'other hooligan activities' not only had great latitude but also varied uncomfortably with the state's changing evaluation of public order. In a standard criminal law textbook, *Xingfa xue* (Criminal Law Science), authored and endorsed by the Ministry of Education in 1983, homosexual behaviour had not been regarded as 'hooliganism'.¹²⁶

In practice, this term 'hooliganism', itself, turned out to be legally abusive.¹²⁷ According to the 1979 CL, the crime of hooliganism can be punished by 7 years' imprisonment. According to the 'Decision of the Standing Committee of the NPC Regarding the Severe Punishment of Criminal Elements Who Seriously Endanger Public Security' (September 2, 1983), a person who committed such a crime could even be sentenced to death. The consequence of convenient application of this provision by many local courts can be very serious. With regard to the definitions of dereliction of duty and profiteering, similar problems existed. In the 1997 CL, these three offences are divided into many more detailed and more explicitly stipulated crimes.¹²⁸

Nulla poena sine lege versus 'flexibility'

The principle, 'the punishment must fit the crime', is basic to the western sense of natural justice, and the 1997 revision needs to be scrutinized in the light of outstanding criticisms of the politically inspired use of analogy and the revised reasoning which alternatively sustained 'no punishment without a law', *nulla poena sine lege*.

The 1979 CL was open-ended in its approach to punishment. Article 59, for example, stipulated that 'where the circumstances of a criminal element are such as to give him [or her] a heavier punishment or a lesser punishment under the stipulations of this law, he [she] shall be sentenced to a punishment within the legally prescribed limits of punishment'. The latter encompassed several alternative types of punishments, such as fixed-term imprisonment, life imprisonment or even the death penalty.

In the case of fixed-term imprisonment, the 1979 CL provided a wide range of prison terms, sometimes from 3 to 10 years or from 5 to 15 years. There was insufficient stipulation to guide judicial personnel in choosing a suitable type of punishment or a certain term of imprisonment. The law did not clearly specify the nature of the relevant circumstances. Given the wide range of the legal limits of punishment, final determination of the sentence often depended on extra-judicial factors such as policies formed during early '1980s anti-crime campaigns, including 'severely and swiftly punishing' (*congzhong congkuai*), and 'strike hard' (*yanda*).

Western scholars really disliked the absence of detailed guidelines for the assignment of punishment in the 1979 CL.[129] Internally, this state of affairs was openly rationalized on the basis of 'flexibility'. Judges were expected to exercise their personal, if not their political, judgment in meting out punishment so as to implement most effectively the policy of 'combining punishment and leniency'. The latter had been directly incorporated into the 1979 criminal code as a 'legitimate' approach to the reform and education of criminals. A similarly deliberate vagueness plagued the 1980–96 NPCSC decisions.[130]

Not surprisingly, flexibility fostered inconsistent sentencing and showcased the irrational fit of punishment to crime. Minor crime often attracted severe punishment and major crime, leniency. The drafters of the 1997 CL responded, stipulating in Article 5 that the 'the severity of punishments must be commensurate with the crime committed by an offender and the criminal responsibility he [she] bears'.[131] For the same reason, these drafters often deleted from the criminal law vague and slippery terminology such as 'when the circumstances are grave', 'the consequences are severe', or 'where the amount of money involved is great'.

The 1997 CL highlighted the issue of 'the punishment must fit the crime' in the hope of remedying the outstanding problems originating with the NPCSC decisions. For instance, the 1983 decision detailing severe punishment of criminals for those who had seriously endangered public security had negated the principle of *nulla poena sine lege* in allowing for the imposition of punishment in excess of the standards stipulated in the 1979 CL. This even allowed for the imposition of non-stipulated capital punishment, and these features of the 1983 decision subsequently came under heavy internal criticism within the legal community.[132]

Influential legal scholars registered their concerns about the excessive resort to capital punishment. This was not so much a rejection of capital punishment, *per se*, but an objection to its flagrant proliferation in application. They often proposed reducing the categories for such punishment while increasing, in comparable cases, possible prison terms from 15 to 20 years. They had argued that such proposed revision would guarantee greater openness, impartiality, and leniency in a more rational assignment of punishment.[133] Some reformers added that such revision would better reflect an essential element of humanitarianism working from within the principles of the criminal law.[134] In short, the revision of the criminal law was part of an ongoing discourse on the punishment fitting the 'crime'.

Retroactivity versus non-retroactivity

The 1997 revision endorsed *nullum crimen sine lege* and *nulla poena sine lege*, and it eschewed retroactivity. According to the legal expert, Jerome Hall, *nullum crimen sine lege, nulla poena sine lege* and non-retroactivity are essential to the principle of legality in western penal law. Non-retroactivity expresses the temporal essence of the principle of legality that the criminal law assumes must have existed when the conduct at issue occurred. In short, was such conduct 'criminal' at the time of its commission? Hall also stated that 'the rationale of non-retroactivity [opposes] the lawless infliction of suffering, aggravated by the fact that this is done by public officials claiming authority to inflict that "punishment"'.[135]

The 1979 CL subscribed to non-retroactivity; however, this principle was insulted in subsequent legislative practice. Alarmed by early 1980s signs of social and economic distress, the NPCSC diverged from the 1979 CL in order to deal with apparently surging criminal activity through the wider application of 'severe punishment'. The NPCSC's 'Decision Regarding the Severe Punishment of Criminals who Seriously Undermine the Economy' (8 March 1982) and 'Decision Regarding the Severe Punishment of Criminal Elements Who Seriously Endanger Public Security' (2 September 1983) violated the 1979 principle of non-retroactivity.

In what was surely a heartening chapter in the struggle to establish the rule of law, some jurists criticized what they regard as an unacceptably political appropriation of the law by NPC law-makers. Luo Shaping, for example, invoked constitutional law, arguing that the NPCSC revisions must be repealed and excluded from the revised criminal law. According to Section 3 of Article 67 of the 1982 Constitution, the Standing Committee of the NPC has powers 'to enact, when the NPC is not in session, partial supplements and amendments to statutes enacted by the NPC provided that they do not contravene the basic principles of these statutes'.[136] The two NPCSC decisions were in fact exposed for having contravened the basic law incorporated in the 1979 CL provisions on non-retroactivity, and they were nullified in the 1997 revision.[137]

Law and 'economic crime' in the marketplace[138]

The 1997 criminal law revision ended any reference to the law as an instrument of class struggle, instead elevating the economic purposes of the law. The attempt to achieve comprehensive and precise stipulation of economic crime was particularly designed to facilitate the law's role in the new socialist market. The 15 articles in Chapter 3 of the 1979 CL, for example, were replaced with Articles 140 through 231 under the newly entitled Chapter 3, 'Crimes of Undermining the Order of Socialist Market Economy'. A new independent chapter (Chapter 8) was created solely to deal with bribery and embezzlement. This particular revision reflected the high political priority assigned to the problem of official malfeasance.

Fifteen articles in the 1997 CL Chapter 8 greatly expanded the two related articles in Chapters 5 and 8 of the 1979 CL. Obviously, this was an attempt to stipulate comprehensively the proliferating types of economic crime and the related changes in procedure; however, at the macro-level of revision there was a new balancing of principles of social control and protection. The revision not only entrenched a new strategy of comprehensive stipulation as against analogy, it also incorporated a strong element of substantive continuity, highlighting the importance of social control in the transitional context of value change and political instability.[139]

This continuity should not have been a surprise. The rule of law had been sold to the Party as necessary to the new economic order and as the only viable remedy against the spreading corruption which was threatening to engulf the regime. Corruption, in law, is largely a matter of 'economic crime'. There was a predisposition to treat the evolving configurations of 'economic crime' under the more compellingly punitive requirements of the criminal rather than economic law; just as the new focus on judicial corruption also required the strengthening of the punitive dimensions of administrative law. Various crimes relating to economic activity had been stipulated in the 1950s regulations governing embezzlement and in the 1979 CL; however, this was a woefully inadequate basis for understanding the complexity of 'economic crime' as it mushroomed in the transition to the socialist market.

Despite new waves of 'criminal' activity, in the early 1980s, the formal definition of 'economic crime' was haphazard and reactive. At the same time, there was, however, growing controversy over the contemporary relevance of counterrevolutionary crime, particularly in relation to the appropriateness of capital punishment in this area during economic modernization. Ironically, even as critics zeroed in on the political nature of the Special Provisions of the criminal law on counterrevolution, the criminal law on capital punishment for economic crime was extended.[140]

The 1982 NPC Standing Committee decisions had expanded the use of capital punishment for serious economic crime, which 'undermines the economy' and causes 'social harm'. Such severe punishment was stipulated for new categories of crime relating to smuggling, profiteering and speculation, selling narcotics and stealing and exporting precious cultural relics. Officials implicated in abetting such crime were presumably to receive more severe punishment than their complicit civilian counterparts as a matter of demonstrating the state's new resolve.[141] These decisions were pushed through the NPC as an alarm bell went off in the Party leadership. However, they produced subsequent controversy within legal circles over the appropriate correlation of crime and punishment, the extension of the death penalty to cover new categories of serious economic crime and the appropriate division of labour between economic and criminal law for dealing with serious economic crime.[142]

The law on economic crime has been continuously expanded so as to keep up with the evolving criminal dimensions of commodity production and illicit market opportunity. The NPCSC on 21 January 1988 passed separate regulations on smuggling and on bribery, embezzlement and the misappropriation of state funds. The latter set of regulations governing criteria of punishment provided public detail relating to state personnel, state-owned enterprise and public institutions which previously was circulated only on a limited and confidential basis.

The Supreme Court and SPP had originally attempted through judicial interpretation to clarify the necessary elements of the crimes of embezzlement in a July 1985 circular, 'Answers to Relating to the Application of Law in Dealing with Economic Crime'.[143] The July 1985 notation quickly became inadequate to the evolving criminal dimensions of commodity production and related illicit market opportunity, and the NPCSC was obliged, on 21 January 1988, to pass separate regulations creating a new distinction between the more serious crime of 'embezzlement', *tanwu*, and the crime of misappropriation of public funds or *nuoyong gongkuan zui*.[144] The inappropriate diversion of funds was separated out from embezzlement in order to satisfy judicial opinion, which had lobbied against the overly severe punishment stipulated for 'embezzlement'. The SPC and SPP further entrenched this distinction in the 6 November 1989 joint circular, 'Answers to the Questions Regarding the Application of the "Complementary Regulations on Embezzlement and Bribery"'.[145]

The issue of state personnel complicity in tax evasion was later covered in the supplementary regulations passed by the NPCSC on 4 September 1992. State personnel in state enterprise and public institutions involved in the economic crime of counterfeiting of trademark

Judicial Justice 217

were dealt with under supplementary regulations passed by the NPCSC in 24 February 1993. The 2 July 1993 NPCSC decision on the production and adulteration of commodities further extended the categories of the death penalty to cover crime relating to the production and sale of adulterated commodities which result in severe harm to consumer health or cause death.[146]

China's jurists debated the utility of severe criminal law punishment, including life imprisonment and capital punishment as the optimal means for controlling economic crime. There was also cognate controversy over the criminal law scope of 'economic crime'. The authoritative 1991 edition of *Faxue da cidian* suggested, for example, that the 'object' of economic crime relates exclusively to damage caused to the economic order in terms of criminal activity jeopardizing the production, exchange, distribution and consumption of commodities.[147] This definition would rather exclusively locate economic crime under Chapter 3 of the Special Provisions of the 1979 Chinese Criminal Law entitled 'Crimes of Undermining the Socialist Economic Order'. Such a strict view left little interpretative room for crimes against property, such as grand theft, fraud and embezzlement – crimes which fell under Chapter 5 of the Special Provisions of the Criminal Law, entitled 'Crimes of Property Violation'.[148]

Chapter 3 of the 1979 CL Special Provisions, however, conflicted with both the 1982 NPCSC revisions to the criminal law regarding serious economic crime and leading contemporary jurist opinion. It was more loosely inclusive in the scattered povisions 'economic crime' under Chapter 3 and 5 as well as under Chapter 6 which relates to crime 'disrupting the order of social administration', covering a multitude of sins such as making, selling, buying and transporting narcotics, smuggling stolen precious cultural relics, and under Chapter 8 which treats bribery under 'dereliction of duty'.[149] Unfortunately, the 1997 revision did not bring closure to all of the outstanding controversies over the real scope of 'economic crime'. It did, however, make headway in terms of a new definition of 'organized crime'.

Analysing the comparative range of economic crime in China and the West, Gu Xiaorong, at the Shanghai Academy of Social Science, noted that, in the West, many 'economic crimes' are considered more innocuously as 'white-collar crime'. While they may potentially disturb the state's economic order and cause harm to society, they are, nonetheless, treated as minor offences requiring only fines as punishment. The same crimes in the PRC, inclusive of crimes against property such as grand theft, fraud, smuggling and the sale of narcotics, may attract severe punishment such as imprisonment and capital punishment. Gu critiqued the 1982 NPCSC revisions for exaggerating the notion of 'economic crime' in the minds of public and judicial officials. Apparently, the NPC decisions had obscured the distinction between minor and serious economic crimes and the rational relation between the punishment and the crime.

Gu put the problem in its social and political context, noting that public expectations of severe punishment were running high in light of the spread of corruption and the government's apparent failure to contain the proliferation of economic crime. Gu, nonetheless, recommended the limitation of economic crime to minor offences. He sought to exclude from the categorization of 'economic crime', offences such as grand theft, fraud, buying and selling narcotics, which directly undermined the state's economic order.[150]

Similarly, Chen Chunjian, a Shijiachuang law scholar, regretted the lack of a scientific definition of 'economic crime'. He argued against what Gao had called 'heavy penalty-ism' which neglected the potential deterrence available in the stipulated correlation of criminal behaviour and punishment. Chen drew on western legal experience to argue that the current *'li er bu yan'* (punishment and no stipulation) had to be modified towards *'yan er bu li'* (stipulation and hardly any punishment).[151]

Apart from this central issue of deterrence and social control, there is continuing controversy over the definition of criminal responsibility. Chinese jurists and law-makers have divided over 'positive' (*kending shuo*), as distinguished from 'negative theory' (*fouding shuo*) on the issue of natural person and legal person responsibility. As the established theory, the latter propounded that the criminal law can only deal with 'natural persons' and that criminal responsibility can only be borne by those who have physically committed a criminal act [152]

However, proponents of 'positive theory' wanted to deploy the punitive dimensions of criminal law in response to economic crime by 'legal persons'. Their theory was suspect in so far as it seemed to invoke British and American criminal law thinking. Nevertheless, foreign capitalists have increasingly assumed the status of legal person, and there may have been a selective disinclination to apply the full rigour of the criminal law to American and European investors for fear of compromising future trade and investment opportunities. Article 30 of 1997 CL, nevertheless, introduced the criminal responsibility of legal persons such as companies, institutions, enterprises, organizations and groups, and Article 31 stipulated potential fines for these persons.

Differentiating 'counterrevolution' and 'endangering state security'

One of the most salient changes in the 1997 CL relates to the deletion of the Special Provisions on the 'crimes of counterrevolution' (*fangeming zui*) and their replacement by 'crimes endangering state security' (*weihai guojia anquan zui*). Some observers have already dismissed this as casuistry. This view appears to be supported in dissembling domestic argument to the effect that all states have to deal with matters like 'counterrevolution' and that the latter is much the same as 'treason' in the foreign context.

Possibly some Chinese legal reformers may have been too eager to highlight the abandonment of such terminology, but a general reading of Chinese politics and ideology should leave no doubt as to the critical importance of this terminology in Party life and ideology. In the authors' opinion, the elimination of 'counterrevolution' is an important part of the underlying shift in the paradigm of Chinese politics; it is, therefore, important to any ongoing assessment of the changing relationship between law and politics. 'Class' had long served as the key construct in the Marxist–Leninist analysis of social change. The continued existence of class struggle had justified the retention of the 1979 CL Special Provisions on Counterrevolution. The continued priority assigned to these special provisions had highlighted the state's political use of law. 'Purpose' (*mudi*) in the formation of 'counterrevolutionary crime was assigned its own distinctive category, setting it apart from the conventional logic of *mens rea* in the construction of the primary elements of other types of crime.

Starting in the early 1980s, legal reformers perennially attacked the unscientific nature of counterrevolutionary 'crime'. Given the changing subjective nature of politics, they contended that establishing in law 'object' (*keti*) of counterrevolutionary crime was an exercise in frustration. 'Object' was one of four necessary components needed to establish criminality, including the physical and mental elements relating to the accused. In short, the nature of such crime may be heinous at a given moment of political life but the law could not retain its legitimacy if it had to adjust constantly to the changing winds of politics.[153] The inconsistency in the elementary constitution of the elements of such 'crime' was revealed in explicit reference to the subjectivity of politics and leadership success.

The related 1979 CL Special Provisions were covered in 14 articles. The 1997 CL articles on state security dropped to 12, but this section is longer due to its more elaborate stipulation. Human Rights Watch analysis has criticized, among other things, the deletion of the 1979 Article 90 wording in the 1997 CL. Article 90 of the 1979 CL stated: '. . . all acts endangering the People's Republic of China committed with the goal of overthrowing the political power of the dictatorship of the proletariat and the socialist system are crimes of counterrevolution'. Apparently, the original wording at least attempted a definition of the 'counterrevolution' whereas the 1997 CL now lacks a 'subjective purpose requirement' and has failed to define precisely 'threats to state security'.[154]

This point, however, ought to weighed in the scales of analysis along with consideration as to whether the 1997 CL, in its new departmental relation to the 1997 CPL, is likely to provide greater clarity and protection of rights as it is premised in a new approach emphasizing specific stipulation rather than flexibility and analogy. However, if the Human Rights Watch/Asia analysis has assumed an underlying Chinese motivation or subterfuge to expand 'threats to state security' to the farthest possible limits, it may have neglected the history and substance of important internal argument for the deletion of Article 90.

Late 1980's legal argument asserted that 'counterrevolution' is a 'political concept' rather than a 'stringent concept of law'. The perceived ambiguity arising from subjective politics made it difficult to establish in law whether an act had been committed for the 'purpose of counterrevolution' (*yi fangeming wei mudi*). The leading law daily, *Fazhi ribao*, in 2 June 1989, editorialized supporting criminal law revision which would liberate the law from having to interpret legally 'purpose' and 'object' in proving 'counterrevolutionary crime'. The latter was neither 'stable' nor 'scientific'. Moreover, it complicated Beijing's relations with Hong Kong and contradicted Deng's 'one country, two systems'. The *Fazhi ribao* called for the deletion of Article 90, reiterated the Soviet decision to abandon this category, and pointed to the problems of extradition in the light of international censure of the political language of 'counterrevolution'.[155] In general, a law which was once deemed appropriate to the establishment of a new regime in the early 1950s, was recognized as counterproductive in the era of economic reform and the open door. In 1989, revision to the law on counterrevolution was overtaken by the Tiananmen Square event, but Party conservatives were subsequently unable to arrest the trend towards the elimination of 'counterrevolutionary' crime.

The related revision of the criminal law in 1997 was premised in the reiteration of arguments which had already been outlined in 1979 and in April, 1989.[156] The 1979 CL Articles 96, 98, 99, 100, 101 and 102 were not included in the 1997 CL, while 1979 Articles 91, 92, 93, 94, 95, 97 and 103 were carried over into the new law with varying degrees of revision. Articles 90, 100, 101 and 102, which had included specific reference to 'for the purpose of counterrevolution', were deleted. The diminution of class struggle and the attempt to narrow the correlation of law and politics was further reflected in the shuffling of 'crime' relating to 'reactionary sects and secret societies' from the Special Provisions relating to 'counterrevolution' to Chapter 6's special principles concerning social management and order.

This is not to say that politics was not taken out of the law. The revision to these special provisions also reflected ongoing response to events in Hong Kong and Tibet as well as lessons learned regarding Tiananmen Square. Legal circles could not ignore the Party's focus on the use of foreign funding and organization to challenge the integrity of the PRC's political system and society. Article 103, which incorporated the previous Article 91 content on 'splitting the nation', included expanded stipulation providing typically calibrated punishment for 'ringleaders' and 'other participants'. From the Chinese point of view, this is consistent with making the punishment fit the crime.

Human Rights Watch/Asia has, however, focused on the retained emphasis on acts of 'instigation' or 'incitement' which not only include incitement to violent action but also any speech which could have the effect of furnishing the Party State's reputation.[157] Possibly the most disappointing facet of this particular revision relates to the new Article 105. The latter brings together originally dispersed elements of the old Articles 92, 98 and 102 providing specification as to the organization, plotting and action 'to subvert the political power of the state'. An ominous resort to 'flexibility' was inserted as follows: 'Whoever instigates the subversion of the political power of the state and overthrow of the socialist system through spreading rumors, slandering or other ways are to be sentenced to not more than five years of fixed-term imprisonment, criminal detention, control, or deprivation of political rights. . . .'

'Other ways' (*qita fangshi*) conflict with the new criminal law approach of comprehensive specific stipulation. Moreover, just as in the case of the last minute revision to Article 23 of the Hong Kong Basic Law on matters relating to subversion,[158] the potential creation of a base against the PRC politically informed the re-drafting of the 1997 CL. Articles 106 and 107 provided for heavier sentencing in cases involving 'collusion' with the outside. There may well be substance to Human Rights Watch/Asia concern over the inappropriate use of state security to derogate freedom of speech; however, the mix of competing factors within Chinese legal reform requires a closer historical examination which analytically contextualizes the entire revision and its rationale.

The question of 'overthrowing the state' is particularly sensitive in any national context. Under China's pressing transitional circumstances, specific stipulations may not always be consistent and progressive, but the challenge to the class-based notions of 'flexibility' and 'purpose' does represent a qualitative departure from the rigid ideological correlation of law and politics of the past. One may argue the degree to which there has been a change in the basic content of politics as it relates to law, but there is a new awareness of the problems that politics poses for the rational development of legal stipulation.

Chapter 1 of the 1979 CL allowed capital punishment for any crime mentioned in Articles 90, 91, 92, 93, 94, 95, 96, 97, 100 and 101 'when the harm to the state and people is especially serious and the circumstances especially odious'. The latter reservation was retained in Article 113 of the 1997 CL. Such vague terminology leaves a lot to be desired, but there is more specific stipulation on the social harm attached to 'endangering state security' than there was originally attached to the provisions on counterrevolution. The above analysis partly disagrees with Human Rights Watch/Asia contention that the 1997 CL is utterly lacking in guidance as to the demonstration of social harm and that 'acts endangering state security' constitute 'a self-evidently obvious class of events requiring no further verification beyond their initial labelling to that effect by the "competent authorities"....'.[159]

The balance of values in the 1997 Criminal Law

This chapter's analysis has stressed the importance of qualitative conceptual change, but it does not ignore the demonstrable element of continuity characterizing the provisions of the 1997 CL. The Party leaders and the legal community are anguished over social instability and value change in the contemporary era of economic reform and marketization. In the light of significant and positive changes elsewhere in the 1997 CL, the increased stipulation of severe punishment in the 1997 CL for the state's explicit purposes of social control is an analytical paradox.

In its attempt to stipulate a wider range of new criminal activity, the 1997 CL naturally has a great many more articles than the 1979 CL. Rather than just comparing the specific numbers of stipulated punishments, it may be appropriate to emphasize the difference in approach and to compare the qualitative punishment levels and categories under the 1997 CL, as distinguished from the 1979 CL. The former was intended to exhaust all stipulated crime while the latter was more open-ended in its inclusion of analogy.

The wider application of capital punishment has occasioned renewed controversy over the death penalty, but there is still very strong public and legal community support for criminal law deterrence, as it is perceived to be rooted in severe punishment. The elimination of class analysis has not entailed a sudden loss of political focus on the importance of social control, but there is an important difference from the past in that the current emphasis on social control diverges from the previous rationale underlying 'combining principle with flexibility'.

Social control under the 1997 CL no longer benefits from politically opportune analogy and the deliberately vague extrapolations from the law's provisions so as to cope with spatial and temporal change. Moreover, the 1997 CL expressly corrected the overly exclusive early to mid-1980s focus on social control. The 1997 CL is informed by new considerations originating in the priorities of economic reform and the deployment of law as against the excesses of state power and judicial corruption. The contemporary emphasis on 'running the country according to the law' incorporates a renewed emphasis on the role that law can play in limiting and guiding how the judicial institutions should exercise their power.[160] The related focus on criminal law is significant in the light of the exclusive leadership focus on anti-crime campaigning in the 1980s.[161]

The 1996 CPL started to limit the powers of public security organization in the independent administrative pursuit of social control. Application of 'custody for investigation' was eliminated. However, control (*guanzhi*; also translated as 'surveillance'), as one of five punishments in the 1979 CL, survived into in the revised criminal law despite vociferous objection to its problematic practice.[162] The persisting focus on control may seem rather impractical, if not counterintuitive. One might argue that comprehensive control is becoming increasingly difficult in China's changing social and organizational circumstances. It still relies on mass participation and surveillance. Mass organization – especially in the non-economic areas of society and culture – has become very diversified in nature.[163]

In practice, it is not easy to draw an analytically neat line between mass-line based action and community orientation in 'civil society'; however, the mass dimensions of social control have always been integral to the internal political assumptions of the regime. The mass line survived the eclipse of class struggle, and mass participation and surveillance in the reform and education of criminals is widely viewed as part of a uniquely Chinese approach to the management of public order. Prior to the 1979 CL, surveillance was used extensively to control 'minor counterrevolutionaries', including those who were identified as having undesirable class origins, such as landlord, rich peasants, and other 'bad elements'. The 1997 CL tossed out the designation 'counterrevolutionary' while retaining 'surveillance' by the public security organ as a 'legitimate' aspect of social control.[164]

Again somewhat inconsistently, Article 4 of the 1997 CL reiterated the principle, equality before the law. This principle had already been stated in 1978, and it was re-stated with greater force in law in the State Constitution of 1982. In that early context, its entrenchment specifically related to the need to prevent recurrence of Cultural Revolution circumstances when people with different social or political background or status were treated differently in the masses arbitrary dispensation of criminal justice. However, the 1997 subscription to equality more immediately relates to the struggle against Party and state corruption.

In open NPC debate in 1996 and 1997, the government, itself, was roundly criticized for failing to address problems of law enforcement and the spread of corruption within the state's own judicial processes. Corrupt officials were only selectively exposed for exploiting personal connections and for the bribery of court and public security personnel. Criminal law prosecutions were put off in favour of less onerous disciplinary action under administrative regulation. The 1997 CL was partly predicated in the direct challenge to the retroactivity of past NPCSC decisions, but it also incorporated a great deal of the conceptual content which had been contained in these same flawed NPCSC decisions.

The death penalty in 1979 and 1997

If analogy was seminal to the 1979 CL, the 1997 CL contained more provisions relating to severe punishment than did the 1979 CL. This trend was clear in the wider application of capital punishment. The use of the death penalty had already become controversial in the drafting of the 1979 CL. According to Gao Mingxuan, the drafters of the 1979 CL believed that capital punishment would protect the social order and deter dangerous offenders.

At that time, many legal experts agreed that if the death penalty could not be applied, the 'class enemy' would not be deterred, and the 'people's anger' would not be quelled. Capital punishment was applied, first and foremost, to crack down upon 'counterrevolutionary crime'. At least 9 articles stipulated the death penalty in the 1979 CL.[165] In the historical dialectics of Party policy, severe punishment had often been combined with 'leniency'. In remonstration against the bloody extremes of the Cultural Revolution, 'kill less' was enshrined as principle in the 1979 CL.[166] The death penalty, in fact, required SPC approval. However, the Party and many of the members of the NPC apparently believed that past experience confirmed the efficacy of the death penalty in stabilizing New China's social and economic order. In response to the worsening social and economic order throughout the country, Deng Xiaoping had instructed that 'the death penalty cannot be abolished, and some criminals must be sentenced to death'.[167]

However, capital punishment, as stipulated in the 1979 CL, was subsequently found not to 'fit the crime'. As a result, the NPC revised the 1979 CL 22 times in a piecemeal fashion during 1980–96. In many of these sporadic amendments, the death penalty was extended to economic crimes involving smuggling, the illegal purchasing of foreign exchange, speculating for huge profits, selling narcotics, stealing and exporting cultural relics, embezzling public property, demanding and accepting bribes, etc. These revisions drastically increased the number of crimes carrying the death sentence from the original 28 in the 1979 CL to 66, accounting for 37 per cent of total crime stipulated in the criminal law.

Some reformers in China's legal community did, however, argue that this extension contradicted rational legal culture.[168] This issue was revisited in the debates surrounding the 1997 revision to the criminal law. Few opposed capital punishment as a cruel and unusual punishment. Criticism centreed on the point that capital punishment should be applied on the basis of a political subscription to a 'killing less' policy.[169] There was a developing consensus among Chinese jurists that the 1979 and the NPCSC decisions contained too many crimes punishable with death penalty. Even the efficacy of capital punishment as a deterrent was challenged.[170]

Referring to the lack of qualitative difference in punishment for minor as distinct from serious crime, Ma Kechang argued that the extensiveness of the death penalty may have actually contributed to the commission of more serious crime.[171] Gao Mingxuan acknowledged that in recent years, the executed criminals were becoming much younger. There was also doubt as to whether the masses had been politically assuaged. Instead of assuaging the masses, the government's more extensive use of the death sentence created disaffection, especially among parents in the cases where an only child was sentenced to death.[172]

Legal scholars exposed the Party's own contradictions on the issue. Zhao Bingzhi and his colleagues contended that the wider capital punishment undermined the Party policy of 'not abolishing death penalty, but limiting the application, and preventing wrongful execution'. They further criticized the NPC for abetting the unreasonable extension of the death penalty in its decisions of 1980–96, without the benefit of careful investigation and scientific research, and in disregard of the requirements of the 1979 CL. They held the NPC and the judicial institutions responsible for abuse of capital punishment.[173]

However, jurist arguments for reducing the use of capital punishment was widely rejected by both law-makers and judicial personnel. The latter still subscribed to the use of capital punishment as an efficient deterrent against serious crime. This viewpoint was apparently anchored in a perception of deep public support, and this partly explains why many deputies in the 5th session of the 8th NPC strongly endorsed a position that '. . . death sentences for existing crimes should remain unchanged to act as a forceful deterrence against wrongdoers' in the new law'.[174] Strong arguments against the proliferation of capital punishment provisions then failed to convince both the Party and the NPC and Wang Hanbin tried to put the best light on the situation protesting that the new law neither increased nor decreased the number of provisions containing the death penalty.[175]

The redefined purposes of the 1997 Criminal Law

By and large, the urgent political focus on the potential collapse of the social and economic order during the transition to the socialist market helps explain the 1997 changes in the criminal law. Economic reform and the open door had witnessed an extraordinary proliferation of 'economic crime'. A large part of the revision was exclusively devoted to such crime. The 1997 CL chapter on economic crime was the largest of the law's 10 chapters. The greatly expanded new Chapter 3, 'Crimes Endangering Socialist Market Economic Order', replaced the 15 articles in the equivalent 1979 CL Chapter, 'Crimes of Undermining the Socialist Economic Order'.

Across 92 articles, organized within 8 discrete sections, Chapter 3 of the 1997 CL considers the multiplicity of economic crime, including manufacturing and selling fake and shoddy goods, smuggling, disrupting the order of company and enterprise administration, undermining the order of financial management, financial fraud, endangering collection and management of taxes, infringing upon intellectual property rights, and disrupting market order. Chapter 3 added more than a dozen new economic crimes to those which had originally been specified in the NPC decisions of 1980–96.

Chapter 3 was augmented by a further 16 articles appearing under Chapter 8, 'Crimes of Embezzlement and Bribery', which dealt discretely with the subject of official corruption. Chapter 9, 'Crimes of Dereliction of Duty', also provided stipulations concerning the punishment of judicial personnel for misconduct and malfeasance.[176] In commenting on the 1979 CL, University of Maryland Law Professor Hungdah Chiu, expressed regret at the lack of criteria by which to judge whether any particular conduct constituted a 'grave violation' of the criminal law.[177] Eventually, this became quite serious in the growing area of economic crime. The most important difference between economic crime and violation of other regulations concerning the market is the seriousness of conduct harmful to economic order. Responding to related internal criticism, the 1997 CL provided detailed descriptions of the elements of 'economic crime'. The easy reference to serious or grave circumstances was reduced significantly in the places where the specific amount of money involved in crime can be meaningfully specified. This is consistent with the underlying approach of the 1997 CL favouring specific stipulation.

The new 1997 chapter on economic crime also moved in yet another direction. Before 1987, the discussion of whether a legal entity or legal person can be held for criminal responsibility was a moot one. There was no provision in law stipulating that a legal person such as a corporation can be indicted for a criminal act of malfeasance. During 1987 to 1996, 12 regulations and laws have been enacted containing provisions stipulating 50 crimes for which legal persons could be held criminally accountable. These laws did not resolve the issue of legal person. The 1997 CL, however, established that 'legal persons' such as state enterprises and work units could be criminally responsible and punished primarily with fines. The persons in charge of the legal person also became liable to fixed-term imprisonment.

The emergence of legislation containing the provisions on legal person suggests that under the rapid development of the socialist market economy, the NPC is concerned more with punishing corporations or legal persons whose economic activities cause public harm than with pure theoretical discussions. In judicial practice, however, very few legal persons have been convicted of any crime. This situation has been partially contributed to the technical inadequacy of the legislation on corporate crime (*danwei fanzui*). The problems include vague definition of the term legal person, vague stipulations of the crimes that can be committed by a legal person, procedural problems such as how to indict and punish a legal person. All of these issues were revisited during the drafting of the 1997 CL.[178] Articles 30 and 31 of the 1997 CL together defined 'legal person', and stipulated criminal responsibility of such persons.

In sum, the 1997 CL embraced a new approach requiring the comprehensive stipulation of the criteria of criminal behaviour. There was at the same time an astonishing break with past assumptions, just as there were also indications of continuing focus on social control through the deployment of the criminal justice system. The deletion of analogy and the new subscription to *nulla crimen sine lege* and *nulla poena sine lege* represented a self-conscious break with the past, but the state's resort to severe punishment was not circumscribed. While faulting the 1980s NPC decisions for their violation of retroactivity, the provisions of the 1997 CL often incorporated the substance of those same decisions. However, class struggle was no longer correlated with the conceptual explanation of society and the legal notion of social control, and the 1997 CL was placed on the new theoretical axis of the socialist market. The law's stipulations have, however, reflected a complex and uneven viewpoint on the rationality of the law as it relates to the protection of rights and interests and the redefined importance of social stability and control.

Conclusion

This chapter began with a basic question as to the changing substantive nature of the newly revised criminal procedure law and criminal law. In any event, transition is likely to present a messy conceptual proposition, but the detailed contrast between 1979 and 1996–97 confirms a largely unrecognized qualitative change to the reasoning that inspires basic law with respect to criminal justice. The undeniable fact that this transition is mixed in nature should not obscure its substantive depth. We may not have 'to imagine the unimaginable'.[179] Even the mixed results of this criminal justice reform represent a qualitative progress towards a new criminal law system and are critical to any analysis of the prospective struggle for 'the rule of law' in China.

At the macro level of explicitly stated general theory, the 1996 CPL and 1997 CL challenged the original purpose of the 1979 CPL and CL. Much of the foundation for this revision was anticipated in the internal legal and political debates of late 1980s. The CCP's political reaction to Tiananmen Square only briefly stalled this progress towards revision.

The mid-1990s revision to the criminal law of procedure culminated in a newly defined relationship between the criminal and criminal procedural laws as well as the introduction of a new conception of balance putting rights protection into the scales of justice along with social control. This new balancing entailed several important departures with respect to the provision of judicial justice. Even if it was qualified in the revision to cognate articles of the 1996 CPL, the NPC's elimination of the police independent power of exercising 'custody for investigation' suggested a greater sensitivity to international opinion on the protection of human rights as well as a new domestic political understanding of how these rights connect with social order in the context of qualitative economic change.

Secondly, the termination of the procuratorate's power in determination of guilt, the negation of 'exemption from prosecution', the developing jurist argument equating 'taking the facts as the basis and the law as the yardstick' with the 'presumption of innocence' and the challenge to 'decide first, trial later' as it had become evident in the people's court's pre-trial examination of the evidence, all represent forward movement in stipulated protection and the reconceptualization of the purposes of law in an arena where the state had heretofore enjoyed unqualified authority.

Even in the widely proclaimed context of 'socialism with Chinese characteristics', the Chinese adaptation to 'internationalization' and 'localization' appears to have been quite complicated, but nonetheless, extensive and substantive. While the NPC has not always been above compromise in dealing with the law and order theme, as advanced by bureaucratic interests within the SPP in particular, it has also shown a great deal of initiative in a self-conscious effort to meet international standards in the criminal justice process based upon 'no guilt without a trial'. The people's court has been instructed to take a neutral position between the defence and prosecution as it moves from an inquisitorial to an adversarial model of trial proceedings.

The 1997 CL, on the other hand, not only subscribed to this newly constructed balance between protection and control but it also constituted a self-conscious challenge to the inappropriate, if not unconstitutional, use of analogy and flexibility on the part of the NPCSC. The latter's attempt to move beyond the interpretation of the law was rebuffed. Even though the revision did bring forward an earlier content relating to 'striking hard', the legally egregious nature of episodic NPCSC decisions was exposed in the healthy criticisms of China's legal circles who preferred progressive stipulation to 'heavy-penalty-ism'. The revision confirmed the break with the anachronistic tendencies of class analysis, and it provided a new perspective on the relationship between the state and law in the socialist market context.

Obviously, the Party continues to invest in the law's utility in the achievement of social control and political stability, but the underlying concept of social control is not the same as before, and there is a need to probe the contemporary rationale for change with respect to what is to be controlled and how. The conventional jurisprudence on the necessity of flexibility collapsed under the stress of the transition to the socialist market. The 1997 CL was self-consciously predicated in a new approach to criminal law development requiring the comprehensive stipulation of law and the adoption of the twin principles of *nulla crimen sine lege; nulla poena, sine lege*.

As compared to 1979, economic crime assumed a greater priority in the specific contents of the 1997 CL. Does this mean that we are now dealing with a sanitized 'state instrumentalism' based upon a soft corporatist approach to law? In the first place, 'economic crime' is a legitimate political as well as legal concern. Ideologically, the Party would still prefer the unity of state and society to the western notion of 'civil society', but the above analysis, nonetheless, confirms an expressed commitment to a new approach to the development of the criminal law itself. In the first place, the formal elimination of the law on counter-revolution was justified in a self-conscious response to the changing nature of crime in the contemporary context of the 'socialist market'. Such law had become an embarrassing anachronism which was deemed to compromise the rationality of law. Although new provisions were simultaneously entrenched in the criminal law so as to expedite state security, the law was finally freed from the last vestiges of large-scale class struggle.

Secondly, the related Marxist position on 'flexibility' collapsed. This is a major event in the modern history of Chinese criminal law which was well celebrated in China, but it seems to have gone largely unnoticed in the West where the media is fixed on China's human rights record, particularly as it relates to the disposition of specific dissidents. An informed analysis explaining the elimination of 'flexibility' ought to contribute greatly to the ongoing evaluation of the development of a Chinese approach to the 'rule of law', and to the state's changing capacity for 'instrumentalism'.

Analogy was placed in contradiction with modern rational legal culture. It became an acknowledged procedural embarrassment, and it was politically regarded as inappropriate to the law's adaptation to qualitative socio-economic change. The 1996 CPL formally created a new balance between control and protection. The 1997 CL greatly contributed to this balance in its substitution of the principles of *nulla crimen sine lege* and *nulla poena sine lege* for analogy and flexibility. At least in the authors' scales of analysis, and despite the vagaries of bureaucratic politics, these principles represented a new approach to judicial justice and the development of law on the basis of comprehensive stipulation and procedural independence.

6
The Law and the Market at the Crossroads of Justice and Efficiency

The foregoing analysis has delved into the reasoning behind conceptual change in the evolving jurist understanding of the purposes of law in China's transition to a 'socialist market'. The analysis and interpretation of new legal thinking is presumed to be useful to the informed understanding of Chinese progress towards rule-of-law making. It accepts the study of the conceptual basis for contemporary legal reform as a legitimate area of academic inquiry; and it disputes impatient assumption that because not all of the new substance of law has been consistently operationalized in practice, the issues of contemporary jurisprudence and related human rights legislation are dubious. On the contrary, a correct and comprehensive knowledge base is necessary to a critically balanced external understanding as to how best to support the positive development of human rights and the rule of law in the complicated circumstances of China's current marketplace.

To borrow from Deng Xiaoping, the 'truth' is a painstaking matter of sorting through various levels of constantly mutating contradictions. The transition to the market has created extraordinary opportunity for the fashioning of rights and interests and their incorporation into law; at the same time, however, the market's operations have accentuated the antithesis of efficiency and social justice. Both this point and counterpoint have been argued well in the domestic context of China's legal reform, and this book's related account of emerging jurisprudence deliberately graphs the plotted implications of the intersecting axes of justice and efficiency.

The main features of 'pluralized jurisprudence'

The Chinese approach to jurisprudence still reflects an explicitly ideological understanding of how law is practically situated in society and politics. The authors have tried to examine the essentials of this content on the basis of what is hopefully a balanced and multidisciplinary approach, drawing on formal legal theory and history, the political science study of institutions, bureaucratic politics and ideology, as well as the sinological area study of political culture and the sociology of law.

To follow through on this approach, it is important to begin with the Chinese telling their own story. This seems especially appropriate on two related counts. In the first place, despite the open door's effects on Chinese scholarship and western access to a new generation of Chinese legal journals and materials, there is still a paucity of English language scholarly literature detailing the emerging outlines of jurisprudence in the era of economic reform. This literature has yet to establish systematically who is contributing what to jurisprudence and why. Much of the literature originating in the western faculties of law deals with the scattered and discrete points of what is truly an exponential production of law, rather than exploring at the macro level the 'balance of values' within newly emerging jurisprudence as it adapts to policy and politics concerning China's economic development and the transition to a market economy. This book's analysis often moves into virgin territory. It looks for confirmation of macro-level developments across the different fields of law and attempts to identify conceptual trends on the basis of a preferred multidisciplinary analysis.

Secondly, the present volume probes the relevance of the largely unknown interior lines of scholarly and political debate concerning jurisprudential controversy in the deliberate recognition of the achievements and frustrations of China's jurists. Virtually all of the legal scholars whom the authors interviewed in Beijing had directly participated in the drafting of new law. To cite a few examples, CASS Professor Shi Tanjing played a central role in the drafting of the 1994 Labour Law. CASS Professor Chen Mingxia was a key player in the drafting of the 1992 Law on the Protection of Women's Rights and Interests. Professor Cui Min of the Beijing Public Security University participated in the drafting of the 1996 revisions to the CPL. The importance of jurist viewpoint was confirmed in the Zhongnanhai series of lectures to top Party leaders. These lectures dealt with a range of issues concerning economic reform and the rule of law. They were published and widely disseminated throughout government at various levels in a mass-line style educational campaign and they had a bearing on the March 1999 revision of the State Constitution.

In China, scholarly advice and the related lines of jurist debate are taken seriously politically, and there are obvious correlates between the debates and the actual legislative stipulation of the law's content. In short, even given the constraints of evolving ideology and bureaucratic politics, the scholars and jurists have played a pivotal role in the rational elaboration of legislative outcomes and in the related formation and introduction of human rights concepts into Chinese law. The present volume is, therefore, dedicated to the significant, but often overlooked, contributions of Chinese scholars and jurists to the development of modern legal culture in China.

Today's Chinese legal scholarship is much more informed about international comparative legal experience. Many leading scholars have either visited or studied at western universities. While many of these scholars, who are interested in vetting legal reform, have opted for a middle-of-the-road accommodation between 'internationalization' and 'localization' of law, the true extent of the influence of western legal concepts and experience on these scholars is not commonly appreciated. Comprehensive analysis requires an accurate and detailed account of this influence. The extent of contemporary 'internationalization' is remarkable, as is the fact that it has taken place on the basis of an open and self-conscious advocacy.

Both jurisprudence and the law are part of the intellectual tension between 'localization', (*bentuhua*) and 'internationalization' (*guojihua* or *quanqiuhua*). The former recommends the law's sensitive adaptation to the underlying values and understandings of a distinctive society, political culture and the pattern of economic development, but its assertion has often been dismissed in western human rights criticism as 'cultural relativism'. Notwithstanding such criticism, the line of analysis separating what might be construed as a positive and 'legitimate' adaptation of domestic experience to international norms and what might be construed as a 'nativist' rejection of these same norms is not so easy to identify in applied analysis.

Critically balanced assessment of Chinese human rights performance must take into account important new internal subscription to the positive prospects of 'internationalization'. Basic changes in Chinese legal thinking are not merely designed to hoodwink foreign critics. It is one thing for domestic reformers to co-opt international pressure so as to consolidate their own human rights agenda and quite another to rely on external pressure as the primary basis for improvements in internal human rights conceptualization and practice. Many of the key examples in this volume of new Chinese legislation and jurisprudence clearly demonstrate a developing inner perspective which accounts for the rejection of past convention and practice and the domestic adaptation to relevant international standards.

Despite the continuing strong political focus on the importance of Chinese history, society and sovereignty, this inner perspective, or 'internationalization', has been articulated in contemporary debate as 'the international developmental process in law in which the particular legal systems of each country in the world, approximate more closely and come together and converge in order to take shape in mutual interdependence and linkage'.[1] Formal subscription to the 'international development process in law' is, in and of itself, evidence of necessary conceptual progress. Cultural clash is not automatic, even in the inflammatory context of international political disagreement over alleged cultural relativism. Chinese jurists have frequently assigned a positive value to the common search for human justice in mutual learning across legal cultures and state jurisdictions.

This volume gives the reader access to a working ledger of the proliferating concepts and perspectives which animate Chinese debate across a wide range of legal controversies. The comprehensive and qualitative analysis of so many strands of debate is an admittedly taxing exercise for a number of reasons. Contemporary jurisprudence is transitional. It lacks the coherence of a new grand theory. It embraces a host of unfamiliar terminological distinctions in the specialized Chinese vocabulary of legal theory. In key areas it has been deliberately 'pluralized' so as to deal with the inchoate mix of newly emerging and relentlessly subjective 'rights and interests' and with the complex and extremely sensitive ideological changes regarding ownership and distribution which have a direct bearing on the legitimacy of the current regime.

Despite the problems originating with contradiction between Chinese self-perception and objective external examination, such analysis is inherently rewarding in that it places the issues relating to the Chinese struggle for the rule of law within the evolving context of the relationship between state and society. China's dialectically balanced jurisprudence records formally recognized change in the new era of market development and social change. This jurisprudence, however, has both a passive and an active voice in the contemporary syntax of change. In its overview of the role of law in society, economics and politics, it not only provides important clues as to the ongoing metamorphosis in the

The readjustment of interests

Reform era jurisprudence witnessed the demise of class struggle and analysis. After the Cultural Revolution, law and its underlying jurisprudence became part of a political strategy of institutionalization, the purpose of which was to pre-empt future extremism. Since late 1992, jurisprudence has attempted a conceptual leap into a new era of pluralized interests, ownership and distribution. This has entailed the self-conscious qualification of traditional 'state instrumentalism'. At the same time, jurisprudence has been deliberately aligned with the preconceived moral basis of Chinese society. However, as was argued in Chapter 5, social control, which had always been at the heart of class politics, is now part of a new structural balance within the criminal and criminal procedural laws. Social control is now balanced against rights protection, and a new emphasis on independent procedure has been grounded in the principles, *nulla crimen sine lege* and *nulla poena sine lege*.

In addition, there is a particular confluence of the changing aspects of law which is likely to have impact on the state–society relationship. The state's once impregnable position vis-à-vis society has been positively qualified by expanding subject equality in civil law, special human rights protection of the vulnerable sectors of society, the articulation of the rights and interests of contract labour, and the procedural protection of citizen's rights and interests in the judicial process. The state's dominant position has also been qualified in the redefinition of judicial justice and the explicit rejection of state instrumentalism, as it was justified in the hard and fast correlation of analogy and 'flexibility'.

In both these positive and qualifying aspects, the traditional unity of state and society has been self-consciously challenged in newly emerging jurisprudence; however, the current transition does, at times, encompass mutually exclusive ends. Chapters 2 and 3 highlighted the growing importance of the Hainan strategy of 'small government, big society', but, at the same time, they plumbed the depths of an interesting, but familiar dilemma.

While much of the rule-of-law argument reiterated the supremacy of the law and importance of the impersonal and independent dimensions of the rule of law vis-à-vis politics, there was also strong argument in favour of an activist state, which would not only consolidate the rule of law, but would also legally and politically support social justice. This argument presumed the need for 'special' or equality rights in the light of the inequality inherent in the conditions of the marketplace. While recognizing 'pluralized labour relations' and participating in the assault on the 'three irons system', the scholarly advocates of fundamental labour law dismissed 'administrative labour relations'. At the same time, they supported the distinction between labour law and civil law. This distinction was politically deployed for the purpose of reinforcing the state's legal responsibility for the 'balance of values', particularly given the inequalities of management–labour relations in the new contractual context. Labour may have lost its 'master' status in practice, but the law was supposed to compensate labour with a new legally entrenched notion of equality.

Taking yet another example from Chapter 2, scholars and politicians entertained different approaches to further gender equality under the rule of law. Some of the more daring reformers distrusted the state's intentions and preferred to use the civil law against traditional village prejudice against women who chose to marry non-villagers, whereas others have strongly promoted a 'direct-effect' constitutional law strategy which would legitimate an aggressive state-imposed remedy on the basis of constitutional law. More generally, public law is, itself, now undergoing a fundamental transition. It must now take into account basic human rights protection as a legitimate function of the law.

The study of civil society in China is fashionable in western scholarship, and there is ongoing controversy on the Chinese state's changing relationship to society.[2] One line of analysis has the state attempting to pre-empt society in the management of a market economy. Jude Howell, for example, has suggested in the following analysis that the state is trying to re-invent itself through adaptation to new market economies:

> Elements of a new market-facilitating state, which is entrepreneurial, legalistic, technocratic and regulatory are emerging. The Chinese state is not in retreat. On the contrary it is in a process of major restructuring, shedding some functions, but taking on others. The web of the command planning state is receding whilst the web of the market-facilitating state is advancing.[3]

One is still left with the question of why the state should not re-invent itself? Certainly, the current Chinese argument for the 'rule of law' is quite sophisticated and not merely a matter of technical convenience.

The study of contemporary jurisprudence, as it highlights rights and interests, has not been well integrated within this larger controversy. Indeed, the orientation within this deliberately 'pluralized jurisprudence' is sometimes difficult to clarify, given the variation of perspective animating the several distinct departments of Chinese law. Change in these departments has incrementally reflected the changing political priorities at the National People's Congress. Such departmental variation is also reflected in scholarly debate over the divide between public and private law and the state's role vis-à-vis the prioritized balancing of efficiency and social justice. Those supporting social justice, for example, focused on reinforcing the distinction between labour law and civil law. The former, it was argued, must have the benefit of state intervention into economic relationships while the latter focused on the development of subject equality vis-à-vis the state.

As discussed in Chapters 2 and 3, the special grouping of the rights and interests of women, children, the disabled and the elderly, often presumed the formation of an activist, progressive state. Wang Jiafu grouped the laws in this politically sensitive area into '*shehuifa*', namely, social laws or legislation. In his view, these laws were located halfway between public and private law. Their purpose was clearly to protect the vulnerable in the new marketplace of opportunity and competition.[4] However, the state no longer enjoys exclusive responsibility for social justice. The Hainan model has exerted an important influence on questions of social justice, and social legislation is formally expected to adhere to a middle course. While permitting an undetermined degree of subscription to market principles of self-regulation so as to facilitate increased productivity based upon efficiency, social legislation assumed that even in a 'bigger society', the state would still foster social justice in the workplace and that social and legal human rights protection would be accorded to the weaker members of society.

Many reform jurists and scholars have invested in what we might tentatively call a 'progressive state' which would ideally protect the rights and interests of the weak and vulnerable in the context of market competition and which would insure the priorities of social justice in the new 'rule of law' economy. Indeed, they were able to advocate such a progressive state, drawing on the existing ideological basis of Deng Xiaoping's 'three favourable directions'. Presumably, these directions were compatible with Deng's instruction, 'efficiency is primary and fairness, supplementary', but at the same time, these directions validated state intervention into the market so as to insure that the market-driven increases in productivity would ultimately promote a general rise in everyone's standard of living.

The efficiency of the market was to be neatly synthesized with social justice in the consolidation of 'socialism with Chinese characteristics'. 'Socialism' was not meant to endorse poverty! All the people's boats were to be floated in the rising tide of the socialist market. However, from within Deng's dialectical legacy, the state is now expected to eschew past arbitrary administrative practice and to work through the law in order to 'readjust rights and interests' and to consolidate 'the system of social protection'.

Possibly, Deng's formulations were deliberately elastic. His successors have been stuck somewhere between the hagiographic antipodes of 'all eating from the same common pot' and 'to get rich is glorious'. Moreover, there are times when experiment on the basis of 'seeking the truth from the facts', rather than leading into a predictable system of legal mediation, seems to have degenerated into open-ended experimentalism. At any rate, since the advent of the socialist market, scholars and jurists have diverged on how exactly to interpret tricky matters of law and jurisprudence while synthesizing the two sides of this dialectic.

If Party history is any guide, the identification of the primary element in such contradiction is likely to cause controversy. This has been especially the case in the arcane terminological battle over the true connotations of property and ownership rights, as outlined in Chapter 4. At the level of formal rhetoric, it would appear that efficiency has triumphed over residual Marxist investment in social justice. But if 'property rights' offer a quick fix to the dilemma of mixed ownership in state enterprise, the political resistance to jurist advocacy of 'ownership rights' suggests a strong underlying commitment to the protection of the state's public assets. The property issue cuts across public and private law in that the state is trying to maintain its legal control over the economy and its public assets, while at the same it recognizes the importance of enterprise self-regulation, and the autonomy and the subject equality, imbedded in the general principles of civil law.

How does the Hainan strategy, with its deliberate contraction of the state, its expansion of the lawful protection of interests, its preference for society's micro-management of economic activity and its rejection of administrative reductionism, fit within this dialectic of efficiency and social justice? Ostensibly, the Hainan strategy attempted to justify the balanced contraction of the naturally inefficient centralized state and the alternative building up of semi-autonomous micro economic organization in society. The empowering of the individual in society, in terms of the provision of welfare on a more diversified institutional basis of financial commitment, entails the reduction of the state's active welfare role and the reduction of its overhead for the sake of efficiency.

Whether this actually empowers the individual or off-loads the state's social justice responsibilities is an interesting, but inherently political, question. This question not only goes to the heart of contemporary Chinese jurist debate over the 'balance of values', but it is also the key question in the context of the economic development of many developed and developing states as they self-consciously respond to the complicated, if not threatening, parameters of economic globalization.[5]

The current 'structure of interests' has given so much new emphasis to the individual that conservative jurists have identified 'rights fundamentalism' as a major threat to the state. Moreover, the state's capacity for trespassing on the rights and interests of the individual has become a recognized subject for political scrutiny and legal remedy. At the same time, there seems to have been little corresponding effort to de-institutionalize morality; and there remains the outstanding tension between the impersonal dimensions of the rule of law in its assumptions of subject equality and the supremacy of law and the regime's need to maintain 'socialist spiritual civilization'.

The law, as in the very clear examples of divorce and family violence, is expected to genuflect before the reconstituted morality recommended in the intuitive leadership of the Party as it grapples with the spiritual consequences of market transition. The detail in Chapter 2's analysis of revision to the marriage law provisions on divorce revealed a naked predisposition towards the use of law as a means of achieving social control against spreading immorality. In these matters, jurists may be as predisposed to conservative morality as politicians.

Not all aspects of past legal theory have quietly passed into history together with class analysis. Despite Li Buyun's stated optimism on this score, this still raises the question as to whether the rule of law has genuinely been liberated from the bonds of 'socialist spiritual civilization'. Even as the Party has reiterated at the highest constitutional level its abiding commitment to the rule of law, it still instinctively focuses on the unity of state and society in its attempt to contain the destabilizing moral implications of rapid economic growth. Even while post-Cultural Revolution politics has continuously focused on the deployment of law against the dangers of persisting feudalism and the state's own predisposition towards 'pan-moralism', the state remains vitally interested in an institutionalized approach to morality.

Obviously, a political emphasis on the family's importance does not have to be placed in antithesis to the rule of law, *per se*. However, this institutionalized approach, as it forms part of 'localization', raises the sensitive, if not universal, issue as to what is the appropriate balance in rule-of-law making between law as a widely accepted medium which reflects notions of justice and society and law which acts as an impersonal predicate on the basis of equality before the law and in deliberate disregard of particular societal and moral factors of a highly personalized and ascriptive nature.

To return to the theme outlined in Chapter 1, the many points of controversy over the 'balance of values' and the purposes of law in the marketplace can be plotted along a continuum which features the intersecting concepts, 'the market economy is a rule of law economy' and 'running the country according to law and establishing a socialist rule-of-law country'. The rule-of-law issue in China predates the current transition to the socialist market. Its basic connotations and perceived implications are not all that new. The policy emphasis on the law's facilitation of the market has, however, raised a fundamental question in Western research as to whether the state is using the transition to the socialist market so as to create a reconstituted but softer variant of 'state instrumentalism'.

In answering this question, however, one need not assume a simple 'legalistic' and 'regulatory' approach on the part of the Chinese. As for the essential political questions, these were raised a long time ago. Leftist extremists in the Cultural Revolution had precipitated a politically debilitating 'legal nihilism' in their adherence to Mao's instruction, 'depend on the rule of man, not the rule of law'.[6] Responding at the outset of economic reform, Dong Likun, a researcher at the Shanghai Academy of Social Science, noted as early as 1980 that all people, including all individuals, organs of state and social groups, must obey the law. Dong drew on Deng Xiaoping's new institutional strategy of democratization and legalization to combat a stubborn and unexpectedly resilient 'feudalism' which had ravaged the political system during the Cultural Revolution. He dared cite the following comment by Rousseau: 'No matter what the form of government in a country, any person within the scope of its jurisdiction who is not required to obey the laws will inevitably come to control the rest of the people.'[7] Dong then indicated that the Party's judicial work was not to be dominated by the party committee and that the Party's 'most important task' was to guarantee the complete implementation of state laws.

The mid-1980s witnessed a debate and a related national educational campaign on the 'rule of law', as an ethos based upon equality and the supremacy of law. The 'rule of law' was placed in antithesis to the feudalism inherent in 'rule by law' and the 'rule of man'.[8] Writing in 1984, Li Buyun hailed the early 1980s' changes to the State and Party Constitutions and attempted to set out the relationship between law and Party leadership. Carefully avoiding any explicit contradiction between law and leadership, he set out two distinctive requirements in the rule of law making: 'The laws of the state must be guided by the policies of the party; however, the policies of the party can only guide the laws in principle, not take the place of the laws'; and 'Once a law is formed, it has a more extensive stable application than that of the policies of the party both in scope and in time.'

In Li's 1984 explanation of the law's supremacy over policy, he was of the opinion that the Party had to respect the laws because 'only those policies which are regarded as relatively mature or considerably stabilized are to be enacted into laws'. Commenting on the related NPCSC issue of 'striking hard', he understood the policy need to punish criminals who seriously harm the social order, but he cautioned the Party: 'However, we . . . cannot disregard the stipulations of the law, nor can we handle affairs not in accordance with the criminal law and code of criminal procedure so as to alter the procedure of legal proceedings and to break through the scope for measuring penalties as we please.'[9]

The second round of debate on the 'rule of law' started in the early 1990s. It survived major leadership change and is still ongoing. It drew extensively from the mid-1980s debate, but the terms of reference were expanded to include reinforcing reference to Deng Xiaoping's Southern Tour theory, which sanctioned the socialist market economy. In its elementary political assumptions, it is historically questionable whether this second round contributed a new set of principles constituting a 'third stage' jurisprudence. In either period there was an ideal assumption that Party would subordinate itself to the rule of law and that Party leadership can be squared with the making of a rule of law.

To be sure, the legal circles were able to capitalize on the policy importance of the market in order to make a reinforced case for the rule of law, as distinct from the mere subscription to 'socialist legality'. Moreover the emphasis on the relation between the rule of law and human rights protection became explicit in the early 1990s debate. Overall, the difference between 1985 and 1993 may lie, however, in the political extent of Party recognition and the importance of the March 1999 amendment to the State Constitution rather than in the creation of fundamentally new content concerning law, policy and political leadership. The abuse of power, the importance of judicial independence, the supremacy of law, and equality before the law, were all reiterated theoretical concerns which received even more attention in the unresolved context of crippling corruption. In both rounds of the debate, the Party leadership was construed as favouring the basic tenets of the 'rule of law'.¹⁰

In lauding Jiang Zemin's new 15th Party Congress formulation, 'running the country according to law and establishing a socialist rule of law country', Sun Guohua and Huang Wenyi more or less borrowed from Jiang Zemin's own wording, and, as was discussed in Chapter 1, Jiang himself had liberally taken what he wanted from Deng Xiaoping's thought. Sun and Huang, nevertheless claimed: 'Meanwhile, relying on law to rule the country signifies a major change in the way the party exercises its leadership. . . . In the new era, governing by the Communist Party means to lead and to support the people in their control of the power of the state. . . .'

Representing a 'conservative Marxist viewpoint' which still presumed the surviving 'will of the ruling class' and the 'master' status of the workers, even in the absence of relevant class struggle, Sun and Huang claimed that a 'socialist rule of law' would rest upon three preconditions. Socialist law would have to express the will and interests of the people, led by the working class. It would also practically embody Deng Xiaoping's 'three favourable directions' in order to ensure healthy social life in the context of great change. Notwithstanding 'rights fundamentalism', it would also have to foster the protection of personal dignity and freedom, the democratic rights, political freedom and economic and other social rights of citizens.

As discussed in Chapter 1, Tong Zhiwei's grand theory insisted on the relevance of obligations rights to interests, and it asserted the importance of state power in the guaranteeing of 'socio-rights'. Tong, however, was criticized for mortgaging rights to state power. In the argument that followed for the 'progressive state' to step into society to support the 'rule of law', Jiang Lishan, of the General Office of the Beijing Municipal People's Government, acknowledged the current confusion over who is the 'subject' [zhuti] in the practicing of the rule of law:

> Theoretically, the answer to the question is quite clear and beyond any doubt. The people are the masters of the country. State power belongs to the people; however, the issue that is being widely debated among legal scholars, is whether or not the people are the subject or the object of the rule of law. . . . Such questions arise not from theory, but from the current rule of law practice in China.¹¹

Jiang Lishan believed that China has been pushed externally into an accelerated process of modernization requiring rapid legal development.

He concluded: 'Therefore... while most Chinese do not have an adequate idea of law, we cannot wait for their sense of law to develop and become sufficient.... The power of the state is deployed to start up large-scale campaigns to spread the knowledge of the law.' In order to make up for this apparent deficit in society and popular consciousness, Jiang Lishan proposed a dual strategy which would remedy the confusion of the subject and object in rule-of-law making in China's self-evident Third World modernizing context.

Noting that many scholars were worried lest too much emphasis be placed upon an activist state initiating top-down reform in the absence of a firm popular grounding in rational legal culture, Jiang hoped to combine top-down state-supported change towards the rule of law with change brought about in bottom-to-top popular adaptation to social reality. Jiang included, in this deliberately complex process, legal development, which builds upon pilot projects vetted by local organization and interests.[12] Indeed, as the detail in the foregoing chapters suggest, basic law at the NPC level often drew extensively upon local provincial experiment in the creation of related regulation.[13]

In his illustrative but controversial perspective on 'internationalization' and 'localization', Jiang argued that, on the one hand, an activist state could be deployed as an important resource in the development of the rule of law in order to reduce the social costs of the transition to the market, and that, on the other hand, an exclusively bottom-up strategy of gradualism and natural evolution would delay China's bid for accelerated social and economic development in the global context of keen economic competition.[14]

For different reasons, the domestic apologists for soft corporatism and the supporters of human rights protection require state activism in the creation of new legal consciousness and practice. But to take a leaf out of Jiang Lishan's stated viewpoint, China's jurists and scholars, in their participation in the formation of jurisprudence and the related drafting of legislation, have already participated in a dual strategy of rule-of-law making. They have often participated in top-down mass-line exercises designed to foster popular identification with the importance of 'running the country according to law and creating a socialist rule of law state', but their role has moved beyond that of the Party's messenger. The jurists and scholars are sometimes in sharp disagreement among themselves, but when there is a trend towards consensus, as was the case in their support of 'no crime without a law, no punishment without a law', they can fundamentally influence the drafting of legislation, pushing it in new directions. In this way, they act as a professional interest group or lobby which attempts to move Party and NPC leadership in a certain legislative direction.

Conclusion

The story of Chinese jurisprudence is still unfolding. The conceptual reality of this jurisprudence is not so much 'unimaginable' as extremely difficult to decipher in its full political and theoretical context. The return to a rigid state instrumentalism based upon extreme class analysis would seem unimaginable. In what may be a worst case scenario, there is the danger that the new emphasis on the rule of law could be eviscerated within a soft corporatist strategy to perpetuate the CCP's power. There is no axiomatic guarantee of the creation of a 'progressive state' in the current transition to the 'socialist' market. It is not hard to imagine an episodic and even a contradictory relationship between social and judicial justice. On the other hand, substantive and progressive development of the rule of law in China has involved a largely unrecognized articulation of new fundamental principles of law. The emphases on equality before the law and supremacy of the law have been self-consciously entrenched in constitutional law and jurisprudence, and responsible external support for such emphasis depends to a large extent upon an accurate understanding of internal perspective and legal thinking.

It is important to stay abreast of the internal discussion on the 'balance of values' which lay at the heart of China's modern developmental predicament. This balancing informs rule-of-law making in China. The everyday assumptions of the western sociology of law were not originally designed to cope with 'pluralized jurisprudence' and rule-of-law making in the transitional context of China's 'socialist' market. Max Weber did not witness the extraordinary and analytically challenging course of post-CCP politics. It is hard to say how he might have dealt with the Chinese attempt to balance social control and rights protection and the anomalous resort to capital punishment in the suppression of economic crime during the transition to a market economy. Weber, however, cautioned against an exaggerated tendency to read too much into the institutional and developmental implications of capitalism as an ideal type. He argued: '. . . economic situations do not automatically give birth to new legal forms, they merely provide the opportunities for the actual spread of legal technique if it is invented'.[15]

Notwithstanding criticism of Chinese 'cultural relativism', there seems to be have been a lot more invention in China than has been commonly recognized in western human rights criticisms. Moreover, the sociology-of-law analysis of this invention, as it relates to 'internationalization and localization', requires the careful consideration of the often legitimate factors, which are studied in the discrete sinological consideration of political culture and China's particular stage of development.

Western research has not comprehensively identified and carefully sifted all of the substantive change that has already taken place within basic Chinese legal thinking. This volume provides the first outline, in English, of the main features of 'pluralized jurisprudence' as it adjusts to new rights and interests in China's marketplace. The readjustment of interests is then placed within the overall context of the trend towards the 'rule of law economy' as it cuts across public and private law to deal with competing factors of justice and efficiency. Certainly this analysis suggests that, even within the very real limitations of contemporary politics, there have been qualitative conceptual breakthroughs in what is admittedly a composite and uneven – but surprisingly positive – trend towards modern rational legal culture in China.

Notes and References

1 Pluralized Jurisprudence in the Socialist Market

1. See 'rights and interests' in Ronald C. Keith, *China's Struggle for the Rule of Law* (Basingstoke and New York: Macmillan and St. Martin's Press, 1994), pp. 81, 97, 112, 114–15, 118, 140. The term's relevance to human rights protection was also discussed in R.C. Keith, 'The New Relevance of "Rights and Interests": China's Changing Human Rights Theories', *China Information*, vol. x, no. 2 (Autumn 1995), pp. 38–62 and in Keith, 'Legislating Women's and Children's "Rights and Interests" in the PRC', *China Quarterly* (hereinafter *CQ*), no. 149, March 1997, pp. 29–55.
2. This chapter significantly expands on the brief discussion of 'pluralized jurisprudence' in Ronald C. Keith, 'Post-Deng Jurisprudence: Justice and Efficiency in a "Rule of Law Economy"', *Problems of Post-Communism*, vol. 45, no. 3, May–June 1998, pp. 48–58. This 1996 article did not have the benefit of reference to crucial 1997–99 textbooks on jurisprudence and a round of related Beijing interviews in 1998 with senior Chinese jurists.
3. Authors' italics. 'Li Ruihan Speech at CPPCC Closing', FBIS-CHI-1999-0312, 11 March 1999.
4. See Liu Shengping's report on collective correspondence on jurisprudence, '*Falixuede gaige yu fazhan – bitanhui*' (Reform and the development of jurisprudence – a forum in writing), *Faxue* (Legal Studies) (Renda) no. 7, 1995, p. 17.
5. It should be pointed out that while Gao was somewhat critical of Deng Xiaoping's specific theory relating to the 16-character formulation concerning law, this book has been taken as an example of how to interpret the 15th Party Congress September 1997 formulation, 'running the country according to law and establishing a socialist rule-of-law country'. See, for example, Li Shuangyuan and Xiao Beigeng, '*Fazhi shehui – Zhongguo fazhi jinchengde zuizhong mubiao*' (The end goal of China's progress towards to the rule of law is a rule-of-law society) *Faxue* (Shanghai), no. 1, 1998, p. 15.
6. Hao Tiechuan, '*Lun faxuejia zai lifazhongde xuo yong*' (On the role of the jurists in law-making) *Zhongguo faxue* (Chinese legal science), no. 4, 1995, pp. 36, 40.
7. Sun Guohua, *et al.*, eds, *Zhonghua faxue da cidian* (The Chinese Encyclopedia of Legal Studies) (Beijing: Zhongguo jiancha chubanshe, 1997), p. 89.
8. See Wang Guochun, *Xiandai falixue: Lishi yu lilun* (Contemporary Jurisprudence: History and Theory) (Hunan chubanshe, 1997), p. 2.
9. See 'Communique of the 3rd Plenary Session of the 11th Central Committee of the Communist Party of China', 22 December 1978, *Peking Review*, no. 52, 29 December 1978, p. 14.
10. Qiao Keyu, ed., *Faxue jiaocheng* (Instructional Program in Jurisprudence) (Beijing: Falu chubanshe, 1997), p. 78.
11. Ibid., p. 79.

12 See Wang Guochun, *Xiandai falixue: Lishi yu lilun*, pp. 1–3.
13 On this distinction see 'Dialectics of Liberating, Developing Productive Forces', *Renmin ribao*, 18 September 1992, p. 5 in FBIS-CHI-92-191, 1 October 1992, pp. 38–9.
14 See Jiang Zemin's Political Report to the 14th Congress, FBIS-CHI-92-198-S, 13 October 1992, p. 27.
15 'Decision of the CPC Central Committee on Some Issues Concerning the Establishment of a Socialist Market Economic Structure', *Beijing Review* (hereinafter *BR*), 22–8 November 1993, p. 12.
16 Donald C. Clarke and James Feinerman, 'Antagonistic Contradictions: Criminal Law and Human Rights in China', *CQ*, no. 141, March 1995, p. 137.
17 Sun Guohua, '*Lun fa yu liyizhi guanxi*' (On the Relation between Law and Interests), *Zhongguo faxue*, no. 4, 1994, p. 37.
18 Xu Xianming, ed., *Gongmin quanli yiwu tonglun* (Introduction to Citizen's Rights and Obligations) (Beijing: Qunzhong chubanshe, 1991), Preface.
19 Ma Changshan, 'Long shimin shehui lilun diu fa benzhi de zai renshi' (Rethinking the essence of law according to the theory of civil society), *Faxue yanjiu*, no. 1, 1995, p. 43.
20 This book details the extent of western influence on domestic discussion of legal change and human rights. For analysis of China's rejoinders to 'human rights diplomacy', see John Cooper, 'Peking's Post-Tiananmen Foreign Policy: the Human Rights Factor', *Issues and Studies*, vol. 30, no. 10, pp. 49–78 and Andrew Nathan, 'Human Rights in Chinese Foreign Policy', *CQ*, no. 139, September 1994, pp. 622–43.
21 Luo Mingda and He Hangzhou, '*Lun renquan de shuxing*' ('On the individual character of human rights'), *Zhengfa luntan* (Tribune of Political Science and Law), no. 1, 1993, p. 56 as cited in R.C. Keith, 'Post-Deng Jurisprudence . . .', op. cit., p. 51.
22 See Li Buyun, '*Lun renquan de shanzhong cunzai xingtai*' (On the three extant forms of human rights), *Faxue yanjiu*, no. 4, 1991, p. 13 as cited in Ronald C. Keith, 'The New Relevance of "Rights and Interests": China's Changing Human Rights Theories', op. cit., p. 48.
23 Yang Haikun, '*Falu, liyi tiaozheng, shehui wending he fazhan*' (Law, interest adjustment, social stability and development), *Faxue* (Renda), no. 10, 1993, p. 24.
24 See the scholarly notations of Chapter 2 for details of the literature.
25 For example, refer to Qin Youtu and Fan Qirong, eds, *Shehui baozhang fa* (Social protection law) (Beijing: Falu chubanshe, 1997).
26 For more on this see Ronald C. Keith, 'Legislating Women's and Children's Rights and Interests in the PRC', op. cit., pp. 47–8.
27 Jiang Zemin's political report in *Zhongguo gongchandang dishiwuzi quanguo daibiao dahui wenjian huibian* (Compiled documents of the Chinese Communist Party 15th National Party Congress) (Beijing: Renmin chubanshe, 1997), p. 25.
28 Ibid., p. 21.
29 Ibid., p. 24.
30 Explanation of the historical and political background and contents of these three concepts was provided in a 9 June 1998 interview with Zhang

Guangxing, a prominent expert at the CASS Institute of Law. Zhang was of the opinion that the substance of Jiang's *chan quan* tended to emphasize 'ownership' rather than 'property rights'.

31 Zhang Wenxian, *Falixue* (Jurisprudence) (Beijing: Falu chubanshe, 1997), pp. 316–17. A similar argument was advanced by Ma Lina who argued that within Deng Xiaoping's emphasis on the primary stage of socialism and in response to the related underdevelopment of productive forces it was necessary to unify fairness and efficiency. See Ma Lina, '*Shehuizhuyi shichang jingji tiaojian xia gongping yu xiaolu de tongyi*' (The unification of fairness and efficiency under the conditions of the socialist market economy), *Zhengfa luntan*, no. 1, Feb., 1998, p. 107.

32 Gong Pixiang, '*Zhongguo fazhi xiandaihua mianlin de si da maodun*' (China is facing four big contradictions in the modernization of its legal system), *Faxue* (Legal science) (Renda), no. 5, 1995, pp. 47–50. Originally published in *Tansuo yu zhengming* (Dialogue and contention), no. 3, 1995, pp. 3–6.

33 Qi Yanping, '*Fade gongping yu xiaolu jiazhi lun*' (Theory on the law's values of fairness and efficiency), *Lilun faxue, fashixue* (Jurisprudence and historical studies), no. 6, 1996, pp. 29–34.

34 Zhang Guangbo, '*Xuexi Deng Xiaoping jianshe you Zhongguo tese shehuizhuyi lilun, yindao faxue yanzhe zhengque daolu xiangqian fazhan*' (Studying Deng Xiaoping's theory on the establishment of socialism with Chinese characteristics so as to develop jurisprudence in the right direction), *Zhongguo faxue*, no. 4, 1995, p. 48.

35 Zhang Guangbo, '*Xuexi Deng Xiaoping jianshe you Zhongguo tese shehuizhuyi lilun . . .*', op. cit., p. 46.

36 Much of the analysis of this theory follows closely on discussion in R.C. Keith, 'Post-Deng Jurisprudence . . .', op. cit., pp. 54–5. For Tong's prize-winning essay and a follow-up essay, see Tong Zhiwei, '*Yong shehui quanli fenxi fangfa chonggou xianfa tixi*' (On reconstructing the system of basic constitutional law studies using the analytical method of socio-rights), *Faxue yanjiu*, no. 5, 1994, pp. 18–24, and Tong Zhiwei, '*Zailun gong shehui quanli fenxi fangfa chonggou xianfaxue tixi*' (Again on reconstructing the system of basic constitutional law studies using the analytical method of socio-rights), *Faxue yanjiu*, no. 6, 1995, pp. 68–77.

37 Sun Xiaoxia, '*Lun falu yu shehui liyi – dui shichang jingji zhong gongping wentide ling yizhong sikao*' (On law and social interests – reflecting on a different idea on the problem of fairness in market economy), *Zhongguo faxue*, no. 4, 1995, pp. 53–4, 58.

38 Zhao Shiyi and Zou Xueping, '*Dui "yong shehui quanli fenxi fangfa chonggou xianfaxue tixi" de zhiyi – yu Tong Zhiwei tongzhi shangque*' (On the validity of 'On reconstructing the system of basic constitutional law studies using the analytical method of socio-rights' – a discussion with Comrade Tong Zhiwei), *Faxue yanjiu*, no. 1, 1995, pp. 49–55.

39 Tong Zhiwei, '*Gongmin quanli guojia quanli dui li tongyi guanxi lun gang*' (An outline of the relationship between citizen's rights and state power – a unity of opposites relationship', *Zhongguo faxue*, no. 6, 1995, p. 19.

40 Tong Zhiwei, '*Lun falixue de gengxin*' (On the renewal of jurisprudence), *Faxue yanjiu* (CASS Journal of Law), no. 6, 1998, pp. 8–10.

41 Liu Han, *'Jieshi quanli yiwu fazhan guilu de yibu li zuo...'* (A masterpiece in revealing the law of development of rights and obligations...), *Zhongguo faxue*, no. 3, 1995, pp. 118–20. See also Albert Chen, 'Developing theories of Rights and Human Rights in China', in Raymond Wack, ed., *Hong Kong, China, and 1997: Essays in Legal Theory* (Hong Kong: Hong Kong University Press, 1993), pp. 123–49.

42 See Ru Xin, *et al.*, *'Xiao zhengfu da shehui'de lilun yu shijian'* (The theory and practice of 'small government and big society') (Beijing: Shehui kexue wenxian chubanshe, 1998), *passim*.

43 Sun Guohua and Hang Jinhua, *'Fa shi "li" yu "li" de jiehe'* (Law is the unity of 'rationality' and 'power'), *Faxue*, no. 1, 1996, pp. 3–5. See also Yang Chunfu and Cai Baogang, *'Falixue yanjiu duixiang shi lun'* (On the research object of jurisprudence), *Lilunfaxue, fashixue*, no. 3, 1996, p. 60, which also attempted to reinstate the significance of 'obligations' in legal theory.

44 See, for example, Zhang Wenxian, ed., *Falixue* (Jurisprudence) (Beijing: Falu chubanshe, 1997), pp. 278–328; Sun Guohua, ed., *Falixue jiaocheng* (Instructional program in jurisprudence) (Beijing: Zhongguo renmin daxue chubanshe, 1994), pp. 103–11; Qiao Keyu, ed., *Falixue jiaocheng* (Instructional program in jurisprudence) (Beijing: Falu chubanshe, 1997), pp. 381–3.

45 Zhang Shaoyu, *'Falixue yanjiu shuping'* (Review of studies in jurisprudence), *Faxue yanjiu*, no. 1, 1995, p. 4.

46 Zhang Shaoyu, op. cit., p. 4.

47 Li Bing, *'Falu jiazhi xiaoyi youxian lun zhiyi'* (Calling into question the theory of efficiency as primary in the evaluation of law), *Faxue yanjiu*, no. 5, 1995, pp. 44–7.

48 Li Bing, op. cit., p. 45.

49 Richard Baum, analysed the September 12, 1997 speech of Jiang Zemin. Baum discussed how Jiang in his view of political reform insincerely commented on '(the putative benefits of "people's democracy", "socialist democracy", and "rule by law"', and concluded that Jiang's speech amounted to 'ritualized repetitions of conventional Communist Party reform rhetoric'. His reference to 'rule by law' misconstrues the issues at stake and ignores new formulation concerning the 'rule of law'. This view does not seem to do justice to the enormous importance attached to the speech by China's jurists. See Richard Baum, 'The Fifteenth National Party Congress: Jiang Takes Command?', *CQ*, no. 153, March 1998, pp. 146–7.

50 Ronald C. Keith, *China's Struggle for the Rule of Law* (London and New York: Macmillan and St. Martin's Press, 1994), Chapter 1.

51 Ibid., p. 12.

52 Wang Liming, *'Yifa zhi guo bushi fazhi'* (A rule-by-law state does not equal the rule of law), *Renmin ribao*, 27 February 1989 as cited in ibid., p. 16, fn. 47.

53 Li Buyun, *'Shixing yi fa zhi guo jianshe shehuizhuyi fazhi guojia'* (Bringing about running the country according to law and creating a socialist rule-of-law country), in Ministry of Justice, *Zhonggong zhongyang fazhi jiangzuo huibian* (The compiled course of CCP Central Committee lectures on the legal system) (Beijing: Falu chubanshe, 1998), p. 134.

54 These lectures are all available in ibid., *passim*. The first four of the six Zhongnanhai lectures appeared earlier in Wang Jiafu, *et al.*, eds, *Yifa zhi guo*,

jianshe shehuizhuyi fazhi guojia (Running the country according to law and establishing a socialist rule-of-law country) (Beijing: Zhongguo fazhi chubanshe, 1996), *passim*. Jiang Zemin was personally involved in approving the lecture topics, and he attended all of the lectures.

55 Much of the following interpretation of the three stages of jurisprudential development in 1949–78, 1979–93 and 1994 to the present, relies on influential discussions of senior jurists at the CASS Institute of Law; however, it should be noted that other scholars have used different periodizations; for example, see Wang Guochun's discussion of four stages including the building stage of 1949 to 1957, the Eighth Party Congress stage of 1957–66, the Cultural Revolutionary stage of destruction, 1966–76 and the current stage of restoration and development, 1976–?) in *Xiandai falixue: Lishi yu lilun*, pp. 135–8. Wang's periodization approximates the conventional periodization of Chinese politics offered in western sinology. The three stage scenario, however, has considerable domestic political significance at the present time and hence the emphasis herein.

56 See Zhang Zhende, '*Lun Deng Xiaoping jianli fazhi shehuide sixiang*' (On Deng Xiaoping's thought on establishing a rule-of-law society), *Zhongguo faxue*, no. 3, 1995, pp. 4–5. For related materials highlighting Deng's contribution to legal theory, see CCP Central Committee Documents Research Office, *Deng Xiaoping tongzhi lun minzhu yu fazhi* (Comrade Deng Xiaoping on democracy and the legal system) (Beijing: Falu chubanshe, 1990) and the Ministry of Justice, *Deng Xiaoping lun minzhu fazhi jianshe* (Deng Xiaoping on establishing democracy and the legal system) (Beijing: Falu chubanshe, 1994). There is a plethora of related academic articles such as Li Long, '*Lun Deng Xiaoping minzhu yu fazhi sixiang de jiben tezheng*' (On the basic features of Deng Xiaoping's ideas on democracy and the legal system), *Zhongguo faxue*, no. 3, 1995, pp. 3–8. Referring to Deng's selected works, Li, on p. 4. of his article, contends that under Deng, for the first time in modern Chinese history, the entwined development of democracy and the legal system was recognized as the basic policy of the state.

57 The impact of Huang Tao's book and the Preface by Guo Daohui is discussed in a review article by Wang Renbo and Zhao Ming, '*Zhaoyue "zhuxin shidai"* – *du "Shehuizhuyi fazhi yishi"*' (Transcend 'the axis of our times' – Notes on "Socialist Rule of Law Consciousness"), *Zhongguo faxue*, no. 5, 1995, pp. 119–20.

58 See Deng Xiaoping, *Selected Works of Deng Xiaoping* (Beijing: Foreign Languages Press, 1984), p. 158 as cited in Ronald C. Keith, *China's Struggle for the Rule of Law*, p. 9.

59 Yang Haikun, '*Falu, liyi tiaozheng shehui wending he fazhan*' (Law, the adjustment of interests, social stability and development), *Faxue* (Renda), no. 10, October 1993, pp. 22–3.

60 See Richard Baum, *Burying Mao* (Princeton: Princeton University Press, 1994), p. 390.

61 'Qiao Shi on Market Socialist Legal Framework', FBIS-CHI-95-034, 21 Feb. 1995, p. 19.

62 See '*Xuexi, xuexi, zai xuexi*' (Study, study and study some more), *Renmin ribao*, 10 December 1994.

63 Qiao Keyu, general ed., *Falixue jiaocheng* (Instructional program in jurisprudence) (Beijing: Falu chubanshe, 1997), p. 160.
64 'Jiang Zemin, Li Peng Attend Law Lecture', *Renmin ribao*, 20 January 1995, FBIS-CHI-95-015, p. 21.
65 *Zhonggong zhongyan fazhi jiangzuo huibian*, p. 128.
66 Ibid., p. 135.
67 See Liu Hainian's preface to Wang Jiafu, *et al.*, *Yifa zhi guo, jianshe shehuizhuyi fazhi guojia* (Running the country according to law and establishing a rule-of-law country) (Beijing: Zhongguo faluzhi chubanshe, 1996), Preface, p. 1.
68 In our June 1998 interview with Li Buyun he seemed to stress the fact that in 1996 Jiang still referred to 'socialist legal system country'. On February 9, 1996, the *Renmen ribao's* account had also cited Jiang's statement to the effect that he favoured strengthening the socialist legal system in order to run the country according to law.
69 A selection of these include: Li Buyun and Zhang Zhiming, '*Kua shijide mubiao: yi fa zhi guo, jianshe shehuizhuyi fazhi guojia*' (Striding towards the goal of the century: running the country according to law, and establishing a socialist rule-of-law-country), *Zhongguo faxue*, no. 6, 1997, pp. 18–25; Liu Hainian, '*Luelun shehuizhuyi fazhi yuanze*' (A brief discussion of the socialist principle of the rule of law), *Zhongguo faxue*, no. 1, 1998, pp. 5–15: Wang Jiafu, '*Yi fa zhi guo, jianshe shehuizhuyi fazhi guojia*' (Running the country according to law, establishing a socialist rule-of-law country) *Qiushi* (Seeking the truth), no. 24, 1997, pp. 9–14; Sun Guohua and Huang Wenyi, '*Yi fa zhi guo: zhiguo fangluede zui jia xuanze*' (Running the country according to law: a fine choice of ends), *Faxuejia* (Jurists), no. 1, 1998, pp. 3–10; Jiang Lishan, '*Zhongguo fazhi daolu chutan*' (Preliminary inquiry as to China's road to the rule of law), *Zhongwai faxue* (Beijing University's law journal), vol. 57, no. 3, 1998; *Fazhi jianshe yanjiu ketizu* (Establishing the rule of law study group), '*Fazhi jianshe lungang*' (Discussing the principle of establishing a rule of law), *Xiangtan daxue xuebao*, no. 5, 1997, pp. 100–6 and No. 6, 1997, pp. 107–11; Wen Zhengban, '*Lun fazhi wenming*' (On rule-of-law civilization), *Xiandai faxue* (Modern law science), no. 2, 1998, pp. 11–20; and running law professor commentary in '*Kaichuang yi fa zhi guode xin jumian*' (Launching the new phase of running the country according to law), *Zhengzhi yu falu* (Politics and law), no. 2, 1998, pp. 5–11.
70 Zhang Chunshen and A Xi, '*Zhunque ba wo fazhide hanyi*' (Correctly understanding the meaning of the rule of law), *Zhongguo faxue*, no. 5, 1998, p. 4.
71 Sun Guohua and Huang Wenyi, '*Lun shehuizhuyi de yi fa zhiguo*' (On the socialist running the country by law), *Zhongguo faxue*, no. 6, 1998, p. 13.
72 Author's italics. See 'Hold High the Great Banner of Deng Xiaoping Theory . . .', Jiang Zemin's Report to the '15th National Party Congress of the Communist Party of China', *BR*, 6–12 October 1997, p. 24.
73 For explanation of the Party's role in the constitution's amendment, see 'Tian Jiyun on Constitution Amendment', FBIS-CHI-1999-0309, 9 March 1999.
74 'Xinhua on Constitutional Amendments', FBIS-CHI-1999-0323, 14 March 1999.

75 'Xinhua on Constitutional Amendments', FBIS-CHI-1999-0323, 14 March 1999.
76 See the discussion of Gao Mingxuan and Mao Zedong Thought as it relates to 'flexibility' in law in Ronald C. Keith and Zhiqiu Lin, 'To Revise or Not to Revise China's Law on Counterrevolution', *China Information*, vol. 5, no. 4, Spring, 1991, pp. 24–41 and Lin and Keith, 'The Changing Substantive Principles of Chinese Criminal Law' *China Information*, vol. xiii, no. 1, Summer 1998, pp. 76–105.
77 The italics are ours. Chen Zexian's comments were reported in Shi Xiuyin, *et al.*, '*Zhongguo shehui fazhan yu quanli baohu*' (The development of Chinese society and the protection of rights), *Faxue yanjiu*, no. 3, 1994, p. 8.
78 Zhang Zhende, '*Lun Deng Xiaoping jianli fazhi shehuide sixiang*' (On Deng Xiaoping's idea of establishing a 'rule-of-law society'), *Zhongguo faxue*, no. 5, 1995, p. 15.
79 Cui Min is author of perhaps the leading treatise on Chinese criminal procedural law. See Cui Min, *Zhongguo xingshi susongfade xin fazhan* (The new development of China's law on criminal procedure) (Beijing: Zhongguo renmin gongandaxue chubanshe, 1996).
80 Jonathan Hecht, *Opening to Reform? An Analysis of China's Revised Criminal Procedure Law* (New York: Lawyers Committee for Human Rights, October, 1996), pp. 77, 79. H.L. Fu recently commented on the former report's suggestion that since the amendment was in contradiction with ingrained practice, there would likely be more procedural infractions to note. Fu noted: '. . . without the Amendment itself, no change at all is likely'. See H.L. Fu, 'Criminal Defence in China: the Possible Impact of the 1996 Criminal Procedural Law Reform', *CQ*, no. 153, March, 1998, p. 32.
81 Stanley Lubman's preface to the special issue of Chinese legal change in 'Introduction: the Future of Chinese Law', *CQ*, no. 139, 1995, p. 21. See also Stanley Lubman, ed., *China's Legal Reform* (Oxford: Oxford University Press, 1996).
82 See Liu Zuoxiang, '*Guanyu jige falixue wenti de sikao*' (Reflection on several questions of jurisprudence), *Zhongguo faxue*, no. 6, 1995, p. 48. Liu reacts to Zhang Guobo's assertion that the emergence of different schools within jurisprudence amounts to the 'pluralization of ideology', indicating that Zhang is, himself, transforming what are academic issues into ideological issues.
83 For example, refer to the May 1998 national conference on this developing crisis.
84 See, for example, Zhao Bingzhi and He Xingwang, 'On special criminal law and the revision of the criminal code', *Zhongguo faxue*, no. 4, 1996, pp. 15–23.

2 The 'Special Grouping' of the Human Rights of Women, Children, Handicapped and Elderly

1 For Deng's original Southern Tour remarks see *Deng Xiaoping wenxuan* (Deng Xiaoping's Selected Works), vol. 3 (Beijing: Renmin chubanshe, 1993), p.

373. See also Zhang Guangbo, 'Xuexi Deng Xiaoping jianshe you Zhongguo tese shehuizhuyi lilun, yindao faxue yanzhe zhengque daolu xiangqian fazhan' (Studying Deng Xiaoping's theory on the establishment of socialism with Chinese characteristics to advance jurisprudence in the right direction), *Zhongguo faxue* (Chinese Legal Science), no. 4, 1995, p. 42.

2 Bruce Gilley, *Tiger on the Brink: Jiang Zemin and China's New Elite* (Berkeley: University of California Press, 1998), p. 289.

3 'Jiang Zeming Delivers Political Work Report', 12 October 1992, Beijing Central Television, *Daily Report*, China, FBIS-CHI-92-198-S, 13 October 1992, p. 28.

4 'The Report of the People's Republic of China on the Implementation of the Nairobi Forward-Looking Strategies for the Advancement of Women', *BR*, October 24–30, 1994, p. 12.

5 'The Situation of Chinese Women', *BR*, June 6–12, 1994, documents, p. 9.

6 Jiang Zemin, 'Hold High the Great Banner of Deng Xiaoping Theory...', *BR*, 6–12 October 1997, p. 19.

7 'Text of the PRC Constitution Amendment', *Xinhua* 16 March 1999, *Daily Report*, China, FBIS-CHI-1999-0316.

8 Jack Donnelly, 'Human Rights and Development: Complementary or Competing Concerns', George Shepherd and Ved Nanda, *Human Rights and Third World Development* (Westport, Connecticut: Greenwood Press, 1985), p. 27. In terms of policy, law and jurisprudence, this book's analysis differs from the assumption in Jiang Wenran that Deng Xiaoping's economic reform introduced an unqualified trade-off of equality for market-based productivity. See Jiang Wenran, 'Human Rights and Development: the Chinese Experience in an International Context', E.P. Mendes and A-M Traeholt, eds, *Human Rights: Chinese and Canadian Perspectives* (Ottawa: The Human Rights Research and Education Centre, 1997), pp. 341–62.

9 See Pitman Potter, 'The Right to Development: Philosophical Differences and Political Implications', in E.P. Mendes and A-M Taeholt, eds, *Human Rights: Chinese and Canadian Perspectives*, pp. 98–9.

10 World Bank, 'Poverty in China: What Do the Numbers Say?', unpublished background note, October 1996 as analysed in Bruce Gilley, *Tiger on the Brink: Jiang Zemin and China's New Elite* (Berkeley: University of California Press, 1998), p. 281.

11 'Decision of the CPC Central Committee on Some Issues Concerning the Establishment of a Socialist Market', *BR*, Nov. 22–28, 1993, p. 23.

12 See Barrett McCormick, Su Shaozhi and Xiao Xiaoming, 'The 1989 Democracy Movement: a Review of the Prospects for Civil Society in China', *Pacific Affairs*, vol. 65, no. 3, Summer 1992, p. 187; Thomas Gold, 'Party-State versus Society in China', in Joyce Kallgren, ed., *Building a Nation-State: China after Forty Years* (Berkeley: Centre for Chinese Studies, China Research Monograph, no. 37), p. 150; Thomas Gold, 'The Resurgence of Civil Society in China', *Journal of Democracy*, Winter, 1990, p. 20; Heath Chamberlain, 'Coming to Terms with Civil Society', *Australian Journal of Chinese Affairs*, no. 31, January 1994, p. 117; Martin Whyte, 'Urban China: a Civil Society in the Making', in Arthur Rosenbaum, ed., *State and Society in China* (Boulder: Westview Press, 1992, pp. 98–9. In commenting on Dorothy Solinger's synthesis of autonomy and control in the Rosenbaum book, Vivi-

enne Shue suggested that even as the state 'erodes' it can also 'reinvent itself, adapting its structure and its ethos to its changing social context'. See Vivienne Shue's review of Rosenbaum's edited volume in *China Quarterly* (hereinafter *CQ*), no. 135, September 1995, p. 606. Shue comments further on the 'state-society paradigm' in her review article, 'Grasping Reform: Economic Logic, Political Logic and the State-Society Spiral', *CQ*, no. 144, December 1995, pp. 1180–1.

13 See Chapter 1's discussion of Chen Mingxia. A similar view was provided by Wu Changshen in an interview of 10 June 1998.
14 Sun Xiaoxia, '*Lun falu yu shehui liyi*' (On law and social interests), *Zhongguo faxue* (Chinese Legal Science), no. 4, 1995, pp. 52–3.
15 This is discussed in detail by David Ding, 'Pre- and Post-Tiananamen Conceptual Evolution of Democracy in Intellectual Circles' Rethinking of State and Society', *Journal of Contemporary China*, 7 (18), 1998, p. 223.
16 See the report on these debates in '*Falixude gaige yu fazhan*' (Reform and Development of Jurisprudence), *Faxue* (Law Studies), (Renda), no. 7, 1995, pp. 16–31. 'Pluralized jurisprudence' is discussed extensively in Ronald C. Keith, 'Post-Deng Jurisprudence: Justice and Efficiency in a "Rule of Law" Economy', *Problems of Post Communism*, vol. 45, no. 3, May–June 1998, pp. 54–5.
17 See Luo Mengda and He Hangzhou, '*Lun renquande geti shuxing*' (On the Individual Character of Human Rights), *Zhengfa luntan* (Forum on Politics and Law), no. 1, 1993, p. 56. On related theory, see Ronald C. Keith, 'The New Relevance of "Rights and Interests": China's Changing Human Rights Theories', *China Information*, vol. X, no. 2, Autumn 1995, pp. 38–61.
18 Tong Zhiwei, '*Lun falixuede gengxin*' (On the Renewal of Jurisprudence), *Faxue yanjiu* (CASS Journal of Law), no. 6, 1998, pp. 4, 7.
19 See Ronald C. Keith, 'Post-Deng Jurisprudence: Justice and Efficiency in a "Rule of Law Economy",' *Problems of Post Communism*, op. cit., pp. 54–5.
20 Theordore Chen, ed., *The Chinese Communist Regime*. Documents and Commentary (New York: Praeger Publishers, 1967), p. 91.
21 For discussion of this law, see '*Zhonghua renmin gongheguo guiqiao qiaojuan quanyi baohu fa*', see Wang Jiafu and Liu Hainian, eds, *Zhongguo renquan bai de quanshu* (Human Rights Encyclopedia of China) (Beijing: Zhongguo da bai de quanshu chubanshe, 1998), p. 714. The State Council on 19 July 1993 passed regulations to implement this law. The Chinese text of this law is in *Zhongguo falu nianjian* (Law Yearbook of China), 1991 (Beijing: Zhongguo falu nianjianshe chubanshe, 1991), pp. 149–50.
22 Text in Theodore Chen, ed., *The Chinese Communist Regime*, pp. 270, 273.
23 This is the English version provided in *Beijing Review* (hereinafter *BR*), no. 11, 16 March 1981, p. 24.
24 For the Chinese text, see *Zhong Hua renmin gongheguo changyong falu daquan* (Compendium of often used laws of the PRC) (Beijing: Falu chubanshe, 1989), pp. 3, 5, 7–9.
25 This July 1, 1988 law is provided in translation in *BR*, no. 10., 6–12 March 1989, Documents, IX–XIV.
26 See 'The Report of the PRC on the Implementation of the Nairobi Forward-Looking Strategies for the Advancement of Women', p. 9.

27 Albert Chen has analysed three different schools of opinion in terms of 'rights-oriented', 'obligations-oriented' and 'equal emphasis on the consistency of rights and obligations', see Albert Chen, "Developing Theories of Rights and Human Rights in China" in Raymond Wacks, ed., *Hong Kong, China and 1997: Essays in Legal Theory* (Hong Kong: Hong Kong University Press, 1993), pp. 123–49.
28 This was explored in the authors' 10 June 1998 discussion with Professor Xia Yinlan.
29 See Ronald C. Keith,'Post-Deng Jurisprudence: Justice and Efficiency in a "Rule of Law Economy",' op. cit., *passim*.
30 See Shao-chuan Leng and Hungdah Chiu, *Criminal Justice in Post-Mao China* (Albany: State University of New York Press, 1985), p. 7. Also refer to Ronald C. Keith's discussion of law and the 'comprehensive management of public order' in *China's Struggle for the Rule of Law* (London: Macmillan, 1994), pp. 18, 29, 106, 118, 149.
31 Back in 1983, Judith Stacey described China's mass associations in terms of their functions to inform the 'public patriarchy', and their lack of ability to initiate policy. See *Patriarchy and Socialist Revolution in China*, p. 228.
32 The notion of '*quanyi*' and its implications were first explored in Ronald C. Keith, *China's Struggle for the Rule of Law* (London and New York: Macmillan Press and St. Martin's Press, 1994), pp. 81, 97, 112, 114–15, 118, 140 and in Ronald C. Keith, 'The New Relevance of "Rights and Interests": China's Changing Human Rights Theories', *China Information*, vol. x, no. 2, Autumn, 1995, pp. 38–62. Western scholarship which deals with the state–society paradigm in China often comments that the Chinese political culture has tended to merge state and society into a continuum of political and social activity and that despite the growth of market relationships the conceptual notion of civil society lacks a strong indigenous equivalent. For the literature on civil society, see n12, above.
33 'Human Rights in China', *BR*, Nov. 4–10, 1991, Documents, p. 9. The distinction between legally defined rights, *fading quanli*, and rights that were socially recognized and enjoyed, *shiyou quanli* was privotal to Li Buyun's major new theory on three forms of human rights. For discussion of Li Buyun, '*Lun renquande sanzhong cunzai xingtai*' (On the Three Extant Forms of Human Rights), *Faxue yanjiu*, no. 4, 1991. See Ronald C. Keith, 'The New Relevance of "Rights and Interests": China's Changing Human Rights Theories', op. cit., p. 48.
34 As explained in Chen Mingxia's 5 June 1998 with the authors. As for the tension between efficiency and fairness, Mme Chen argued that these two concepts have to be given equal emphasis. She also wanted to emphasize active state involvement in rights protection and attitudinal change and at the same time she recognized the need for new organizational initiatives within society.
35 Authors' italics 'PRC: Text of Law on Protecting Elderly', *Xinhua*, Beijing, 29 August 1996 in FBIS-CHI-96-173, *Daily Report*, China, 29 August 1999.
36 Ru Xin *et al.*, eds, '*Xiao zhengfu da shehui*' *de lilun yu shijian* (The Theory and Practice of Small Government Big Society), p. 64.

37 See Ronald C. Keith, *China's Struggle for the Rule of Law*, pp. 116–18 and also Ronald C. Keith and Zhiqiu Lin, 'Coping with Economic Crime in a "Rule of Law Economy",' *China Report*, vol. 35, no. 2, 1999, pp. 143–61.
38 Li Lin provides this definition. See his '*Quanqiuhua beijingxide Zhongguo lifa fazhan*' (China's Legislative Development in the Globalization Context), *Falixue, fashixue* (Jurisprudence and Legal History), no. 3, 1998, p. 31. In his 4 June 1998 interview with the authors, Lu Buyun offered the following definition: 'Internationalization includes generating links with the international community which includes increasing participation in international convention and the convergence of the spirit, purpose and form of law between China and the West.' Also see Ronald C. Keith, ' "Internationalization" and "Localization" in the Chinese Search for Human Justice', October 1999 published proceedings of 'Globalization: Social, Economic and Political Dimensions', Eastern Mediterranean University, November 1998.
39 See 'Human Rights in China', *BR*, 4–10 November 1991, pp. 8–45.
40 Shen Zongling, '*Nuquanzhuyi faxue shuping*' (A Commentary on Feminist Jurisprudence), *Zhongguo faxue*, no. 3, 1995, p. 51.
41 Paul McKenzie, 'China and the Women's Convention: Prospects for the Implementation of an International Norm', *China Law Reporter*, v. vii, no. 1, 1991, Introduction, p. 34.
42 'Beijing Declaration', *BR*, 16–22 October 1995, p. 9.
43 Sixteen of these regulations have been translated in Yuanling Chao and Richard Sao, eds, 'Provincial Laws on the Protection of Women and Children', *Chinese Law and Government*, v. 27, no. 1, Jan.–Feb., 1994, *passim*.
44 'The Situation of Children in China', *BR*, April 22–9, 1996, p. 21.
45 'The Report of the PRC on the Implementation of the Nairobi Forward-Looking Strategies for the Advancement of Women', *BR*, 24–30 October 1994, p. 10. Also see the June 1994 white paper, 'The Situation of Chinese Women', which highlights this law in its discussion of equal legal status in *BR*, 6–12 June 1994, pp. 12–13.
46 Wang Rong, 'Women's Rights Awareness Drive Put on the Move', *China Daily*, 10 June 1992, p. 3.
47 'Chen Muhua Profiled', *Xinhua*, 4 September 1995 in FBIS-CHI-95-171, 5 September 1995, pp. 31–2.
48 'An Outline of Chinese Women's Development 1995–2000', in FBIS-CHI-95-154, 10 August 1995, pp. 13–19. The Chinese text is available in *Xin Hua yuebao*, no. 10, 1995, pp. 48–55. The Beijing Declaration was carried in the *BR*, no. 42, 16–22 October 1995, pp. 8–10.
49 'Speech by Chen Muhua: Equality, Development and Peace are the Common Pursuit of Women all over the World', *Xinhua*, 2 September 1995 in FBIS-CHI-95-174, 8 September 1995, pp. 4, 6.
50 'Text of Jiang's Speech', FBIS-CHI-95-171, 5 September 1995, pp. 21–2.
51 Hillary Rodham Clinton, 'Women's Rights Are Human Rights', in *Vital Speeches of the Day*, vol. lxi, no. 24, 1 October 1995, pp. 738–40.
52 'The PRC Law for the Protection of the Handicapped', *Xinhua*, Beijing, 29 December 1990, FBIS-CHI-91-003, 4 January 1991, pp. 22–7. For the Chinese text *see* '*Zhonghua renmin gongheguo canjifen baohu fa*', in *Zhongguo*

falu nianjian, 1991 (Law Yearbook of China, 1991) (Beijing; Zhongguo falu nianjianshe chubanshe, 1991), pp. 152–6.
53 Authors' italics, 'Song Rufen on Draft Law Revisions', *Xinhua*, Beijing, 27 December 1990, FBIS-CHI-90-250, 28 December 1990, p. 18.
54 'Commentator on Legislating Law for Handicapped', *Renmin ribao*, 29 December 1990, p. 1, FBIS-CHI-91-003, 4 January 1991, p. 27.
55 'I am just as good as anyone else!', *China Daily*, 15 March 1985, p. 5.
56 Ibid., p. 18.
57 This background was originally provided in Ronald C. Keith, *China's Struggle for the Rule of Law*, p. 115.
58 A short list of such works might include: Phyllis Andors, *The Unfinished Liberation of Chinese Women 1949–1980* (Bloomington: Indiana University Press, 1983); Margery Wolf and Roxane Witke, eds, *Women in Chinese Society* (Stanford: Stanford University Press, 1975); Judith Stacey, *Patriarchy and Socialist Revolution in China* (Berkeley: University of California Press, 1983); Elizabeth Croll, *The Politics of Marriage in Contemporary China* (Cambridge: Cambridge University Press, 1981); Dalia Davin, *Woman-Work: Women and the Party in Revolutionary China* (Oxford: Clarendon Press, 1976); Kay Ann Johnson, *Women, the Family and Peasant Revolution in China* (Chicago: University of Chicago Press, 1983); Deborah Davis and Stevan Harrell, eds, *Chinese Families in the Post-Mao Era* (Berkeley: University of California Press, 1993). Christina Gilmartin, Fail Hershatter, *et al.*, eds, *Engendering China: Women Culture, and the State* (Cambridge, MA: Harvard Contemporary China Series, no. 10, 1994; Ellen Judd, *Gender and Power in Rural North China* (Stanford: Stanford University Press, 1994); 'Family Background, Gender and Educational Attainment in Urban China', *CQ*, no. 145, March 1996, pp. 53–86.
59 This issue of the relative priority of 'rights and interests' in the 1991 law was explored during the authors' 10 June 1998 discussion with Wu Changshen who emphasized that, unlike women, the handicapped and the elderly, children do not have the right to work.
60 'The Progress of Human Rights in China', *BR*, Special Issue, 1996, p. 21.
61 See Articles 1 and 3, 'Law on Minors', *Xinhua*, Beijing, 4 September 1991, in FBIS-CHI-91-1974, 9 September 1991, p. 36.
62 Ibid., p. 37.
63 'PRC Law Protecting Women's Rights and Interests', *Xinhua*, Beijing, 7 April 1992, FBIS-CHI-92-072-S, 14 April 1992, p. 17.
64 Shao Dengsheng claims that there are two basic views on the causal connection between the Cultural Revolution and the subsequent rise of juvenile deliquency. His own view is: 'Without the "cultural revolution", this peak period would never have occurred.' Shao does recognize another view which holds that holds that '. . . it is too simplistic to attribute juvenile deliquency to the cultural revolution alone. . . .' Shao, *Preliminary Study of China's Juvenile Deliquency* (Beijing: Foreign Languages Press, 1992), p. 56. Borge Bakken has challenged the proponents of Shao's view arguing that the government in its defence of Chinese moral and cultural values 'vastly over-reacted' to juvenile deliquency as a 'perceived threat to social order'. See Borge Bakken, 'Crime, Juvenile Deliquency and Deterrence

Policy in China', *Australian Journal of Chinese Affairs*, no. 30, July 1993, p. 29.
65 'The Situation of Children in China', p. 20. Kay Johnson has raised the very pertinent criticism that while the poorer segments of China's population have witnessed increasing prosperity, Chinese orphanages are still disproportionately filled with girls. See Kay Johnson, 'Chinese Orphanages: Saving China's Abandoned Girls', *Australian Journal of Chinese Affairs*, no. 30, 1993, pp. 61–88.
66 According to Professor Yu Shutong, adviser to the Internal and Judicial Affairs Committee of the NPC. See 'NPC Adviser on Protecting Minors' Rights', *Xinhua*, 6 December 1991, FBIS-CHI-91-235, 6 December 1991, p. 24.
67 'Law on Minors', op. cit., p. 37.
68 See Wang Zhongfan, ed., *Zhongguo shehui zhian zenghe zhili de lilun yu shijian* (Theory and Practice of Comprehensive Management of Public Order) (Beijing: Qunzhong chubanshe, 1989), p. 4.
69 For discussion of this sector of the law refer to Ronald C. Keith and Lin Zhiqiu, 'Economic Crime and China's Transition to a "Rule of Law Economy",' *China Report*, vol. 35, no. 2, 1999, pp. 143–61.
70 The Chinese text of this law is in *Funu he weichengnianren falu baohu quan shu* (Complete volume on the legal protection of women and children) (Beijing: Zhongguo jiancha chubanshe, 1991), pp. 10–16. The English text is in FBIS-CHI-91-174, 9 September 1991, pp. 36–40.
71 'PRC Law Protecting Women's Rights and Interests', *Xinhua*, Beijing, 7 April 1992, FBIS-CHI-92-072-S, 14 April 1992, p. 18.
72 'Song Rufen Reviews Draft Laws', *BR*, 3 September 1991, FBIS-CHI-91-172, 5 September 1991, p. 27.
73 'Minors Protected Under the Law', *BR*, June 22–28, 1992, p. 25.
74 This kind of approach was previously explicit at the provincial level; for example refer to 'Regulations of Heilongjiang Province on the Protection on Women's and Children's Lawful Rights and Interests', *Chinese Law and Government*, vol. 27, no. 1, Jan.–Feb., 1994, p. 11.
75 Ronald C. Keith, *China's Struggle for the Rule of Law*, p. 111.
76 'Adoption Law of the PRC', *Xinhua*, 29 December 1991, FBIS-CHI-91-251, 31 December 1991, pp. 18–20.
77 As explained in the author's 15 June 1998 discussion with Li Mingxuan.
78 Dang Rihong, '*Hunyinfa de xiugai yu funu yuanyi de baohu*' (Revision of the Marriage Law and the Protection of Women's Rights and Interests), *Zhonghua nuzi xueyuan xuebao*, vol. 10, 1998, Supplementary Issue, p. 17.
79 'The Report of the PRC on the Implementation . . .', op. cit., p. 10.
80 This was confirmed in a 10 June 1998 interview with Wu Changshan.
81 *BR*, June 6–12 1994, p. 13.
82 'Implementation of the Law on Safeguarding the Rights and Interests of Women', *BR*, 4–10 September 1995, p. 12.
83 See 'Women and Reform' *China News Analysis*, 1477, Jan 15, 1993, p. 3 and Ronald C. Keith, *China's Struggle for the Rule of Law*, pp. 112–13.
84 'Women's Conference Participant Issues Protest', *Eastern Express*, 22 September 1995, p. 13 in FBIS-CHI-95-185, p. 23.

85 'PRC Law Protecting Women's Rights and Interests', FBIS-CHI-92-072, 14 April 1992, pp. 18–21.
86 'Important Legal Weapon for Protecting Women's Rights, Interests', *Renmin ribao*, 10 April 1992, p. 1, FBIS-CHI-92-075, 17 April 1992, p. 39.
87 'The Report of the PRC on the implementation . . .', op. cit., p. 8.
88 The latest 1998 Chinese figures indicate that women account for 21.82 per cent of the NPC delegates and 15.5 per cent of the delegates at the Chinese People's Political Consultative Conference. The later is up over the 1994 figure of 9.2 per cent. The greatest increases have occurred with an increase of 46.47 per cent over the last five years at the provincial leadership level. See State Council Information Office, '*1998 nian Zhongguo renquan shiye de jinzhan*' (Employment progress for the year 1998 in China's human rights) (Beijing: Wuzhou zhuanbo chubanshe, 1999), pp. 18–19.
89 Stanley Rosen, 'Women and Political Participation in China', *Pacific Affairs*, vol. 68, no. 3, Fall 1995, p. 339.
90 Han Henan '*Xin Zhongguo can zheng funu qunti jiegou de bianhua ji qi yuanyin yu yingxiang*' (Changes in the structure of the political participation of women's groups and their causes and effects), *Zhonghua nuzi xueyuan xuebao* (Journal of the Chinese Women's College), no. 3, 1998, pp. 36–7.
91 This is based on the explanation of Ma Yinan who states a preference for fixing the pool of candidates in '*Guanyu wanshan funu quanyi baochang fa de ruogan sikao*' (Several thoughts on the perfection of the law on the protection of women's rights and interests), *Zhongguo faxue*, no. 5, 1994, p. 102. Ma has indicated that the provincial response to Article 10, Part 2 of the new women's law was robust and that she, herself, preferred a system which focused on women candidates rather than women deputies. See Ma Yinan, 'Chinese Law and the Protection of Women's Human Rights', in E.P. Mendes and A.-M. Traeholt, eds, *Human Rights: Chinese and Canadian Perspectives*, p. 455.
92 Ma Yinan, '*Guanyu wanshan funu quanyi baochang de ruogan sikao*', pp. 104–5.
93 Li Mingshun, '*Funu fa lilun yanjiuzhong de liangge wenti*' (Two questions in the theory of women's law), *Zhonghua nuzi xueyuan xuebao* (*Journal of the Chinese Women's College*), no. 2, 1997, p. 28. In this article Li was particularly concerned that even given its great importance, the 1992 law not be taken as the sum of the law on women.
94 Ming Chenxia discussed this with the authors on 5 June 1998. See also Shao Fen, 'Women's Legal Status and Protection of Rights and Interests in China', *Funu yanjiu*, no. 4, 1994, pp. 36–43.
95 For the Chinese text of the new labour law, see *Zhonghua renmin gongheguo falu fenlei zonglan: Guojia fa, xingzheng fa juan* (General Compendium of All Classes of PRC Law) (Beijing: Falu chubanshe, 1994, pp. 661–8.
96 According to the author's 15 June 1998 discussion with Li Mingshun. Apparently as a result of the 1997 revision to the criminal law, selling and kidnapping were again brought together as two different behaviours placed within the same criminal category.
97 Ronald C. Keith, *China's Struggle for the Rule of Law*, pp. 107–8.
98 5 June 1998 interview with the authors at the Institute of Law.

99 Author's 10 June 1998 discussion with Xia Yinlan.
100 For example, see Li Huiying, 'Mianxiang 21 shiji de funu fazhan zhanlue (xia)', (Towards a 21st strategy for women's development, part 2), *Funu yanqiu* (Women's Studies) (Renda), no. 1, 1997, p. 13.
101 Li Mingshun, '*Luelun woguo xin xingfa dui funu quanyide teshu baohu*' (Sketching out the Special Protection of Women's Rights and Interests in China's New Criminal Law), *Zhonghua nuzi xueyuan xuebao* (Journal of Chinese Women's College), no. 3, 1997, p. 13.
102 'Minister on New Maternal, Infant Health Care Law', Hong Kong *AFP*, 14 Nov. 1994, in FBIS-CHI-94-219, 14 November 1994, p. 55.
103 'Standing Committee Hears Amendments to Draft Laws', *Xinhua*, 26 October 1994, p. 33.
104 'Officials on Goal of Health Care Law', *Xinhua*, 14 November 1994, p. 56.
105 Yu Min, '*Lun nannu pingdeng de xianfa yuance zai "minshi lingyu" nei de zhijie xiaoli*' (On the direct effect of the constitutional principle of gender equality in the sphere of civil affairs), *Zhongguo faxue*, no. 6, 1995, p. 106.
106 Dang Rihong, '*Hunyinfa xiugai yu funu quanyi de baohu*', op. cit., p. 17.
107 Yang Dawen, Ma Yinan, '*Xin zhongguo huanyin jiating faxue de fazhan ji women de sikao*' (The development of the study on new China's marriage and family law and our thinking), *Faxue yanjiu* (CASS Journal of Law), no. 6, 1998, p. 36. Wu Changzhen has argued that marriage and family law ought to be considered a separate department of law as this will give it more profile than if it were a subset of civil law. See Wu, '*Xiugai Zhongguo hunyinfade silu he gouxiang*' (Conceptualizing and thinking about revision to China's Marriage Law), *Zhonghua nuzi xueyuan xuebao*, vol. 10, Special Issue, pp. 2–3.
108 Wu Hong, '*Dui woguo xianxing hunyinfa xiugai de yijian he kanfa*' (Ideas and viewpoint on the revision of China's current marriage law), *Zhonghua nuzi xueyuan xuebao*, vol. 10, 1998, Supplementary Issue, pp. 25–7.
109 Li Mingshun, '*Luelun woguo xin xing fa dui funu quanyi de teshu baohu*', op. cit., p. 15.
110 Yu Jing, '*Hunyin jiatingfazhong falu he daode fa guanxi wenti yanjiu*' (Studying questions concerning the relation between law and morality in the marriage and family law), *Zhonghua nuzi xueyuan xuebao* (Journal of the Chinese Women's College), no. 10, 1998, Supplementary Issue, p. 19.
111 Zhuo Dongqing, '*Qianyi lihun xianzhi*' (Brief Opinion on Divorce Restriction), *Zhonghua nuzi xueyuan xuebao*, vol. 10, 1998, Supplementary Issue, p. 54.
112 Zhang Qinmian and Wang Shengluan, '*Wanshan woguo fuqi zaichanzhi; huoying shichan jingjide fazhan*' (Perfecting China's system of marital property relations and enlivening the development of the market economy), *Zhonghua nuzi xueyuan xuebao*, vol. 10, 1998, Supplementary Issue, p. 47.
113 Chen Wei (A study of divorce parents' custody of children), p. 43.
114 'PRC Law on Protecting Rights and Interests of the Elderly', *Xinhua*, Beijing, 29 August 1996, FBIS-CHI-96-173, 29 August 1996. For the Chinese text, see '*Zhonghua renmin gongheguo laonianren quanyi baohu*', in *Zhonghua falu nianjian 1997* (Law Yearbook of China, 1997) (Beijing: Zhonghu falu nianjianshe chubanshe, 1997), pp. 295–7.

115 UN figures analysed by Sun Xiuping, *China's Social Security System* (Beijing: Foreign Languages Press, 1996), p. 61.
116 Ibid., p. 6.
117 Wang Shunhua, ed., *Laonianjen quanyide falu baozhang* (The legal guarantees of the rights and interests of the elderly) (Beijing: Jingji guanli chubanshe, 1995), pp. 13–14, 20, 31. See also the gloss on Articles 5 and 6 of the 1996 law in Meng Liankun, *et al.*, eds, *Zhonghua renmin gongheguo laonianren quanyi baozhang fa shiyi* (Explanations of the PRC law on the rights and interests of the elderly) (Beijing: Hualing chubanshe, 1997), pp. 12–15.
118 Ibid., p. 70.
119 Ibid., p. 74.
120 Shi Jichun, '*Woguo minfa tongze yu waiguo chuantong minfa zongze de bijiao*' (Comparing [China's] General Principles of Civil Law with the traditional civil law principles of foreign countries), *Shehui kexue*, no. 7, 1986, p. 24.

3 Justice and Efficiency in Contractual Labour Relations

1 'Premier Zhu Rongji on Rule of Law', FBIS-CHI-1999-0304, 5 March 1999.
2 Fifth National People's Congress, *Constitution of the People's Republic of China* (Beijing: Foreign Languages Press, 3rd edn, 1994), p. 14.
3 'Tian Jiyun on Constitution Amendment', 9 March 1999, FBIS-CHI-1999-0309, 23 March 1999.
4 Sun Xiuping, *China's Social Security System* (Beijing: Foreign Languages Press, 1996), p. 118.
5 Ibid., p. 117.
6 See Articles 16, 17 and 45 of the 1982 State Constitution of the PRC.
7 See Jiang Zemin's Political Report in *Zhongguo gongchandang dishiwuzi quanguo daibiao dahui wenjian huibian* (Compiled Documents of the Chinese Communist Party 15th National Party Congress) (Beijing: Renmin chubanshe, 1997), p. 25.
8 Sun Xiuping, *China's Social Security System*, p. 102.
9 Zhu Rongji, 'Government Work Report', *Daily Report, China*, FBIS-CHI-1999-0305, 8 March 1999.
10 Ibid., p. 45.
11 Wang Jiafu, '*Guanyu yi fa zhiguo jianshe shehuizhuyi fazhi guojia de lilun he shijian wenti*' (On the questions concerning the theory and practice of ruling the country according to law and establishing a rule of law country) in *Zhonggong zhongyang fazhi jiangzuo huibian* (Collection of Lectures on the Legal System to the Central Committee of the CCP) (Beijing: Falu chubanshe, 1998), p. 116.
12 Wang Jiafu, '*Shehuizhuyi shichangjingji faluzhidu jianshe wenti*' (On the questions concerning the creation of the legal system under the socialist market economy) *in Zhonggong zhongyang fazhi jiangzuo huibian* (Collection of lectures on the legal system to the Central Committee of the CCP) (Beijing: Publishing House of Law, 199), pp. 61–83.
13 See Ru Xin, *et al.*, eds, '*Xiao zhengfu da shehui*' *de lilun yu shijian* (The theory and practice of 'small government and big society') (Beijing: Shehui kexue wenxian chubanshe, 1998), pp. 25–33.

14 Sun Xiuping, *China's Social Security System*, p. 27.
15 Ibid., pp. 78–9.
16 Guan Huai, Ren Fushan, and Chan Wenyun (eds), *Laodong faxue* (Labour Law Science) (Beijing: Falu chubanshe, 1996), pp. 92–3.
17 Wang Quanxing, *Laodong fa* (Labour Law) (Beijing: Falu chubanshe, 1997), p. 82.
18 'Labour Relations in Foreign Enterprises Viewed', *BR*, 15–21 May 95, no. 2, pp. 17–21; FBIS-CHI-95-092, *Daily Report*, China, 12 May 1995; see also '*Guanyu "Zhonghua renmin gongheguo laodongfa (caoan)" shuoming*' (Explanation about the 'PRC Labour Law (draft)' by Minister of labour, Li Boyong to the Standing Committee of the NPC in *Laodong fa jiben lilun yu shiwu jiangzuo* (Lectures on basic theory and practice of the labour law, compiled by the Supreme People's Court Labour Training Group) (Beijing: Falu chubanshe 1995), p. 151.
19 Wang Yantian, 'Commentary Views Passage of Labour Law', *Renmin ribao*, in FBIS-CHI-94-149, *Daily Report*, China, 28 July 1994, 'Commentator Welcomes Newly Promulgated Labour Law' FBIS-CHI-94-133, *Daily Report*, China, 6 July 1994, translated from Commentator's article, 'Conscientiously Safeguard Labourers' Legitimate Rights and Interests' in *Renmin ribao*, 6 July 1994, and 'Labour Relations in Foreign Enterprises Viewed', *BR*, 15–21 May 1995, no. 2, pp. 17–21, *Daily Report*, China, FBIS-CHI-95-092, 12 May 1995.
20 Hilary K. Josephs, 'Labour Law in a "Socialist Market Economy": The Case of China', *Columbia Journal of Transnational Law*, 1995, vol. 33, 1995, p. 568. Articles 38, 41, and 44 of the 1994 LL explicitly stipulated overtime should not exceed one hour a day, no more than 36 hours a month, and at least one day off from work each week. Overtime pay shall be 150 per cent of regular wage on work days, at least 200 per cent on off-days, and 300 per cent during legal holidays.
21 For a general introduction on Chinese labour law, see Vai Lo, 'Labour and Employment in the People's Republic of China: From A Nonmarket-Driven to A Market-Driven Economy' *Indiana International and Comparative Law Review*, vol. 6, no. 2, 1996, pp. 337–411.
22 See Guan Huai (ed.), *Zhonghua renmin gongheguo laodong fa daodu* (Introduction to PRC Labour Law) (Beijing: Falu chubanshe, 1994), p. 4 and Wang Quanxing, *Laodong fa*, p. 73.
23 See Guo Jie, Liu Zun and Yang Sun, *Laodong faxue* (Labour Law Science) (Beijing: Zhongguo zhengfa daxue chubanshe, 1997), p. 14.
24 See Guan Huai, Ren Fushan and Chan Wenyun (eds), *Laodong faxue*, p. 141.
25 For a brief history of post-1949 Chinese labour legislation, see Guan Huai, *et al.*, *Laodong faxue* (Labour Law Science), 1996, pp. 122–42.
26 Guan Huai (ed.), *Zhonghua renmin gongheguo laodong fa daodu*, p. 29.
27 See H. Josephs, 'Labour Law in a "Socialist Market Economy": The Case of China', *Columbia Journal of Transnational Law*, 1995, vol. 33, p. 100. She also pointed out that 'the law does not indicate any change in the government's repressive attitude toward independent union activity, the rights of association, and the right to strike and engage in collective bargaining over terms and conditions of employment'.

28 To facilitate the implementation of 1994 LL in January 1995, the Ministry of Law promulgated 17 supplementary regulations, including: 'The Circular on Enforcing the Minimum Wage System'; 'The Procedures for Managing Labour Supervisors'; 'The Regulations Governing Personnel Reductions in Enterprises due to Business Considerations'; 'The Interim Regulations Governing the Management of the Interprovincial Migration of Rural Labour'; 'The Regulations Governing the Medical Leave of Enterprise Worker Resulting from Illness or Non-Job-related Injuries'; 'The Procedures for Providing Economic Compensation for Violations or the Termination of Labour Contracts'; 'The Regulations Governing Wage Payments'; 'The Regulations Governing the Special Protection of Minors'; 'The Procedures for Approving the Enforcement of the Work System Based on Irregular Hours and the Work System Based on the Comprehensive Calculation of Work Hours'; 'The Regulations Governing the Management of Vocational Training Entities'; 'The Procedures for Managing Mining Safety Supervisors'; 'The Procedures for Carrying out Safety Supervision in Mining Construction'; 'Experimental Measures for Enterprise Workers' Child-Bearing Insurance'; and 'The Measures of Punishment for Violations of the Labour Law'. See also Ministry of Labour, 'Supplementary Labour Laws', FBIS-CHI-95-024, 6 February 1995, p. 31. This legislative trend continued throughout 1996–98.

29 See Labour Minister Li Boyong's 'explanation' in *Laodong fa jiben lilun yu shiwu*, p. 151.

30 For instance, based on the provisions of the 1982 constitution, Professor Guan Huai argued that there should be eight principles in the 1994 LL, including: citizens have rights and obligations to work; the reform labour system promotes production efficiency; distribute according to labour and improve wages and welfare based on development of economy; labour have rights to rest and labour protection; labour has the right of material assistance; labour has the obligation to observe labour discipline; workers have the freedom of assembly, organization and rights to participate in the democratic management of enterprises; equality between female and male and between different ethical groups in terms of labour-related issues. See Guan Huai *et al.*, (eds), *Laodong faxue*, pp. 18–20.

31 See Jiang Zemin's 1997 Political Report in *Zhongguo gongchandang dishiwuzi quanguo daibiao dahui wenjian huibian*, p. 25.

32 See Guo Jie, Liu Zun and Yang Sun, *Laodong faxue*, pp. 46–53.

33 See '*Guanyu "Zhonghua renmin gongheguo laodong fa (caoan)" shuoming*', op. cit., p. 151. Article 1 of the 1994 LL also states that 'based on the state constitution, this law is enacted to protect lawful rights and interests of labour, to adjust labour relations, to establish and maintain a socialist market economy labour system and to promote economic development and social progress'.

34 See Guo Jie, Liu Zun and Yang Sun, *Laodong faxue*, p. 46.

35 This theory is elaborated fully in Dong Baoha, *Laodong fa yu laodong zhengyi shiyong shouce* (Practical Handbook on Labour Law and Labour Disputes Settlement) (Beijing: Zhongguo jiancha chubanshe, 1994), cited in Guo Jie, Liu Zun and Yang Sun, *Laodong faxue*.

36 This theory is discussed extensively in Wu Chaomin, Wang Quanxing and Zhang Guowen, *Zhongguo laodong fa xinlun* (New Studies in Chinese Labour Law) (Beijing: Zhongguo jingji chubanshe, 1994), cited in Guo Jie, Liu Zun and Yang Sun, *Laodong faxue*.
37 Guo Jie, Liu Zun and Yang Sun, *Laodong faxue*, pp. 71–2.
38 See Li Jingsen and Wang Cangsuo (eds), *Laodong faxue* (Labour Law Science) (Beijing: Chinese People's University Press, 1996), p. 41.
39 See Article 4 of the 1994 LL.
40 See Liang Shuwen and Hui Luming, *Laodong fa jipeitao guiding xinshi xinjie* (New interpretations of 1994 Labour Law and Related Regulations) (Beijing: Renmin fayuan chubanshe, 1997), p. 35.
41 See Li Jinsen and Wang Cangsuo, eds, *Laodong faxue*, p. 247.
42 Li Buyun, '*Shixing yifa zhiguo jianshe shehuizhuyi fazhi guojia*' (Ruling the Country According to Law, and Establishing a Socialist Rule of Law Country) in *Zhonggong zhongyang fazhi jiangzuo huibian*, p. 146. He also criticized some of the existing local legislation that did not satisfy this fundamental requirements of law focusing on rights protection.
43 '*Gongren ribao* commentator,' Labour Law Implementation Marks Milestone' FBIS-CHI-95-060, *Daily Report*, China, 27 January 1995. Some scholars also connect the protection of rights and interests in the 1994 LL with restoration of the master status of labourers, although the argument is ideologically charged and without any grounding in reality. For a discussion, see Guo Jie, Liu Zun and Yang Sun, *Laodong faxue*, p. 9.
44 See Guo Jie, Liu Zun and Yang Sun, *Laodong faxue*, p. 7.
45 Guan Huai, *Zhonghua renmin gongheguo laodong fa daodu*, pp. 39–41. For a detailed account of the employment system under the planned economy before the reform, see Yanjie Bian, *Work and Inequality in Urban China* (New York: State University of New York Press, 1994).
46 Gordon White, 'The Politics of Economic Reform in Chinese Industry: the Introduction of the Labour Contract System', *CQ*, no. 111 (September, 1987), p. 356. Also in this article White provides a detailed treatment on the politics of introducing the labour contract system in state-owned enterprises during the period 1978–86.
47 R.H. Folsom and J.H. Minan, *Law in The People's Republic of China: Commentary, Readings and Materials* (Boston: Martinus Nijhoff Publishers, 1989), p. 508.
48 A series rules and regulations were issued for this purpose, including the 1980 'Regulations concerning Labour Management in Sino-Foreign Joint Enterprises' by the State Council and the 1983 'Notice on the Active Trial Implementation of the Contract Employment System' by the Ministry of Labour and Personnel, the 1986 'Regulations on Contract Employment', the 1986 'Provisional Regulations of Implementation of Labour Contract System in State-Owned Enterprises', the 1986 'Provisional Regulations concerning Hiring Workers in State-Owned Enterprises' and the 1989 'Provisional Regulations Concerning Labour Management in Private Enterprises', issued by the State Council. Chinese texts of these regulations are in Liang Shuwen and Hui Luming (eds), *Laodong fa jipeitao guiding xin shixijie*.

49 See articles 16–35 of the 1994 LL.
50 An example is the 1994 'Methods of Financial Compensation in Cases Where Labour Contract Was Terminated and Breached' by the Ministry of Labour.
51 See Guan Huai, Ren Fushan and Chan Wenyun (eds), *Laodong faxue*, p. 215, and Tian Ying, 'On Theory and the Practice of Relying on Working Class', *Daily Report*, China, FBIS-CHI-96-211, August 1, 1996. For more on changes to worker status in state-owned enterprises, see Gordon White, 'The Politics of Economic Reform in Chinese industry: the Introduction of the Labour Contract System', op. cit., p. 365.
52 Mao-chang Li provides a useful discussion concerning implications of recent development in Chinese labour legislation to international investors. See Mao-chang Li, 'Legal Aspects of Labour Relations in China: Critical Issues for International Investors', *Columbia Journal of Transnational Law*, 1995, vol. 33, pp. 521–57.
53 Liang Shuwen and Hui Luming, *Laodong fa jipeitao guiding xinshi xinjie*, p. 222. The issue of treating labour as a commodity in the marketplace is not without controversy among western labour law scholars. For instance, Steven Anderman observed that '... for whereas general principles of freedom of contract were rigorously applied to give the employer the opportunities to treat labour as a pure market commodity, those principles gave way to older, almost feudal, notions of hierarchical duty when it came to regulating the extent of the employee's obligations to obey the employer'. See S. Anderman, *Labour Law: Management Decisions and Workers' Rights* (London: Butterworths, 1992), p. 4.
54 Guan Huai (ed.), *Zhonghua renmin gongheguo laodong fa daodu*, p. 90.
55 Shi Tanjing, '*Lun shehuizhuyi shichang jingji yu laodong fa*' (On the socialist market economy and labour law), *Faxue yanjiu*, no. 1, 1994, pp. 54–62.
56 Chen Wenyuan, '*Guanyu laodong fa de jige jiben wenti chutan*' (A Preliminary Study of Certain Fundamental Problems of Labour Law), *Zhengfa luntan*, no. 60, October 1994, p. 56.
57 See Article 16 of the 1994 LL.
58 The 1986 'Provisional Regulations Concerning the Implementation of the Labour Contract System in State-owned Enterprises', issued by the State Council also required workers to sign a contract to establish employment relations. But the regulations are only applicable for the workers in state-owned enterprises recruited after October 1 1986. At that time, this labour contract employment system was not fully implemented, partly because this system was not well received. For many, including legal scholars, the labour contract system is in direct conflict with the important political notion that labourers are masters of the nation and the enterprises, especially the state-owned enterprises. The labourers as the masters could not sign a labour contract with either the state or the enterprises. This debate is still continuing. For more discussion see Josephs, *Labour Law in China*, *passim*.
59 'Journal Welcomes Adoption of Labour Law', *Banyuetan*, no. 15, 10 August 1994, pp. 16–18, in *Daily Report*, China, 10 August 1994. FBIS-CHI-94-192.
60 See Article 19 of the 1994 LL.

61 See Li Boyong's explanation in *Laodong fa jiben lilun yu shiwu jiangzuo*, pp. 156–7.
62 See Article 14 of the the 1986 GPCL. For a detailed discussion on 1986 GPCL, see William Jones (ed.), *Basic Principles of Civil Law in China* (London: M.E. Sharpe, Inc. 1989).
63 Liang Shuwen and Hui Luming, *Laodong fa jipeitao guiding xinshi xinjie*, p. 322.
64 See Articles 17 and 18(1) of the 1994 LL.
65 Shi Tanjing, '*Lun shehuizhuyi shichang jingji yu laodong fa*', op. cit., pp. 54–62.
66 *Laodongfa jiben lilun yu shiwu jiangzuo*, p. 9.
67 Liang Shuwen and Hui Luming, *Laodongfa jipeitao guiding xinshi xinjie*, p. 35.
68 Article 26 of the 1994 LL.
69 Liang Shuwen and Hui Luming, *Laodongfa jipeitao guiding xinshi xinjie*, p. 362.
70 Article 27 of the 1994 LL.
71 *Laodongfa jiben lilun yu shiwu jiangzuo*, p. 10.
72 See Articles 28 and 30 of the 1994 LL. Articles 20 and 21 of the 1995 'Foreign-Funded Enterprises Labour Law' provide a detailed formula for payment. For the English text of the law, see 'Text of Foreign-funded Enterprises Labour Law', *Daily Report*, China, FBIS-CHI-95-057, 24 March 1995, p. 48.
73 Article 32 of the 1994 LL.
74 Liang Shuwen and Hui Luming, *Laodong fa jipeitao guiding xinshi xinjie*, pp. 370–4.
75 *Laodongfa jiben lilun yu shiwu jiangzuo*, p. 11.
76 Chen Wenyuan, '*Guanyu laodong fa de jige jiben wenti chutan*', op. cit., p. 58.
77 Shi Tanjing, '*Lun shehui zuyi shichang jingji yu laodong fa*', op. cit., pp. 54–62. For a discussion on legal development concerning China's trade union activities before the 1994 LL, see Sara Biddulph and Sean Cooney, 'Regulations of Trade Unions in the People's Republic of China', *Melbourne University Law Review*, vol. 19, no. 2, December 1993, pp. 253–92.
78 Guan Huai, Ren Fushan and Chan Wenyun (eds) *Laodong faxue*, p. 468.
79 See Yijiang Ding's account, 'Corporatism and Civil Society in China: an Overview of the Debate in Recent Years', *China Information*, vol. 12, no. 4, Spring 1998, p. 56.
80 *Xinhua*, 30 July 1995 in FBIS-CHI-95-146 (31 July 1995), pp. 32–3 as cited in Yijiang Ding, 'Corporatism and Civil Society . . .', op. cit., p. 56.
81 Chen Wenyuan, '*Guanyu laodong fa de jige jiben wenti chutan*', op. cit., p. 58.
82 Steven D. Anderman, *Labour Law: Management Decisions and Workers' Rights*, p. 270.
83 For example, in response to strikes in 1956, Mao indicated: 'We do not approve of disturbances, because contradictions among the people can be resolved through the method of "unity – criticism – unity", while disturbances are bound to cause some losses and are not conducive to the advance of socialism.' See Mao Zedong, 'Correct Handling of Contradictions Among the People', *Selected Works of Mao Zedong*, vol. v (Beijing: Foreign Languages Press, 1977), p. 415.

84 See Folsom and Minan, *Law in the People's Republic of China*, p. 508.
85 Chen-chang Chiang provides a useful discussion on the Party's attitude towards the independent trade union prior to 1994 LL. He also lists several reasons for illegal strikes before the 1990s, such as the decline in living standards resulting from price rises, discontent of contracted labourers with their working conditions and income, laying off of surplus workers, workers' disatisfaction with the unreasonable terms forced upon them by factory managers, and the arbitrary violation of contracts by investors. See Chen-chang Chiang, 'The Role of Trade Union in Mainland China', *Issues and Studies*, vol. 26, no. 2, Feb. 1990, pp. 75–98.
86 See Articles 32 and 34 of 'Gansu Regulations on Unions in Foreign-Invested Enterprises', *Lanzhou Gansu ribao*, 8 June 1996, p. 6 in *Daily Report*, China, FBIS-CHI-96-207, 8 June 1996.
87 Shen Tongxian makes a similar argument in '*Zhongwai jiti hetong zhidu de bijiao he pingxi*' (Comparison and analysis of the collective contract system between China and foreign countries), *Zhongguo faxue*, no. 4, 1996, August 9, 1996, p. 81.
88 '*Gongren ribao* commentator: Labour Law Implementation Marks Milestone', *Daily Report*, China, FBIS-CHI-95-060, 27 January 1995.
89 For more discussions on the trade union's struggle for more independence from the party, see Chapter 3 of G. White, J. Howell and Shang Xiayuan, *In Search for Civil Society: Market Reform and Social Change in Contemporary China* (Oxford: Clarendon Press, 1996).
90 '*Gongren ribao* commentator: Labour Law Implementation Marks Milestone', FBIS-CHI-95-060, *Daily Report*, China, 27 January 1995.
91 'Official Urges Firms To Set Up Trade Unions', *Xinhua*, 27 June 1994, FBIS-CHI-94-124, *Daily Report*, China, 27 June 1994. *Xinhua* reported on a decree issued by the State Council stipulating that 'Overseas-funded enterprises must establish trade unions within one year from the start of business'.
92 'Labour Relations in Foreign Enterprises Viewed', *BR*, no. 20, 15–21 May 1995, pp. 17–21, *Daily Report*, China, FBIS-CHI-95-092, 12 May 1995.
93 'Party Circular Warns of Spread of Illegal Trade Unions', *South China Morning Post*, 4 June 1996, p. 1 in FBIS-CHI-96-109, 4 June 1996.
94 See H. Josephs, *Labour Law in China*, p. 100.
95 See Professor Shen's discussion in Guan Huai, *et al.* (eds), *Laodong faxue*, pp. 501–8.
96 See 'Authorities Alarmed At Increase in Labor Disputes', *South China Morning Post*, 15 August 1996, p. 10, in *Daily Report*, China, FBIS-CHI-96-159, 15 August 1996.
97 *Laodongfa jiben lilun yu shiwu jiangzuo*, p. 105.
98 See Article 78 of the 1994 LL.
99 See, for example, Article 79 of the 1994 LL and also Liang Shuwen and Hui Luming, *Laodongfa jipeitao guiding xin shixiejie*, passim.
100 Liang Shuwen and Hui Luming, *Laodong fa jipeitao guiding xinshi xinjie*, p. 866.
101 Donald Clarke, Dispute Resolution in China', *Journal of Chinese Law*, no. 5, 1991, p. 245. The same article details the treatment of dispute resolution procedures before the 1994 LL.

102 Hilary Josephs, 'Labour Law in a "Socialist Market Economy": The Case of China', op. cit., p. 100.
103 Article 80 of the 1994 Labour Law and Article 7 of 'The Regulations of Organizations and Operation of Enterprise Labour Disputes Settlement Mediation Committee'.
104 For example, see 'The Regulations for Adjudicating Labour Disputes by the Labour Disputes Arbitration Committee', the State Council, June 1993; 'The PRC Regulations on Labour Disputes Settlement in Enterprise' issued by the State Council,' July 1993; 'The Regulations for the Organization of Labour Disputes Arbitration Committees', the Ministry of Labour, November 1993, and 'The Regulations for the Arbitration of Disputes by Arbitration Committee', the Ministry of Labour, October 1993, in Liang Shuwen and Hui luming, *Laodong fa jipeitao guiding xin shixijie*.
105 See H. Josephs, 'Labour Law in a "Socialist Market Economy": the Case of China', op. cit., pp. 110–11. See also Article 81 of the 1994 LL.
106 See Article 83 of the 1994 LL.
107 *Laodong fa jiben lilunyu shiwu jiangzuo*, p. 124.
108 *Laodong fa jiben lilunyu shiwu jiangzuo*, p. 96 and 'Hainan Provisions on Labour Disputes', *Haikou Hainan ribao*, 27 June 1997, p. 10, in *Daily Report*, China, FBIS-CHI-97-205, 24 July 1997.
109 Guan Huai, Ren Fushan and Chan Wenyun (eds), *Ladong faxue* (Labour Law Science) (Beijing: Falu chubanshe, 1996), pp. 271–3.
110 Liang Shuwen and Hui Luming, *Laodong fa jipeitao guiding xinshi xinjie*, pp. 496–97.
111 *Laodong fa jiben lilun yu shiwu jiangzuo*, p. 68.
112 Regarding such calculation refer to the following 1993 Ministry of Labour regulations, 'The Provisional Regulations on the Total Expense on Wages in Public Overship Enterprises' issued in 1993, and 'The Handbook on the Use of Total Budget for Wages'. See also 'Market Mechanism to Determine Wage Levels', Beijing Zhongguo Xinwen she, 24 September 1994, *Daily Report*, China, FBIS-CHI-94-186, 24 September 1994.
113 See Article 49 of the 1994 LL.
114 See Article 50 of the 1994 LL.
115 'Official Comment on Social Security System', *Qiye guanli* (Enterprise Management), no. 3, March 1995, pp. 4–5, in *Daily Report*, China, FBIS-CHI-95-147.
116 *Laodong fa jiben lilun yu shiwu jiangzuo*, p. 79.
117 Sun Xiuping, *China's Social Security System*, p. 13.
118 *Laodong fa jiben lilun yu shiwu jiangzuo*, p. 96.
119 Wang Quanxing, *Laodong fa*, p. 70.
120 Guo Jie, Liu Zun and Yang Sun., *Laodong faxue*, p. 14.
121 See Articles 1 to 5 of the 'Opinion' in Liang Shuwen and Hui Luming, *Laodong fa jipeitao guiding xinshi xinjie*, p. 17.
122 Chen Wenyuan, 'A Preliminary Study of certain fundamental problems of labour law', op. cit., p. 55.
123 Shi Tanjing, '*Lun shehuizhuyi shichang jingji yu laodong fa*', op. cit., p. 56.
124 See Liang Shuwen and Hui Luming, *Laodong fa jipeitao guiding xinshi xinjie*, p. 112.
125 See 'Professor on Economic Benefits of Transient Labour', *Daily Report*, China, FBIS-CHI-95-015, 24 January, 1995.

270 Notes and References

126 'Chen Juncheng Discusses Handling Surplus Rural Labour', *Beijing nongmin ribao*, 29 October 1996, p. 1 in *Daily Report*, China, FBIS-CHI-96-220, 29 October 1996.
127 Dorothy Solinger, *Contesting Citizenship in Urban China; Peasant Migrants, the State and the Logic of the Market* (Berkeley: University of California Press, 1999), pp. 2–3. Dr Solinger's analysis notes the related emergence of 'true citizens, second-class citizens, ersatz citizens (outside the state), and noncitizens', p. 279.
128 There was a 43 per cent increase in Beijing, 53 per cent in Shanghai, 50 per cent in Guangzhou, and a high of 97 per cent in Shenzhen. The rising crime rate among rural migrants is directly connected to the influx of rural unemployed workers.
129 'Article Reviews Influx of Migrant rural workers', *Daily Report*, China, FBIS-CHI-15-058, 25 March 1995. Lora Sabin indicates that in the period of 1978–80 China's urban unemployment rate was at 4.9–5.3 per cent. See Lora Sabin, 'New Bosses in the Worker's State: the Growth of Non-State Sector Employment in China', *CQ*, no. 140, December 1994, p. 945. Both Margaret Maurer-Fazio and Ching Kwan Lee discussed the ways by which Chinese authorities dealt with unemployed and redundant workers by developing labour intensive, tertiary sectors such as food services, transport, domestic services, retailing and tourism. See Margaret Maurer-Fazio, 'Building A Labour Market in China', *Current History*, vol. 94, no. 593, September 1995, p. 286 and Ching Kwan Lee, 'Labour Politics of Market Socialism: Collective Inaction and Class Experiences among State Workers in Guangzhou', *Modern China*, vol. 24, no. 1, January 1998, pp. 3–31. In Chinese, '*xiagang*' conveys 'unemployed'. '*Dagang*', however, connotes 'waiting to be called back to their duties'. In the former case, the government provides social assistance and in the latter, it is provided by the work unit.
130 'NPC Deputies Discuss Rural Labour Flow', *Daily Report*, China, FBIS-CHI-97-041, 2 March, 1997.
131 Enterprise receives 3000 *yuan* per local resident hired; however, the fine for hiring a migrant labourer was a paltry 50 *yuan*. Lin Zhe, '*Quanli buchang: xiandai fazhi shehui de jiben yaoqiu*' (Rights Supplement: a Basic Requirement of Modern Rule of Law Society), *Zhongguo faxue*, no. 2, 1997, p. 51.
132 Lin Zhe, '*Quanli buchang: xiandai fazhi shehui de jiben yaoqiu*', op. cit., p. 51.
133 See 'State to Promote Orderly Migration of Rural Workers', *Daily Report*, China, FBIS-CHI-96-070, 10 April 1996. The revised 1995 draft of the Beijing City Regulations suggests a strong intent to implement a tight control on this segment of population. The migrant rural labourers are required to obtain residence permission cards in order to get employed. For such an identification, they are required to report their status in terms of marriage and child-bearing, and to sign contracts with local social security and family planning agencies. See 'Revised Draft Law to Regulate Transient Labourers', *Daily Report*, China, FBIS-CHI-95-072, 14 April 1995, p. 16.
134 See Chapter 3 of White, *et al.*, *Search for Civil Society: Market Reform and Social Change in Contemporary China*.

4 Sorting Out Property and Ownership Rights

1. George Woodcock, *Pierre-Joseph Proudhon: His Life and Work* (New York: Schocken Books, 1972), pp. 45–50.
2. Karl Marx, 'The Manifesto of the Communist Party', in Robert C. Tucker, *Marx–Engels Reader*, 2nd edn (New York: W.W. Norton & Co., 1978), p. 484.
3. Karl Marx, 'The Origin of Family, Private Property and the State', Robert Tucker, *The Marx–Engels Reader*, p. 473.
4. 'Law is the Cornerstone of Progress', *China Daily*, 22 August 1987, p. 4 as cited in Ronald C. Keith, *China's Struggle for the Rule of Law*, p. 6.
5. For example, see the entry under *'suoyouzhi'* in Liu Peixian, ed., *Makesizhuyi yu dangdai cidian* (Dictionary of Marxism and the Contemporary Era) (Beijing: Zhongguo renmin daxue chubanshe, 1988), p. 470. The latest encyclopedia of jurisprudence carries an entry on 'ownership', *suoyouquan*, but does not refer to 'ownership system'. See Sun Guohua, *Zhonghua faxue da cidian*, p. 420 of which puts ownership rights in the context of the Continental law tradition.
6. The *classicus locus* for this theory is in Zhang Chunqiao, 'On Exercising All-Round Dictatorship over the Bourgeoisie', *BR*, no. 14, 4 April 1975, pp. 5–11.
7. Chinese Communist Party, Eleventh Central Committee, 6th Plenary Session, *Resolution on CPC History (1949–81)* (Beijing: Foreign Languages Press, 1981), pp. 13, 76, 84.
8. Edward J. Epstein, 'General Principles of Civil Law: Theoretical Controversy in the Drafting Process and Beyond', *Law on Contemporary Problems*, vol. 52, no. 2, 1989, pp. 208–9.
9. 'Basic Differences Between Socialist Demoracy and Capitalist Democracy', *Renmin ribao*, October 22, 1989 in FBIS-CHI-89-206, 26 October 1989, p. 16.
10. Maurice Meisner, *The Deng Xiaoping Era: an Inquiry into the Fate of Socialim 1978–1994* (New York: Hill and Wang 1996), p. 513.
11. Edward Steinfeld, *Forging Reform in China: the Fate of State-Owned Industry* (Cambridge: Cambridge University Press, 1998), p. xv, pp. 7, 27.
12. There are some English studies on China's property rights reforms from an economics perspective. These studies focus primarily on the nature of effects of the recent property rights reform on economic productivity in a variety of economic sectors. These studies also point out the complexity and diversities of the emerging forms of property relations in China which are not entirely consistent with the property rights reforms in other former communist countries. For detailed discussions on China's property rights reforms from an economics perspective, see Russel Smyth, 'Property Rights in China's Economic Reforms' *Communist and Post-Communist Studies*, 1998, vol. 31, no. 3, pp. 235–48; and Peter Nolan and Wang Xiaoqiang, 'Beyond Privatization: Institutional Innovation and Growth in China's Large State-Owned Enterprises', *World Development*, 1999, vol. 27, no. 1, pp. 169–200.
13. Xie Cichang, *'Guojia shuoyouquan lilun zai shijianzhong de yunyong he fazhan'* (Application and Development of the Theory of National Ownership in Practice), *Zhongguo faxue* (Chinese Legal Sciences), 1996, no. 6, p. 36.

14 Jiang Zemin's political report in *Zhongguo gongchandang dishiwuzi quanquo daibiao dahui wenjian huibian* (Compiled Documents of the Chinese Communist Party 15th National Party Congress) (Beijing: Renmin chubanshe, 1997), p. 23.
15 See *Zhonggong zhongyang fazhi jiangzuo huibian* (Collection of Lectures on the Legal System for the Central Committee of the CCP) (Beijing: Falu chubanshe, 1998), p. 66.
16 Huang Sujian, 'CASS Researcher Views Debate on Property Rights', *Liaowang* (Outlook), no. 1, 2 January 1995, pp. 26–7, *Daily Report*, China, FBIS-CHI-95-060, 2 January 1995.
17 For an authoritative introduction on Chinese Civil law and its theories by a Chinese distinguished civil law expert, Profressor Tong Rou, see William C. Jones, ed., *Basic Principles of Civil Law in China* (London: M.E. Sharpe, Inc., 1989).
18 'Decision of the CCP Central Committee on Some Issues concerning the Establishment of a Socialist Market Economic Structure', *BR*, 22–28 November 1993, Document.
19 Jainfu Chen, *From Administrative Authorisation to Civil Law: a Comparative Perspective of the Developing Civil Law in The People's Republic of China* (Boston: Martinus Nijhoff Publishers, 1995), p. 139.
20 Ibid., p. 143.
21 See 'Jiang Zemin Urges Further Enterprise Reform', *Xinhua*, 7 March 1996, *Daily Report*, China, FBIS-CHI-96-131.
22 Huang Sujian, 'CASS Researcher Views Debate on Property Rights', op. cit.
23 The meaning of the concept of 'property right' was already controversial in the process of drafting the 1986 General Principles of Civil Law. For an extensive discussion on Chinese debates on this concept and the relationship between Chinese understanding of the concept and similar debates in the former Soviet Union, see Edward J. Epstein, 'General Principles of Civil Law: Theoretical Controversy in the Darfting Process and Beyond', *Law and Contemporary Problems* , vol. 52, no. 2, 1989, pp. 179–216.
24 See Shi Jichun, *Guoyou qiye falu* (On Law of State-owned Enterprise) (Beijing: Falu chubanshe, 1997), pp. 188–9.
25 Liu Shujun, *'Woguo guoyou qiye chanquan wenti de falu sikao'* (Legal Thinking over the Question of State Enterprise Ownership), *Minshang faxue* (Civil and Commercial Laws), *Renda*, no. 6, 1996, p. 8.
26 Ibid.
27 9 June 1998 interview with Zhang Guangxing at the Institute of Law.
28 See Jiang Zemin's Political Report *in Zhongguo gongchandang dishiwuzi quanquo daibiao dahui wenjian huibian 1997* (Compiled Documents of the Chinese Communist Party 15th National Party Congress) (Beijing: Renmin chubanshe, 1997), p. 23.
29 For a more extensive discussion of the debate on this issue and social and political implications of the controversies, see Ronald Keith, *China's Struggle for the Rule of Law*, Chapter 5, 'Law as the Contactual Predicate of Ownership Rights'.
30 See Article 71 of the GPCL. The General Principles of Civil Law were adopted by the 4th Session of the 6th NPC, 1986. An English text can be found in Folson and Minan (eds), *Law in the People's Republic of China: Com-*

mentary, Readings, and Materials (Boston: Martinus Nijhoff Publishers, 1989), pp. 1055–76.
31 Chan Huabin, *Wuquan fa yuanli* (Principles of Law on Rights in Things) (Beijing: State Administration College Press, 1997), p. 183.
32 See Tong Rou, Wang Liming and Ma Zunju, (ed.) *Zhongguo min fa* (Chinese Civil Law) (Beijing: Falu chubanshe, 1998), p. 232.
33 Gao Shangquan and Chi Fulin (eds) *Reforming China's State-Owned Enterprises* (Beijing: Foreign Languages Press, 1997), p. 7
34 See Su Xing, 'Article Stresses Deng Thinking on State Firms', *Renmin ribao*, 22 February 1995, p. 9, in *Daily Report*, China, FBIS-CHI-95-060, 22 February 1995.
35 National Legal Education Office and State Economic System Reform Commission, eds, *Gufenzhi yu gufen hezuo zhi falu zhengce zhishi wanda* (The Questions and Answers concerning Laws and Policies of Joint Stock System and Shareholding Cooperative System) (Beijing: Falu chubanshe, 1998), p. 223 and Su Xing, 'Article Stresses Deng Thinking on State Firms', *Renmin ribao*, 22 February 1995 in *Daily Report*, China, FBIS-CHI-95-060, p. 9.
36 Jianfu Chen, 'From Administrative Authorisation to Civil Law . . .', op. cit., p. 205.
37 See Jiang Zemin's Political Report in *Zhongguo gongchandang dishiwuzi quanguo daibiao dahui wenjian huibian* (Compiled Documents of the Chinese Communist Party 15th National Party Congress) (Beijing: Renmin chubanshe, 1997), p. 22.
38 'Liu Guoguang on Inflation, Enterprise Reform', *Caimao jingji*, no. 9, 1995, 11 September 1995 in *Daily Report*, China, FBIS-CHI-95-021, 11, September 1995, pp. 4–8, 39.
39 'Xinhua Backgrounder on Enterprise Reform', *Xinhua*, Hong Kong, 24 October 1997, *Daily Report*, China, FBIS-CHI-97-305, 1 November, 1997.
40 Yuan Mu, 'Paper further Examines State Enterprise Reform', 3 March 1995, *Daily Report*, China FBIS-CHI-95-053.
41 Kong Xiangjun, 'Qiye faren zaichan quan yanjiu' (Studies in the property rights of the enterprise legal person), *Minshang faxue*, Renda, no. 9, 1996, pp. 40–8.
42 Xie Cichang, 'Guojia shuoyou quan lilun zai shijianzhong de yunyong he fazhan' op. cit., p. 36.
43 Shi Jichun, *Guoyou qiye falu*, p. 154.
44 Kong Xiangjun, 'Qiye faren zaichan quan yanjiu', op. cit., p. 41.
45 Ibid., pp. 40–8.
46 Wang Chuang and Zhang Han, 'Minfa xue yanjiu shuping' (A Review of the Chinese Civil Law Studies in 1996), *Faxue yanjiu*, no. 1, 1997, p. 48.
47 Ibid., p. 48.
48 Kang Dequan, 'Shuoyouquan shuoyou zhi dui ying guanxi bo lilun he xiandai qiye zhidu' (Distinguishing ownership from ownership system and the establishment of modern enterprise system), *Faxue yanjiu*, no. 6, 1994, p. 48.
49 Wang Jianping, 'Faren caichanquan yanjiu' (Studies in property right of legal person), *Minshang faxue*, no. 10, 1996, p. 23.
50 *Zhonggong zhongyang fazhi jiangzuo huibian*, p. 73.
51 Wang Jianping, 'Faren caichanquan yanjiu', op. cit., p. 23.
52 Ibid., p. 23.

274 Notes and References

53 Shi Jichun, *Guoyou qiye falu*, pp. 201–2.
54 Wang Chuang and Zhang Han, 'Minfa xue yanjiu shuping', op. cit., p. 48.
55 Shi Jichun, *Guoyou qiye falu*, p. 219.
56 Kong Xiangjun, '*Lun xiandai gongside chanquan jiegou*' (On the structure of property rights in modern corporations (part 1)), *Zhengfa luntan* (Tribune of Political Science and Law), 1994, no. 3, pp. 46–50.
57 Liu Shujun, '*Woguo guoyou qiye chanquan wentide falu sikao*', op. cit., pp. 6–8.
58 Yin Wenquan, 'Study on Separating Enterprises from Government', *Jingji yanjiu*, 20 February 1998, pp. 38–45 in *Daily Report*, China, FBIS-CHI-98-110, 20 April 1998.
59 Wang Chuang and Zhang Han, 'Minfaxue yanjiu shuping', op. cit., p. 48.
60 Yu Junwen, *et al.*, eds, *Makesizhuyi baike cidian* (Encyclopedia of Marxism), vol. 1 (Shenyang: Dongbei shifan daxue chubanshe, 1987), pp. 399–400.
61 Chen Jianfu, *From Administrative Authorisation to Civil Law*, p. 117.
62 Ibid.
63 Louis Putterman, 'The Role of Ownership and Property Rights in China's Economic Transition', *CQ*, no. 144, 1995, p. 1052.
64 For an extensive discussion on the development and reform of urban collective enterprises before 1985, see Jianzhong Tang and Laurence J.C. Ma, 'Evolution of Urban Collective Enterprises in China', *CQ*, no. 104, December 1985, pp. 614–40; and Howard Chao and Yang Xiaoping discussed several methods of denationalization of small state-owned enterprises in China, including contracting with a collective enterprise or leasing to individuals for operation, converting into collective enterprises before 1987. See Howard Chao and Yany Xiaoping, 'The Reform of the Chinese System of Enterprise Ownership', *Stanford Journal of International Law*, no. 23, 1987, pp. 383–5.
65 Shi Xiaoyi, 'Researcher Analyzes Township Enterprise Reform', *Guanli shijie* (Management World), no. 5, 24 September 1994, pp. 142–9, in *Daily Report, China*, FBIS-CHI-95-016, 24 September 1994.
66 Ibid.
67 Chen Jiangung and Pan Libing, 'Current Development of Township Enterprises', *Nongmin ribao*, 24 October 1996, in *Daily Report*, China, FBIS-CHI-96-247, 24 October 1996.
68 Shi Xiaoyi, 'Researcher Analyzes Township Enterprise Reform', op. cit.
69 'Interview with Li Dewei on Shareholding System', *Jingji cankao bao*, 4 November 1997, *Daily Report*, China, FBIS-CHI-97-335 1 December 1997.
70 Shao Bingren, 'Develop and Improve [the] Shareholding Cooperative Economy', *Jingji ribao*, 12 August 1997, p. 2 in *Daily Report*, China, FBIS-CHI-97-267.
71 'Interview with Li Dewei on Shareholding System' , *Daily Report*, FBIS-CHI-97–335, 12 January 1997, 335.
72 Gu Gongyun suggests that cooperative enterprises are actually equivalent to partnership enterprise in law. See Gu Gongyun, '*Gufen hezuozhi qiye lifade ruogan yinan wenti yanjiu*' (Studies in several difficult issues concerning shareholding cooperative enterprises) in *Jingji fa, laodong fa* (Economic Law and Labour Law), *Renda*, no. 2, 1998, p. 6.
73 See 'Interview with Li Dewei on Shareholding System', *Daily Report*, China, FBIS-CHI-97-335, 12 January 1997; Shao Bingren, 'Develop and Improve [the] Shareholding Cooperative Economy', op. cit., p. 2.

74 *Gufenzhi yu gufen hezuo zhi falu zhengce zhishi wanda*, p. 333.
75 Ibid., p. 333.
76 Shao Bingren, 'Develop and Improve Shareholding Cooperative Economy', op. cit., p. 2.
77 Ma Yuejin, *'Lun nongcun gufen hezou qiye de guquan jiegou'* (On the Shareholding Rights Structure of Rural Shareholding Cooperative Enterprise), *Zhongguo faxue*, no. 3, June, 1997, p. 83.
78 *Gufenzhi yu gufen hezuo zhi Falu Zhengce zhishi wanda*, p. 333.
79 Gu Gongyun, *'Gufen hezuozhi qiye lifade ruogan yinan wenti yanjiu'*, op. cit., p. 6; Shao Bingren, 'Develop and Improve Shareholding Cooperative Economy', op. cit., p. 2.
80 *Gufenzhi yu gufen hezuo zhi Falu Zhengce zhishi wanda*, p. 333.
81 Zhao Yousu, *'Gufen hezuozhi falu xingzhi yanjiu'* (Studies in the Legal Characteristics of Shareholding Cooperative Enterprises), *Jingji fa, laodong fa*, Renda, no. 2, 1998, p. 47.
82 'Township Enterprises Report', *Xinhua*, 23 April 1997, *Daily Report*, China, FBIS-CHI-97-081, 23 April 1997.
83 Han Yuanqin, 'Rural Collective Economy Must be Amply Emphasized', *Zhenli de zhuiqiu*, no. 3, 11 March 1997, pp. 20–30, *Daily Report*, China, FBIS-CHI-97-107, 11 March 1997.
84 Ibid.
85 See Zong Han, 'Basic Principles of Modern Enterprise System', *Zhenli de zhuiqiu*, no. 10, 11 October 1997, pp. 11–18, in *Daily Report*, China, FBIS-CHI-98-002, 2 January 1998.
86 Articles 14–16 of the 1998 constitutional revisions in *Renmin ribao*, Overseas, 17 March 1999, p. 1.
87 Tong Rou, Wang Liming and Ma Zunju, (eds) *Zhongguo minfa*, p. 232.
88 Professor Zhang Guangxing's 9 June 1998 interview with the authors.
89 See the 'Law of People's Republic of China on Chinese–Foreign Joint Ventures', 1979, in *China's Foreign Economic Legislation*, vol. I (Beijing: Foreign Languanges Press, 1986), pp. 1–8; and 'The Regulations for the Implementation of the Law of the People's Republic of China on Chinese–Foreign Joint Venture' in *China's Foreign Economic Legislation*, vol. III (Beijing Foreign Languages Press, 1987), pp. 1–19; *'Zhonghua renmin gongheguo zhongwai hezuo jingying qiye fa'*. The Law of the PRC on Chinese–Foreign Joint Cooperative Enterprises) in Kong Xiangzun, Jiang Tianbe, Wang Ze, eds, *Gongsifa ji peitao guiding xinshi xinjie* (New Interpretation of Company Law and Related Regulations), vol. 2 (Beijing: People's Court Press, 1997), pp. 2250–8.
90 Ibid.
91 'Interim Regulations on Private Enterprises of the People's Republic of China', *BR* [no?] 1989, pp. IX–XIV. For the Chinese, see Kong Xiangzun, Jiang Tianbe and Wang Ze, eds, *Gongsifa ji peitao guiding xinshi xinjie* (New Interpretation of Company Law and Related Regulation), vol. 2 (Beijing: Renmin fading chubanshe, 1997), pp. 1708–16.
92 See Articles 7–11 of 'Sichuan Regulations on Private Enterprises', *Sichuan ribao*, 2 August 1994, p. 8, in *Daily Report*, China, FBIS-CHI-94-182, February 8 1994. The Yunnan provincial government issued similar regulations. See 'Yunnan Regulations on Private Enterprises, *Yunnan ribao*, 14 January 1995, p. 3, in *Daily Report*, China, FBIS-CHI-95-067, January 14, 1995.
93 Tong Rou, Wang Liming and Ma Zunju (eds) *Zhongguo minfa*, p. 259.

94 Jianfu Chen, *From Administrative Authorisation to Civil Law*, p. 4.
95 Xiao Yong, 'Upcoming PRC Constitutional Revisions', *Ching pao*, no. 12, 1 December 1997, Hong Kong, pp. 16–17, in *Daily Report*, China, FBIS-CHI-98-058, 27 February 1998.
96 Ibid.
97 Jianfu Chen has drawn a similar conclusion in *From Administrative Authorisation to Civil Law*, passim.
98 Jiang Ping and Zhang Chu, *'Minfade benzhi tezheng shi sifa'* (The Essential Characteristic of Civil Law is Private Law) *Zhongguo faxue*, no. 6, December 1998, p. 30.
99 See *Zhonggong zhongyang fazhi jiangzuo huibian*, p. 75.
100 For a discussion of Chinese debates on the nature of civil law in the process of drafting the 1986 General Principles of Civil Law, see Jianfu Chen, *From Administrative Authorisation to Civil Law*, pp. 50–65.

5 Balancing Society and the Individual in Judicial Justice

1 This same point was made in 'Concepts of Law in the Chinese Anti-Crime Campaign', *Harvard Law Review*, vol. 98, 1985, p. 1908 which reviewed the interpretation of criminal law concepts within the highly politically charged circumstances of the early 1980s anti-crime campaigns.
2 Jonathan Hecht, *Opening to Reform? An Analysis of China's Revised Criminal Procedure Law* (New York: Lawyers Committee for Human rights, October 1996), p. 80.
3 'People's justice' and the explicitly political dimensions of mass-line criminal justice were, for example, reviewed in Shao-chuan Leng, 'The Role of Law in the PRC as Reflecting Mao Tse-tung's Influence', *Journal of Criminal Law and Criminology*, November 1977, pp. 356–73. See also Jerome Cohen, 'The Party and the Courts: 1949–1959', *CQ*, no. 38, April/July 1969, pp. 120–57; L.S. Tao, 'Criminal Justice in Communist China', Parts 1 and II, in *Issues and Studies*, June 1977, vol. xiii, no. 6, pp. 15–41 and vol. xiii, no. 7, July 1977, pp. 19–50. One might also note, for example, the following point in another of Cohen's articles: 'Indeed, Max Weber's appraisal of the traditional system as "a type of patriarchal obliteration of the line between justice and administration" would appear to apply to the Communist System'. See Jerome Cohen, 'The Chinese Communist Party and "Judicial Independence": 1949–59,' *Harvard Law Review*, vol. 82, no. 5, March 1969, p. 129 at footnote 148. Speaking of periodic emphasis on legality and pendulum swings between political relaxation and rigidity, Tao-tai Hsia emphasized the continuous focus on the coordination of legal development with direct mass action. See Hsia, 'Legal Developments Since the Purge of the Gang of Four', *Issues and Studies*, November 1978, pp. 1–26.
4 Jerome Alan Cohen, 'Tiananmen and the Rule of Law', in George Hicks, ed., *The Broken Mirror: China After Tiananmen* (Longman-Group UK Limited, 1990), p. 340. For another reading of the effects of Tiananmen Square on the struggle for the rule of law, see Ronald C. Keith, *China's Struggle for the Rule of Law* (London and New York: Macmillan and St. Martin's Press, 1994), pp. 208–25.

5 This same principle was stipulated in the 1954 state constitution and the 1954 Organic Law of the People's Courts. For analysis of its content and application, see Shao-chuan Leng, 'Criminal Justice in Post-Mao China: Some Preliminary Observations', *The Journal of Criminal Law and Criminology*, vol. 73, no. 1, 1982, pp. 228–32.
6 For further discussion on the political use of counterrevolution and the evolution of criminal law, see Ronald C. Keith, *China's Struggle for the Rule of Law*, pp. 152–71.
7 Shao-chuan Leng, for example, referred to outstanding 'deficiencies', but also noted that there was general agreement that the 1979 CL and its companion law on criminal procedure represented impressive and concise pieces of legislation. See 'Criminal Justice in Post-Mao China: Some Preliminary Observations', op. cit., pp. 213, 135. Also see Shao-chuan Leng, 'Criminal Justice in Post-Mao China: Some Preliminary Observations', *CQ*, no. 87, September, 1981, pp. 440–69; and Hungdah Chiu, 'China's New Legal System', *Current History*, September 1980, p. 31. In the past, change favouring legal procedure was often described in terms of the alternation of 'jural' and 'societal models' of Chinese politics and legal development.
8 See Gao Mingxuan, *Zhonghua renmin gongheguo xingfade yunyu he dansheng* (The embryo and birth of the criminal code of the People's Republic of China) (Beijing: Falu chubanshe, 1980).
9 See 'A Major Step Toward an Ideal Criminal Code – Sidelights on Deliberations on Draft Criminal Code Amendments', by *Xinhua* reporters, *Daily Report*, FBIS-CHI-96-252, 30 Dec., 1996.
10 See 'Commentary on Revised Criminal Law', *Daily Report*, China, FBIS-CHI-97-079, 20 March 1997.
11 Chen Guangzhong and Zheng Xu, 'Xingshi susong faxue ershi nian' (Twenty Years of Criminal Procedural Law Study), *Zhongguo faxue* (Chinese Legal Science), no. 4, 1998, p. 16. The second stage in this particular interpretation seems to correspond with the 'third stage' discussed in Chapter 1.
12 Cui Min, 'Xingshi susong fa shishizhong de wenti yu jiangyi' (Issues and suggestions in the process of implementation of the criminal procedure law), *Xiandai faxue* (Modern Law Science) no. 1, 1998, p. 18.
13 Zhang Zipei (ed.) *Xingshi susongfa jiaocheng* (Lectures on Criminal Procedure Law) (Beijing: Qunzheng chubanshe, 1982), p. 5.
14 See Shen Jiaban, et al., 'Memorial to the throne regarding trial implementation of procedure law' in Zhou Mi, *Zhongguo xingfa shi* (The History of the Chinese Criminal Law) (Beijing: Qunzheng chubanshe, 1985), p. 347.
15 4 June 1998 interview with Fu Kuaizhi at the Institute of Law, CASS.
16 See Zuo Weimin, 'Ershi shiji Zhongguo de xingshi susong fa xue' (China's Criminal Procedure Law Science in the 20th Century) 'Xingshi faxue, sifa zhidu' (Procedural Law and Legal System) (*Renda*), no. 2, 1998, p. 230.
17 Wang Minyuan, 'Qingchengxu de xianxiang, yanyin jiqi jiaozheng' (The reasons for despising processes and its remedy), *Faxue yanjiu* (Studies in Law), no. 5, 1994, p. 89; for a more extensive discussion on this issue, see also Song Yinghui, *Xingshi susong mudi lun* (On the purposes of criminal procedure) (Beijing: Chinese Public Security University Press, 1995).
18 Zhang Lingjie, 'Chengxufa de jige jiben wenti' (Essential Problems on the Processes of Law), *Faxue yanjiu*, no. 5, 1994, p. 35.

19 Mao Guohui, 'Lun fazhi shehui yu xiandai chengxufa linian de chong su' (On the rule of law society and reconceptualization of modern procedure law), *Xingshi faxue, sifa zhidu*, no. 8, 1998, p. 4.
20 Herbert L. Packer, in his article entitled 'The Courts, the Police and the Rest of Us', *Journal of Law and Criminology and Police Science*, 57:238 (1966), classified criminal process into two models: crime control and due process models.
21 Zuo Weimin, 'Ershi shiji zhongguo de xingshi susong fa xue', op. cit., p. 230.
22 Song Yinghui, 'Lun woguo xingshi susong zhidu gaige de mubiao moshi), woguo xingshi (On China's model for criminal procedure system), *Xingshi faxue, sifa zhidu*, no. 2, 1996, pp. 16–17.
23 Li Fuyan, Hou Zunjing, Zhao Houxuan, 'Lun xingshi susong mude' (On the Purposes of Criminal Procedure), *Xingshi faxue, sifa zhidu*, no. 10, 1997, p. 5.
24 Song Yinghui, 'Lun woguo xingshi susong zhidu gaige de mubiao moshi', op. cit., p. 61.
25 Long Zhongzhi and Zuo Weimin, 'Zhuanzhe yu zhanwang' (Turning Points and Prospects) *Xingshi faxue, sifa zhidu* (Procedural Law and Legal System), *Renda*, no. 5, 1996, p. 9.
26 Cui Min, *Zhongguo xingshi susong fa de xin fazhan: xingshi susong fa xiugai yantao de quanmian huigu* (New Development of Chinese Criminal Procedure Law: a Comprehensive Review of the Deliberations on the Revisions of Criminal Procedure Law) (Beijing: People's Public Security University Press, 1996), pp. 1–2.
27 'Officials on Amended Criminal Procedure Law' *Daily Report*, China, FBIS-CHI-96-133, May 26, 1998.
28 Wang Guiwu, 'Bixu chongfen zhongshi he renzhen zhixing xingshi susong fa' (We must implement criminal procedure law fully and strictly) *Faxue jikan* (Law Quarterly) no. 2, 1982, p. 19.
29 Gu Angran, 'Guanyu xingshi susong fa de xiugai yuanze' (On principles in revising the Criminal Procedure Law), *Xingshi faxue, sifa zhidu*, no. 2, 1996, p. 13.
30 See Cui Min, *Zhongguo xingshi susongfa de xin fazhan*, p. 24.
31 See Song Yinghui, 'Lun woguo xingshi susong zhidu gaige de mubiao moshi', op. cit., p. 17.
32 Cui Min, *Zhongguo xinshi susongfa de xin fazhan*, pp. 22–4.
33 'PRC: Ren Jianxian, Wang Hanbin on Amended Criminal Procedure Law', *Xinhua*, 19 April 1996, FBIS-CHI-96-078, 22 April 1996, p. 38.
34 Jonathan Hecht, *Opening to Reform?*, p. 79.
35 Ibid.
36 Article 38 of the 1979 CPL, in *The Criminal Law and the Criminal Law of Procedure* (Beijing: Foreign Languages Press, 1984), pp. 125–6.
37 Article 39 of the 1979 CPL, ibid., p. 126.
38 Article 40 of the 1979 CPL, ibid., pp. 126–7.
39 Article 43 of the 1979 CPL ibid., p. 128
40 See Article 44 and 48 of the 1979 CPL, ibid., pp. 128–9.
41 Wang Shangxin, 'Xingshi susong fa xiugaide ruogan wenti' (Several issues in the revision to criminal procedural law) *Faxue yanjiu*, no. 5, 1994, p. 76.
42 Cui Min, *Zhongguo xingshi susong fa de xin fazhan*, p. 90.
43 Ibid.

44 See Article 61 of the revised CPL. See 'PRC: Amended PRC Criminal Procedure Law', *Xinhua*, 23 March 1996, in FBIS-CHI-96-069, 9 April 1996, p. 31.
45 Cui Min, *Zhongguo xingshi susong fa de xin fazhan*, p. 90.
46 Cui Min, *Zhongguo xingshi susong fa de xin fazhan*, p. 102.
47 Cui Min's interview with the authors at the Beijing Public Security University, 13 June 1998.
48 See Long Zhongzhi and Zuo Weimin, op. cit., p. 11 and Cui Min, *Zhongguo xingshi susong fa de xin fazhan*, pp. 90–103.
49 J. Hecht, *Opening to Reform?*, p. 30.
50 For a good summary of the debate on the presumption of innocence before 1980s, see T.A. Gelatt, 'The People's Republic of China and the Presumption of Innocence' *The Journal of Criminal Law and Criminology*, vol. 73, 1982, no. 1, pp. 259–316.
51 See Ronald C. Keith, *China's Struggle for the Rule of Law*, p. 36.
52 Article 87, *The Basic Law of the Hong Kong Special Administrative Region of China* (Beijing: Foreign Languages Press, 1991), p. 132.
53 See Cui Min, *Zhongguo xingshi susong fa de xin fazhan*, pp. 226–39 and 45.
54 'Newly adopted "Presumption of Innocence" Principle', *Daily Report*, China, FBIS-CHI-96-187, 06/10/96.
55 Wang Minyuan, op. cit., p. 89.
56 See article 6 of the 1996 CPL.
57 Yi Lihua and Li Yuxia, *'Xingshi Susong fa de xin tedian'* (New Characteristics of the Criminal Procedure Law) *Xingshi faxue, sifa zhidu*, Renda, no. 4, 1996, p. 27.
58 Hecht, op. cit., p. 44.
59 Ibid., p. 63.
60 Article 95 of the 1979 CPL also mentioned about 'exemption from prosecution'. It states that 'a people's procuratorate shall review and make a decision in all cases in which it is necessary to initiate a public prosecution or exemption from prosecution'.
61 Wang Shangxin, *'Xingshi susong fa xiugaide ruogan wenti'* (Several issues in criminal procedure law revisions) *Faxue yanjiu*, no. 5, 1994, p. 80.
62 See Article 27 of the 1979 CPL; according to Article 112 and 126 of the 1979 CPL, prosecutors are not involved in the cases where criminal conduct is relatively minor or in the cases of private prosecution.
63 Article 28 of the 1979 CPL.
64 Article 29 of the 1979 CPL.
65 Article 110 of the 1979 CPL.
66 Article 33 of the 1996 CPL.
67 Article 34 of the 1996 CPL.
68 Article 96 of the 1996 CPL.
69 Ibid.
70 J. Hecht, op. cit., p. 40.
71 See Zhang Zipai (ed.) *Xingshi susong fa jiaocheng*, p. 87.
72 'Daxing County People's Court open for the People' in FBIS, JPRS, *China Report*, 30 March, 1979, p. 9.
73 For a discussion on other related problems concerning China's trial proceeding under the 1979 CPL, see Donald Clark and James Feinerman, 'Antagonistic Contradictions: Criminal Law and Human Rights in China' in Stanley Lubman, ed., *China's Legal Reform*, p. 140.

74 Article 151 of the 1996 CPL.
75 Article 149 of the 1996 CPL; for a discussion on the nature of China's adjudication system under the 1979 CPL, see Donovan, D.A. 'The Structure of the Chinese Criminal Justice System: a Comparative Perspective' *University of San Francisco Law Review*, vol. 21, Winter/Spring 1987, pp. 234, 241.
76 Article 151 of the 1996 CPL.
77 Article 157 of the 1996 CPL.
78 Cui Min, *Zhongguo xingshi susong fa de xin fazhan*, p. 162.
79 Cui Min, *Zhongguo xingshi susong fa de xinfazhan*, p. 168.
80 Professor Ronald Brown of University of Hawaii Law School suggests that in fact the entire Chinese legal system, not just trial proceedings, is more 'inquisitorial' than 'adversarial'. See Ronald. C. Brown, *Understanding Chinese Courts and Legal Process: Law with Chinese Characteristics* (Boston: Kluwer Law International, 1997), p. xxi.
81 Long Zhongzhi and Zuo Weimin, op. cit., p. 10.
82 Stanley Lubman, op. cit., p. 10.
83 See Herbert L. Packer 'The Courts, the Police and the Rest of Us', *Journal of Criminal Law and Criminology and Police Science*, 57:238 (1966).
84 Long Zhongzhi and Zuo Weimin, op. cit., p. 13.
85 See Keith, *China's Struggle for the Rule of Law*, p. 215.
86 Long Zhongzhi and Zuo Weimin, 'Zhuanzhe yu zhanwang', op. cit. p. 12.
87 Cui Min, *Zhongguo xingshi susong fa de xin fazhan*, op. cit., p. 263.
88 Ronald C. Keith, 'Socialist Legality and Proletarian Democracy in China', *Canadian Journal of Political Science*, vol. xiii, no. 3, September 1980, pp. 578–79.
89 Bai Xiuyun, 'Lun xingshi beigaoren de quanshe baozhang' (On Protection of the Rights and Interests of Defendants), *Xingshi faxue, sifa zhidu*, no. 9, 1998, p. 46.
90 Bai Xiuyun, 'Lun xingshi beigaoren de quanshe baozhang', op. cit., p. 48.
91 Song Yinghui, *Xingshi susong mudilum* (The purposes of criminal procedure) (Beijing Zhonggeo renmin gonggan daxue chubanshe, 1995), pp. 200–48.
92 Ibid., pp. 240–8.
93 Gao Mingxuan, 'Ershi nian lai woguo xingshi lifade huigu yu zhanwang' (A review of the last twenty years of criminal law legislation and future prospects), *Zhongguo faxue*, no. 6, 1998, p. 27.
94 The significance of economic reform for the development of the 'rule of law' in contemporary China is generally discussed in Stanley Lubman's prefatory remarks to the *China Quarterly*'s special issue on Chinese legal change. See Stanley Lubman, 'Introduction: the Future of Chinese Law', *China Quarterly* (hereinafter *CQ*), no. 138, 1995, pp. 1–21. Professor Lubman discusses the possibility of legal reform accelerating social change 'by creating a vocabulary of concepts' and notes on p. 21: 'Although prospects for growth of the rule of law as that concept is understood in the West presently seem dim, it may be necessary to imagine the unimaginable.'
95 Donald C. Clarke and James Feinerman, 'Antagonistic Contradictions: Criminal Law and Human Rights in China', *CQ*, no. 138, 1995, p. 134. For discussion of some of the newly emerging human rights theory, see Ann Kent, *Between Freedom and Subsistence: China and Human Rights* (Hong Kong: Oxford University Press, 1993); and Ronald C. Keith, 'The New Relevance

of 'Rights and Interests': China's Changing Human Rights Theories,' *China Information*, vol. x, no. 2, 1995, pp. 38–61 and Ronald C. Keith, 'Legislating Women's Children's Rights and Interests in the PRC,' *CQ*, no. 149, March 1997, pp. 29–55.

96 See Zhao Bingzhi and He Xingwang, *'Lun tebie xingfa he xingfa xiugai'* (On special criminal law and the revision of the criminal code) *Zhongguo faxue*, no. 4, 1996, pp. 15–23.

97 'Justice Minister on Criminal Law', March 23, 1997, *Daily Report*, China, FBIS-CHI-97-082.

98 For discussion of related jurisprudence, see Ronald C. Keith, 'Post-Deng Jurisprudence: Justice and Efficiency in a "Rule of Law Economy"', *Problems of Post-Communism*, vol. 45, no. 3, (May–June 1998), pp. 48–57.

99 See Ronald C. Keith, *China's Struggle for the Rule of Law*, Chapters 4 and 5.

100 Jiang Zemin, himself, informed the China Law Association of his personal commitment to the 'rule of law' as an 'important indicator and guarantee for social civilization and progress'. See *Zhongguo faxue*, no. 2, 1997, p. 5.

101 Sun Yihai and Li Kai, *'Lun shuli shehuizhuyi shichang jingji xing fa guan'* (On Establishing the 'Socialist Market Economy': Perspectives in the Criminal Law), *Faxue (Renda)*, no. 6, 1996, pp. 5–8.

102 Zhao Bingzhi and He Xingwang, *'Lun tebie xing fa he xing fa xiugai'*, op. cit., pp. 15–23.

103 See Sun Yihai and Li Kai, *'Lun shuli shehuizhuyi shichang jingji xing fa guan'* (On establishing the 'socialist market economy': perspectives in the criminal law), *Faxue (Renda)*, no. 6, 1996, pp. 5–8.

104 Indeed, the outline of the 1997 revision with the major exception of reference to the death penalty, was already explicit in the proposals at a 1994 symposium of the Criminal Jurisprudence Research Society. See Shan Min, 'Market Economy and Revision and Perfection of the Criminal Law ... ,' translated under 'Scholars View Criminal Law Reform, Market Economy', FBIS-CHI-95-026, 8 February 1995, pp. 10–13.

105 Murray Scott Tanner makes a similar point in his analysis of law-making process in China. See M.S. Tanner, 'The Erosion of Communist Party Control over Lawmaking in China', *CQ*, no. 138, 1994. pp. 381–403.

106 H.J. Berman, S. Cohen and M. Russell, ' A Comparison of the Chinese and Soviet Codes of Criminal Law and Procedure', *The Journal of Criminal Law and Criminology*, vol. 73, no. 1 (1982), pp. 238–58.

107 See Article 1 of the 1979 CL.

108 See Article 1 of the 1997 CL.

109 Gao Mingxuan, *Zhonghua renmin gongheguo xingfade yunyu he dansheng* (The Embryo and Birth of the PRC Criminal Code) (Beijing: Falu chubanshe, 1980). M.J. Meijer also notes the existence of the analogy in China's earlier Criminal Codes, such as Qing Criminal Code. See Meijer, 'The New Criminal Law of the People's Republic of China', *Review of Socialist Law*, no. 2, 1980, p. 132.

110 As outlined in Marxism–Leninism Mao Zedong Thought, the other four of the five criteria included 'objective criteria' in establishing criminality and punishment, the correlation of punishment with the severity of the crime, the emphasis on class struggle and dictatorship and adhering to 'seeking the truth from the facts', Gao Mingxuan, *Zhonghua renmin gongheguo xing*

fa de yunyu he dansheng, p. 17. For more analysis, see Ronald C. Keith and Lin Zhiqiu, 'To Revise or not To Revise China's Law on Counterrevolution', *China Information*, no. 4 (Spring 1991), pp. 29–30.

111 See R.H. Folsom and J.H. Minan (eds) *Law in the People's Republic of China: Commentary, Readings and Materials* (Boston: Martinus Nijhoff Publishers, 1989), p. 56. Shao-Chuan Leng makes a similar point in his article 'Criminal Justice in Post-Mao China: Some Preliminary Observations', op. cit., pp. 204–37.

112 See Gao Mingxuan, *Zhonghua renmin gongheguo xing fa de yunyu he dansheng*, 1980, p. 17.

113 See Zhao Bingzhi and Xiao Zhonghua, *'Xing fa xiugai zhong leitui zhidu cunfei zhizheng de jiantao'* (Discussions on the analogy system in the process of revising the Criminal Code), *Faxue* (Renda), no. 11, 1996, pp. 13–26.

114 In fact, in order to give the NPC Standing Committee power to amend the criminal law, in 1982, the 1978 Constitution was amended on the issues of power of the Standing Committee. The 1978 Constitution gave the Standing Committee only power to interpret laws and regulations. The 1982 Constitution granted the Standing Committee of the NPC not only power to interpret laws, but also power to revise laws. The Standing Committee has used this power in the past 15 years to issue 22 decisions concerning crime and punishment. This is also a primary reason why the analogy has not been used extensively in judicial practice.

115 See Gao Mingxuan, 'On Several Issues Concerning Reform of Criminal Law of China', *Zhongguo Faxue*, no. 6, 1996, pp. 12–18.

116 Ma Kechang, *'Jiada gaige lidu, xiugai, wanshan xingfa'* (Expanding the strength and power of reform, revising and perfecting the criminal code) *Faxue (Renda)*, no. 11, 1996, pp. 4–11.

117 Zhao Bingzhi and Xiao Zhonghua, *'Xing fa xiugai zhong leitui zhidu cunfei zhizheng de jiantao'*, op. cit., p. 18.

118 Zhao Bingzhi and Xiao Zhonghua, *'Xing fa xiugai zhong leitui zhidu cunfei zhizheng de jiantao'*, op. cit., pp. 13–26.

119 Gao Mingxuan, 'On Several Issues concerning Reform of the Criminal Law of China', op. cit., pp. 12–18.

120 See Article 3 of the 1997 CL.

121 Gao Mingxuan, 'On Several Issues concerning Reform of the Criminal Law of China', op. cit., pp. 12–18.

122 'Justice Minister on Criminal Law' China, *Daily Report*, FBIS-CHI-97-082, March 23, 1997.

123 See Articles 118, 160, and 187 of the 1979 CL.

124 See 'A Major Step Toward an Ideal Criminal Code – Sidelights on Deliberations on Draft Criminal Code Amendments' by *Xinhua* reporters, FBIS-CHI-96-252, *Daily Report*, 30 December 1996.

125 *Xing shi fa gui huibian* (Collection of Laws and Regulations concerning Criminal Matters) (Harbin: Heilongjiang renmin chubanshe, 1990), p. 854.

126 Gao Mingxuan, ed., *Xing fa xue* (Criminal Law Science) (Beijing: Falu chubanshe, 1983), pp. 523–6.

127 See Zhao Bingzhi, Hao Xingwang, Yan Maokun and Xiao Zhonghua, 'Problems on Amendments of the Criminal Law of China', op. cit., pp. 3–68.

128 For new stipulations concerning hooliganism in the 1997 CL, see Articles 290 to 294; for new stipulations of crimes of dereliction of duty, see Chapter

9; the crime of profiteering has been deleted and many new crimes concerning the market, including the financial market, are stipulated in Chapter 3 of the 1997 CL.
129 H.J. Berman, S. Cohen and M. Russell, 'A Comparison of the Chinese and Soviet Codes of Criminal Law and Procedure', *The Journal of Criminal Law and Criminology*, vol. 73, no. 1, 1982, p. 249 and Kim Chin, *The Criminal Code of the People's Republic of China*, The American Series of Foreign Penal Codes (Rothman, 1982), p. 17.
130 For a good example on this issue, see Zhang Baoqiang and Zhang Chen, 'Guanyu chengzhi weifan gongsifade fanzuide jueding jidai xiding' (NPCSC's Decisions Regarding the Punishment of Crime concerning the Corporate Law Needs to be Revised Urgently), *Faxue* (Renda), no. 6, 1996, pp. 14–15.
131 See 'A Major Step Toward an Ideal Criminal Code – Sidelights on Deliberations on Draft Criminal Code Amendments' by *Xinhua* reporters, FBIS-CHI-96-252, *Daily Report*, 30 December 1996.
132 See 'Decision of the Standing Committee of the National People's Congress Regarding the Severe Punishment of Criminal Elements who Seriously Endanger Public Security' in *The Criminal Law and the Criminal Procedure Law of China* (Beijing: Foreign Languages Press, 1984).
133 See Zhao Bingzhi, He Xingwang, Yan Maokun and Xiao Zhonghua, 'Problems on Amendments of the Criminal Law of China', *Faxue yanjiu*, vol. 18, no. 5, 1996, pp. 3–68.
134 Zhao Bingzhi, ed., *Xing fa xin tansuo* (New Probing into Criminal Law) (Beijing: Qunzhong chubanshe, 1993), p. 599.
135 Jerome Hall, *General Principles of Criminal Law*, 2nd edn. (New York: the Bobbs-Merrill Company Inc. 1960), p. 63.
136 Luo Shaping, 'Legislative Completion of the System of the Limitation of Time in the Criminal Law of China', *Faxue yanjiu* (CASS Journal of Law) vol. 18, no. 5, 1996, p. 90.
137 See appendix 1 of the 1997 CL.
138 The following analysis follows very closely upon the detailed discussion of corruption and economic crime in Ronald C. Keith and Zhiqiu Lin, '"Economic Crime" in China's Transition to the "Rule of Law Economy"', *China Report*, vol. 35, no. 2, 1999, pp. 143–61.
139 For the text of the new criminal law, see FBIS-CHI-97-056, 17 March 1997.
140 See Stephen Davis, 'The Death Penalty and Legal Reform in the PRC', *Journal of Chinese Law*, vol. 1, no. 2, Fall 1987, pp. 304–5.
141 'Decision of the Standing Committee of the National People's Congress Regarding the Severe Punishment of Criminals Who Seriously Undermine the Economy', 8 March 1982, in *The Criminal Law and Criminal Procedure Law of China*, pp. 229–33.
142 Ronald C. Keith, *China's Struggle for the Rule of Law*, pp. 171–3.
143 Supreme Court and Supreme Procuratorate, 'Guanyu danq qian banli jingji fanxui anjian zhong zhuti yingyong falu de ruogan wenti de jieda' (Answers Relating to the Application of Law in Dealing with Eco-nomic Crime), in *Zhonghua renmin gongheguo falu fenlei zonglan* (*Xingshi falu juan*) (The Classified Assemblage of the Law of the People's Republic of China, Criminal Law) (Beijing: Falu chubanshe, 1994), pp. 54–8.
144 See sections no. 1 and no. 3 of National People's Congress, 'Guanyu chengzhi tanwu zhuihuilu zui de buchong guiding' (Supplementary Regulations on Pun-

ishment for Embezzlement and Bribery), in *Zhonghua renmin gongheguo falu fenlei zonglan* (*Xingshi falu juan*) (The Classified Assemblage of the Law of the People's Republic of China, Criminal Law) (Beijing: Falu chubanshe, 1994), pp. 21–2.
145 Jean-Louis Rocca's description of 'embezzlement' appears to have incorrectly included the misappropriation of public funds within *'tanwu'*. See Rocca, 'Corruption and its Shadow: an Anthropological View of Corruption in China,' *CQ*, June 1992, p. 405.
146 National People's Congress Standing Committee, *'Guanyu chengzhi shengchan xiaoshou weilue shangpin fanzuide guiding'* (Decision on Punishment for the Adulteration of Market Commodities), in *Zhonghua renmin gongheguo falu fenlei zonglan, Xingshi falu juan* (Classified Assemblage of the Law of the People's Republic of China, Criminal Law) (Beijing: Falu chubanshe, 1994), pp. 37–8.
147 Zhou Yu and Gu Ming, general editors, *Faxue da cidian* (Encyclopedia of Chinese law) (Beijing: Zhongguo zhengfa daxue chubanshe, 1991), p. 1121.
148 The parallel English and Chinese texts are available in *The Criminal Law and the Criminal Procedure Law of the People's Republic of China* (Beijing: Foreign Languages Press, 1984).
149 See 'Talking About the Issues Concerning Economic Crime' in Zhou Daoluan, ed., *Zhongguo xingfa* (Chinese Criminal Law) (Beijing: Zhongguo zhengfa daxue chubanshe, 1991).
150 Gu Xianrong, *'Lun jingji fanzui de gainian he fanwei'* (On the Definitions and Range of Economic Crime), *Faxue yanjiu*, no. 2, 1990, pp. 15–8.
151 Chen Chunjian, *'Qianyi chengzhi jingji fanzui de xingshi lifa sixiang'* (Critical Discussions of the Thought of Lawmaking in Economic Crime), *Faxue zazhi*, no. 4, 1992, pp. 15–16 in *Faxue* (Renda), no. 9, 1992, pp. 82–3.
152 Ronald C. Keith, *China's Struggle for the Rule of Law*, pp. 172–3.
153 For more explanation, see Ronald C. Keith and Lin Zhiqiu, 'To Revise or not to Revise China's Law on Counterrevolution', op. cit., p. 26.
154 Human Rights Watch/Asia, 'China: Whose Security? "State Security" in China's New Criminal Code', *Human Rights in China*, vol. 9, no. 4 (C), (April 1997), pp. 13–14.
155 *'Dui fangeming zui de xiugao jianyi'* (Proposals for the Revision of 'Counterrevolutionary Crime'), *Fazhi ribao* (Law Daily), 2 June 1989, p. 3.
156 For example, Zhou Daolun's high profile article treats 'counterrevolutionary crime' as a political rather than a legal concept. See Zhou Daolun, *'Xingfa wanshan chuyi'* (Preliminary Discussions on Perfecting the Criminal Law), *Faxue zazhi* (Law Magazine), no. 4, 1996, pp. 11–13. Almost the same arguments were presented in Zhao Bingzhi, ed., *Xing fa xin tansuo* (New Probing into Criminal Law) (Beijing: Qunzhong chubanshe, 1993), p. 613.
157 'China: Whose Security?', op. cit., p. 17.
158 For 'subversion' in the Hong Kong example, see Ronald C. Keith, *China's Struggle for the Rule of Law*, pp. 194–7.
159 See Human Rights Watch/Asia, 'China: Whose Security? "State Security" in China's New Criminal Code', op. cit., p. 15.
160 For a more elaborated Chinese discussion on this point, see Liu Zuexiang, 'The Concatenation of Rights and Powers in a Society Ruled by Law', *Faxue yanjiu*, vol. 18, no. 4, 1996, pp. 69–79.

161 Note on 'Concepts of Law in the Chinese Anti-Crime Campaign', *Harvard Law Review*, vol. 98, 1985, pp. 1890–908.
162 See Article 21 of the 1997 CL and Article 33 of the 1979 CL.
163 See Yijiang Ding, 'Corporatism and Civil Society in China: an Overview of the Debate in Recent Years', *China Information*, vol. xii, no. 4, Spring 1998, pp. 44–59.
164 See Article 38 of the 1997 CL.
165 Gao Mingxuan, *Zhonghua renmin gongheguo xingfade yunyu he dansheng*, p. 73.
166 See Articles 43, 44 and 46 of the 1979 CL and Gao Mingxuan, 'On Several Issues concerning Reform of the Criminal Law of China', *Zhongguo faxue*, op. cit., pp. 12–18.
167 Deng Xiaoping, *Fundamental Issues in Present-day China* (Oxford: Pergamon Press, 1987), p. 137.
168 For example, see Zhao Bingzhi and He Xingwang, *'Lun tebie xingfa he xingfa xiugai'*, op. cit., pp. 15–23.
169 Gao Mingxuan, 'On Several Issues concerning Reform of the Criminal Law of China', op. cit., pp. 12–18.
170 See Wang Fengzhi, 'Use of Death Penalty should be Reduced', *Zhengfa Luntan* (Politics and Law Tribune), August 1995, no. 64, pp. 23–7, in *Daily Report*, China FBIS-CHI-96-014, 22 January, 1996.
171 Ma Kechang, *'Jiada gaige lidu, xiugai, wanshan xing fa'*, op. cit., pp. 4–11.
172 Gao Mingxuan, 'On Several Issues concerning Reform of the Criminal Law of China', op. cit., p. 16.
173 See Zhao Bingzhi, He Xingwang, Yan Maokun and Xiao Zhonghua, 'Problems on Amendments to the Criminal Law of China' op. cit., p. 35. Zhao Bingzhi and He Xingwang, *'Lun tebie xingfa he xingfa xiugai'*, op. cit., pp. 15–23.
174 See 'Lawmakers Support Changes to Criminal Law', *Daily Report*, China, FBIS-CHI-96-249, 26 December 1996.
175 See 'Further on Amendments to Criminal Code', *Xinhua*, FBIS-CHI-96-249, 24 Dec, 1996.
176 See Articles 399–402 of the 1997 CL.
177 See Hungdah Chiu, 'China's New Legal System', *Current History*, September 1980, p. 31. For instances of this terminology, see Articles 116 and 117 of the 1979 CL.
178 Gao Mingxuan, 'On Several Issues concerning Reform of the Criminal Law of China', op. cit., pp. 12–18.
179 This is Stanley Lubman's phraselology in his 'Introduction: the Future of Chinese Law', op. cit., p. 21.

6 The Law and the Market at the Crossroads of Justice and Efficiency

1 See Li Lin, *'Quanqiuhua beijingde Zhongguo lifa fazhan'* (China's legislative development in the context of globalization), *Falixue, fashixue* (Jurisprudence and Legal History), no. 3, 1998, p. 31. As cited in Ronald C. Keith, '"Internationalization" and "Localization" in the Chinese Search for

286 Notes and References

Human Justice', published conference proceedings, 'Globalization, Social, Economic and Political Dimensions', Eastern Mediterranean University, 19 November 1998.

2   A selection of related literature is cited in n12 of Chapter 2.
3   Jude Howell, *China Opens Its Doors* (Hemel Hempstead: Harvester Wheatsheaf, 1993), pp. 182–93.
4   Wang Jiafu, '*Shehuizhuyi shichang jingji falu zhidu jianshe wenti*' (Issues relating to the establishment of the legal system of the socialist market economy), in Ministry of Justice, ed., *Zhonggong zhongyang fazhi jiangzuo huibian* (Compiled course of CCPCC lectures on the legal system) (Beijing: Falu chubanshe, 1998), p. 78.
5   See, for example, Dusan Polonc, 'Efficiency and Justice', *International Journal of Political Economy*, vol. 26, no. 1, Spring 1996, pp. 3–90.
6   'Completely Smash the Feudal, Capitalist and Revisionist Legal Systems', *Fan Peng-Lo heixian* (The anti-Peng/Lo blackline), no. 2, July 1968, in *Survey of China Mainland Magazines*, no. 625, 3 September 1968, p. 23.
7   Dong Likun, 'No One Can Stand Above the Law: a Discussion of the Relationships Between the Law and Individuals, the Party, the Government and Politics', *Shehui kexue* (Shanghai), no. 1, February 1980, pp. 7–12 in *Joint Publications Research Service* (JPRS), 77155, no. 155, 12 January 1981, p. 9.
8   See Ronald C. Keith, *China's Struggle for the Rule of Law*, passim and Ronald C. Keith, 'Chinese Politics and the New Theory of the "Rule of Law"', *CQ*, no. 125, March 1991, pp. 109–18.
9   Li Buyun, 'Certain Questions Concerning the Relationship Between Party Policies and State Laws', *Faxue jikan* (Law Quarterly), no. 3, July 1984, pp. 3–7 in *China Report*, JPRS-CPS-84-068, 15 October 1984, pp. 32, 33 and 39.
10 A review of the ten points outlined by Li Buyun to the authors, for example, suggests that the only really new theme that emerged in the 1990s conceptualization of the rule of law's content related to the protection of human rights. See Chapter 1 discussion of the authors' 4 June 1998 interview with Li Buyun.
11 Jiang Lishan, '*Zhongguo fazhi daolu chutan – shang*' (Initial exploration of the road to the rule of law in China – part 1), *Zhongwai faxue* (Chinese and Foreign Jurisprudence), no. 3, 1998, pp. 16–28, as reprinted in *Falixue, fashixue* (Jurisprudence and the History of Law), no. 10, 1998, p. 37.
12 Ibid., p. 41.
13 For example, see the discussion in Chapter 2. For the '*Shanghai shi qingnian baohu tiaoli*' (Shanghai municipal regulations on the protection of minors), see *Faxue* (Renda) no. 7, 1987, pp. 72–7. These provided a important reference point in the drafting of related 1991 national legislation, and as Chen Mingxia indicated to the authors, there is some expectation that new law on family violence will move from the local to the national level.
14 Jiang Lishan, '*Zhongguo fazhi daolu wenti taolun – xia*' (A discussion of problems on the road to a Chinese Rule of Law – part 2), *Zhongwai faxue*, no. 4, 1998, pp. 21–33, reprinted in *Falixue, fashixue*, no. 10, 1998, p. 43.
15 Max Weber as cited in Guenther Ross and Claus Wittich, eds, *Economy and Society*, vol. 2 (Berkeley: University of California Press, 1994), pp. 6–7.

Abbreviated Listing of Prominent Jurists

Cao Jianming	曹建明	East China University of Political Science and Law
Chen Guangzhong	陈光中	Chinese University of Political Science and Law
Chen Mingxia	陈明侠	Institute of Law, Chinese Academy of Social Science (CASS)
Chen Shirong	陈世荣	Institute of Law, CASS
Chen Wenyuan	陈文渊	Chinese University of Political Science and Law
Cui Min	崔 敏	Chinese Public Security University
Fu Kuanzhi	付宽芝	Institute of Law, CASS
Gao Mingxuan	高铭暄	Faculty of Law, Chinese People's University
Gao Shangquan	高尚全	President, China (Hainan) Institute for Reform and Development
Gu Angran	顾昂然	Chairman, Legal System Working Committee of the NPC
Gu Xiaorong	顾肖荣	Institute of Law, Shanghai Academy of Social Science
Guan Huai	关 怀	Faculty of Law, Chinese People's University
Guo Daohui	郭道晖	Chief Editor, Chinese Legal Science
Guo Jie	郭 捷	Northwest China Political and Law College
Han Henan	韩贺南	Chinese Women's College
Hao Tiechuan	郝铁川	East China University of Political Science and Law
He Xingwang	赫兴旺	Faculty of Law, Chinese People's University
Huang Jinhua	黄金华	Faculty of Law, Chinese People's University
Huang Wenyi	黄文艺	Faculty of Law, Jilin University
Jiang Ping	江 平	Chinese University of Political Science and Law
Kong Xiangjun	孔祥俊	Fair Trade Bureau, National Industry and Commerce Administration Bureau

Li Bing	李兵	Faculty of Law, Nanjing University
Li Buyun	李步云	Director of the Center of Human Rights, Institute of Law, CASS
Li Mingshun	李明舜	Department of Law, Chinese Women's College
Liang Huixing	梁慧星	Institute of Law, CASS
Liang Shuwen	梁书文	Legal expert at the Supreme People's Court
Liu Hainian	刘海年	Institute of Law, CASS
Liu Han	刘瀚	Institute of Law, CASS
Liu Junhai	刘俊海	Institute of Law, CASS
Long Zhongzhi	龙宗智	Southwest China University of Political Science and Law
Luo Shuping	罗书平	Sichuan Provincial Higher People's Court
Ma Kechang	马克昌	Faculty of Law, Wuhan University
Ma Yinan	马忆南	Department of Law, Beijing University
Ma Yuejin	马跃进	Shanxi Institute of Economics Management
Ma Zunju	马俊驹	Faculty of Law, Wuhan University
Shen Tongxian	沈同仙	Faculty of Law, Suzhou University
Shen Jiaban	沈家本	An eminent Qing jurist (1840–1913)
Shen Sibao	沈四宝	University of Foreign Economic Trade
Shen Zongling	沈宗灵	Beijing University
Shi Jichun	史际春	Faculty of Law, Chinese People's University
Shi Tanjing	史探径	Institute of Law, CASS
Song Yinghui	宋英辉	Chinese University of Political Science and Law
Sun Guohua	孙国华	Faculty of Law, Chinese People's University; General Editor, 1997 ZhongHua Faxue Da Cidian (The Chinese Encyclopedia of Legal Studies 1997)
Sun Xiaoxia	孙笑侠	Faculty of Law, Hangzhou University
Tong Rou	佟柔	Faculty of Law, Chinese People's University
Tong Zhiwei	童之伟	Institute of Politics and Administration, Wuhan University
Wang Baoshu	王保树	Institute of Law, CASS
Wang Jiafu	王家福	Institute of Law, CASS
Wang Liming	王利明	Faculty of Law, Chinese People's University
Wang Minyuan	王敏远	Institute of Law, CASS

Wang Quanxing	王全兴	South China Politics and Law College
Wang Shengluan	王生栾	Chinese Women's College
Xia Yinglan	夏吟兰	Secretary-General of China Family Law Association; Chinese University of Political Science and Law
Xia Yong	夏 勇	Institute of Law, CASS
Xiao Zhonghua	肖中华	Faculty of Law, Chinese People's University
Xie Cichang	谢次昌	China State Property Management Bureau
Yang Dawen	扬大文	Faculty of Law, Chinese People's University
Yang Haikun	扬海坤	Faculty of Law, Suzhou University
Yu Jing	于 晶	Department of Law, Chinese Youth Political College
Yu Min	喻 敏	People's Court of Xinjin County, Sichuan Province
Zhang Guangbo	张光博	Faculty of Law, Jilin University
Zhang Guangxing	张广兴	Institute of Law, CASS
Zhang Lingjie	张令杰	Institute of Law, CASS
Zhang Qinmian	张芹棉	Chinese Women's College
Zhang Xianyu	张贤钰	East China University of Political Science and Law
Zhang Zipei	张子培	Chinese University of Political Science and Law
Zhao Bingzhi	赵秉志	Faculty of Law, Chinese People's University
Zhao Shiyi	赵世义	Faculty of Law, Wuhan University
Zou Xueping	邹平学	Faculty of Law, Wuhan University
Zuo Weimin	左卫民	Faculty of Law, Sichuan University

Select Glossary of Chinese Political/Legal Terms

actual rights	*shiyou quanli* 实有权力
adjustment of interests	*liyi tiaozheng* 利益调整
administrative labour relations	*laodong xingzheng falu guanxi* 劳动行政法律关系
alienationism	*fenlie zhuyi* 分裂主义
analogy	*leitui* 类推
arrest	*daibu* 逮捕
balancing of rights and interests	*quanyi pingheng* 权益平衡
basic theory of law	*faxue jichu lilun* 法学基础理论
breakdown of affection	*ganqing polie* 感情破裂
breakdown of the marriage	*hunyin polie* 婚姻破裂
change in objective conditions	*keguan qingkuang bianhua* 客观情况变化
citizens' rights	*gongmin quan* 公民权
city registration	*chengshi hukou* 城市户口
clarification of property rights	*minque chanquan* 明确产权
collective welfare	*jiti fuli* 集体福利
combining remuneration according to work and multiple patterns of distribution	*an lao fenpei yu duozhong fenpei fangshi xiangjiehe* 按劳分配与多种分配方式相结合
common duty	*gong tong zeren* 共同责任

comprehensive management of public order	shehui zhi'an zonghe zhili 社会治安综合治理
concubines	er nai 二奶
contractual society	qiyue shehui 契约社会
control (also translated as 'surveillance')	guanzhi 管制
corporate crime	danwei fanzui 单位犯罪
crime of misappropriation of public funds	nuoyong gongkuan zui 挪用公款罪
crimes endangering state security	weihai guojia anquan zui 危害国家安全罪
crimes of counterrevolution	fangeming zui 反革命罪
criminal law science	xingfa xue 刑法学
decide first, trial later	xianding, houshen 先定，后审
deletion theory	feichu shuo 废除说
democratize	minzhuhua 民主化
detention	juliu 拘留
disguised form of corporal punishment	bianxiang tifa 变相体罚
dual purposes theory	shuangchong jiazhi shuo 双重价值说
economic ownership	jingji suoyouquan 经济所有权
efficiency is primary and fairness, supplementary	xiaoyi weizhu, gongzheng weifu 效益为主，公正为辅
embezzlement	tanwu 贪污
employment contract system	laodong hetongzhi 劳动合同制
enterprises running society	qiyie ban shehui 企业办社会

establishment of a socialist market economy legal system	shehuizhuyi shichang jingji falu zhidu jianshe 社会主义市场经济法律制度建设
exemption from prosecution	mianyu qisu 免于起诉
external correlation	wai xietiao 外协调
fairness, justice	pingdeng, zhengyi 平等，正义
first establish the rules and then handle affairs	xian li guiju, hou banshi 先立规矩，后办事
flexibility	linghuoxing 灵活性
formal justice	xingshi zhengyi 形式正义
general stipulations are better than specific ones	yi cu bu yi xi 宜粗不宜细
general theories of law	fade yiban lilun 法的一般理论
group	qunti 群体
hooliganism	liumang zui 流氓罪
human rights	renquan 人权
impairing marriage	fanghai hunyin 妨害婚姻
impartiality	gongzheng yuanze 公正原则
independent control	zhipei 支配
independent purposes theory	duli jiazhi shuo 独立价值说
individual economic organization	geti jingji zuzhi 个体经济组织
individual industrial and commercial households	geti gongshang hu 个体工商户
individual ownership under the socialist system	shehuizhuyi zhidu xia de geren suoyouzhi 社会主义制度下的个人所有制

interest relations	liyi guanxi 利益关系
interior correlation	nei xietiao 内协调
intermediary property management organization	zhongjie jigou 中介机构
jurisprudence	falixue 法理学
just rights and interests	zhengdang quanli he liyi 正当权利和利益
justice and due process	gongzheng he youxu 公正和有序
labour object theory	laodongli shuo 劳动力说
law on rights in things	wuquan fa 物权法
lawful subject	hefa zhuti 合法主体
legal ownership	falu suoyouquan 法律所有权
legal rights	fading quanli 法定权利
legal system	fazhi 法制
legal theory	fali 法理
living at home under surveillance	jianshi juzhu 监视居住
localization	bentu hua 本土化
malpractice	yingsi wubi 营私舞弊
market economy is a rule of law economy	shichang jingji shi fazhi jingji 市场经济是法治经济
methods and tasks	fangfa yu renwu 方法与任务
mixed ownership	hunhe chanquan 混合产权
mixed ownership economy	hunhe suoyou zhi jingji 混合所有制经济

must, should	bixu, yingdang 必须,应当
negative theory	fouding shuo 否定说
network of natural phenomena	ziran xianxiang zhi wang 自然现象之网
objects, subjects	keti, zhuti 客体,主体
obtaining a guarantor and awaiting trial	qubao houshen 取保候审
operational management right	jingying quan 经营权
ownership right of legal person	faren suoyouquan 法人所有权
ownership system, ownership rights, rights in things	suoyouzhi, suoyouquan, wuquan 所有制,所有权,物权
pan-moralism	fan daode zhuyi 泛道德主义
people visiting system	renmin laifang zhidu 人民来访制度
plurality of subjects before the law	liyi zhuti duoyuanhua 利益主体多元化
pluralization of enterprise ownership	qiye chanquan duoyuanhua 企业产权多元化
pluralized jurisprudence	duoyuan de falixue 多元的法理学
positive theory	kending shuo 肯定说
presumption of innocence	wuzui tuiding 无罪推定
property ownership rights	caichan suoyouquan 财产所有权
property relationships	caichan guanxi 财产关系
property rights	caichan quan 财产权
property rights of legal person	faren chanquan 法人产权
protection of women's lawful rights and interests	baozhang funu de hefa quanyi 保障妇女的合法权益

public ownership as primary and the common development in the economy of various forms of ownership	gongyou zhi wei zhuti, duozhong suoyouzhi jingji gongtong fazhan 公有制为主体，多种所有制经济共同发展
punishment and no stipulation	li er bu yan 厉而不严
purpose	mudi 目的
purpose of counterrevolution	yi fangeming wei mudi 以反革命为目的
rationalize	kexuehua 科学化
reform faction	gaige pai 改革派
relative ownership	xiangdui suoyouquan 相对所有权
relying on law to govern the country	yi fa zhi guo 依法治国
retention theory	baoliu shuo 保留说
right of possession	zhanyou quan 占有权
right to benefits or usufruct	shouyi quan 受益权
right to dispose of property	chufen quan 处分权
right to use	shiyong quan 使用权
rights and interests	quanyi 权益
rights and obligations relations	quanli guanxi he yiwu guanxi 权利关系和义务关系
rights fundamentalism	quanli benweizhuyi 权利本位主义
rights in things belonging to oneself	ziwu quan 自物权
rights in things belong to others	tawu quan 他物权
roaming about	liudang 流荡

rough outlines to detailed rules	*yi cu bu yi xi* 宜粗不宜细
rule of law economy	*fazhi jingji* 法治经济
rule of law society	*fazhi shehui* 法治社会
rule of law state	*fazhi guo* 法治国
rule of law	*fazhi* 法治
rule of man	*renzhi* 人治
ruling the country in accordance with law	*yifa zhiguo* 依法治国
ruling the people in accordance with law	*yifa zhimin* 依法治民
running the country according to law and establishing a socialist rule-of-law country	*yifa zhiguo, jianshe shehuizhuyi fazhi guojia* 依法治国，建设社会主义法治国家
rural management responsibility contract household	*nongcun geti chenbao hu* 农村个体承包户
self-determination	*zijue* 自决
separating ownership from operational management rights	*suoyouquan yu jingyingquan fenli* 所有权与经营权分立
severely and swiftly punishing	*cong zhong cong kuai* 从重从快
sexual harassment	*xing saorao* 性骚扰
shareholding cooperation	*gufen hezuo* 股份合作
shareholding cooperative system	*gufen hezuo zhi* 股份合作制
showing-examples-ism	*lishi zhuyi* 例示主义
small government, big society	*xiao zhengfu, da shehui* 小政府，大社会
social protection law	*shehui baozhang fa* 社会保障法
socialist collective ownership of the working masses	*shehuizhuyi laodong qunzhong jiti suoyouzhi* 社会主义劳动群众集体所有制

Select Glossary of Chinese Political/Legal Terms

socialist ownership by the whole people	shehuizhuyi quanmin suoyouzhi 社会主义全民所有制
society fundamentalism	shehui benwei zhuyi 社会本位主义
socio-rights	shehui quanli 社会权利
special grouping	teshu qunti 特殊群体
special labour subjects groups	teshu laodongzhe qunti 特殊劳动者群体
state and society	guojia he shehui 国家和社会
state legal person	guojia faren 国家法人
stipulation and hardly any punishment	yan er bu li 严而不厉
strike hard	yanda 严打
structure of interests	liyi jiegou 利益结构
shift in trial proceeding from the inquisitorial to the adversarial	bian jiuwen shi wei kongbian shi 变纠问式为控辩式
substance, form	ti, yong 体，用
substance and form	neirong yu xingshi 内容与形式
substantial justice	shizhi zhengyi 实质正义
system of ownership of the means of production	shengchan ziliao suoyouzhi 生产资料所有制
system of rights	quanli tixi 权利体系
system of social protection	shehui baozhang zhidu 社会保障制度
taking facts as the basis and the law as the yardstick	yi shishi wei genju, yi falu wei zhunsheng 以事实为根据，以法律为准绳
theories of state and law	guojia yu fade lilun 国家与法的理论
theory on principal and supplementary objects	jiben keti yu fuzu keti shuo 基本客体与辅助客体说

three capital enterprises	*sanzi qiye* 三资企业
three catch-all crimes: dereliction of duty, hooliganism, and profiteering	*koudai zui* 口袋罪
three favourable directions	*sange youli yu* 三个有利于
ultimate ownership	*zhongji suoyouquan* 终级所有权
unity of rights and obligations	*quanli yiwu xiang tongyi* 权利义务相统一
use law to administer	*yi fa xingzheng* 依法行政
using general principles-ism	*gaikuo zhuyi* 概括主义
voluntary participation	*ziyuan* 自愿

Select English and Chinese Bibliography

Chinese reference books

China, *Zhong Hua renmin gongheguo changyong falu daquan* (Compendium of often used laws of the PRC) (Beijing: Falu chubanshe, 1989).
China, *Zhongguo falu nianjian, 1991* (Law Yearbook of China, 1991) (Beijing: Zhongguo falu nianjianshe chubanshe, 1991).
Deng Xiaoping, *Deng Xiaoping wenxuan* (Deng Xiaoping's Selected Works) (Beijing: Renmin chubanshe, 1993).
China, *Zhongguo gongchandang dishiwuci quanguo daibiao dahui wenjian huibian* (Compiled Documents of the Chinese Communist Party 15th National Party Congress) (Beijing: Renmin chubanshe, 1997).
Dong Baoha, *Laodongfa yu laodong zhengyi shiyong shouze* (Practical Handbook on Labour Law and Labour Disputes Settlement) (Beijing: Zhongguo jingji chubanshe, 1997).
Gao Mingxuan, *Zhonghua renmin gongheguo xingfade yunyu he dansheng* (The Embryo and Birth of the Criminal Code of the People's Republic of China) (Beijing: Falu chubanshe, 1980).
Liu Peixian (ed.), *Makesizhuyi yu dangdai cidian* (Dictionary of Marxism and the Contemporary Era) (Beijing: Zhongguo renmin daxue chubanshe, 1988).
Ministry of Justice (ed.), *Zhonggong zhongyang fazhi jiangzuo huibian* (The Compiled Course of CCP Central Committee Lectures on the Legal System (Beijing: Falu Chubanshe, 1998).
Qin Youtu and Fan Qirong (eds), *Shehui baozhang fa* (Social Protection Law) (Beijing: Falu Chubanshe, 1997).
Song Yinghui, *Xingshi susong mudi lun* (On the Purposes of Criminal Procedure) (Beijing: Chinese Public Security University Press, 1995).
Sun Guohua *et al.* (eds), *Zhonghua faxue da cidian* (The Chinese Encyclopedia of Legal Studies) (Beijing: Zhongguo jiancha chubanshe, 1997).
Wang Jiafu and Liu Hainian (eds), *Zhongguo renquan baike quanshu* (Human Rights Encyclopedia of China) (Beijing: Zhongguo da baike quanshu chubanshe, 1998).
Wu Chaomin, Wang Quanxing and Zhang Guowen, *Zhongguo laodongfa xinlun* (New studies in Chinese Labour Law) (Beijing: Zhongguojingji chubanshe, 1994).
Yu Junwen, *et al.* (eds), *Makesizhuyi baike cidian* (Encyclopedia of Marxism) vol. 1 (Shenyang: Dongbei shifan daxue chubanshe, 1987).
Zhou Mi, *Zhongguo xingfa shi* (The History of the Chinese Criminal Law) Beijing: Qunzheng chubanshe, 1985).
Zhou Yu and Gu Ming (general eds), *Faxue da cidian* (Encyclopedia of Chinese law) (Beijing: Zhongguo zhengfa daxue chubanshe, 1991).

Chinese legal and political journals

Note: The titles only of journals are cited herein. Detail regarding specifically cited articles are given in full in the chapter notes. This listing is representative of the major law journals in Chinese, but it is not exhaustive. Please note the invaluable compendiums of extracted materials, provided by the Information Centre of People's University, under the general title, *Fuyin baokan ziliao* (Duplicated materials from newspapers and journals). These compendiums are indicated with an asterisk in the listing below.

Falixue, fashixue (Jurisprudence and History of Laws) Beijing
Faxue (Legal Studies) Beijing
Faxue (Legal Studies) Shanghai
Faxue jikan (Law Quarterly), Chongqing
Faxue yanjiu (Studies in Law) Beijing
Faxue yuekan (Law Monthly) Beijing
Faxuejia (Jurists)
Funu yanjiu (Women's Studies) Beijing
Gongren zuzhi yu huodong (Workers' organization and movement) Beijing
Jingji fa (Ecnomic Law) Beijing
Jingji faxue. laodong faxue (Studies in Economic Law and Labour Law) Beijing
Lilun faxue, fashixue (Jurisprudence and Historical Studies) Beijing
Min shang faxue (Civil and Commercial Law) Beijing
Qiushi (Seeking the truth, formerly *Hongqi*, Red flag) Beijing
Shehui kexue (Social Science) Shanghai
Susong faxue. sifa zhidu (Studies in Procedure Law, Judicial System) Beijing
Tansuo yu zhengming (Dialogue and Contention) Beijing
Xiandai faxue (Modern Law Science) Chongqing
Xianfaxue. xingzheng faxue (Studies in the Constitution and Administration Law) Beijing
Xiangtan daxue xuebao (Journal of Xiangtan University) Xiangtan
Xingshi faxue (Studies in Criminal Law) Beijing
Xinhua yuebao (New China Monthly) Beijing
Zhengfa luntan (Tribune of Political Science and Law) Beijing
Zhengzhi yu falu (Politics and Law) Shanghai
Zhongguo falu (Chinese Law Quarterly) Hong Kong
Zhongguo faxue (Chinese Legal Science) Beijing
Zhonghua nuzi xueyuan xuebao (Journal of Chinese Women's College) Beijing
Zhongwai faxue (Chinese and Comparative Legal Studies) Beijing

Chinese books

CCP Central Committee Documents Research Office, *Deng Xiaoping tongzhi lun minzhu yu fazhi* (Comrade Deng Xiaoping on democracy and legal system) (Beijing: Falu chubanshe, 1990).
Chan, Huabin, *Wuquanfa yuanli* (Principles of law on rights in things) (Beijing: State Administration College Press, 1997).

China, *1998 nian Zhongguo renquan shiye de jinzhan* (Employment progress for the year 1998 in China's human rights) (Beijing: Wuzhou chuanbo chubanshe, 1999).
China, *Funu he weichengnianren falu baohuquanshu* (Complete volume on the legal protection of women and children) (Beijing: Zhongguo jiancha chubanshe, 1991).
China, *Zhonggong zhongyang fazhi jiangzuo huibian* (Collection of lectures on the legal system to the Central Committee of the CCP) (Beijing: Publishing House of Law, 1998).
China, *Zhongguo falu nianjian, 1991* (Law Yearbook of China, 1991) (Beijing: Zhongguo falu nianjianshe chubanshe, 1991).
China, *Zhonghua renmin gongheguo changyong falu daquan* (Compendium of often used laws of the PRC) (Beijing: Falu chubanshe, 1989).
China, *Zhonghua renmin gongheguo falu fenlei zonglan: Guojia fa, xingzheng fa juan* (General compendium of all classes of PRC law) (Beijing: Falu chubanshe, 1994).
Cui Min, *Zhongguo xingshi susong fa xin fazhan* (The new development of China's law on criminal procedure) (Beijing: Zhonguo renmin gongan daxue chubanshe, 1996).
Dong Baoha, *Laodongfa yu laodong zhengyi shiyong shouze* (Practical handbook on labour law and labour disputes settlement) (Beijing: Zhongguo jingji chubanshe, 1997).
Faxue yanjiu bianji bu, (ed.), *Faxue yanjiu yibai qi youxiu lunwen* (The outstanding articles selected from the 100 issues of studies in law) (Beijing: 1995).
Gao Mingxuan, *Zhonghua renmin gongheguo xingfa de yunyu he dansheng* (The embryo and birth of the criminal code of the People's Republic of China). (Beijing: Falu chubanshe, 1980).
Guan Huai (ed.), *Zhonghua renmin gongheguo laodong fa daodu* (Introduction to PRC labour law) (Beijing: Falu chubanshe, 1997).
Guan Huai, Ren Fushan and Chan Wenyun (eds), *Laodong faxue* (Labour Law Science) (Beijing: Falu chubanshe, 1996).
Guo Jie, Liu Zun and Yang Sun, *Laodong faxue* (Labour Law Science) (Beijing: Zhongguo zhengfa daxue chubanshe, 1997).
Li Jingsen and Wang Cangsuo (eds), *Laodong faxue* (Labour Law Science) (Beijing: Chinese People's University Press, 1996).
Liang Shuwen and Hui Luming (eds), *Laodongfa ji peitao guiding xin shixijie* (New interpretations of the 1994 LL and related regulation) (Beijing: Renmin fayuan chubanshe, 1997).
Liu Suping, (ed.), *Hunyin faxue cankao ziliao* (Marriage law reference materials) (Beijing: Zhongguo renmin daxue chubanshe, 1989).
Meng Liankun *et al.* (eds), *Zhonghua renmin gongheguo laonianren quanyi baozhang fa shiyi* (Explanations of the PRC law on the rights and interests of the elderly) (Beijing: Hualing chubanshe, 1997).
Ministry of Justice (ed.), *Deng Xiaoping lun minzhu fazhi jianshe* (Explanations of Deng Xiaoping on establishing democracy and the legal system) (Beijing: Falu chubanshe, 1994).
National Legal Education Office and State Economic System Reform Commission (ed.), *Gufenzhi yu gufen hezuo zhi Falu Zhengce zhishi wenda* (Questions and

answers concerning legal policies of joint stock system and shareholding cooperative system) (Beijing: Falu chubanshe, 1998).

Qiao Keyu (ed.), *Falixue jiaocheng* (Instructional program in jurisprudence) (Beijing: Falu chubanshe, 1997).

Ru Xin et al., *Xiao zhengfu da shehui de lilun yu shijian* (The theory and practice of 'small government and big society') (Beijing: Shehui kexue wenxian chubanshe, 1998).

Shen Zongling and Zhang Wenxian (eds), *Falixue* (Jurisprudence) (Beijing: Gaodeng jiaoyu chubanshe, 1994).

Shi Jichun, *Guoyou qiye falu* (On law of state-owned enterprises) (Beijing: Falu chubanshe, 1997).

Sun Guohua (ed.), *Falixue jiaocheng* (Instructional program in jurisprudence) (Beijing: Zhongguo renmin daxue chubanshe, 1994).

Sun Guohua and Zhu Jingwen (ed.), *Falixue* (Jurisprudence) (Beijing: Falu chubanshe, 1994).

Supreme People's Court Labour Training Group (ed.), *Laodongfa jiben lilun yu shijian jiangzuo* (Lectures on basic theory and practice of the labour law) (Beijing: Falu chubanshe, 1995).

Tong Rou, Wang liming, and Ma Zunju (eds), *Zhongguo minfa* (Chinese civil law) (Beijing: Falu chubanshe, 1998).

Wang Guochun, *Xiandai falixue: Lishi yu lilun* (Contemporary jurisprudence: history and theory) (Hunan chubanshe, 1995).

Wang Jiafu et al. (eds), *Yifa zhiguo, jianshe shehuizhuyi fazhi guojia* (Running the country according to law and establishing a socialist rule-of-law country) (Beijing: Zhongguo fazhi chubanshe, 1996).

Wang Quanxing, *Laodongfa* (Labour law) (Beijing: Falu chubanshe, 1997).

Wang Shunhua (ed.), *Laonianren yuanyi de falu baozhang* (The legal guarantees of the rights and interests of the elderly) (Beijing: Jingji guanli chubanshe, 1995).

Wang Zhongfan (ed.), *Zhongguo shehui zhi'an zonghe zhili de lilun yu shijian* (Theory and practice of comprehensive management of public order) (Beijing: Qunzhong chubanshe, 1989).

Xu Xianming (ed.), *Gongmin quanli yiwu tonglun* (Introduction to citizen's rights and obligations) (Beijing: Qunzhong chubanshe, 1991).

Yu Changmiao and Li Wei (eds), *Shiwu da yihou de Zhongguo* (China after the 15th congress of the CCP) (Beijing: Renmin chubanshe, 1997).

Zhang Wenxian, *Falixue* (Jurisprudence) (Beijing: Falu chubanshe, 1997).

Zhang Zipei (ed.), *Xingshi susongfa jiaocheng* (Lectures on criminal procedure law) (Beijing: Qunzhong chubanshe, 1982).

Zhou Mi, *Zhongguo xingfa shi* (The history of the Chinese criminal law) (Beijing: Qunzhong chubanshe, 1985).

Zhu Jingzhe (eds), *Wo guo xingfa dui Funu he ertong hefa quanyi de baohu* (Our country's criminal law's protection of women and children's legal rights and interests) (Beijing: Qunzhong chubanshe, 1993).

Articles, books and documentation in English

Alford, William, 'Tasselled Loafers for Barefoot Lawyers: Transformation and Tension in the World of Chinese Legal Workers', in Stanley Lubman

(ed.), *China's Legal Reforms* (New York: Oxford University Press, 1996) pp. 22–38.
Anderman, S., *Labour Law: Management Decisions and Workers' Rights* (London: Butterworth, 1992).
Andors, Phyllis, *The Unfinished Liberation of Chinese Women* (Bloomington: Indiana University Press, 1983).
Bakken, Borge, 'Crime, Juvenile Delinquency and Deterrence Policy in China', *Australian Journal of Chinese Affairs*, no. 30, July 1993, pp. 29–58.
Baum, Richard, *Burying Mao* (Princeton: Princeton University Press, 1994).
Baum, Richard, 'The Fifteenth National Party Congress: Jiang Takes Command?', *CQ*, no. 153, March 1998, pp. 146–7.
'Beijing Declaration', *Beijing Review*, 16–22 October 1995.
Brown, Ronald C., *Understanding Chinese Courts and Legal Process: Law with Chinese Characteristics* (Boston: Kluwer Law International, 1997).
Chamberlain, Heath, 'Coming to Terms with Civil Society', *Australian Journal of Chinese Affairs*, no. 31, January 1994, p. 113–17.
Chao Yuanling and Richard Sao, (eds), 'Provincial Laws on the Protection of Women and Children', *Chinese Law and Government*, vol. 27, no. 1, Jan.–Feb., 1994.
Chen Jianfu, *From Administrative Authorisation to Private Law: a Comparative Perspective of the Developing Civil Law in the People's Republic of China* (Boston: Martinus Nijhoff Publishers, 1995).
Chen, Albert, 'Developing Theories of Rights and Human Rights in China', in Raymond Wacks, ed., *Hong Kong, China, and 1997: Essays in Legal Theory* (Hong Kong: Hong Kong University Press, 1993), pp. 123–49.
Chen, Theodore (ed.), *The Chinese Communist Regime, Documents and Commentary* (New York: Praeger Publishers, 1967).
China, 'Adoption Law of the PRC', *Xinhua*, 29 December 1991, FBIS-CHI-91-251, 31 December 1991, pp. 18–20.
China, 'An Outline of Chinese Women's Development 1995–2000', FBIS-CHI-95-154, 10 August 1995, pp. 13–19.
China, *The Basic Law of the Hong Kong Special Administrative Region of China* (Beijing: Foreign Languages Press, 1991).
China, *The Criminal Law and the Criminal Law of Procedure* (Beijing: Foreign Languages Press, 1984).
China, Chinese Communist Party, Eleventh Central Committee, 6th Plenary Session, *Resolution on CPC History (1949–81)* (Beijing: Foreign Languages Press, 1981).
China, 'Gansu Regulations on Unions in Foreign-Invested Enterprises', FBIS-CHI-96-207, *Daily Report*, China, 8 June 1996.
China, 'Decision of the CPC Central Committee on Some Issues Concerning the Establishment of a Socialist Market Economic Structure', *Beijing Review*, 22–28 November 1993, p. 12.
China, Fifth National People's Congress, *Constitution of the People's Republic of China* (Beijing: Foreign Languages Press, 3rd edn, 1994).
China, 'Human Rights in China', *Beijing Review*, Nov. 4–10, 1991, pp. 8–45.
China, 'Law on Minors', *Xinhua*, Beijing, 7 April 1992, FBIS-CHI-94-1974, 9 September 1991, p. 36.

China, 'Newly adopted "Presumption of Innocence" Principle', *Daily Report*, China, FBIS-CHI-96-187, 06/10/96.

China, 'PRC: Amended PRC Criminal Procedure Law', *Xinhua*, 23 March 1996, in FBIS-CHI-96-069, 9 April 1996.

China, 'PRC Law for the Protection of the Handicapped', *Xinhua*, Beijing, 29 December 1990, FBIS-CHI-91-003, 4 January 1991, pp. 22–7.

China, 'The Situation of Children in China', *Beijing Review*, April 22–9, 1996, p. 21.

China, 'PRC Law on Protecting Rights and Interests of the Elderly', *Xinhua*, Beijing, 29 August 1996, FBIS-CHI-96-173, 29 August 1996.

China, 'PRC Law Protecting Women's Rights and Interests', *Xinhua*, Beijing, 7 April 1992, FBIS-CHI-92-172-S, 14 April 1992, p. 17.

China, 'Revised Draft Law to Regulate Transient Laborers', FBIS-CHI-95-072, *Daily Report*, China, 14 April 1995, p. 16.

China, 'Text of Foreign-funded Enterprises Labor Law', FBIS-CHI-95-057, 24 March 1995, p. 48.

China, 'Text of Jiang's Speech', FBIS-CHI-95-171, 5 September 1995, pp. 21–2.

China, 'Xinhua on Constitutional Amendments', FBIS-CHI-1999-0323, 14 March 1999.

Chiu, Hungdah, "China's New Legal System" *Current History* (September 1980), p. 31.

Clarke, Donald C. and James Feinerman, 'Antagonistic Contradictions: Criminal Law and Human Rights in China', *CQ*, no. 141, March 1995, p. 137.

Clinton, Hillary Rodham 'Women's Rights Are Human Rights', in *Vital Speeches of the Day*, vol. xi, no. 24, 1 October 1995, pp. 738–40.

Cooper, John, 'Peking's Post-Tiananmen Foreign Policy: The Human Rights Factor', *Issues and Studies*, vol. 30, no. 10, pp. 49–78.

Croll, Elizabeth, *Politics of Marriage in Contemporary China* (Cambridge: Cambridge University Press, 1981).

Davin, Dalia, *Women-work: Women and the Party in Revolutionary China* (Oxford: Clarendon Press, 1976).

Davis, Deborah and Stevan Harrell (eds), *Chinese Families in the Post-Mao Era* (Berkeley: University of California Press, 1993).

Deng Xiaoping, *Selected Works of Deng Xiaoping* (Beijing: Foreign Languages Press, 1984).

Ding Yijiang, 'Corporatism and Civil Society in China: an Overview of the Debate in Recent Years', *China Information*, vol. 12, no. 4, Spring 1998, pp. 44–67.

Ding, David, 'Pre- and Post-Tiananamen conceptual Evolution of Democracy in Intellectual Circles' Rethinking of State and Society', *Journal of Contemporary China*, 7 (18), 1998, p. 223.

Donnelly, Jack, 'Human Rights and Development: Complementary or Competing Concerns?', George Shepherd and Ved Nanda, *Human Rights and Third World Development* (Westport, Connecticut: Greenwood Press, 1985), p. 27.

Donovan, D.A. 'The Structure of the Chinese Criminal Justice System: A Comparative Perspective', *University of San Francisco Law Review*, vol. 21, Winter/Spring 1987, pp. 234, 241.

Folsom, R.H. et al. (eds), *Law in The People's Republic of China: Commentary, Readings and Materials* (Boston: Martinus Nijhoff Publishers, 1989).

Fu, H.L. 'Criminal Defence in China: the Possible Impact of the 1996 Criminal Procedural Law Reform', *CQ*, no. 153, March, 1998, p. 32.

Gao Shangquan and Chi Fulin (eds), *Reforming China's State-Owned Enterprises* (Beijing: Foreign Languages Press, 1997).
Gelatt, A., 'The People's Republic of China and the Presumption of Innocence' *The Journal of Criminal Law and Criminology*, vol. 73, 1982, no. 1, pp. 259–316.
Gilley, Bruce, *Tiger on the Brink: Jiang Zemin and China's New Elite* (Berkeley: University of California Press, 1998). p. 281.
Gilmartin, Christina *et al.* (eds), *Engendering China: Women Culture, and the State* (Cambridge, MA: Harvard Contemporary China Series, 1994).
Gold, Thomas, 'Party-State Versus in China', in Joyce Kallgren, (ed.), *Building a Nation-State: China after Forty Years* (Berkeley: Center for Chinese Studies, China Research Monograph, no. 37, 1990).
Gold, Thomas, 'The Resurgence of Civil Society in China', *Journal of Democracy*, Winter, 1990.
Hecht, Jonathan, *Opening to Reform? An Analysis of China's Revised Criminal Procedure Law* (New York: Lawyers Committee for Human Rights, October, 1996).
Heufers, Rainer (eds), *The Impact of the Administrative Procedure Law on Legal Security in the People's Republic of China* (Beijing, China: 1996).
Hong Kong, *China and 1997: Essays in Legal Theory* (Hong Kong: Hong Kong University Press, 1993).
Jiang Wenran, 'Human Rights and Development: The Chinese Experience in an International Context', E.P. Mendes and A-M Traeholt, eds, *Human Rights: Chinese and Canadian Perspectives* (Ottawa: The Human Rights Research and Education Centre, 1997), pp. 341–62.
Jiang Zemin, 'Hold High the Great Banner of Deng Xiaoping Theory...', *BR*, 6–12, October 1997, p. 19.
Johnson, Kay Ann, *Women, the Family and Peasant Revolution in China* (Chicago: University of Chicago Press, 1983).
Johnson, Kay, 'Chinese Orphanages: Saving China's Abandoned Girls', *Australian Journal of Chinese Affairs*, no. 30, 1993, pp. 61–88.
Jones, William (ed.), *Basic Principles of Civil Law in China* (London, England: M.E. Sharpe, Inc. 1989).
Josephs, Hilary K., 'Labour Law in a "Socialist Market Economy": The Case of China', *Columbia Journal of Transnational Law*, 1995, 33:100.
Judd, Ellen, *Gender and Power in Rural North China* (Stanford: Stanford University Press, 1994).
Keith, Ronald C., *China's Struggle for the Rule of Law* (London and New York: Macmillan and St. Martin's Press, 1994).
Keith, Ronald C. and Zhiqiu Lin, 'Economic Crime and China's Transition to a "Rule of Law Economy"', *China Report*, vol. 35, no. 2, 1999, pp. 143–61.
Keith, Ronald C., '"Internationalization" and "Localization" in the Chinese Search for Human Justice', published proceedings of 'Globalization: Social, Economic and Political Dimensions', Eastern Mediterranean University, October,1999.
Keith, Ronald C., 'Legislating Women's Children's Rights and Interests in the PRC', *CQ*, no. 149 (March 1997), pp. 29–55.
Keith, Ronald C., 'The New Relevance of "Rights and Interests": China's Changing Human Rights Theories', *China Information*, vol. X, no. 2, Autumn, 1995. pp. 48–57.

Keith, Ronald C., 'Post-Deng Jurisprudence: Justice and efficiency in a "Rule of Law" Economy', *Problems of Post Communism*, vol. 45, no. 3, May–June 1998, pp. 54–5.
Keith, Ronald C. and Lin Zhiqiu, 'To Revise or Not to Revise China's Law on Counterrevolution', *China Information*, vol. 5, no. 4, Spring, 1991, pp. 24–41.
Kent, Ann, *Between Freedom and Subsistence: China and Human Rights* (Hong Kong: Oxford University Press, 1993).
Leng, Shao-chuan and Hungdah Chiu, *Criminal Justice in Post-Mao China* (Albany: State University of New York Press, 1985).
Leng, Shao-chuan, 'Criminal Justice in Post-Mao China: Some Preliminary Observations', *CQ*, no. 87 (September 1981), pp. 440–69.
Leng, Shao-chuan, 'Criminal Justice in Post-Mao China: Some Preliminary Observations', *The Journal of Criminal Law and Criminology*, vol. 73, no. 1, 1982, pp. 228–32.
Lin Zhiqiu and Ronald C. Keith, 'The Changing Substantive Principles of Chinese Criminal Law', *China Information*, vol. xiii, no. 1, Summer 1998, pp. 76–105.
Lubman, Stanley (ed.), *China's Legal Reform* (Oxford University Press, 1996).
Lubman, Stanley, 'Introduction: The Future of Chinese Law', *CQ*, no. 138, 1995. pp. 1–21.
Mao Zedong, *Selected Works of Mao Zedong*, vol. v (Beijing: Foreign Languages Press, 1977).
McCormick, Barrett, Su Shaozhi and Xiao Xiaoming, 'The 1989 Democracy Movement: a Review of the Prospects for Civil Society in China', *Pacific Affairs*, vol. 65, no. 3, Summer 1992, pp. 182–202.
McKenzie, Paul, 'China and the Women's Convention: Prospects for the Implementation of an International Norm', *China Law Reporter*, vol. vii, no. 1, 1991, Introduction.
Meisner, Maurice, *The Deng Xiaoping Era: an Inquiry into the Fate of Socialism 1978–1994* (New York: Hill and Wang 1996).
Nathan, Andrew, 'Human Rights in Chinese Foreign Policy', *CQ*, no. 139, September 1994, pp. 622–43.
Packer, Herbert L., 'The Courts, the Police and the Rest of Us', *Journal of Law and Criminology and Police Science*, 57:238, 1966.
Potter, Pitman B, *Domestic Law Reforms in Post-Mao China* (Armonk, N.Y.: M.E. Sharpe, 1994).
Potter, Pitman B, *Economic Contract Law of China: Legitimation and Contract Autonomy in the PRC* (Seattle: University of Washington Press, 1992).
Potter, Pitman, 'The Right to Development: Philosophical Differences and Political Implications', E.P. Mendes and A.-M. Traeholt, eds, *Human Rights: Chinese and Canadian Perspectives* (Ottawa: The Human Rights Research and Education Centre, 1997), pp. 98–9.
Rosen, Stanley, 'Women and Political Participation in China', *Pacific Affairs*, vol. 68, no. 3, Fall 1995, pp. 315–41.
Shao Dengsheng, *Preliminary Study of China's Juvenile Delinquency* (Beijing: Foreign Languages Press, 1992).
Shen Tongxian, 'Comparison and Analysis of the Collective Contract System between China and Foreign Countries', *Chinese Legal Sciences* 1996 no. 4, August 9, 1996.

Shue, Viviene, 'Grasping Reform: Economic Logic, Political Logic and the State–Society Spiral', *CQ*, no. 144, December 1995, pp. 1180–1.

Solinger, Dorothy, *Contesting Citizenship in Urban China; Peasant Migrants, the State and the Logic of the Market* (Berkeley: University of California Press, 1999).

Stacey, Judith, *Patriarchy and Socialist Revolution in China* (Berkeley: University of California Press, 1983).

Steinfeld, Edward, *Forging Reform in China: the Fate of State-Owned Industry* (Cambridge: Cambridge University Press, 1998).

Sun Xiuping, *China's Social Security System* (Beijing: Foreign Languages Press, 1996).

Tucker, Robert C., ed., *Marx–Engels Reader*, 2nd edn (New York: W.W. Norton & Co., 1978).

Weber, Max et al. (eds), *Economy and Society*. vol. 2. (Berkeley: University of California Press, 1978).

White, G. et al. (eds), *In Search for Civil Society: Market Reform and Social Change in Contemporary China* (Oxford: Clarendon Press, 1996).

Whyte, Martin, 'Urban China: A Civil Society in the Making', in Authur Rosenbaum (ed.), *State and Society in China* (Boulder: Westview Press, 1992), pp. 77–102.

Wolf, Margery and Roxane Witke (eds), *Women in Chinese Society* (Stanford: Stanford University Press, 1975).

Woodcock, George, *Pierre-Josehp Proudhon: His Life and Work* (New York: Schocken Books, 1972).

Yanjie Bian, *Work and Inequality in Urban China* (N.Y: State University of New York Press, 1994).

Zhu Rongji, 'Government Work Report', 5 March 1999, FBIS-CHI-1999-0305, 8 March 1999.

Index

A Xi 37
'abstract interests' 24
'adjustment of interests' 9, 44, 53, 82, 91, 132, 236–45
analogy 39, 42, 48, 180, 204, 206–12, 215, 229, 236
All China Federation of Trade Unions (ACFTU) 108, 109, 121, 124
All China Women's Federation (WF) 63, 64, 75–7, 82
Anderman, Steven 122
Anti-crime campaigns and 'severely and swiftly punishing' 199, 212, 213
Anti-Rightist Movement 77
Aristotle 37

Baucus, Max 50
Bai Xiuyun 201–2
'balance of values' 19, 25–7, 43, 48, 49, 93, 98, 115, 137, 162, 233, 237, 239, 240, 245
Beijing Declaration and Action Program, *see* United Nations
Berman, H.J. 115, 207
'breakdown of affection' as contrasted with 'breakdown of marriage' 84–5
'building the socialist legal system' 33, 34

Cao Jianming 32
capital punishment 42, 196, 215, 216, 218, 223, 224–6
'change in objective conditions' 117
Chen Chunjian 218
Chen Guangzhang 183
Chen Guangzhong 181, 187
Chen Jianfu 143–4, 150, 160, 173
Chen Jiangguang 161
Chen Mingxia 14, 79, 233

Chen Minzhang 81
Chen Muhua 65
Chen Shirong 31
Chen Wenyuan 112, 120, 122, 133
Chen Zexian 40
Cheng Yunsheng 23
Chi Fulin 149
children 12; after divorce 83, 86; child labour 45, 72–3; 'dying rooms' 70; Human Rights Watch/Asia report 70; infanticide 71; National Program of Action for Child Development 64; 'roaming about' 72; rights and interests 704; 'school protection' 89
China's Struggle for the Rule of Law ix 27
Chinese People's Political Consultative Conference 3
Chinese Communist Party (CCP) 1, 30, 31, 32, 34, 36, 37, 38, 39, 44, 50, 53, 55, 58, 60, 61, 69, 70, 71, 89, 97, 109, 122, 123, 139, 144, 148, 156, 158, 159, 179, 222, 240; 14 November 1993 decision on socialist market structure 7, 143; 12th National Party Congress 142; 14th CPC Central Committee 140; 14th National Party Congress 166, 178, 181, 183, 215; 14th Party Congress 10, 17, 50, 140, 149, 150, 153, 154, 181; 15th National Party Congress 27, 34, 35, 38, 51, 97, 142, 147, 150, 155, 168, 273, 181, 242
civil law 6, 174, 175, 189, 233, 236, 239, 242; indirect effect of 82
civil society 5, 10, 53–4, 58, 61, 63, 81, 82, 89, 93, 178, 223, 230
Clarke, Donald 8, 127, 204
class struggle and analysis 3, 8, 15,

21, 49, 53, 89, 132, 139, 140, 180, 221, 223, 224, 245
Clinton, Hillary Rodham   65
Cohen, Jerome   178
'collective welfare'   131
'combining punishment and leniency'   194
'combining remuneration according to work and remunerating according to factors of production put in'   16
'common duty'   72, 87
'community cooperative economic organization'   168
'comprehensive management of public order'   61, 79, 89
constitutional law   27; 1999 constitutional amendments   27, 38, 51, 55–6, 69, 82, 90, 94, 96, 122, 123, 174; direct effect of   82
'consultative authoritarianism'   53, 178
'contractual society'   20, 39
'corporate crime'   227
counterrevolution   179, 203, 207, 208, 215, 219–21
'crime control' and 'due process' models   200
'Crimes Disrupting Marriage and the Family'   83
'crimes endangering state security'   219–22
'Crimes Infringing on the Rights of the Person and the Democratic Rights of Citizens'   83
'Crimes of Undermining the Order of Socialist Market Economy'   217
criminal law and procedure   40, 47–8, 178–231
Croll, Elizabeth   68
Cui Min   41, 185, 186, 191, 193, 198, 223
'cultural relativism'   51, 89, 233, 245
Cultural Revolution   6, 14, 69, 77, 102, 122, 139, 179, 186, 191, 224, 225, 241, 245
'custody for investigation'   189–91, 223, 229

Dai Yuzhong   198
death penalty, *see* capital punishment
'decide first, trial later'   195, 197, 229
'Decision Regarding the Severe Punishment of Criminals who Seriously Undermine the Economy'   205
defence counsel   195–6, 199
Deng Xiaoping   5, 6, 7, 10, 16, 28, 29, 30, 31, 161, 232, 239, 241; 16 character formulation   29–30; Deng Pufang   68; legal theory   29–30; 'one country, two systems'   220; 'seeking the truth from the facts'   192, 239; 'socialism with Chinese characteristics'   34, 204, 143, 161; 'Southern Tour Theory'   7, 28, 30, 140, 205, 242, 243; 'three favourable directions'   61, 50, 51, 99, 130, 238, 243
detention   189
'disguised form of corporal punishment'   73
distribution   163, 167
divorce   83, 86–8, 240
Dong Likun   241
Donnelly, Jack   51

'economic crime'   41, 214–29, 226, 230
'embezzlement'   216
'efficiency as primary and fairness as supplementary'   8, 16, 17, 29, 26, 39, 93, 97, 109
'egalitarianism'   19, 49, 129, 161, 166, 176
'enterprises running society'   131
'equality before the law'   9, 30, 43, 179, 180, 206, 224
'eugenics'   81
'exemption from prosecution'   192–5, 201, 229
'external correlations'   6

Feinerman, James   8, 204
'first establish the rules and then handle affairs'   99
'flexibility'   39, 41, 48, 118, 180,

191, 204, 205, 208, 209, 210, 214, 222, 229, 230, 231, 236
formal justice 48
'fragmented authoritarianism' 178
Fu Kuaizhi 182

'Gang of Four' 139, 168, 208
Gao Mingxuan 202, 203, 208, 209, 210, 224, 225
Gao Shangquan 149
gender equality 78
'general stipulations are better than specific ones' 42, 181, 206
'getting rich is glorious' 7, 239
globalization 98, 100, 240
Gong Pixiang 19, 24, 54, 29, 66
'grasping the big, while enlivening the small' 151
Great Leap Forward 102
'group' 26, 65; group interest 154
Gu Angran 115, 116, 117, 133, 183
Gu Gongyun 163, 167
Gu Xiaorong 21718
Guan Huai 101-2, 111, 121, 126, 129
Guo Daohui 4, 29
Guo Jie 104, 105, 132

Hainan model 60, 67, 87, 90, 107, 129-30, 137, 238-9
Hall, Jerome 214
Han Henan 77
Han Yuanqin 168
Hao Tiechuan 4
Hao Yichun 81
He Hangzhou 10, 54
He Xingwang 205
'heavy-penalty-ism' 203, 218, 229
Hecht, Jonathan 41, 178, 188, 191, 196
Hershatter, Gail 68
'hooliganism' 80, 211-12
Howell, Jude 236
Hu Xiaoyi 131
Huang Jinhua 24
Huang Sujian 145, 147
Huang Tao 29
Huang Wenyi 243

Hui Luming 107, 111, 116, 117, 120, 129
human rights 2, 5, 10, 11, 12, 13, 16, 36, 40, 44, 45, 52, 59, 62, 66, 90, 92, 137, 187
Human Rights Watch 220-21
Hungdah Chiu 57, 208, 227
Huang Tao 29

'impairing marriage' 30
'independent purposes theory' 182
'individual rights' 24
Institute of Law, Chinese Academy of Social Sciences 18, 23, 31, 33, 35, 36, 46, 98, 133, 140, 147, 170, 183, 193
'institutionalized morality' 49, 81-6, 89
'internationalization' 14, 24, 29, 37, 61-66, 99, 229, 233, 244, 246
'inquisitorial and adversarial methods' 198

Jiang Lishan 243, 244
Jiang Ping 145
Jiang Zemin 18, 28, 32, 50, 51, 65, 94, 142, 145, 147, 150, 151, 155, 158, 171, 242, 243, 244; and Deng Xiaoping 38; 'core faction'; 'property rights' 17-18, 147; 'public ownership as primary and the common development in the economy of various forms of ownership' 17; 'running a country according to the law' 35; September 12, 1997 speech 35, 37; shareholding power 151
Johnson, Kay 68, 70
Josephs, Hilary K. 101, 103, 126, 128
Judd, Ellen 68
'judicial independence' 16, 36, 201
'jural' (formal) and 'societal' (informal) models 57-8
Jurisprudence 1-3; class-based 10; defined 5-6; Western feminist 62-3; 'pluralized' 5, 7, 8, 14, 43, 44, 54, 104, 148, 233-6, 246; 'third

Index 311

stage' 29, 31, 33, 54, 89, 242; 'unified' 14, 44
juvenile deliquency 60, 61, 70, 71, 90

Kang Deguan 195
Keith, Ronald C. 27
Kong Xiangjun 153, 154, 158

labour: labour contract 109–19; labour discipline and dismissal 107, 116, 117; labour dispute settlement 102, 125–9; labour management 132; 'labour administrative relations' 93, 106; 'labour object theory' 105; 'legal labour relations' 106; 'pluralized labour relations' 96, 126, 136; rights and obligations relations' 126; right to strike 12, 120, 122, 123; 'theory on principal and supplementary objects' 105
Laws of the PRC: 1951 PRC Labour Insurance Law 101; 1992 Trade Union Law 101; 1993 Company Law 140, 147, 151, 174, 180; 1994 Labour Law 93–4, 100, 101–9; Criminal Laws (1979 and 1997) 40, 79, 80, 172, 179–80, 214–24, 229; Criminal Procedural Laws (1979, 96) 41, 179–80, 185, 187, 188–202; General Principles of Civil Law 18, 56, 71, 83, 91, 113, 140, 143, 154, 174; Inheritance Law 81; Hong Kong Basic Law 192, 221; Labour Law 46, 66, 78, 93–137; Law of Administrative Procedure 78; Law of Civil Procedure 56, 66, 90; Law on Adoption 69, 74; Law on Maternal and Infant Care 69, 81; Law on Protecting the Rights and Interests of the Elderly 12, 59, 86–9; Law on the Rights and Interests of Women 12, 13, 45, 64, 66, 68–70, 74–7, 80, 90, 233; Law on the Prevention and Control of Infectious Diseases 69; Law on the Protection of the Handicapped 66–8; Law on Protecting the Rights and Interests of the Elderly 86–8; Law on the Protection of Minors 12, 69, 71–4; Mandatory Education Law 66, 69; Marriage Laws (1950, 1980) 45, 55, 66, 74, 83, 86
'lawful subject' 8, 114
'legal' as distinguished from 'actual rights' 59
legal culture 16, 36
'legal person' 140; state legal person 159
'legal positivism' 178
'legalization' 6, 38
Li Bing 31
Li Boyong 104
Li Buyun 28, 31, 33, 35, 36, 52, 98, 99, 108, 239, 241, 242
Li Dewei 162, 163, 164, 165
Li Fuyan 185
Li Jingsen 106
Li Mingshun 78
Li Peng 17, 32, 147
Li Ruihuan 3, 32
Li Yining 143
Liang Huixing 33
Liang Shuwen 107, 111, 116, 117, 120, 129
'liberation of productive forces' 20, 50
Lin Zhe 136
Liu Hainian 33, 35
Liu Han 23
Liu Huaqing 32
Liu Shujun 146, 158
'living at home under surveillance' 189
'localization' 25, 37, 40, 62, 66, 229, 233, 240, 246
Long Zhongzhi 196, 198, 199, 200, 204
Lu Fei 198
Lu Zhongya 192
Lubman, Stanley 43, 200
Luo Mingda 10, 54
Luo Shaping 214

Ma Changshan 10
Ma Kechang 209, 225

Ma Yinan 77–8
Ma Yuejin 166
Ma Zunju 170
Mao Guohui 183
Mao Zedong 8, 18, 29, 32, 40, 43, 94, 97, 122, 127, 136, 174, 241
'market economy is a rule of law economy' 1–2, 18, 40, 48, 198, 206, 241
Marx 138
Marxism–Leninism Mao Zedong Thought 14, 207
mass associations 14, 91, 128, 132, 223
mass-line approach 14, 57–8, 64, 71, 75, 103, 244
'mature totalitarianism' 6, 178
McKenzie, Paul 63
Meese III, Edwin 139
Meisner, Maurice 141, 143, 167, 177
'method of addition and abstraction' 222; *see also* Tong Zhiwei
'Methods of Economic Compensation for Breach and Termination of the Labour Contract' 118
Minan, J.H. 110, 123
Ministry of Agriculture 161, 162
Ministry of Education 212
Ministry of Justice 5, 32, 65
Ministry of Labour 102, 102, 103, 107, 111, 112, 113, 118, 119, 121, 129, 132, 134, 136
Ministry of Public Security 190, 199
'mutual cooperation and restriction' 201

National People's Congress (NPC) 40, 65, 66, 72, 75, 76, 87, 202, 188, 190, 191, 192, 193, 194, 196, 199, 200, 201, 208, 224, 228, 229, 238, 244; Eighth National People's Congress 103, 85, 226; Seventh NPC 79; Law Committee 66–7, 71, 74, 77; Legal System Work Committee 115, 186, 187; Standing Committee 31, 56, 65, 76, 104, 117, 123, 195, 205, 214, 215, 216, 217, 229, 242; Special Group for Women and Children of the Committee for Internal and Judicial Affairs 63
'neo-authoritarianism' 6
'no crime without a law; no punishment without a law' 40–2, 181, 204, 205, 206, 207–14, 228, 230, 231, 236, 244
'no guilt without a trial' 94, 229

'obligations' 13, 14, 23, 54, 67, 88, 108; 'obligational fundamentalism' 9, 57; 'off duty' 158
'obtaining a guarantor and waiting for trial' 189
'organizing others for prostitution' 79
'organized crime' 217
ownership 138–9: 'corporate enterprise ownership' 155; 'dual ownership theory' 157; 'economic ownership' 146; ideological notion of ownership system 138–40, 148, 167; 'individual ownership under the socialist system' 159; 'legal ownership' 146; 'mixed ownership' 96, 158; 'ownership by the whole people 117; ownership in the Continental and Common Law traditions 143–4, 147, 159, 176; ownership rights' 141, 142, 146, 148, 155, 175; 'pluralized ownership' 17, 94, 138, 164, 175; 'ownership right of legal person' 140–1, 146, 152–9; 'pluralization of enterprise ownership 158; 'power and function of ownership' 157; private ownership 169–75; 'relative ownership' 146; 'right to benefits 148; right to dispose of property 148; right to use 148; rights in things' 148, 157, 173; 'separating ownership from operational management rights' 47, 142, 144; shareholder ownership theory 156; shareholding cooperative system'

162–7; 'socialist collective ownership of the working masses' 159, 160; 'socialist ownership by the whole people' 159, 170, 173; 'socialist public ownership system' 166; 'system of the ownership of the means of production' 139; 'ultimate ownership' 146, 175; *see also* property rights

Packer, Herbert 184, 200
Pan Libing 19, 161
'people visiting system' 126
'personal property rights' 145
'positive' versus 'negative theory' 218
'presumption of innocence' 192–4, 199, 202, 229
'property ownership rights' 145
'property rights' 17, 47, 142, 145, 147, 249, 159, 239; 'property rights of legal person' 140, 153, 154, 155, 158, 176; property versus ownership rights 143–9, 175; *see also* ownership
Proudhon, Pierre Joseph 138
'public interests' 22
'public society' 26
'punishment and no stipulation' 218
Putterman, Louis 160

Qi Yanping 20
Qiang Shigong 25
Qiao Keyu 33
Qiao Shi 31, 32

Rawls, John 26
'red hat' phenomena 171, 176
'relying on education while making punishment secondary' 71
'retention' versus 'deletion theory' 209
Ren Fushan 120
'retroactivity' 214
'rights and interests' 1, 12, 16, 23, 53–7, 64, 81, 91, 92, 191, 235; 'balancing rights and interests' 185; 'rights and interests in a market economy' 11–16; 'rights are but obligations, and obligations, rights' 56; 'rights fundamentalism' 12, 20–5, 137, 184
Roosevelt, Franklin D. 50
Rosen, Stanley 76–7
'rough outlines to detailed rules' 84
Rousseau 241
'rule of law society' 4, 29
'rule of law state' 4
'ruling the people with law' 40
'running the country according to law and establishing a socialist rule of law country' 2, 27, 29, 33, 35, 37, 38, 48, 181, 182, 188, 206, 209, 223, 240

'sexual harassment' 45, 61, 79, 80
Shan Dongshan 123
Shao Bingren 162, 164, 165–6
Shekou Industrial Zone 125
Shen Mingzhao 35
Shen Sibao 32
Shen Zongling 62
Shi Jichun 147, 153, 157
Shi Tanjing 46, 109, 112, 114, 15, 120, 122, 123, 133, 233
Shi Xiaoyi 161, 162
'should': as distinguished from 'must' 14, 59–60, 66, 72, 75, 108
'small government, big society' 13, 24, 44, 60, 97, 99, 130, 137, 174
Smith, Adam 54
social protection law 12
Socialist Economic Reconstruction Movement 102
'socialist market economy' 6, 19, 35, 49, 53, 95, 143, 177
'socialist spiritual civilization' 14, 35, 240
'society fundamentalism' 184
'socio-powers' 22
'socio-rights' 20–2, 34–5, 54–5, 242; *see also* Tong Zhiwei
Solinger, Dorothy 134
Song Yinghui 184, 185, 202
'special grouping of rights' 12, 13, 15, 45, 46, 49, 52, 61–6, 88, 97, 118

'special labour subjects groups' 132
'special rights' 62, 81
Stacey, Judith 68
'state and society' approach 58, 67, 75, 88, 91
State Council 87, 101, 103, 108, 127, 129, 140, 147, 148, 172; National State Property Management Bureau 153; State Economic System Reform Commission 150, 164, 165; Working Committee on Women and Children 64
Steinfeld, Edward 141
'subjects' 44
substantive justice 19, 182
Sun Guohua 5, 7, 8, 20, 24, 28, 38, 243
Sun Xiaoxia 22, 54
Sun Xiuping 95, 99
'supremacy of law' 9, 16, 36, 43, 44, 236, 242
Supreme People's Court (SPC) 107, 114, 197–8, 209, 211, 216
Supreme People's Procuratorate (SPP) 187, 194, 199, 211, 216, 229

'theories of state and law' 5
three capital enterprises 125, 127, 129, 170
'three irons system': 'iron chair'; 'iron rice bowl'; iron salary 97, 115, 136
'three ones theory' 38
Tiananmen Square 29, 56, 68, 140, 178, 220, 221, 228
Tong Rou 120
Tong Zhiwei 21–3, 54–5, 92, 242
township enterprise reform 159–69
trade unions 76, 106, 118, 119–25
'transplantation' 20, 92

United Nations: Beijing Declaration 62, 63, 65; Convention on the Rights of Children 62, 71; Convention on the Elimination of All Forms of Discrimination Against Women 63, 74; Decade for the Handicapped, 1983–92 68; Fourth World Conference of Women 62, 64–5, 74, 75, 78, 79, 80; State of the World's Children Report 70; World Action Program on the Handicapped 67; World Declaration on Survival, Protection and Development of Children 64
'unity of rights and obligation' 13, 34
US Lawyers Committee for Human Rights 41

'waiting to return to their positions' 158
Wang Baoshu 33
Wang Cangsuo 106
Wang Chuang 154
Wang Hanbin 188
Wang Jiafu 33, 34, 35, 98, 100, 108, 142, 156, 174, 238
Wang Jianping 155
Wang Liming 28, 170
Wang Minyuan 183, 193
Wang Quanxing 100
Wang Shengluan 85
Weber, Max 19, 47, 207, 245
White, Gordon 109
'will of the ruling class' 10, 95, 139
Wolf, Margery 68
Women 56; female infanticide 65, 100; maternity benefits 118; Nairobi Forward-Looking Strategies 50, 64, 70, 74, 76; 'Outline of Chinese Women's Development (1995–2000)' 65; rights and interests 68–70; rape 80, 81; selling and kidnapping 79; white paper on 50
Woo, Margaret 60
Wu Jingliang 143, 148

Xi Jieying 73
Xia Young
Xiao Yang 186, 205
Xiao Zhonghua 209, 210
Xie Cichang 153
Xu Xianming 9–10
Xue Ju 81
Xue Zhaojun 121

Yang Dawen 84
Yang Haikun 11, 30
Yin Wenquan 1
Yu Min 82, 89
Yuan Mu 152

Zhang Chunshen 37
Zhang Guangbo 20, 23, 54
Zhang Guanxing 1, 47, 155, 170, 171, 173
Zhang Lingjie 183
Zhang Qigong 187
Zhang Qinmian 85
Zhang Wenxian 19, 23

Zhang Xianyu 80
Zhang Zhende 29, 40
Zhang Zipei 182
Zhao Bingzhi 205, 209, 210, 225
Zhao Shiyi 2
Zhao Zhenjiang 25
Zheng Xu 181
Zhongnanhai 'six lectures' 28, 32–6, 108, 174, 233
Zhu Rongji 97
Zou Xueping 22
Zuo Weimin 184, 196, 198, 199, 200, 204